HINDU SAṀSKĀRAS

HINDU SAṀSKĀRAS

SOCIO-RELIGIOUS STUDY OF THE HINDU SACRAMENTS

Rajbali Pandey

MOTILAL BANARSIDASS
Delhi Varanasi Patna
Bangalore Madras

Second Revised Edition : Delhi, 1969
Reprint: Delhi, 1976, 1982, 1987

MOTILAL BANARSIDASS
Bungalow Road, Jawahar Nagar, Delhi 110 007
Branches
Chowk, Varanasi 221 001
Ashok Rajpath, Patna 800 004
24 Race Course Road, Bangalore 560 001
120 Royapettah High Road, Mylapore, Madras 600 004

ISBN: 81-208-0396-5

PRINTED IN INDIA
BY JAINENDRA PRAKASH JAIN AT SHRI JAINENDRA PRESS, A-45 NARAINA INDUSTRIAL AREA, PHASE I, NEW DELHI 110 028 AND PUBLISHED BY NARENDRA PRAKASH JAIN FOR MOTILAL BANARSIDASS, DELHI 110 007.

समर्पणम्

श्रीभारतोज्ज्वलविशालपवित्रकीर्ति-
दिव्यावदानमहनीयमहानुभावः ।
भव्यस्फुरच्छ्रुतिसमादृतधर्मवर्म-
सन्मूर्तिमान् मदनमोहनमालवीयः ॥
तस्मै महामहिममान्यवदान्यधन्य-
हिन्दूसुसंस्कृतिनिधानविधानभूम्ने ।
सोल्लासमर्पयति मत्कृतिपुष्पमालां
श्रद्धानुरागसुपरागसुगन्धबन्धाम् ॥

PREFACE

In the following pages an attempt has been made to trace the Hindu Saṁskāras through their origin and development. They have a long and varied past. Many of them go back to a hoary antiquity and some of them still survive. In course of time, they have undergone many changes and modifications. The Saṁskāras are described in some hymns of the Vedas, a few Brāhmaṇas, the Gṛhyasūtras, the Dharmasūtras, the Smṛtis and the later treatises. But as these works were intended to be manuals or codes for a particular time and locality, they do not present the Saṁskāras in their historical evolution. So, an endeavour has been made here to link and piece together these scattered materials into a comprehensive whole and to supply a historical perspective for their proper understanding.

For doing so not merely chronological sequence is traced but the connection between various changes is also shown. It has also been explained that the Saṁskāras were based on religious beliefs and social conditions. What was in the beginning purely natural became more cultural. Here it will be found that many social elements entered into the precincts of religious ceremonies and many cultural devices were introduced to mould the Saṁskāras in order to produce the desired effects.

The Saṁskāras are, in a fact, expressive and symbolic performances. They also contain dramatic utterances and theological gestures. Without an inkling into these aspects of the Saṁskāras they appear as fanciful puerile pranks. In order to make them intelligible, the symbols are unfolded and explained and suggestions are made more articulate . This has been done without overrationalising. The Saṁskāras give expression to aspirations and ideals of the Hindus. They are brought out wherever found.

Many constituents of the Saṁskāras were meant to be means of intercourse with, and influence upon, spiritual beings that were believed to guide and interfere with the course of human actions. But while the mind of the performers was bent on religious intent, their knowledge of the arts of life helped to bring about the object in view. In this connection the religious beliefs of the Hindus are analysed and their knowledge of the arts of life shown. As the aim of the Saṁskāras was to secure the welfare of the recipient and to develop his personality, every contrivance towards the same is pointed out.

All the rites, ceremonies and customs, that form the Saṁskāras, are, more or less, universal. They have all a recognized place in ancient cultures and they are still represented within the limits of modern religions. So, in order to make the historical development of the Saṁskāras more comprehensible, parallels in other religions are referred to wherever possible.

Many people, looking at the Saṁskāras from the modern practical point of view, regard them as ridiculous and meaningless. But few, who will care to understand the general principles of ancient religions, will ever think them so. They will also find that their knowledge is not superfluous to the common stock of human interest. The sacramental beliefs and practices, far from being an irrational priest-craft are consistent and logical in a high degree, though working under a mental condition which was different from what it is to-day.

As regards the intrinsic merits of the study of the Saṁskāras, it has been made clear that these had practical utility and intention when and wherever they originated, though they, now, appear obscure and purposeless, for they have been carried on, without adaptation, into a new state of society where their original sense is lost. Therefore, a study of the Saṁskāras forms an important part of investigation into the origin and development of civilization.

For treatment in the present thesis, only those Smārta Saṁskāras are taken which were performed at the various epochs in the life of an individual from conception to crematorium. Their theatre was the home, their chief actor the householder and the presiding deity the domestic Fire, by the side of which they were staged. The Śrauta sacrifices, for the performance of which the administration of priests was required, the Yajamāna being a passive agent, are excluded from the list of the Saṁskāras. They being Kāmya (optional) ceremonies, were not binding on every individual, and so they do not come under the Saṁskāras proper, which were compulsory.

The whole work can be divided into two parts. In the first part, sources of inquiry, the meaning and the number of the Saṁskāras, the purpose of the Saṁskāras and the constituents of the Saṁskāras are discussed in their historical growth. In the second part of the work the entire Saṁskāras are grouped under the following heads and the conclusions are given in the end:

1. The Pre-natal Saṁskāras.
2. The Saṁskāras of Childhood.
3. The Educational Saṁskāras.
4. The Marriage Saṁskāra.
5. The Funeral Ceremonies.

While dealing with a particular Saṁskāra, first its origin is traced and then its subsequent development discussed. The creative period of the Saṁskāras has passed away. Many of them, e.g. the pre-natal Saṁskāras and a few of the childhood are not generally performed at present; so they have become a thing of the past. The rest are performed by orthodox families only and, here too, in a distorted form. The only current Saṁskāras are the Upanayana (Initiation), not performed by all the twice-born today, the Vivāha (Marriage Ceremonies) and the Antyeṣṭi (Funeral Ceremonies). The revival of the Saṁskāras by reform societies like the Arya-Samāja is very recent, but times do not seem to be propitious for such attempts.

As the Saṁskāras include many essential preliminary considerations and ceremonies relating to social rules, taboos, restraints and, as they are well recognized by authoritative works, they have found their proper place in the treatment of the subject. In the end the ritual proper is described with possible interpretations and significance thereof.

This work was originally written as a thesis, which was approved by the Banaras Hindu University for the degree of Doctor of Letters in 1936. It could not be sent to the press earlier for various reasons, but mainly due to the press and paper difficulties during the Second World War, which started in 1939. The long gap has, however, been utilized in the revision and the improvement of the original work.

It is a pleasant duty of the author to acknowledge his deep gratitude to Dr. A. S. Altekar, M.A., LL.B., D.Litt., Head of the Department of Ancient Indian History and Culture, Banaras Hindu University, under whom he worked as a Research Scholar and whose learned guidance and help were available at all times. He also owes grateful thanks to Dr. R. S. Tripathi, M.A., Ph.D., Head of the Department of History, Banaras Hindu University, who readily offered many valuable suggestions on various topics in this work. His indebtedness to individual authors is acknowledged in the footnotes. The author is deeply indebted to Pt. Nagesh Upadhyaya, M.A., the Proprietor of the Vikram Panchang Press, Banaras, and his staff for undertaking the publication of this work in the midst of their multifarious and pressing duties. His thanks are due to Shri Nemi Kumar, B.A. for taking great pains in preparing the Index of this work. The author, more than any body else is conscious of many defects and blemishes, especially typographical, which have crept into the book. For these he craves the indulgence of the reader.

Banaras Hindu University
Ram-navami, Vikrama Samvat 2006
March, 1949

R. B. PANDEY

PREFACE TO THE SECOND EDITION

The second edition of the "Hindu Saṁskāras" is a revised and improved version of the original work. At places, new and additional materials have been provided. I hope this edition will be found more comprehensive and useful to the scholars of Indian studies.

RAJ BALI PANDEY

26–1–69

ABBREVIATIONS

A.A.	.. Aitareya Āraṇyaka
A.B.	.. Aitareya Brāhmaṇa
Āp.D.S.	.. Āpastamba Dharmasūtra
Āp.G.S.	.. Āpastamba Gṛhyasūtra
Āp.Ś.S.	.. Āpastamba Srautasūtra
Ā.G.S.	.. Āśvalāyana Gṛhyasūtra
A.S.	.. Atri-Smṛti
A.U.	.. Aitareya Upaniṣad
A.V.	.. Atharvaveda
A.V.Par	.. Atharvaveda Pariśiṣṭa
B.U.	.. Bṛhadāraṇyaka Upaniṣad
B.D.S.	.. Baudhāyana Dharmasūtra
B.G.S.	.. Baudhāyana Gṛhyasūtra
B.G.	.. Bhagavadgītā
B.S.S.	.. Baudhāyana Śrautasūtra
Bh.G.S.	.. Bhāradvāja Gṛhyasūtra
Bh.P.	.. Bhaviṣya Purāṇa
Ch.U.	.. Chāndogya Upaniṣad
D.S.	.. Dakṣa-Smṛti
De.S.	.. Devala-Smṛti
G.B.	.. Gopatha Brāhmaṇa
G.D.S.	.. Gautama Dharmasūtra
G.G.S.	.. Gobhila Gṛhyasūtra
H.D.S.	.. Hārīta Dharmasūtra
H.G.S.	.. Hiraṇyakeśi Gṛhyasūtra
H.D.S.	.. Hiraṇyakeśi Dharmasūtra
H.S.	.. Hārīta-Smṛti
J.G.S.	.. Jaiminīya Gṛhyasūtra

Kh.G.S.	..	Khadira Gṛhyasūtra
K.S.	..	Kauśika Sūtra
M.Bh.	..	Mahābhārata
M.D.S.	..	Mānava Dharmasūtra
M.G.S.	..	Mānava Gṛhyasūtra
M.S.	..	Manu Smṛti
M.U.	..	Maitrāyaṇī Upaniṣad
N.S.	..	Nārada-Smṛti
P.Br.	..	Pañchaviṁśa Brāhmaṇa
P.G.S.	..	Pāraskara Gṛhyasūtra
P.S.	..	Parāśara-Smṛti
R.V.	..	Ṛgveda
S.Ch.	..	Saṁskāra-Chandrikā
Ś.Br.	..	Śatapatha Brāhmaṇa
Ś.G.S.	..	Śāṅkhyāyana Gṛhyasūtra
S.M.	..	Saṁskāra Mayūkha
S.U.	..	Śvetāśvatra Upaniṣad
S.V.	..	Sāmaveda
T.A.	..	Taittirīya Ārṇyaka
T.Br.	..	Taittirīya Brāhmaṇa
T.U.	..	Taittirīya Upaniṣad
V.G.S.	..	Vārāha Gṛhyasūtra
V.D.S.	..	Vasiṣṭha Dharmasūtra
Viṣ.D.S.	..	Viṣṇu Dharmasūtra
V.M.S.	..	Vīramitrodaya-Saṁskāra Prakāśa
Yāj.S.	..	Yājñavalkya-Smṛti
Y.V.	..	Yajurveda

THE SYSTEM OF TRANSLITERATION ADOPTED IN THE BOOK

अ = a	क = ka	ढ = ḍha	य—ya
आ = ā	ख = kha	ण = ṇa	र = ra
इ = i	ग = ga	त = ta	ल = la
ई = ī	घ = gha	थ = tha	व = va
उ = u	ङ = ṅa	द = da	श = śa
ऊ = ū	च = cha	घ = dha	ष = ṣa
ऋ = ṛ	छ = chha	न = na	स = sa
ए = e	ज = ja	प = pa	ह = ha
ऐ—ai	झ = jha	फ = pha	क्ष = kṣa
ओ = o	ञ = ña	ब = ba	त्र = tra
औ = au	ट = ṭa	भ = bha	ज्ञ = jña
अं = aṁ	ठ = ṭha	म = ma	
अः = aḥ	ड = ḍa		

CONTENTS

X. CONCLUSION

CHAPTER I

THE SOURCES OF INQUIRY

1. *Introductory*

The Gṛhyasūtras, the oldest manuals of the Hindu Saṁskāras, do not cite their authorities as the Dharmasūtras do for their contents. The cause of this silence is that the Saṁskāras, mostly being domestic rites and ceremonies, were based more on precedent and popular traditional usages than on any definite written code. The Dharmasūtras, the Smṛtis and the mediaeval treatises produce authorities on Dharma or Law, both sacred and secular. But these works do not go deep into ritualistic details and are mainly concerned with the social aspects of the Saṁskāras. Therefore, for the full information about the Saṁskāras, we have to ransack other sources also ignored by them.

2. *The Vedas*

The Vedas are universally recognised as the primary source of the Hindu Dharma. According to the Gautama-Dharmasūtra[1] "the Veda is the source of Dharma and the tradition and practices of those who know it." Other Dharmasūtras and the Smṛtis endorse the above view.[2] From the perusal of the Vedas also we arrive at the same conclusion.

The oldest document of the religious literature of the Indo-Aryans is the Ṛgveda. Though the religious picture painted in it is by no means complete, as it contains hymns used by the priests in the sacrifices to high gods, we catch glimpses of popular religion at several places. Moreover, there are a few specific hymns that are particularly concerned with popular rites and ceremonies. The wedding,[3] the funeral[4] and the conception[5] are narrated in them.

1. वेदो धर्ममूलम् । तद्विदां च स्मृतिशीले । i. 1–2
2. ĀP. D.S. i. 1. 1–2; V. D. S. i. 4. 5.
3. X. 85,
4. X, 14, 16, 18.
5. X. 183. 184.

The narrations or descriptions may not be ritualistically exact but they are historically approximate. The later-day Saṁskāras, the Vivāha, the Antyeṣṭi and the Garbhādhāna were direct descendants of these hymns. Then, there are those hymns of the Ṛgveda that are of general applicability in the sacramental rituals. They are recited at different occasions, which show that they were not originally composed for a particular Saṁskāra. But their connection with popular ceremonies cannot be denied altogether. Again, we find in the Gṛhyasūtras many citations homonymous to the Vedic Mantras. This fact indicates that a large number of the items of the Saṁskāras were suggested by the Vedic verses in question and they originated in the later Vedic or the post-Vedic period.

As regards the details and regulations of the Saṁskāras, it must be confessed that the Ṛgvedic hymns do not contain positive rules. They contain many incidental references which throw light on the Saṁskāras. In fact, the Vedic hymns were composed under inspirations for invoking the help of gods in events, public and private, that immediately interested the Vedic people. There are invocations relating to a life of hundred years with children and grand children, securing wives, children and other domestic articles,[7] and the destruction of the demon who kills offsprings.[8] These and similar references have a great correspondence with the Saṁskāras that were performed at the various important occasions in the life of a man. Besides, there are other refernces in the Ṛgveda that bear on the social aspects of the Saṁskāras. For example, it was difficult to secure a husband for a brotherless girl. "Like a woman growing old in her parents' house etc."[9] Different forms of marriages are also hinted at. The purchase of a bride (Āsura marriage) was prevalent in the Ṛgvedic period. The Vasiṣṭha-Dharmasūtra[10] quotes a passage from the Maitrāyaṇīya-Saṁhitā[11] which runs, "she, who being purchased by husband." The Gāndharva form is also referred to in these words, "when the bride is finelooking and well-adorned,

---

6. शतमिन्नु शरदो अन्ति देवा यत्रा नश्चक्रा जरसं तनूनाम् ।
पुत्रासो यत्र पितरो भवन्ति मा नो मध्यारीरिषतायुर्गन्तोः ॥ R. V. i. 89. 9.

7. Ibid. IX 67. 9. 11. VIII, 35. 10. X. 183.

8. R. V. X. 162.

9. अमाजूरिव पित्रोः सचा सती समानाद्य सदसत्वामिये भगम् । ibid. II, 17.7.

10. Ibid. I, 36. 37.

11. Ibid. I. 11. 12.

she seeks by herself her friend among many men."[12] The Ṛgveda[13] praises the stage of a student.

The Sāmaveda almost entirely borrowed from the Ṛgveda, supplies hardly any material worth the name for the history of the Saṁskāras. It is mainly interesting for its musical tune. It was sung at great sacrifices and other auspicious occasions, e. g. marriage etc. The Vārāha-Gṛhyasūtra prescribes Vādana and Gāna (music) as a part of the marriage ceremonies. But as regards the form of the Saṁskāras, the Sāmaveda has nothing to contribute.

The Yajurveda represents an advanced stage in the progress of rituals. During the period of its composition the functions of different priests were specialized. In it all those formulas are fixed, which were used by the Adhvaryu and his assistants in the performance of the great sacrifices. But the Yajurveda is concerned with the Śrauta sacrifices only. So we do not get any material help from it for the study of the Saṁskāras. The only useful reference found in it is to the shaving ceremony, a common feature, which preceded a Śrauta sacrifice—where prayers are offered to the shaving razor and directions are given to the barber.[14] This reference supplies a link between the Śrauta and the Gṛhya ceremonies.

In contradistinction with the other Saṁhitās, the Atharvaveda is rich in information about popular religion, rites and ceremonies. Here we get mantras for almost every end of human life. The wedding[15] and the funeral[16] hymns are more elaborated in the Atharvaveda than in the Ṛgveda. To the praise of the Vedic Brahmachāri a full hymn is devoted.[17] The act of conception has found mention in a larger number of hymns than in the Ṛgveda.[18] In the book XVIII of the Atharvaveda there are prayers for long life that are called Āyuṣyakarmāṇi, "hymns achieving long life." These prayers were used chiefly at domestic rituals, such as the first haircutting of the boy, the first shaving of the youth and the initiation. It also contains hymns that refer to marriage and love and form a separate

---

12. भद्रा वधूर्भवति यत्सुपेशाः स्वयं सा मित्रं वनुते जने चित् । ibid, X. 27. 12.

13. Ibid. X. 109. 5.

14. vi. 15.

15. A. V. xiv. 1, 2.

16. Ibid XVIII. 1–4.

17. Ibid. XI. 5.

18. Ibid. III. 23; Vt. 81,

class. Kauśika calls them 'Strīkarmāṇi' or women's rites. Through them a maiden tried to obtain a bridegroom or a young man a bride by stimulating love in indifferent lovers and unresponsive sweethearts, benedictions upon the bride were offered, conception was accelerated and the birth of a male child effected. These hymns have also got prayers for the protection of the pregnant woman,[19] the unborn and the new-born child, and so on. Considering this popular character of the Atharvaveda, Ridgeway concludes that it is not a record of the Aryan religion but represents the beliefs of the aboriginal people. This view cannot be accepted. It is just possible that the Indo-Aryans assimilated many non-Aryan elements in their religion, but the lower strata of the Aryan community were not less interested in the lower side of religion than the non-Aryan population. The Atharvaveda reflects the faith and rites of the common people rather than the highly specialized religion of the priests.

3. *The Brāhmaṇas*

After the Vedas, we come to the Brāhmaṇas as the source of our information. They are thorough treatises on the Vedic rituals. The Brāhmaṇas give rules for the performance of the Śrauta sacrifices and the Arthavāda or explanation of the purpose and meaning of the sacrificial acts. They contain many discussions on the sacrifices, give interpretations of Vedic hymns, trace etymology of words and try to explain symbols. But the Brāhmaṇas are mostly occupied with the Śrauta sacrifices that were the supreme religious concern of the time. In them, however, we get sporadic references that supply some data for constructing the history of the Saṁskāras. A fragmentary account of the Upanayana is found in the Gopatha Brāhmaṇa.[21] The Śatapatha[22] gives a different account of it and the word "Brahmacharya" used here denotes the condition of the life of a student. The word 'Antevāsin' (living with a teacher) in the sense of a student is used both by the Śatapatha[23] and the Aitareya[24] Brāhmaṇas. Ajina 'the deer-skin' is mentioned in the Śatapatha-Brāhmaṇa.[25] Godāna ceremonies are described in the same

19. A. V. VI. 6.

20. Dramas and the Dramatic Dances of non-European Races. p. 122.

21. i. 2. 1–8.

22. Xi. 3. 3. 1.

23. V. 1. 5. 17.

24. iii. 2. 6.

25. V. 2. 1 21.

Brāhmaṇa.[26] Recognition of marriage within the third or the fourth degree is also found in it.[27] The Tāṇḍya-Brāhmaṇa mentions the Vrātyas and the Vrātyastoma sacrifices through which they were reclaimed to the Aryan community. The Śatapatha-Brāhmaṇa, Books XI-XIV, besides appendices to the preceding books also contain a few interesting sections on the subjects which are otherwise not dealt with in the Brāhmaṇas e.g. on the Upanayana,[28] the initiation of a pupil, on the daily Vedic Study[29] and on the death ceremonies or the raising of the mound.[30]

4. *The Āraṇyakas and the Upaniṣads*

The Āraṇyakas and the Upaniṣads are mainly concerned with philosophical subjects and do not condescend to deal with rituals. But the Vedic sacrifices and rituals were still very popular in their times and they have found mention, here and there, in them. From the point of view of the Saṁskāras, the Taittirīya Āraṇyaka is important. From it we learn that late marriages[31] were general, as unmarried pregnant girls were looked upon as sinful. The Brahmayajña or the Daily Study is praised.[32] The sixth chapter called "Pare" gives the Mantras required for the Pitṛmedha, 'the burning of the dead'.

In the Upaniṣads we have many references relating to the Upanayana-Saṁskāra. The theory of the four Āśramas seems to have been established. The Brahmachārin resided and boarded at the house of the guru and in return rendered many personal services such as tending his cows. The importance of the guru was recognized even for studying the Brahmavidyā and one had to approach a teacher for this purpose.[33] Admission of a student to the guru is described in the Chāndogya-Upaniṣad.[34] The restrictions on the

26. iii. 1. 2. 5, 6.

27. i. 8. 3. 6.

28. Xi. 5. 4.

29. Ś. P. Br. Xl. 5. 6.

30. Ibid. Xiii.

31. कुमारीषु कानीनीषु जारिणीषु च ये हिताः। i 27.

32. Ibid. ii 9.

33. आचार्यस्तु ते गतिर्वक्ता आचार्यदेव विद्या विदिता साधिष्ठं प्रापयति।
CH. U iv. 14. 1.

34. iv 4.

teaching are found in the Maitrāyaṇi-Upaniṣad, in the dialogue of Bṛihadratha and Śākāyana which runs thus: "This knowledge should not be imparted to a sceptic and so on."[35] The usual period of Brahmacharya is mentioned in the Chāndogya-Upaniṣad.[36] In the Bṛhadāraṇyaka-Upaniṣad,[37] the sacred Gāyatri Mantra is esoterically explained. Many practical instructions of very high value are given in the Taittirīya-Upaniṣad,[38] such as those to the student who leaves his college. As regards marriage, polygamy was possible as shown by the case of Yājñavalkya and his two wives. Early marriage is referred to in the Chāndogya-Upanisd.[38] Here Āṭiki wife is mentioned. The word is explained by later writers as a wife married when she was very young. It was, however, derided. The same Upaniṣad[40] contains many references to the system of naming. In the Bṛhadāraṇyaka-Upaniṣad[41] we have a detailed sacrificial rite for begetting a learned son versed in all the Vedas. The custom of not performing any funeral ceremony of an ascetic is mentioned in the Chāndogya-Upaniṣad.

5. *The Ritual Literature proper*

Th first systematic treatment of the Vedic sacrifices and domestic rites is found in the Sūtra literature. The Śrautasūtras contain directions for the laying of the sacred sacrificial fire, for the Agnihotra, the Darśapaurṇamāsya, the Chāturmāsya, the Paśuyāga and the great Aśvamedha, the Rājasūya and the Vājapeya sacriqces. But as they are mainly occupied with the Vedic sacrifices, they do not yield any material relating to the Saṁskāras. It is in the Gṛhyasūtras that we find directions for all sorts of usages, ceremonies, rites, customs and sacrifices, the performance and observance of which were binding on the Hindu householder. Among these are found the Saṁskāras that were performed from the moment when the individual was conceived in the womb till the hour of his death and even further through the funeral ceremonies. The Gṛhyasūtras generally begin with the Vivāha, 'marriage ceremonies' and go on describing the Garbhādhāna, the

35. असूयकायानृजवेऽयताय न मा ब्रूया वीर्यवती तथा स्याम्। Chap. I.

36. Vi. 1. 2.

37. V. 15.

38. i. 11.

39. i. 10. 1,

40. V. 15.

41. Vi. 5.

Puṁsavana, the Sīmantonnayana, the Jātakarma, the Nāmakaraṇa, the Niṣkramaṇa, the Annaprāśana, the Chūḍākarma, the Upanayana and the Samāvartana. Then, they describe the sacrifices and rites to be performed by a married couple, and in the end deal with the Antyeṣṭi or funeral ceremonies. They give every detail of a Saṁskāra and lay down Mantras and formulas to be recited at different stages of a particular Saṁskāra. Many Gṛhyasūtras omit the funeral ceremony as it was regarded inauspicious and was described in separate Pariśiṣṭas or addenda and the Pitṛmedha-sūtras. The ritual aspects of the Saṁskāras are emphasised and minutely described in the Gṛhyasūtras. Their social sides are simply hinted at or briefly described. The Gṛhyasūtras belong to the different Vedic schools; so, in matters of details, they differ from one another to some extent.

There are other branches of the ritual literature, which, though of later date, should be classed with the Gṛhyasūtras. These are various Kalpas, the Pariśiṣṭas, the Kārikās, the the Prayogas and the Paddhatis. The Śrāddhakalpas[42] and the Pitṛmedhasūtras, which contain rules for funeral ceremonies and ancestral sacrifices follow many of the Gṛhyasūtras. Next come the Pariśiṣṭas or "addenda" in which certain features of the Saṁskāras are dealt with in a greater detail, that were briefly described in the Gṛhyasūtras. Other works on the Saṁskāras are the Prayogas, "practical handworks", the Paddhatis "outlines", and the Kārikās, "versified presentations of rituals". These works supplement the Gṛhyasūtras and introduce new materials in course of time. They deal either with the complete rites and ceremonies of that school, or are only concerned with special rites. There are also exhaustive works of this class of literature on important Saṁskāras like the marriage, the Upanayana, the funeral etc. There is a continuous stream of the ritual literature from the most ancient period up to the present time.

6. *The Dharmasūtras*

The Dharmasūtras are closely connected with the Gṛhyasūtras and they were perhaps written in continuation with them. By "Dharma" the Hindus mean 'right, duty, law' and also 'religious custom and usage.' So, at many places the contents of the Dharmasūtras and the Gṛhyasūtras overlap each other. The latter des-

---

42. The most important of them are the मानव, the कात्यायन, the शौनक, the पैप्पलाद, the गौतम, the बौधायन and the हिरण्यकेशी श्राद्धकल्पs.

cribe the domestic rites which the householder was required to perform in his individual capacity, whereas the former were concerned with rules and regulations about the conduct of men as the members of the Hindu community and do not describe rituals of any kind. The Dharmasūtras deal with the Varṇas (castes) and the Āśramas (stages of life). It is under the Āśrama-Dharmas that the rules about the Upanayana and the Vivāha are given exhaustively. They also contain rules about the Samāvartana, the Upākarma, the Anadhyāyas, Āśaucha, the Śrāddhas and the Madhuparkas. They take up and develop the social aspects of the Saṁskāras that were simply suggested in the Gṛhyasūtras.

7. *The Smṛtis*

The Smṛtis represent a later and a more systematic development of the Dharmasūtras. Like the Dharmasūtras, they are also mainly concerned with the social conduct of men rather than with rituals. Their contents can be classified under three heads, Āchāra, Vyavahāra and Prāyaśchitta. Under the first head the Saṁskāras are (mentioned and the rules regulating them are) given. The most exhaustively treated Saṁskāras are the Upanayana and the Vivāha, as they inaugurated the first and the second stages of the life of an individual. The Pañcha-mahāyajñas or 'five great sacrifices' also figure very prominently in the Smṛtis. Manu[43] gives a very important place to them and describes them at length. The Smṛtis also offer us a mass of information about prayers and sacrifices, household duties, eschatology, funeral ceremonies and sacrifices to the dead. We find in them discussions on the right of performing the Saṁskāras, minor ceremonies and rites, the worship of new Paurāṇika deities at various occasions in life, all unknown to the Gṛhyasūtras and the Dharmasūtras. Not all the Smṛtis deal with the Saṁskāras. Some, like the Nārada-Smṛti, are entirely devoted to Vyavahāra or Law, while others like the Parāśara, are given to the prescription of Prāyaśchittas. Under the Prāyaśchitta, however, ceremonial impurity due to birth and death are described. The main features of the Smṛtis, as regards the Saṁskāras, are that they mark the transition from the Vedic to Smārta and Paurāṇika Hinduism. They omit almost all the Vedic sacrifices and introduce new types of worship and ceremonies. Greater restrictions are placed on social sides of the Saṁskāras, e.g., the total rejection of intercaste marriages in the latest Smṛtis.

---

43. iii. 67–75.

8. *The Epics*

The epic literature also gives some information about the Saṁskāras. The Brāhmaṇas, who were the custodians of literature, utilized the epics, as they became popular, for propagation of their culture and religion. So, many religious and ceremonial elements which did not originally belong to it, entered the huge body of the Mahābhārata and it became a reference book for the Hindu religion. The Mahābhārata was regarded as a Samhitā as early as before the fifth century A.D.[44] Profuse quotations from the Mahābhārata are found in the commentaries and the treatises, bearing on the various topics of the Saṁskāras,[45] "Bhārate" or in the "Mahābhārata" is an oftused phrase in the treatises on the Dharmaśāstra. Moreover, there is a close relation between the Mahābhārta and the Smṛtis. The Manusmṛti and the Mahābhārta possess many common verses. The Vṛddha Gautama,[46] the Bṛhaspati and the Yama-Smṛtis originally formed part of the Mahābhārata. The Rāmayaṇā and other epics like the Raghuvaṁśa, the Kumārasaṁbhava, and the plays like the Uttara-Rāmacharita supply apt illustrations elucidating many tangled points in the Saṁskāras.

9. *The Purāṇas*

The Purāṇas are not less important than the epics for the study of the Saṁskāras. Their influence on the Dharmaśāstra literature is considerable. Even the earliest Dharmasūtras bear witness to the popularity of the Purāṇas which they often quote. They are in many ways connected with the Smṛtis. The Āpastamba-Dharmasūtra[47] refers specially to the Bhaviṣya-Purāṇa.[48] Caland, while writing on Śrāddha, traced close relation between the Mārkaṇḍeya-Purāṇa and the Gautama-Smṛti, the Viṣṇudharmottara-Purṇāa and Viṣṇusmṛti, the Chaturviṁśati-Purāṇa and the Mānava-Śrāddha-Kalpa, the Kūrma-Purāṇa and the Uśanas-Smṛti, and the Brāhma-purāṇa and the rites of the Kaṭhas. We also come across identical descriptions of many topics relating to the Saṁskāras in the Smṛtis and the Purāṇas.

---

44. Bühler and Kirste, contrib. to the history of the Mahābhārata. Siteungsher wien, 1892. 4—27.

45. Cf. VMS; S. C. etc.

46. The Dharmaśāstra-Saṁgraha, Calcutta, 1876, vol. 2. 497-635. Cf. Islampurkar 1. c. Preface notes 6-9.

47. Áp D. S. i. 24, 6.

48. Altind Ahneneult. 68. 79. 112,

Thus, the Śrāddhakalpa of the Yajñavalkya-Smṛti is the same as given in the Agni and the Garuḍa Purāṇas. Long passages from the first three chapters of the Manusmṛti are borrowed by the Bhaviṣya-Purāṇa. The Laghu-Hārīta-Smṛti is nothing but an extract from the Narasiṁha-Purāṇa.

The Purāṇas deal with ceremonies, customs and usages and fasts and feasts of the Hindus and thus throw light on many parts of the Saṁskāras. Astrological consideration that played an important part in the Saṁskāras are developed in the Purāṇas. Divinations regarding different marks on the body, that determine the suitability of the bride or the bridegroom are given in the Liṅgapurāṇa.[49] The Purāṇas also served as an abrogative agency and came to rescue the Hindu society in the middle ages. Many old customs and usages that had become obsolete or obnoxious to the society were tabooed under Kalivarjya by the Brāhma[50] and the Āditya-Purāṇas.[51]

10. *The Commentaries*

The commentaries on the existing Gṛhyasūtras, the Dharmasūtras and the Smṛtis also give further and later information about the Saṁskāras. Though they propose to explain and expound the ancient texts, they do some thing more. They not only explain, but they supplement and restrict also. Thus they reflect a new state of society where many of the old provisions of the Dharmaśāstra had become out of date, and new ones were urgently needed. They were able to do so by means of ingenious interpretations, extenstion, restrictions and overruling. Really speaking the commentators are more important than the texts, as the Hindus of the different provinces follow the particular commentary prevalent in them. Modern Pandits reject even sacred authorities if they are not quoted by the commentators.

11. *The Mediaeval Treatises*

The Nibandhas or the mediaeval treatises gave a new orientation to the Saṁskāras. The Gṛhyasūtras and the Dharmasūtras

---

49. Quoted in VMS. Vol. I.

50. गोत्रान्मातुः सपिण्डाच्च विवाहो गोवधस्तथा ।
नराश्वमेधौ मद्यं च कलौ वर्ज्यं द्विजातिभिः ॥ Quoted in N.S. p. 261.

51. On Kalivarjya quoted in the CVC, and the N.S. p. 262.

belonged to different Vedic schools and even the Smṛtis were connected with them to some extent. But the Nibandhas do not owe allegiance to any single Vedic school. Rather they are scholarly works universal in their nature and treatment. The Nibandhas are huge compilations from ancient sources on various topics of Dharma. The Saṁskāras are treated under separate sections allotted to them and called Saṁskāra-kāṇḍa,[52] Saṁskāra-Prakāśa[53] etc. Many ancient and out of date Saṁskāras are also repeated in them. The texts are arranged according to the convenient opinions of the writers. They pay hardly any attention to the chronological differences and try to rationalize the ancient texts in their own way. Different Nibandhas are current in different provinces. So they contain divergent opinions on the same topics.

12. *The Customs*

Customs have been recognized from the very beginning as a source of the Hindu Dharma. The Gautama, the Baudhāyana, the Āpastamba and the Vasiṣṭha Dharmasūtras and the Manu and the Yājñavalkya-Smṛtis all include customs in the lists of their authorities.[54] But no branch of the Hindu Dharma is more based on customs than the Saṁskāras that originated from popular beliefs and usages, and developed independently without any state interference. The Gṛhyasūtras generally refer to the customs of one's own family in the performance of the Saṁskāras. Really speaking, customs were the only source of the Saṁskāras before they were codified in the Gṛhya manuals. But there was still a mass of floating customs that could not be codified but was recognized as authority on the Saṁskāras. The Āśvalāyana Gṛhyasūtra[55] while laying down rules about the Vivāha Saṁskāra says, "the customs and usages of different provinces and villages are high and low, that is variant. They should be all consulted in marriage. We prescribe what is common." The difference was bound to be in rites and ceremonies that were performed at such happy and joyous occasions like marriage, birth etc. according to the taste and refinement of the people concerned. In the funeral ceremonies Āpastamba[56] refers to the authority of ladies in particular as they are the most conservative elements in society.

---

52. In S.C.

53. In VM.

54. See Ante pp 1 & 2.

55. अथ खलूच्चावचा जनपदधर्मा ग्रामधर्माश्च तान् विवाहे प्रतीयात् । यत्तु समानं तत् वक्ष्यामः ।

56. यत् स्त्रियः आहुः तत्कुर्युः । Ap. D.S. ii. 6.

Baudhāyana,[57] on Āśaucha, says, "In the rest the people should be referred to," for the funeral ceremonies were closely connected with local beliefs and superstitions. Thus, not written in a code book, customs were a dynamic force that introduced necessary and welcome changes from time to time. They also played an important part in determining the procedure of a rite of ceremony.

Customs can be broadly divided into three groups. The first group consists of the Deśāchāras or customs prevalent in a particular province, e.g., marrying the daughter of a maternal uncle in the South, which is generally prohibited elsewhere.[58] The second group includes the Kulāchāras or the family customs, for example, the keeping of sacred knot or Śikhā was determined by the Pravara of a man.[59] The last group coincides with the Jātyāchāras or customs current in a caste, for instance, the Rākṣasa and the Gāndharva forms of marriages were, on the whole, not desirable. Yet they were recommended for the Kṣatriyas.[60]

13. *Indo-Iranian, Indo-European and Semitic Sources*

The sources of information about the Hindu Saṁskāras are not exhausted with the Indian literature and customs. A few Saṁskāras, and many constituents of the Saṁskāras in general, can be traced back to the pre-Vedic times, when the Indo-Iranian and even some of the Indo-European people were living together, sharing the same beliefs and performing the same rites. The religion of the Avesta bears close resemblance with the Vedic religion and Parsism still preserves a few sacraments akin to the Hindu Saṁskāras, e.g., the birth ceremonies, the first eating of food and the initiation ceremonies. The worship of fire and the cult of sacrifice were common to Hinduism and Parsism both. The Greek and the Roman religions were also sacrificial and their rituals, in many respects, resembled the Hindu Saṁskāras. For example, the marriage ceremonies of the Greeks were similar to those of the Hindus in their broad out-lines. For studying the Hindu Saṁskāras the knowledge of these religions supplies a proper perspective.

---

57. शेषक्रियायां लोकः अनुरोध्यः। B. P. S.

58. B. D. S. i. 1.17.

59. चूडाः कारयेत दक्षिणतः कमुजावसिष्ठानाम् उभयतोऽत्रिकाश्यपानां, मुण्डाः भृगवः Laugakṣi, quoted in V.M.S. vol. 1. p. 315.

60. M. S. iii. 23. 24.

The religious ceremonies being universal in ancient times, we find many parallel rites in non-Indo-European races also. Semitic religions have many sacraments of very old origin which are performed at important occasions in the life of a man. The Christian sacraments evolved from Semitic sources, though later on they assimilated many Aryan elements in the course of this spread in Europe. Christianity and Islam both have religious ceremonies like baptism, confirmation, matrimony etc. These serve as means of comparison between the Hindu and the Semitic rites which originated from the same process of ideas.

14. *The Relative Importance of Sources*

The information derived from the Vedas, mostly being incidental, is highly reliable. Here the poet, unlike the priests, was not superimposing ceremonies on the people but drawing on the popular sources and incorporating the popular rites in his compositions. The specific hymns, e.g., the wedding and the funeral hymns reproduce very approximately their respective rites. Winternitz[61] calls the wedding hymn "a narrative ballad." But even if we grant that it was so, we cannot deny that the narrating poet must have tried to be true to reality as far as it was possible. The theory also that the Vedic hymns were poetic outpourings of heart and had no connection with rituals, does not negate the possibility of the Vedic singers being influenced by ritualistic atmosphere they were breathing in. The same is also the case with other incidental references found in the Upaniṣads, the Purāṇas and the epics. They have corroborative as well as supplementary value. In the Brāhmaṇas, the discussions on the rituals are very speculative and interpretation and explanations highly fantastic. Therefore, we cannot take them at their face value. Making allowance, however, for exaggeration and fancy, we get the mental picture of a people who believed in the miraculous efficacy of sacrifices and rituals. Ritualistic details found in the Brāhmaṇas have been utilized and amplified by the later literature, the Sūtras. So, there is hardly any doubt that these details are trustworthy for their times. In the ritual literature proper there is a great elaboration of the simple rites of ancient days. For the development of rituals the priest was responsible to a great extent. But rites and ceremonies were not his fabrications; rather he mainly drew on common practices, though he gave a polish and supplied a rationale to them. Had these rituals not been popular

61. A History of Indian Literature. vol. I, p. 154.

in their origin, they could not have become so universal and lasting. We have mostly relied on this class of literature while describing the Saṁskāras. The Dharmasūtras and the Smṛtis that prescribe the rules and regulations are not so natural to the Saṁskāras as the Gṛhyasūtras. In them there was much ideal and only partially followed by people. But as the hold of religion on men was very strong in ancient times, these rules and regulations were respected and observed to a great extent. The Dharmasūtras and the Smṛtis were not closely connected with any Vedic School and they were followed universally. So, in the present thesis their rules and regulations have been understood and utilized as such. The views of the commentaries and the treatises are more reliable for their times than the texts, because the texts were written in a time far back in the past under different circumstances. Their interpretations, however, of ancient texts cannot be accepted for every time as they try to show.

CHAPTER II

THE MEANING AND THE NUMBER OF THE SAMSKĀRAS

1. *The Meaning of the word 'Saṁskāra'*

The word Saṁskāra defies every attempt at its correct translation into English. Ceremony or Latin caerimonia does not give the full meaning of this word. Rather it corresponds with Sanskrit Karman, religious act in general. Saṁskāra does not mean "more outward religious rite. polite observances, empty form, stately usage, formalities and punctilious behaviour"[1] as it is generally understood by some people. Nor does it mean rites and rituals alone by which we understand "form of procedure, action required or usual in a religious or solemn ceremony or observance, or a body of usages characteristic of a church."[2] A better approach to the rendering of Saṁskāra in English is made by the word sacrament which means "religious ceremony or act regarded as outward and visible sign of inward and spiritual grace", applied by the Eastern, pre-reformation Western, and Roman Catholic churches to the seven rites of baptism, confirmation, the eucharist, penance, extreme unction, orders and matrimony. Sacrament also means confirmation of some promise or oath; things of mysterious significance, sacred influence and symbol."[3] Thus it overlaps many other religious spheres which, in the Sanskrit literature, are covered by "Śuddhi, purification," Prāyaścitta, "atonement;" Vratas, "vows" etc.

The word Saṁskāra is derived from the Sanskrit root Saṁskṛghañ and is used in a variety of ways. It is seldom found in the early Vedic literature. But its allied word 'Saṁskrita' occurs frequently enough. In the Ṛgveda (V. 76. 2) it is used in the sense of 'purified' : 'The two Aśvins do not harm the *gharma* (vessel) that has been purified." The Śatapatha Brāhmaṇa (1.1.4.10) uses the term in the sense of preparing or purifying *havis* (offering) for the gods. The Mimāṁsakas[4] mean by it the ceremonious purification of sacri-

1. The Oxford Dictionary, under the word, 'Ceremony'

2. Ibid. under the word, 'Rite'.

3. Ibid. under the word, 'Sacrament'.

4. प्रोक्षणादिजन्यसंस्कारी यज्ञाङ्ग पुरोडाशेष्विति द्रव्यधर्मः। Vāchaspatya-brhadābhidhāna, V. p. 5188.

ficial materials. In the Sūtras of Jaimini the word 'Saṁskāra' has been applied several times in the sense of some purificatory rite (III. 1. 3; III. 2, 15; III. 8. 3; IX. 2, 9, 42–44). Śābra, the commentator on the Jaiminisūtras (III. 1. 3) explains the term Śaṁskāra' as an act which makes a certain thing or person fit for a certain purpose.[5] The Tantravārtika (p. 1078) regards 'Saṁskāra' as those acts and rites that impart fitness and further adds, "fitness is of two kinds." It arises from the removal of taints (sins) or by the generation of fresh qualities. Saṁskāras generates fresh qualities, which *tapas* brings about the removal of sins." The Advaita Vedantists[6] regard it the false attribution of physical action to the soul. The Naiyayikas use it in the sense of self-reproductive quality or faculty of impression recognised by the Vaiśeṣikas as one of the twenty four guṇas. In the classical Sanskrit literature the word Saṁskāra is used in a very wide sense :–in the sense of education, cultivation, training;[7] refinement, perfection and grammatic purity;[7a] making perfect, refining, polishing;[8] embelishment, decoration and ornament;[9] impression, form, mould, operation, inbuence;[9a] the faculty of recollection, impression on the memory;[10] a purificatory rite, a sacred rite or ceremony;[11] consecration, sanctification and hallowing; idea, notion and conception; effect of work, merit of action etc.[12]

So we find that the word "Saṁskāra" has got its own peculiar associations gathered round it through its long history. It means religious purificatory rites and ceremonies for sanctifying the body, mind and intellect of an individual, so that he may become a full-fiedged member of the community. But the Hindu Saṁskāras also

---

5. संकारो नाम स भवति यस्मिज्जाते पदार्थों भवति योग्य: कस्यचिदर्थस्य।

6. स्नानाचमनादिजन्या: संस्कारादेहे उत्पद्यमानापि तदभिमानि जीहें कल्प्यन्ते। *Ibid.*

6a. निसर्ग संस्कारविनीत इत्यसौ नृपेण चक्रे युवराज शब्दभाक्।
Ragh. V. iii. 35.

7. संस्कारवत्येव गिरा मनीषी तया स पूतश्च विभषितश्च।
Kumārasmbhava, 1.28.

8. प्रयुक्तसंस्कार इवाधिकं बभौ। Ragh. V. iii. 18.

9. स्वभावसुन्दरं वस्तु न संस्कारमपेक्षते The Śakuntalā vii. 23.

9a. यन्नवे भाजने लग्न: संस्कारो नान्यथा भवेत्। The Hitopadeśa 1. 8.

10. संस्कादिजन्यं ज्ञानं स्मृति:। The Tarkasmgraha.

11. कार्य: शरीरसंस्कार: पावन: प्रेत्य चेह च। M. S. ii. 26.

12. फलानुमेया प्रारम्भा: संस्कारा: प्राक्तना इव। Ragh V. i. 20.

combine a number of preliminary considerations and rites and other accompanying regulations and observances, all aiming at not only the formal purification of the body but at sanctifying, impressing, refining and perfecting the entire individuality of the recipient. The Saṁskāras with their paraphernalia were regarded as producing a peculiar indefinable kind of merit for the man who underwent them a "a peculiar excellence due to the rites ordained (by the Śāstrās) which resides either in the soul or the body."[13] It was in this collective sense that the word Saṁskāra was used.

Though many of the Saṁskāras originated in, or even before, the Vedic period, as the ritualistically specific hymns[14] of the Vedas indicate, the word 'Saṁskāra' does not occur in the Vedic literature. The Brāhmaṇa literature also does not mention the word, though some sections of it contain fragments of a few Saṁskāras like the Upanayana, the funeral etc.[15] The Mimāṁsakas[16] used the word in the sense of not purificatory rites concerning individuals but in the sense of cleansing and purifying sacrificial materials before they were offered into fire.

2. *The Extent and Number of the Saṁskāras*

(i) The Gṛhyasūtras. The Saṁskāras, in the strict sense, fall within the jurisdiction of the Gṛhyasūtras. But here too we do not find the word "Saṁskāra" used in its proper sense. They too use the word in the sense of the Mimāṁsakas and speak of the Pañcabhūsaṁskāras[17] and the Pāka-Saṁskāras by which they mean sweeping, sprinkling and purifying the sacrificial ground and boiling or preparing food for sacrifice. The hold of sacrifices on the social mind was great. They classify the entire domestic rituals under the names of different sacrifices.[18] The bodily Saṁskāras are included in the list of the Pākayajñas.[19] The Pāraskara-Gṛhyasūtra divides

13. आत्मशरीरान्यतरनिष्ठो विहितक्रियाजन्योऽतिशयविशेषः संस्कारः।
V. M. S. vol. I. p. 132.

14. See ante p. 2. footnotes.

15. Ś. Br. Xi Xiv.

16. ब्रीह्यादेश्च यज्ञाङ्गताप्रदानाय वैदिकमार्गेण प्रोक्षणादिः।
The Vāchaspatya-bṛhadabhindhāna Vol. V. P. 5158.

17. A G.S. i. 3. i; P.G.S.

18. i. 1. 9; Kh. GS. i 2 1 P.G.S. i. 4 1; A.G.S. i. 1. 2.

19. B.G.S. i. 1. 1-12.

the Pāka-yajñas into four classes, the huta, the āhuta, the prahuta and the prāśita. The Baudhāyana-Gṛhyasūtra classifies the Pākayajñas under seven heads, the huta, the prahuta, the āhuta, the Śūlagava, the baliharaṇa, the pratyavarohaṇa and the aṣṭakāhoma. It explains them as follows. Where the offerings are thrown into the fire it is called huta. This class includes the Saṁskāras from the Vivāha (marriage) to the Sīmantonnayana (hair-parting). Where, after making offerings to the fire, presents are given to the Brahmans and others it is called prahuta. This group contains the Saṁskāras from the Jātakarma (birth ceremonies) to the Chaula (tonsure). That kind of sacrifices are called āhuta where after making offerings to the fire and presents to the Brahmans, one receives presents from others. The Upanayana and the Samāvartana Saṁskāras are included in this list. Thus, here what are later on, called the Saṁskāras are treated as domestic sacrifices. There seems to be no clear idea about sanctifying the body and perfecting personality. The gods are the centre of religious activities and not individuals. So the sacrifices, including even the bodily Saṁskāras, were offered for their propitiation.

In the Vaikhānasa-Smārtasūtras[20] we find a clearer distinction between the bodily Saṁskāras and the sacrifices, that were performed at various occasions to propitiate the gods. Here eighteen bodily Saṁskāras (Aṣṭādaśa Saṁskāraḥ Śārīrāḥ), from the Ṛtusaṁgamana (conception) to the Vivāha (marriage) are mentioned. Again, the same work mentions the twenty-two sacrifices separately.[21] These sacrifices include the Pañcamahāyajñas, the seven Pāka-sacrifies, the seven Havisacrifices and the seven Soma sacrifices. Properly speaking, these are not personal Saṁskāras but daily and seasonal sacrifices.

The Gṛhyasūtras generally deal with the bodily Saṁskāras beginning with Vivāha and ending with Samāvartana. The majority of them omit the funeral. Only a few, e.g., the the Pāraskara, the Āśvalāyana and the Baudhāyana describe it. The following are the numbers of Saṁskāras dealt with in the Gṛhyasūtras. They fluctuate from twelve to eighteen and the lists are slightly varying in names of some particular Saṁskāras or in some additions and omissions.

---

20. i. 1.

21. Ibid.

Āśvalāyana G.S.	Pāraskara G.S.	Baudhāyana G.S.
I	II	III
1. Vivāha	1. Vivāha	1. Vivāha
2. Garbhālambhana	2. Garbhālambhana	2. Garbhālambhana
3. Puṁsavana	3. Puṁsavana	3. Puṁsavana
4. Sīmantonnayana	4. Sīmantonnayana	4. Sīmantonnayana
5. Jātakarma	5. Jātakarma	5. Jātakarma
6. Nāmakaraṇa	6. Nāmakaraṇa	6. Nāmakaraṇa
7. Chūḍākarma	7. Chūḍākarma	7. Upaniṣkramaṇa
8. Annaprāśana	8. Annaprāśana	8. Annaprāśana
9. Upanayana	9. Cūḍākarma	9. Cūḍākarma
10. Samāvartana	10. Upanayana	10. Karṇavedha (Gṛhya Śeṣa)
11. Antyeṣṭi	11. Keśānta	11. Upanayana
	12. Samāvartana	12. Samāvartana
	13. Antyeṣṭi	13. Pitṛmedha

(I) Vārāha G. S.	(II) Vaikhānasa G.S.
1. Jātakarma	1. Ṛtusaṁgamana
2. Nāmakaraṇa	2. Garbhādhāna
3. Dantodgamana	3. Sīmanta
4. Annaprāśana	4. Viṣṇubali
5. Chūḍākarṇa	5. Jātakarma
6. Upanayana	6. Utthāna
7. Veda-Vratāni	7. Nāmakarana
8. Godāna	8. Annaprāśana
9. Samāvartana	9. Pravāsāgamana
10. Vivāha	10. Piṇḍavardhana
11. Garbhādhāna	11. Chaulaka
12. Puṁsavana	12. Upanayana
13. Sīmantonnayana	13. Pārāyaṇa
	14. Vratabandhavisarga
	15. Upākarma
	16. Utsarjana
	17. Samāvartana
	18. Pāṇigrahaṇa

(ii) The Dharmasūtras, being mostly occupied with the Hindu laws and custom, not all of them care to describe or enumerate the Saṁskāras. They contain rules about the Upanayana, Vivāha, Upākarma, Utsarjana, Anadhyāyas and Āśaucha. The Gautama-Dharmasūtra gives a list of altogether forty Saṁskāras with eight virtues of the soul (Chatvārinśatsaṁsakārāḥ Aṣṭau Ātmaguṇāḥ).

1.	Garbhādhāna	2.	Puṁsavana
3.	Sīmantonnayan	4.	Jātakarma
5.	Nāmakaraṇa	6.	Annaprāśana
7.	Chaula	8.	Upanayana
9-12	Chatvāri Veda-Vratāni	13.	Snāna
14.	Sahadharma-chāriṇī-Saṁyoga		
15-19.	Pañca-Mahāyajñas	20-26	Aṣṭakā, Pārvana, Śrāddha, Srāvaṇī, Āgrahayani, Chāitre Āśvayaji-iti Sapta-Pāka-Yajña-Saṁsthaḥ
27-33.	Agnyādheyam, Agnihotram, Darśa-Paurṇamāsya, Chāturmāsya, Āgrayāṇeṣti, Nirūḍha-paśubandha, Sautrāmaṇi-iti Sapta-Haviryajña-Saṁsthāḥ	34-40	Agnistoma, Atyagnistoma, Uktha, Ṣoḍaśī, Vājapeya, Atirātra, Āptoryāma-iti Sapt-Somayajña-Saṁsthāḥ.

Here too we do not find a clear distinction between the Saṁskāras proper and the sacrifices. All the domestic rites and many Śrauta sacrifices elaborately described in the Brāhmaṇas and the Śrautasūtras, are placed with the Saṁskāras in the above list. The word "Saṁskāra" is used in the sense of religious rites in general.

According to Hārita,[23] a later Smṛti-writer, the sacrifies are to be taken as the Daiva Saṁskāras and other ceremonies, that were performed at the various occasions in the life of an individual, as the Brāhma Saṁskāras. Only the latter are to be taken as the Saṁskāras in the proper sense. No doubt, indirectly the sacrifices were of purificatory nature,[24] but their direct purpose was to propitiate gods at different seasons, whereas the main object of the Saṁskāras proper was to sanctify the personality of the recipient.[25] Many of the sacrifices, e.g. Chaitrī, Āśvayujī, were seasonal festivals that later on crystallised into popular feasts and rejoicings.

(iii) The Smṛtis. When the Smṛtis arose, the sacrificial religion and with them the Daiva Saṁskāras were on the wane. The Smṛtis generally mean by Saṁskāras only those sacramental rites that were performed for sanctifying the personality of an individual, though some of them include the Pākayajñas also in their lists. According to Manu[26] the Smārta Saṁskāras or the Saṁskāras proper are thirteen, from conception to death. Beginning from the conception they are:

1. Garbhādhāna
2. Puṁsavana
3. Sīmantonnayana
4. Jātakarma
5. Nāmadheya
6. Niṣkramaṇa
7. Annaprāśana
8. Chūḍākarma
9. Upanayana or Maunjibandhana
10. Keśānta
11. Samāvartan
12. Vivāha and
13. Smaśāna

---

23. पाकयज्ञहविर्यज्ञसौम्याश्चेतिदैवः। ब्रह्मसंस्कारसंस्कृत ऋषीणां समानतां सलोकतां सायुज्यं गच्छति। दैवेनोत्तरेण संस्कृतो देवानां समानतां सलोकतां सायुज्यं गच्छति। इति।
H. D.S. XI. 1. S. Quoted in S.C. I. p. 13; Paraśara-Mādhaviya I part 2, p. 18. The MS of H.D.S. in referred to by the editor of the Parāśara-Mādhavīya.

24. यज्ञो दानं तपश्चैव पावनानि मनीषिणाम्। B.G. xviii. 5

25. संस्कारार्थं शरीरस्य। M.S. ii. 66.

26. Ibid. ii. 16, 26, 29; iii. 1-4.

The Yājñavalkya Smṛti[27] also enumerates the same Saṁskāras except the Keśānta which was omitted from the list owing to the decline of the Vedic studies and its confusion with the Samāvartana. The Gautama-Smṛti[28], following the tradition of its school, enumerates the forty Saṁskāras, though it does not seem oblivious of the fact that the Vedic sacrifires had fallen in disuse and consequently the Daiva Saṁskāras were not regarded as the Saṁskāras proper. The list of Angirā[29] contains twenty-five Saṁskāras. Here the Pākayajñas are also enumerated with the bodily Saṁskāras mentioned in Manu and Yājñavalkya. The later Smṛtis supply the list of sixteen Saṁskāras. According to the Vyāsa-Smṛti[30] the Saṁskāras are Garbhādhāna, Niṣkrama, Annaprāśana, Vapanakriyā, Karṇvedha, Vratādeśa, Vedārambha, Keśānta, Snāna, Udvāha, Vivāhāgniparigraha and Tretāgnisaṁgraha. In this list Karṇavedha and the last two Saṁskāras are added to the number given in Manu and Yājñavalkya. This late addition was due to the fact that Karṇavedha was regarded as a Saṁskāra only later, originally being meant for decoration. Jātūkarṇya[31] also provides a list of sixteen Saṁskāras, but he includes the Four Vows of the Vedic study instead of Vedārambha and retains Antya or funeral, dropping the last two Saṁskāras of Vyāsa.

(iv) Treatises. The mediaeval treatises generally devote one section to the Saṁskāras and in the introduction lists of Gautama, Aṅgirā, Vyāsa, Jātūkṛṇya etc. are compiled. The majority of them exclude the Daiva Saṁskāras or the pure sacrifices from their treatment. For example, the Vīramitrodaya[32] and the Smṛtichandrikā,[33] the Saṁskāramayūkha[34] quote the list of Gautama but they deal with only the Brāhma or Smārta Saṁskāras from Garbhādhāna to Vivāha. So, by Saṁskāras' they mean only the bodily Saṁskāras. They also, like the majority of the Smṛtis, exclude the funeral which was described in separate books. The Nibandhas, besides the classical Smārta Saṁskāras, describe a large number of minor rites and wor-

---

27. I. 2.

28. viii. 2.

29. Quoted in VMS. vol. I.

30. i. 13-15.

31. Quoted in the Saṁskāradīpaka, Part II. p. 1.

32. VMS. vol. I. P. 37.

33. Anhika, Prakaraṇa I.

34. Saṁskāroddeśa p. 10.

ships which were either the offshoot of the major Saṁskāras or were included in them. They were popularly performed but were not elevated to the position of a separate Saṁskāra.

(v) The Paddhats and the Prayogas. The Paddhatis and the Prayogas also deal with only the Brāhma Saṁskāras and leave the Daiva Saṁskāras altogether, partly because they have now become obsolete and partly the current Pākayajñas are described elsewhere. The funeral is always treated separately. The usual number of the Saṁskāras in them is from ten to thirteen (from Garbhadhāna to Vivāha). Many of the Paddhatis are actually called "The Daśakarma-Paddhati,"[35] or "The Manual of Ten Ceremonies."

3. *The Sixteen Saṁskāras*

At present sixteen are the most popular Saṁskāras, though the enumeration differs in different books. The latest Paddhatis have adopted this number. The Smṛtyarthasāra (p. 3) contains: 'Here are the Saṁskāras from *Garbhādhāna* (conception) to *Vivāha* (marriage). There are necessary main Saṁskāras sixteen in number. The digest usually enumerate sixteen Saṁskāras. The Saṁskāravidhi[36] of Svāmi Dayanand Sarasvati and the Ṣoḍaśa-Saṁsāra Vidhi[37] of Pandit Bhimasena Śarmā contain only the sixteen Saṁskāras.

As already pointed out, Antyeṣṭi or the funeral Saṁskāra is not enumerated by Gautama in his long list of forty-eight Saṁskāras, it has been generally omitted by the Gṛhyasūtras, the Dharmasūtras and the Smṛtis and neglected by later works on the Saṁskāras. The reason underlying this exclusion or indifference was that the funeral was regarded as an inauspicious ceremony[38] and it should not be described with auspicious ones. It was, perhaps, also due to the fact that the life history of an individual closes with the advent of death and the post-mortem ceremonies had no direct bearing on the cultivation of personality. Nevertheless, Antyeṣṭi was recognised as a Saṁskāra. Some Gṛhyasūtras describe it, Manu, Yājñavalkya, Jātūkarṇya enumerate it in the list of the Saṁskāras. The funeral

35. The Daśakarmapaddhatis of Gaṇapati, Nārāyaṇa, Pṛthvidhara, Bhūdeva etc.

36. Published from the Vaidika Yantralaya, Ajmer.

37. Published from the Brahma Press, Etawah.

38. M. Williams, Hinruism. p. 65.

belongs to the class of ceremonies in which Vedic Mantras were recited[39], and these Mantras are mostly taken from Vedic funeral hymns.[40] In the present thesis, where there is no psychological bias against it, Antyeṣṭi has found its proper place among the Saṁskāras.

---

39 ३९. निषेकादिस्मशानान्तो मंत्रैर्यस्योदितो विधि:। M.S. 11. 16.

40. R. V. X. 14, 16, 18; A.V., XVIII. 1-4.

CHAPTER III

THE PURPOSE OF THE SAMSKĀRAS

1. *Introductory*

An investigation into the real purpose and significance of ancient institutions like the Hindu Saṁkāras is beset with many difficulties. First of all, the peculiar circumstances under which they arose are buried deep under thick crusts of ages, and around them have clustered a mass of popular superstitions. So, at such a distance of time, it requires a well-trained imagination coupled with a through knowledge of facts to probe into the problem. The second difficulty is that of national sentiment, which looks only at the bright side of the past and clouds the critical *vision so essential* for any research work. But a more stubborn difficulty is presented by the *a priori* tendencies of the modern mind. It is apt to assume that any thing ancient must be superstitious; it is suspicious of spiritual values of life; and it is impatient of understanding strict discipline, which is a great characteristic of ancient religions. A student of ancient culture has to guard himself against credulity on the one hand and the ultrascepticism on the other. He should study the Saṁskāras with due reverence to the past and full sympathy with human nature through its various stages of development.

2. *Two-fold Purpose*

We can broadly divide the purpose of the Saṁskāras into two classes. The first class is popular and superstitious, which is motived by unquestioned faith and naive simplicity of the unsophisticated mind. The second class is priestly and cultural. Its origin is due to conscious forces governing the development and evolution of society, when human beings try to improve upon nature. The priest, though not beyond the common run of people, was above the ordinary man in the street, and he introduced considerable refinment and culture into social customs and rites in a variety of ways. Saṁskāras of both the types have continued to figure in society from the very beginning, they have reacted on each other and they are still represented in Hinduism.

3. *The Popular Purpose*

To begin with the popular purpose, the ancient Hindus, like other nations of the world, believed that they were surrounded by superhuman influences which were potent enough for good or evil consequences. They thought that these influences could interfere in every important occasion in man's life. Therefore, they tried to remove hostile influences and attract beneficial ones, so that man may grow and prosper without external hindrances and receive timely directions and help from gods and spirits. Many items and ramifications of the Saṁskāras arose out of these beliefs.

(i) The Removal of Hostile Influences. For removing the unfavourable influences the Hindus adopted several means in their Saṁskāras. The first of them was propitiation. Goblins, demons and other uncanny spirits were offered praise, oblations and food, so that they may return satisfied with offerings, without causing injury to the individual. The householder was anxious to protect the life of his wife and children and regarded it his duty to deal with them. During the pregnancy of a woman, at the birth of a child, during childhood etc., such propitiation took place. In the birth ceremonies "if the disease-bringing demon, Kumāra attacks the child, the father murmurs........" Kurkura, Sukurkura, who holds fast children, Chet ! Chet ! doggy let him loose. Reverence be to thee, the Sisara, a barkar, a bender."[1] The second method was that of deception. Sometimes propitiation was thought unnecessary or purposely avoided. For example, at the time of tonsure, the severed hair was mixed with cowdung and buried in a cowstall or thrown into a river, so that none could play magic upon it.[2] Deception is also evident in the funeral ceremonies. At the approach of death the image of a man was burnt before his death to deceive it.[3] The motive underlying this act was that death while haunting the proper body of its victim would mistake him for an already dead person. But when propitiation and deception both proved inefficient, a third drastic step was taken. Mischievous spirits were plainly asked to go away, threatened and directly attacked. During the birth ceremonies the father pronounces, 'May Śuṇḍa and Marka, Upavīra and Śauṇḍikeya, Ulūkhala and Malimlucha, Droṇāsa and Chyavana, vanish hence. Svāhā"[4] ! The householder also invoked the help of gods and deities to drive away foul influences. While performing

1. P.G.S. i 16. 20; A.G.S. i. 15; G.G.S. ii. 7. 17. Gadādhara commenting on P.GS. says. ततस्तुष्टो एनं कुमारं मुञ्च।

2. अनुगुप्तमेतं सकेशं गोमयपिण्डं निधाय गोष्टे पल्वलमुदकान्ते वा।
P.G.S. ii. 1. 20.

3. K.S. xlviii. 54 ff; 39 ff.

4. P.G.S. i. 16. 19; AP. G.S. i. 15.

the Chaturthikarma (the Fourth Day after marriage) the husband invites Agni, Vāyu, Sūrya, Chandra and Gandharva to remove the injurious elements from the newly married wife.[5] But sometimes, he himself, by means of water and fire, frightened and drove them off.

Other devices were also used for this purpose. Water was invariably used in every Saṁskāra. It washed away physical impurities and warded off demons and goblins.[6] Noise was made at the time of burial to scare away lurking spirits. Sometimes the man himself asserted his boldness. He equipped himself with weapons to face any odds that might come in his way. For instance, the student was given a staff.[7] He was forbidden to part with it and asked always to keep it close to his body. When this staff was thrown away at the end of studentship, he was provided with a stronger bamboo-staff at the time of Samāvartana.[8] It is clearly stated that it was used not merely for protection against animals and human foes but also against Rākṣasas and Piśāchas.[9] Shaking was also a means to remove evil influences. Combing the hair at the time of the Sīmantonnayana (Hair-parting) was done for the same purpose.[10] Selfishness of man sometimes compelled him to transfer bad influences form his side to that of others. The marriage custume worn by the bride was given to a Brahman, as it was thought injurious to her. In this case, however, the Brahman was thought too powerful to be attacked by evil influences. The nuptial clothes were also put in a cowpen or hung on a tree.[11]

(ii) Attraction of Favourable Influences. Just as untoward influences were tried to be got rid of, so the favourable influences were invited and attracted for the benefit of the recipient of a particular Saṁskāra. The Hindus believed that every period of life was presided over by a deity. Therefore, on every occasion, that deity was invoked to confer boons and blessings on the man. At the time of the Garbhādhāna (Conception) Viṣṇu was the chief deity, at the

5. अग्ने प्रायश्चित्ते त्वं देवानां प्रायश्चित्तिरसि ब्राह्मणस्त्वा नाथकाम उपधावामि याऽस्यै पतिघ्नी तनूस्तामेस्यै नाशय स्वाहा। etc. P.G.S. i. 11. 2. 1-5.

6. आपो हि वै रक्षोघ्नी। Ś. Br.

7. A.G. i. 19. 10; P.G.S. ii. 5. 16.

8. वैणवं दण्डमादत्ते। .G.S. ii. 6. 26.

9. विश्वाभ्यो मा नाष्ट्राभ्यस्परिपाहि सर्वंत इति। P.G.S. ii. 6. 26.

10. Āp. G.S. xiv; H.G.S. ii. 2.

11. A.V. xiv. 2. 48-50; K.S. lxxvi. 1; lxxix. 24.

time of the Vivāha Prajāpati, and at the time of the Upanayana Bṛihsapati and so on. But there was no entire dependence on gods only. Men helped themselves also by various means. Suggestion and reference to analogous phenomena played a great part. Touch exercised a magic power. By touching things that were beneficial in themselves one expected good influences to follow. In the Sīmantonnayana ceremonies a branch of the Udumbara (fig) tree was applied to the neck of the wife.[12] Here touch was believed to bring about fertility. Mounting a stone brought about nrmness and was therefore prescribed for a student and a bride.[13] Touching the heart was thoughtt to be a sure means of union and producing harmony between student and teacher or husband and wife.[14] As breath was a symbol of life, the father breathed thrice on the new-born child to strengthen its breaths.[15] For securing a male child the expectant mother was required to eat a barley corn with two beans and curd attached to it.[16] The reason is obvious. The things which the expectant mother took were symbolical of the male sex and were expected to impart it to the embryo. To produce offsprings the juice of a many-rooted and luxuriant banyan-tree branch was inserted into the right nostril of the wife.[17] Anointment produced love and affection. In the marriage ceremonies the bride's father anointed the couple while the bridegroom pronounced, "May all gods, may water unite our hearts......[18] Avoidance of ugly and inauspicious sights, and giving up contact with impure persons preserved the purity of an individual. The Snātaka was forbiddes even to pronounce a word beginning with an unlucky letter, or containg a repugnant idea.[19] Sometimes dramatic utterances were also requisitioned to bring about the desired thing. In the Sīmantonnayan ceremonies the wife was asked to look at a mess of rice whereupon the husband inquired whether she

---

12. औदुम्बरेण त्रिवृतमाबध्नाति—'अयमूर्ज्जावतो वृक्षः उर्ज्जीव फलिनी भव। P.G.S. i. 15. 4. 6, G.G.S. ii. 7. 1.

13. In the Upanayana and the Vivāha Saṁskāras.

14. Ibid.

15. In the Jātakaima.

16. H.G.S. ii. 2. 23; A.G.S. i. 13. 2.

17. P.G.S. i. 14. 3.

18. अथेनौ समञ्जयति—'समंजन्तु विश्वे देवाः समीपो हृदयानि नौ। सम्मातरिश्वा सन्धाता समुदेष्ट्री दधातु नः। P.G.S. i. 4. 15; G.G.S. ii. 1. 18.

19. गर्भिणो विजन्येति। सकुलमिति नकुलम्। भगालमिति कपालम्। P.G.S. ii. 7. 11-13. A.G.S. iii. 9. 6.

was seeing into *its* offsprings, cattle, prosperity and long life for him.[20]

(iii) The Material Aim of the Saṁskārs. The material aims of the Saṁksāras were the gain of cattle, progeny, long life, wealth, prosperity, strength and intellect. The Saṁskāras were domestic rites and naturally during their performance things essential for domestic felicity were asked from gods. It was a belief of the Hindus that by prayer and appeal their desire and wishes were communicated to the deities who responded to them in form of animals, children, corn, a good physique and a sharp intellect.[21] These material aims of the Saṁskāras are very persistent and they are found uppermost, even now, in the minds of common people. The priest has always welcomed and blessed the material aspirations of people. He has tried to sanctify and thereby make them legitimate for a householder.

(iv) Saṁskāras as Self-expression. The hauseholder was not only an ever terror-stricken man, nor was he a professional beggar of gods. He performed the Saṁskāras also to express his own joys, felicitations and even sorrows at the various events of life. The possession of a child was a coveted thing, so on its birth the joy of the father knew no bounds. Marriage was the most festive occasion in the life of a man. Every land-mark in the progressive life of a child brought satisfaction and gladness in the household. Death was a tragic scene which brought forth mach pathos. The householder expressed his happy feelings in the shape of decoration, music, feast and presents, his sorrows were manifested in the funeral ceremonies.

4. *The Cultural Purpose.*

While fully recognizing the popular purpose of the Saṁskāras, the great writers and lawgivers have attempted to interoduce higher religion and sanctity of life into them. Manu[22] says, "By performing the Saṁskāras, conception, birth-rites, tonsure, and Upanayana, semi-

---

20. किं पश्यसि प्रजां पशून् सौभाग्यं मह्यं दीर्घायुष्टं पत्युः। The Sāmaveda-mantrabrūhmaṇa i. 5. 1-5.

21. एकमिषे विष्णुस्त्वां नयतु द्वे ऊर्जे त्रीणि रायस्पोषाय चत्वारि मयोभवाय पञ्च पशुभ्यः षड्ऋतुभ्यः। This verse is recited in the great Saptapadī A. i. G.S. i. 7 19; ś. G. ś. i. 14. 5.

22. गार्भैं होमैर्जातकर्म चौड-मौञ्जीनिबन्धनैः।
वैजिकं गार्भिकं चैनो द्विजानामवमृज्यते॥ M.S. ii. 27.

nal and uterine impurities are washed away." He[23] again adds. "The bodily Saṁskāras of the twice-born sanctify this life as well as the other." Yājñavalkya[24] also endorses the same view. Some kind of impurity was attached to the physical side of procreation and lying in the womb.[25] Therefore, it was thought necessary to remove that impurity from the body by performing various Saṁskāras. The idea of sin (*enas*) associated with the physical process of birth as mentioned in the Mamsmṛti (II.27) is differently interpreted by by different commentators. In the opinion of Medhātithi here 'sin' means mere imparity. According to Kullūka blemishes of seed are those arising from intercourse in a prohibited manner and the blemish of womb in that which arises from staying in the womb of an impure mother. The Mitāṣarā commenting on the Yajñavalkya-smṛti (I. 13) explain that the saṁskāras are calculated to remove the bodily defects transmitted from the parents but they are not intended to remove the tint of sin arising from immoral parents. The whole body was also consecrated to make it a fit dwelling place for the soul. According to Manu,[26] "the body is made Brāhmī by studies, observing vows, offering oblations, performing sacrifices, procreating children and undergoing the Pañca-Mahāyajñas."

Hārīta as quoted in the Saṁskāra-tattva (p. 857) maintains that 'when a person has an intercourse according to the procedure of garbhādhāna he establishes in the wife a foetus that becomes fit for the reception of the Veda. The theory was also current that every man is born a Śūdra, who requires refinement and polish before he becomes a full-fledged Aryan: "By birth every one is a Śūdra, by performing the Upanayana he is called a twice-born, by reading the Vedas he becomes a Vipra and by realizing Brahman he attains the status of a Brāhmaṇa."[27]

---

23. वैदिकैः कर्मभिः पुण्यैर्निषेकादिर्द्विजन्मनाम् ।
कार्यः शरीरसंस्कारः पावनः प्रेत्य चेह च ।। M.S. ii, 26.
24. Yāj. S. I. 16.
25. बीजगर्भसमुद्भवैनोविदर्हणोजातकर्मादिजन्यः । V.M.S. vol. 1. p. 132.
26. स्वाध्यायेन व्रतैर्होमैस्त्रैविद्येनेज्यया सुतैः ।
महायज्ञैश्च ब्राह्मीयं क्रियते तनुः ।। M.S. ii 28.
27. जन्मना जायते शूद्रः संस्काराद्द्विज उच्यते । etc.
जन्मना ब्राह्मणो ज्ञेयः संस्कारैर्द्विज उच्यते ।
विद्यया याति विप्रत्वं श्रोत्रियस्त्रिभिरेव च ।। Atri, 141-142.

Social privileges and rights were also connected with the Saṁskāras. The Upanaya was a passport for admission into the Aryan community and its sacred literature. It was also a special privilege to the twice born and denied to the Śūdras.[28] To mark the end of education and for entering the married life one had to perform the Samāvartana Saṁskāra. The Upanayana and the Vivāha Saṁskarās with Vedic hymns entitled a person to perform all kinds of sacrifices befitting an Aryan and increasing his status in the society.

Another purpose of the Saṁskāras was the attainment of heaven and even Mokṣa or liberation.[29] When great sacrifices ceased to be mere propitiation of gods and became a means for securing heaven,[30] the Saṁskāras, which were domestic sacrifices, also rose in their efficacy. Hārita[31] speaks about the fruits of the Saṁskāras, "One who is consecrated with the Brāhma Saṁskāras attains the status of Ṛṣis, becomes their equal, goes to their world and lives in their close vicinity. One who is consecrated with the Daiva Saṁskāras attains the status of gods etc." As the heaven was regarded the ultimate goal of life by common people in ancient times, the Saṁskāras naturally became instrumental in the attainment of that coveted state of existence. Śaṇkha-Likhita remarks, "Purified by the Saṁskāras and always practising the eight virtues of the soul, one gets, merits and heaven, he goes to the world of Brahman and reaches the state of Brahmanhood from where he never falls.[32]"

5. *The Moral Purpose.*

In course of time a moralizing feature emerged from the material body of the Saṁskāras. Gautama[33] after enumerating forty Saṁskāras, gives 'eight good qualities of the soul," viz., mercy,

28. अशूद्राणामदुष्टकर्मणामुपनयनम् । Ap. D.S. i. 1. 16.

29. नहि कर्मभिरेव केवलै ब्रह्मत्वप्राप्तिः प्रज्ञानकर्मसमुच्चयात्किलमोक्षः ।
एतैस्तु संस्कृतः आत्मनोपासनास्वाधिक्रियते । Medhātithi on M.S. ii. 28.

30 स्वर्गकामो यजेत् । The Pūrvamimaṁsā.

31. Quoted in V.M.S. vol. I. p. 139.

32. संस्कारैः संस्कृतः पूर्वैरुत्तरनुसंस्कृतः ।
नित्यमष्टगुणैर्युक्तो ब्राह्मणो ब्राह्मलौकिकः ।
ब्राह्मं पदमवप्नोति यस्मान्नच्यवते पुनः ।। Quated in V. M. S. vil. I. p. 142.

33. G.D.S. viii 24.

forbearance, freedom from envy, purity, calmness, right behaviour, and freedom from greed and covetousness. He[34] further says, "He that has performed forty sacraments but has not the eight good qualities enters not into union with Brahman. But he that has performed only a part of the forty Saṁskāras and has eight good qualities enters into union with Brahman and into the heaven of Brahman."

The Saṁskāras were never regarded as ends in themselves. They were expected to grow and ripen into moral virtues. For every stage of life rules of conduct were prescribed in the Saṁskāras.[35] No doubt, in them there is much that is religious and superstitious, but ethical attempt for the moral uplift of an individul is also visible. This stage of the Saṁskāras marks a great advance over the individual benefits that were solicited in them.

6. *The Formation and Development of Personality*

The cultural purpose that evolved from the ancient rites and ceremonies of the Hindus was the formation and development of personality. Aṅgirā[36] giving the analogy of a painting says, "Just as a picture is painted with various colours, so the character of an individual is formed by undergoing various Saṁskāras properly". The Hindu sages realized the necessity of consciously moulding the character of individuals instead of letting them grow in a haphazard way. They utilised the Saṁskāras, already prevalent in the society, for this purpose.

The Saṁskāras cover the full span of life, and they even try to influence and impress the individual after his death through the cult of soul. They were arranged in such a way that they may produce suitable impressions from the very beginning of one's life. The Saṁskāras were a guide that directed the life of an individual according to his growth. So a Hindu was required to live a full life of discipline and his energies flowed into a well-guarded and purposive channel. The Garbhādhāna Saṁskāra was performed at the proper time when the couple were physically fit and in a healthy condition, when they knew each other's heart and had intense desire

34. Ibid. viii. 25.

35. Cf. गर्भिणींधर्माः अनुपनीतधर्माः ब्रह्मचारिधर्माः etc.

36. चित्रकर्म यथाऽनेकैरङ्गैरुन्मील्यते शनैः।
ब्राह्मण्यमपि तद्वत्स्यात्संस्कारैर्विधिपूर्वकम्॥ Parāśara, VIII. 19

for possessing a child. Their whole thought was concentrated towards the act of procreation and a pure and congenial atmosphere was produced by means of sacrifices and recital of apt hymns. Throughout her pregnancy the wife was guarded and protected against evil influences physical and superphysical and her conduct was regulated to influence the growing child in the womb.[37] At the time of birth, Āyuṣya (for long life) and Prajñājanana (for talent) ceremonies were performed when the new-born was blessed to become firm like a stone, strong and crushing like an axe and grow into an intellectual man.[38] On every occasion during the childhood joys and felicitations of an optimistic life were thrown into atmosphere which was breathed in by the budding child. After the Chūḍākaraṇa or tonsure when the child grew into a boy, his duties were prescribed and his responsibilities explained before him without encumbering his mind and body with book-knowledge and school discipline. The Upanayana and other educational Saṁskāras formed the great cultural furnace where the emotions, desires and will of the boy were melted and shaped and he was prepared for an austere but a rich and cultured life. The Samāvartana was an entrance and probation for the life of a married householder. The marriage arrangement was a developed code of eugenics and the nuptial ceremony a homily on the life of a married couple. . The various sacrifices and vows prescribed for a householder were introduced to remove selfishness clinging to one's individuality and make him realize that he was the part and parcel of the whole community.

The death of a man was made easy by previous arrangement and his soul was given solace and help in its journey to the other side of life. No doubt, there are many itmes in the Saṁskāras that may be called a matter of faith. But none can deny the operation of the cultural motive underlying the Saṁskāras, though one may not concede them a place for a perfect scientific scheme.

By making the Saṁskāras compulsory, the Hindu sociologists aimed at evolving a type of humanity uniform in culture and character and having the same ideal in life. They were successful to a great extent in their attempt. The Hindus form a peculiar race with a wide cultural background. They influenced and assimilated the people who came in contact with them by their cultural scheme, and they are still living as a nation.

---

37. See the pre-natal Saṁskāras.

38. Āp. G S xiv; P.G.S. i. 16; J.G.S. i. 8.

7. *Spiritual Significance*

Spiritualism is a chief feature of Hinduism and every phase of Hindu religion is tinctured with it. This general outlook of the Hindus transformed the Saṁskāras into a spiritual Sādhanā. The spiritual purpose and significance of the Saṁskāras cannot be given an open demonstration nor can it be evidenced with paper documents. It is the experience of those who have received the sacraments. To a Hindu the Saṁskāras conveyed more than their constituents. They were "an outward visible sign of an inward spiritual grace." He looked beyond the ceremonial performances and felt something invisible which sanctified his whole personality. So, for the Hindus the Saṁskāras were a living religious experience and not a dead formalism.

The Saṁskāras served a mean between the ascetic and the materialistic conception of the body. The advocates of the first school try to worship the spirit while discarding the body--an absurd procedure in the world of elements.[39] The upholders of the second view do not go beyond the body and deny the spiritual aspect of man's life, and therefore they are deprived of that peace and joy that are nestled in the calm recesses of the spirit.[40] It was the business of the Saṁskāras to make the body a valuable possesson, a thing not to be discarded, but made holy, a thing to be sanctified, so that it might be a fitting instrument of the spiritual intelligence embodied in it.

The Saṁskāras were a gradual training in spiritualism. Through them the racipient realized that all life, properly understood, is a sacrament and every physical action should be referred to, and connected with, the spiritual reality. It was the way in which an active life of the world was reconciled with spiritual realization. In this system of living the body and its functions ceased to be hindrances, and became helpers in attaining perfection. By performing these Saṁskāras the life of an ordinary Hindu, with whom the world would have been too much but for timely intervention of spiritual discipline, was made a grand sacrament. Thus, duly celebrating the rites and ceremonies, the Hindus believed that they escaped the physical bondage and crossed the ocean of death.[41]

---

39. The Jains, the Buddhists and the neo-Vedantists,

40. The Chārvākas and the Vāmamārgis.

41. विद्याञ्चाविद्याञ्च यस्तद्वेदोभयं सह ।
अविद्ययामृत्युं तीर्त्वा विद्ययाऽमृतमश्नुते ॥ The Iśopaniṣad, 11

8. *Different Stages*

Such was the purpose of the Hindu Saṁskārs, when they formed the part and parcel of the life of the Hindus, who felt and acted accordingly. The Saṁskāras in their creative period were true to life, a flexible and living institution and not a fixed rigid ritualism. They were adapted to different localities and different times.[42] Every Vedic family performed the ceremonies in its own way. Then set in the intellectual classification of the Saṁskāras, when they were codified. At this time the creative period was drawing to its close and an attempt was made to settle every thing finally. There are numerous discussions and options about the various details of the Saṁskāras. Minutest details were recorded and no departure from them was desired. But change was still possible. The Hindu mind was not stagnant as yet. Then came a third period in the religious life of the Hindus. They thought that their energy was exhausted, they could not create any thing new and their only business was to collect and preserve. They regarded even a slight variation from the fixed course of the Saṁskāras a sin and they felt that they could not turn even a pebble, or utter a single word without the prescription of the ancient Ṛṣis. To make the matter worse, the language of the procedure and Mantras became unintelligible in course of time. This was the stage when the true spirit of the Saṁskāras departed and their sepulchures were left behind to be worshipped by their blind followers. The Saṁskāras ceased to be refined, elevated and adapted to the specific needs of the time. Therefore, they became, more or less, a defunct institution not serving their real purpose. In modern times reformist religious movements have tried to simplify and unify the Saṁskāras to serve the Hindu society as a whole. There have been also attempts at their rationalisation.

42. That is why there are so many variations in the Gṛhysūtras.

CHAPTER IV

THE CONSTITUENTS OF THE SAMSKĀRAS

1. *Introductory*

The Saṁskāras are a complex combination of various elements. They express beliefs, sentiments and knowledge of the ancient Hindus about the nature of human life and the universe and their relation with the superhuman powers that were supposed to guide or control the destiny of man. The Hindus believed that man requires protection, consecration and refinement. For this, to a great extent, they depended on gods whose existence they seriously felt and whose help they invariably asked. But while they sought aids from gods, they also helped themselves by the knowledge they possessed of natural and supernatural world. So we find a mixture of religious and secular factors in the Saṁskāras, though they have all assumed a religious garb in course of time.

2. *Fire*

The first and the most permanent constituent of the Saṁskāras was Agni or Fire which was always kindled in the beginning of every Saṁskāra. The importance of Agni in the Aryan religion is as old as Indo-European period. Its equivalents are found in Latin ignis and Luthianian ugni. During the Indo-Iranian period also it was worshipped as a chief domestic deity. As it is called the "houselord" in the Ṛgveda, so Atar (Avestan word for fire) is called the "houselord of all houses" in the Avesta.[1] Its contact with man was very congenial in cold winters of northern countries. Consequently, it became the chief domestic deity that was a constant source of help in secular as well as sacred life of the householder. The family hearth was the first "holy of the holies." The fire that was kept burning in every house became a perpetual sign for all influences that bound men with family and social relations, and became the centre of all domestic rites and ceremonies. It was not the case with the Vedic Indians alone. The Romans and the Greeks also made the hearth the centre of religious faith and rite.

We can well appreciate the high position given to Agni it the Saṁskāras, if we know what beliefs the Vedic Indian cherished

1. Yasna. 17. 11.

about it. By virtue of its services, Agni assumed the role of Gṛhapati, "the lord of the house":

Doing his work he dwells in earthly houses,
Though god he wins the fellowship of mortals[2]
Who over the Five Tribes bearing away,
Has set him down in every home,
Sage, youthful, master of the house.[3]

Agni was believed to be a great and renowned protector against illness, demons and other hostile spirits. Therefore, at various Saṁskāras it was propitiated and recognized as such because one of the objects of the Saṁskāras was to ward off evil influences.

To the sage Agni render praise,
Him of true rules in sacrifice.
God banisher of illness.[4]
Agni expells the Rākṣasas,
God of clear radiance, deathless one,
Bright cleansing, worthy to be praised.
Agni protect us from distress,
With hottest flames, unaging god,
Burn those against our enemies.[5]

To the ancient Hindus Agni was not only the "house-lord" and protector but also the high priest and mediator and messenger between gods and men. In the first capacity it supervised the ceremonies and in the second it bore offerings to gods.

Agni I praise, domestic priest,
God minister of sacrifice,
The Hotar, giver best of gifts.[6]

---

2. स चेतयन्मनुषो यज्ञबन्धुः प्र तं मह्या रशनया नयन्ति।
स क्षेत्यस्य दुर्यासु साधन्देवो मर्तस्य सद्यनित्वमाप।। R. V. iv. 1. 9.

3. यः पञ्च चर्षणीरभि निजसाद दमे दमे।
कविर्गृहपतिर्युवा।। R. V. VII. 15. 2.

4. कविमग्निमुपस्तुहि सत्यऽधर्माणमक्ष्वहै।
देवममीव चातनम्।। ibid. i. 12. 7.

5. अग्नि रक्षांसि सेधति शुक्रशोचिरमर्त्यः।
शुचिः पावक ईड्यः।। ibid.
अग्ने रक्षाणो अहंसः प्रति ष्म देव रीषतः।
तपिष्ठैरजरो दह।। ibid. vii. 15. 10, 13.

Through thee who art their mouth the guiltless deathless gods.

All eat the offering which is sacrificed to them.[6a]

O Agni, mayest thou announce
Among the gods this newest song
Of ours, a potent Gāyatra.[7]
Agni doth send the sacrifice to heaven.[8]
Hotar is he, he knows the work
Of messenger; goes to and for

"Twixt heaven and earth, knows heaven's ascent.[8a]

The Hindus regarded Agni as the director of rites and guardian of morality. Every rite was performed and contract and bond executed by Agni. It was an eternal witness around which, during the Upanayana and the Vivāha ceremonies, the student, and the husband and wife made circumambulations, so that their ties may be valied and permanent.

King of the clans, the wonderful
Director of the rites, I praise
This Agni, may he hear our call.[9]
Thou who art king of holy rites,
Guardian of ṛta, shining one,
Increasing in thy own abode.[10]

3. *Prayers, Appeals and Blessings*

The second class of constituents includes prayers, appeals and blessings. According to Tylor "prayer is soul's sincere desire, uttered

6. अग्निमीळे पुरोहितं यज्ञस्य देवमृत्विजम् ।
होतारं रत्नधातमम् ।। ibid. i. 1. 1.

6a. Ibid. ii. 1. 14.

7. इममूषु त्वमस्माकं सनिं गायत्रं नव्यासम् ।
अग्ने देवेषु प्रवोचः ।। ibid. i. 27. 4.

8. अग्निर्दिवि हव्यमाततान । ibid. X. 80. 4...

8a. Ibid. vii. 5. 1.

9. विशां राजानमद्भुतमध्य धर्मणामिमम् ।
अग्नि मीळे स उ श्रवत् ।। ibid. viii. 43. 24.

10. राजन्तमध्वराणां गोपामृतस्यदीदिवम् ।
वर्धमानं स्वे दमे ।। ibid. i. 1. 8.

or unexpressed, and is the address of personal spirit to personal spirit."[11] When, lateron, ceremonies and rites evolved, the animistic prayer became co-extensive with ritual prayers. Because prayer originated in the early stage of culture and was applied to domestic ceremonies, it was, more or less, unethical in the beginning. Gods were prayed to for the accomplishment of desire, but desire was as yet limited to personal or family interest. The Saṁskāras, as already said, were domestic rites. During their performance, generally, prayers were offered for protection and prosperity of a family consisting of children, animals, corn, strength and other felicities. For example, the husband, while taking with his wife the great "Seven Steps" (Saptapadī) prayed to Lord Viṣṇu, "One for sap, two for juice, three for the prospering of wealth, four for comfort, five for cattle, six for the seasons. Friend, be with seven steps (united to me). So be thou devoted to me."[12] In more cultural Saṁskāras like the Upanayana, the worshipper adds to his entreaty for prosperity the claim for help towards virtue and against vice, and prayer became an instrument of morality. In the Upanayana prayers were offered for intellectual stimulation, purity, Brahmacharya etc. The famous and the most sacred Gāyatri mantra says, "Let us meditate on the most excellent light of the Creator (the Sun); may he guide our intellect."[13] The pupil at the time of making offerings to Fire prays, "May I be full of insight; not forgetful; may I become full of glory, of splendour, of holy lustre etc."[14] While tying the girdle round his loin the student said, "Here has come to me, keeping away evil words, purifying my kinds as a purifier, clothing herself by (power of) inhalation and exhalation, with strength, this sisterly goddess, this blessed girdle."[15]

During the performance of the Saṁskāras blessings were also expressed. They differed from prayers in this that while the prayers were made for one's own good, the blessings conveyed good feelings towards others. These were wishes or appeals on the part of those interested, which were uttered by a spirit or a god. They symbolised

11. Primitive Culture, vol. I. p.

12. P. G. S. i. 8. 1; A. G. S. i. 19. 9.

13. तत्सवितुर्वरेण्यं भर्गो देवस्य धीमहि ।
धियो यो न प्रचोदयात् । G.G.S. ii. 10. 35.

14. A.G.S. i. 22. 1.

15. यं दुरक्तं परिबाधमाना वर्णं पवित्रं पुनती म आगात् ।
प्राणापानाभ्यां बलमादधाना स्वसा देवी सुभगा मेखलेयम् ।। P.G.S. ii. 2. 11.

the object desired for. The man believed that his blessings would transmit the good and thus influence the individual aimed at. The objects of blessings were almost the same as those of prayers. The husband presenting the under-garment to the bride uttered, "Live to old age; put on the garment; be a protectress of the human tribes against imprecation. Live a hundred years full of vigour. Cloth thyself in wealth and children. Blessed with life put on this garment!"[16] The father at the birth rite blessed his child, "Be a stone, be an axe, be imperishable gold. Thou indeed art the self called son; thus live a hundred autumns."[17]

4. *Sacrifice*

Another important constituent of the Saṁskāras was sacrifice. Its origin belongs to the same period of culture and it evolved from the same anthropological belief which gave birth to prayer. They have, moreover, stood in close connection with each other in their long career. Men believed that gods, like men, were propitiated by praise and prayer. It was equally natural to their mind that, like men, they also liked and accepted presents and gifts. The Saṁskāras with the solitary exception of the funeral, were performed at the blooming and festive occasions in the life of a man. Therefore the recipient of the Saṁskāras or, if he were a minor, his or her parents offered presents, paid homage or tribute to the beneficient gods in token of gratitude, or in anticipations of further blessings. Even at the funeral, sacrifices were made to gods requesting them to help the dead. The sacrifices were offered invariably in the beginning of, and through the course of a Saṁskāra. Special deities were believed to preside over a particular period of life. So they were specifically invited, placated and feasted. But other gods were also entertained, as their spheres of influence were often overlapping.

5. *Lustration*

The next class of constituents consisted of bath, sipping water and lustration or baptismal sprinkling of water over persons and things. "The animistic theory of the universe which underlies all

16. जरां गच्छ परिधत्स्व वासो भवाकृष्टीनामभि शस्तिपावा। शतं च जीव शरदः सुवर्चा रयिं च पुत्राननुसंव्ययस्वायुष्मतीदं परिधत्स्व वासः ॥ P.G.S. i. 4. 13.

17. अश्मा भव परशुर्भव हिरण्यमस्रुतं भव। ibid. i. 16. 14; H. G. S. ii. 3. 2.

ancient religion and philosophy suggested that water was a living being, which in so far as it assisted the process of growth and aided men in other ways, might be presumed to be beneficient."[18] But, besides this animistic theory, water seemed living to ancient people on account of its motion, sound and power. That is why the Hebrews called it "living water." The purifying effects of water and its invigorating influence were revealed to men, as after having a plunge in its cool waves he found himself purified and refreshed. Other ideas were also associated with water. Many springs, lakes, wells and rivers had miraculous healing property, so it was thought that some divinity lived in each of them. The water was also supposed to possess the power of removing evil influences and killing demons.[19] It was quite natural that having all these powers it was used by the Hindus as one means of removing the contagion, influence of spirits, and at a higher stage the guilt of sin. Bath was complete washing off of physical, moral and spiritual impurities. Sipping water and lustration were partial or symbolic baths. Ceremonial purification was a universal feature in almost all the Saṁskāras. The Hindu led a life regularly purified by water from his conception in the womb up to his death and even after it. The father was required to bathe after the Garbhādhāna[20] and in the Jātakarma (birth ceremonies.[20a] Bathing was one of the initial steps that preceded the Cūḍākaraṇa and the Upanayana.[21] At the end of his student career the youth was sumptuosuly bathed.[22] The bride and the bridegroom were bathed before the nuptial ceremonies.[23] The dead body was washed before it was burnt.[24] Sipping many times in a day as well as ceremonial sipping in every Saṁskāra are prescribed by the scriptures. Sprinkling was also a common feature of the Saṁskāras. Entire material was sprinkled with water before a Saṁskāra began. In the tonsure ceremonies the child's head was sprinkled, a Snātaka was sprinkled with water for fame,

---

18. Encyclopaedia of Religion and Ethics. vol. 114 p. 367.

19. R.V. vii. 47, 49; X. 9. 30.

20. ऋतौ तु गर्भशंकित्वात्स्नानं मैथुनिनः स्मृतम् । Apastaṁba, quoted by गदाधर on P. G. S.

20a. श्रुत्वा जातं पिता पुत्रं सचैलं स्नानमाचरेत् । Vasiṣṭha. ibid.

21. माता कुमारमादायाप्लाव्य । A.G.S. i. 17.

22. P.G.S. ii. 6; G.G.S. iii. 4. 6.

23. G. G. S. ii. 1. 10–17.

24. The B.P.S.

glory, learning and holy lustre.[25] the bride was sprinkled on her head for, health, peace and happiness etc.[26]

6. *Orientation*

Orientation was another element of the Saṁskāras. It was based on the picturesque symbolism of the path of the sun and myths according to which different directions were ruled by different deities. In men's mind the eastern direction was associated with light and warmth, life and happiness and glory; the west with darkness and chill, death and decay. According to Indian mythology, south is the direction of Yama, the god of death, so it was regarded inauspicious. These beliefs gave rise to various practices concerning the position of man in the Sāṁskāras. In all the auspicious Saṁskāras the recipient faced the east indicating his preparedness to receive light and life. While making circumambulation in the Saṁskāras, the course of the sun was followed. In inauspicious Saṁskāras the direction was reversed. During the funeral ceremonies the head of the dead was kept towards the south when it was placed on the funeral pyre and the soul was on its journey to the abode of Yama. At special occasions the position of persons and things was determined by ideas suggested on that time.

7. *Symbolism*

Symbolism played a great part in the Hindu Saṁskāras. It was a material object to convey mental and spiritual significance. It was mostly suggested by analogous objects. Men believed that like things produce like effects. So, by their contact, it was thought, men were bestowed with similar characteristics. Stone was a symbol of fixity and one who mounted it was supposed to be invested with firmness in his or her character.[27] The student in the Upanayana and the bride in the Vivāha ceremonies were required to step on a stone suggesting their steadfastness in their devotion to the teacher and the husband. Looking at the pole star was productive of similar effects.[28] Sesamum and rice were symbols of fertility and prosperity.[29] Anointment was symbolic of love and affection;[30] eating

---

25. तेन मामभिषिञ्चामि श्रियै यशसे ब्रह्मणे ब्रह्मवर्चसाय ।
26. Ibid. i. 8. 5.
27. आरोहेममश्मानमश्मेव स्थिरा भव । P. G. S. i. 7. 1.
28. ध्रुवमसि ध्रुवं त्वा पश्यामि ध्रुवैधिपोष्ये मयि । ibid. i. 8. 9.
29. इमांल्लाजानवपाम्यग्नौ समृद्धिकरणं तव । A. G. S. i. 7. 8.
30. समञ्जन्तु विश्वे देवा समञ्जन्तु हृदयानि नौ । G. G. S. ii. 1. 18.

together was a symbol of union;[31] touching the heart symbolized joining hearts;[32] grasping the hand was a sign of taking full responsibility;[33] looking towards the sun indicated brilliance and lustre;[34] a male constellation ensured conception and so on.[35]

8. *Taboos*

Numerous taboos observed at various points of the Saṁskāras constituted a different category. Taboo is a Polynesian word said to mean "what is prohibited." The ethical conception of man in early times was influenced by magical determination of things injurious. The science of medicine and hygiene were also helped by it. There were many taboos connected with the conception of life. Life was the central mystery of the world for early man. He attached mystery and danger with every thing connected with it. Its genesis, growth and end were all mysterious. It was thought necessary to take precautions against dangers and to give vent to the sense of mystery at various occasions of life. This gave birth to various restrictions that later on crystallised into well defined taboos about pregnancy, birth, childhood, adolescence, youth, marriage, death and corpse.

There were taboos connected with lucky and unlucky days, months and years.[37] People believed that injurious influences arising from various objects and present in the air associated themselves with some months, days and years when things might or might not be done with safety and advantage. Unfavourable incidents, economic and astronomical, and occasions like death, desease and defeat stamped days, months and years as unlucky. There are many such beliefs, the origin of which is lost in a remote antiquity. Out

31. अथैनां स्थालीपाकं प्राशयति––'प्राणैस्ते प्राणान्सन्दधामि अस्थिभिरस्थीनि मांसै मासानि त्वचा त्वचम्'। P. G. S. i. 11. 5.

32. मम व्रते ते हृदयं दधामि ममचित्तमनुचित्तं तेऽस्तु। ibid. i. 8. 8.

33. G. G. S. ii. 2–16.

34. तच्चक्षुर्देवहितं पुरस्ताच्छुक्रमुच्चरत्। P. G. S. i. 17. 6.

35. Ibid. i. 11. 3.

37. जन्मर्क्षे जन्ममासे जन्मदिवसे शुभं त्यजेत्। Ratnakoṣa quoted by Gadādhara on the P. G. S. i. 4–8.

श्रावणेऽपि च पौषे वा कन्या भाद्रपदे तथा।
चैत्राश्वयुक्कार्तिकेषु याति वैधव्यतां खलु॥ Vyāsa, ibid.
अयुग्मे दुर्भगा नारी युग्मे तु बिधवा भवेत्। Rājamārtaṇḍa, ibid.

of the vast experience of a community there evolved a system of taboos connected with them. But there were other prohibitions also that were based on rational grounds. During natural calamity, political revolution, death of a person, monthly course of a woman etc. the Saṁskāras were postponed.[38]

Taboos connected with food were also numerous. A particular food was prescribed in a particular Saṁskāra.[39] The object in view was that food should be light, free from injurious ingridients and symbolic of the occasion. Sometimes food was altogether prohibited.[40] The underlying idea here was that the weakness and impurity of the flesh should be removed before the man could enter into communion with a deity at the time of the Saṁskāra. Fasting was sometimes also meant for producing ecstasy. By observing abstinence from food man felt elevated and moving in an atmosphere quite different from that of ordinary men.

9. *Magic*

Magical elements are also found in the Saṁskāras. Dangers and problems of early life were more acute, in certain directions, than those that confront the civilized society to-day. They demanded constant vigilence, careful investigation and prompt action. As already said, early men recognized supernatural agencies. But they did not always supplicated to these agencies. Sometimes they attempted to avail of, and control, these forces. Magic originated from this tendency of man. It is essentially a directive and coercive procedure and differs in this respect from full-fledged religion, which is essentially submissive and obedient to supernatural powers. The method of magic is based on sequence of incidents and on imitation of nature and man. In the Atharva-veda there is a large number of magic formulas which are used by Kauśika in his sūtras at various ceremonies. A hymn of the Atharvaveda begins as follows, "Let

---

38. दिग्दाहे दिनमेकं च गृहे सप्तदिनानि तु।
भूकम्पे च समुत्पन्ने त्र्यहमेव तु वर्जयेत् ॥
उल्कापाते त्रिदिवसं धूम्रे पञ्चदिनानि च।
वज्रपाते चैकदिनं वर्जयेत्सर्वकर्मसु ॥
विवाहव्रतचूडासु यस्य भार्या रजस्वला।
तदा न मंगलं कार्यं शुद्धौ कार्यं शुभेप्सुभिः॥ Vrddhamanu, ibid.

39. त्रिरात्रमक्षारलवणाशिनौस्याताम् P. G. S. i. 8. 21.

40. Ibid. iii. 10. 25-26.

the up-thruster thrush thee up; do not abide in thine own lair, the arrow of love that is terrible therewith I pierce thee in the heart."[41] This hymn is used by Kauśika[42] in a charm for winning a woman under one's control, by pushing her with a finger, piercing the heart of an image of her, etc. Other Gṛhyasūtras also utilize magic formulas in the Sṁskāras. But here, magic being beneficient is different from black magic. For example, magic was performed for safe and easy delivery,[43] for warding off evil spirits etc.[44]

In the Hindu Saṁskāras religion was more important than magic. On the whole, in the beginning, there was hardly any difference between a priest and a magician. But later on, as a consequence of progress and refinement in religion, conflict arose between the two. Ultimately, though not completely, the priest succeeded in ousting the magician, who was in league with uncanny world. The Buddhist and Jain monks were forbidden to devote themselves to the exorcism of the Atharvaveda and magic. The Brahmanical law-books declared sorcery as a sin; the magicians were classed with rogues and scoundrals and the king was asked to punish them.[54]

10. *Divination*

Divination also played an important part in the performance of the Saṁskāras. Divination is the science that seeks to discover the will of supernatural powers. Men desired to learn the causes of the present and the past misfortunes and the story of the future that they may know at any moment what is the best course to pursue. It was supposed that these things are indicated by appearances and movements of the various objects of the world. Natural phenomena indicated the purpose of the superhuman forces, as it was believed that gods could not but so reveal themselves. It was man's task to disecover the laws of phenomenal revelations. The question of rationale did not arise, as it was held that gods were friendly, and anxious to guide the uncertain footsteps of man.

---

41. iii. 25. 1.

42. K. S. xxxv. 22.

43. The Soṣyanti karma.

44. In the Jatakarma Ceremonies.

45. उत्कोचकाश्चोपधिका: कितवास्तथा।
मंगलादेशवृत्ताश्च भद्राश्च क्षणिकै: सह ॥ M.S. ix. 258.
अभिचारेषु च सर्वेषु कर्तव्यो द्विशतो दम:। ibid. ix. 290

Of all divinatory methods astrology played the greatest role in the history of the Saṁskāras. It derived its prominence from the splendour and myths of the sidereal heavens and the belief that all heavenly bodies were divine or controlled by divine beings, or abode of the dead.[46] So, it was natural that the astral movements should be looked on as giving signs of the will of the gods. In the early Gṛhyasūtras astrological considerations are very few and simple. With the development of astrology they became amplified and developed. Detailed astrological rules are formulated in the later treatises for every Saṁskāra. Every care was taken that a Saṁskāra should be performed under an auspicious planet.[47]

Sacredness of human body also lent divinatory power to several marks on body. The Liṅga-purāṇa has exhaustively dealt with this subject and is quoted in the examination of the bride and the bridegroom.[48] Other methods were also adopted for divination. Gobhila admits the limitation of human knowledge and recommends to examine the future of the bride by means of various clods of earth.[49] After the Annaprāśana, the occupation of the child was determined by its choosing one of the objects placed before it. And so on.[50]

11. *Cultural Elements*

In addition to the above religious beliefs, rites and ceremonies, the Saṁskāras contained social customs and usages and rules about eugenics, ethics, hygiene, medicine etc. In ancient times, different spheres of life were not departmentalized. The whole life was a compact unity saturated with the all-pervading idea of religion. As the Saṁskāras covered the full life of an individual, his physical, mental and spiritual training was combined with them. The social status of a man played an important role throughout the Saṁskāras. The right of performance and the procedure of ceremonies were often determined by castes. Marriage settlements were made ac-

46. द्यावा पृथिवी are the parent-gods from which the Hindu Pantheon sprang up.

47. I large number of astrological works have come into existence for this very purpose.

48. Quoted in the V.M.S. vol. II. p. 752.

49. G.G.S. ii. 1. 11.

कृतप्राशनमुत्संगाद् धात्री बालं समुत्सृजेत् ।
कार्यं तस्य परिज्ञानं जीविकायाः अनन्तरम् ॥
Quoted in V.M.S. vol. I.

cording to social customs and rules. In selection of bride and bridegroom, in copulation, pregnancy and rearing of children the rules of eugenics and racial purity were followed. The life of a Kṛtachūḍa (one who has undergone the tonsure ceremonies), a Brahmacāri, a Snātaka and a householder were regulated according to the moral laws of the time. Life was protected not only against demons and goblins but also against desease and accidents by prescribing rules of health, diet and medicine. Rules of sanitation were also observed during the monthly course of a woman, confinement, and death in a family and other occasions in life.

12. *Common-sense Elements*

Common-sense elements were also found in the Saṁskāras, which were not closely connected with the religious idea and they will continue to be there whatever change may occur in the religious idealogy of people. Invitations were sent to all the relatives and friends to attend the ceremonies. A new canopy was erected in the Vivāha, the Chūḍākaraṇa, the Keśānta, the Upanayana and the Sīmanta ceremonies. Mirth was expressed by decoration of the house with sprouts, leaves, flowers etc. and dressing the recipient with fitting costumes. During the Samāvartana the Snātaka was presented garments, garlands, staf and other necessities and comforts of a householder. In the Vivāha ceremonies both the husband and the wife were dressed and ornamented according to their social status. Music was also employed to echoe the general happiness and to entertain the guests. The Vārāha Gṛhyasūtra raises the Vādanakarma or instrumental music to the position of a regular constituent of the Vivāha ceremonies.

13. *A Spiritual Atmosphere*

These rules and regulations and commonsense elements were social in their origin. But in course of time they were given a religious shape. The whole scramental atmosphere was fragrant with spiritual significance. Under the sacramental canopy the recipient felt himself exalted, elevated and sanctified.

CHAPTER V

THE PRE-NATAL SAMSKĀRAS.

1. THE GARBHĀDHĀNA (CONCEPTION)

(i) *The Meaning*

The rite through which a man placed his seed in a woman was called Garbhādhāna.[1] Śaunaka gives the similar definition though in slightly different words; "The rite by the performence of which a woman receives semen scattered (by her husband) is called Garbhālambhanam or Garbhādhāna."[2] So this is quite clear that this rite was not a religious fiction but a ceremony corresponding to fact, though its adherents, later on, fought shy of, and ultimately, abandoned it.

We know nothing about sentiments and rites, if any, regarding the procreation of children and the ceremonial procedure accompanying it in the pre-Vedic times. It must have taken a very long period for the evolution of this Saṁskāra. In the beginning, procreation was a natural act. A human pair copulated, whenever there was a physical demand for it, without any anticipation of progeny, though it was a usual consequence. The Garbhādhāna Saṁskāra, however, presupposed a well established home, a regular marriage, a desire of possessing children and a religious idea that beneficient gods helped men in begetting children. So the origin of this Saṁskāra belongs to a period when the Aryans were far advanced from their primitive conditions.

(ii) *The Vedic Period*

In the Vedic period we see that parental instincts found their expression in many utterences containing prayers for children.[3]

1. गर्भः संधार्यते येन कर्मणा तद्गर्भाधानमित्यनुगतार्थं कर्मनामधेयम् ।
पूर्वमीमांसा अध्याय 1 पाद 4 अधि 2 Quoted in V.M.S. under this Saṁskāra.

2. निषिक्तो यत्प्रयोगेण गर्भः सन्धार्यते स्त्रिया ।
तद् गर्भलम्भनं नाम कर्म प्रोक्तं मनीषिभिः ।। Quated in V.M.S.

3. प्रजां च धत्तं द्रविणं च धत्तम् । R.V. viii. 35. 10;
पुत्रासो यत्र पितरो भवन्ति । ibid. i. 89. 9.

Heroic sons were regarded as boons conferred by gods on men. The theory of Three Debts was in the process of evolution in the Vedic period.[4] A son was called "Ṛinachyuta"[5] or one who removes debts, which may denote parental and economic both and the begetting of children was regarded a sacred duty binding on every individual. Moreover, there are many similes and references in the Vedic hymns bearing on how to approach a women for conception.[6] Thus an idea and, perhaps, a simple ceremony regarding conception were coming into existence in the Vedic period.

Though the ritual procedure adopted in the Garbhādhāna must have assumed a fairly ceremonious shape before the codification of the Saṁskāras in the Gṛhyasūtras, we do not get an exact information about it in the pre-Sūtra period. But we come across many prayers in the Vedic hymns pointing to the act of conception. "Let Viṣṇu prepare the womb; let Tvaṣṭar adorn thy form; let Prajāpati pour on; let Dhātar place the embryo. Place the embryo, O Sarasvati; let both the Aśvins garlanded with blue lotus set thine embryo."[7] "As Aśvattha has mounted the Śamī; there is made the generation of a male; that verily is the obtainment of a son; that we bring into women. In the male indeed grows the seed. That is poured along into the women; that verily is the obtainment of a son; that Prajāpati said."[8] A verse in the Atharvaveda contains an invitation to wife to mount the bed for conception: "Being happy in mind, here mount the bed; give birth to children for me, your husband."[9] Descriptions of actual copulation are also found in the pre-Sūtra literature.[10] From the above references we gather that

4. जायमानो वै ब्राह्मणस्त्रिभिर्ऋणवान् जायते ब्रह्मचर्येण ऋषिभ्यो यज्ञेन देवेभ्यः प्रजया पितृभ्यः। एष वा अनृणो यः पुत्री यज्वा ब्रह्मचारी वा स्यादिति। the Taittiriya-Samhitā, vi. 3. 10. 5.

5. R.V. x. 142. 6.

6. शमीमश्वत्थमारूढस्तत्र पुंसवनं कृतम्।
तद्वै पुत्रस्य वेदनं तत् स्त्रीष्वाभरामसि॥ etc. A.V. vi. 9.

7. R.V. x. 184.

8. A.V. vi. 9. 1, 2.

9. Ibid xiv. 2. 2.

10. तां पूषन् शिवतमामेरयस्व यस्यां बीजं मनुष्याः वपन्ति।
या न ऊरू उशती विश्रयाति यस्यामुशन्तः प्रहराम शेपम्॥ R.V. x. 85. 37.
अथ यामिच्छेत्। गर्भं दधीतेति तस्यामथ निष्ठाप्य मुखेन मुखं सन्धायापान्यामिप्रारायादिन्द्रियेणा रेतसा रेते आदधामीति गर्भिण्येव भवति।
The Bṛhadāraṇyakopaniṣad.

in the pre-Sūtra period the husband approached the wife, invited her for conception, prayed to gods for placing the embryo into her womb and then finished fertilization. The procedure was very simple. No other details are available. It is just possible that some kind of ceremony was performed on this occasion, but we are quite in dark about it. The reason why this ceremony is not described in details seems to be that originally it formed a part of the marriage ritual.

(iii) *The Sūtra period*

The Garbhādhāna ceremonies are, for the first time, systematically dealt with in the Gṛhyasūtras. According to them, since marriage the husband was required to approach the wife in every month when she was ceremoniously pure after her monthly course. But before the conception, one had to observe various vows according to the desire of possessing different types of sons-Brāhmaṇa, Śrotriya (one who has read one Śākhā), Anūchāna (who has read only the Vedāṅgas), Ṛṣikalpa (who has read the kalpas), Bhrūṇa (who has read the sūtras and the Pravachanas), Ṛṣi (who has read the four vedas) and Deva (who is superior to the above).[11] At the end of the vow, cooked food was offered to the fire. After this, the pair were prepared for cohabitation. When the wife was decently decorated, the husband recited Vedic verses containing similes of natural creation and invocations to gods for helping the woman in conception.[12] Then embracing began with verses containing metaphors of joint action of male and female forces, and the husband rubbed his own body with verses expressing his fertilizing capacity.[13] After embracing, conception proper took place with prayers to god Pūṣan and an indication to scattering semen.[14] The husband, then, touched the heart of the wife, reclining over her right shoulder with the verse, "O thou whose hair is well parted. Thy heart that dwells in heaven, in the moon, that I know; may it know me. May we see a hundred autumns."[15]

11. B. G. S. i. 7. 1–8.

12. Ibid. i. 7. 37–41.

13. अथेनां परिष्वजति—'अमूहमस्मि सा त्वं द्यौरहं पृथ्वी त्वं रेतोऽहं रेतोभृत्त्वम्'। etc. ibid. i. 7. 42.

14. Ibid. i. 7. 44.

15. P.G.S. i. 12. 9.

(iv) *The Dharmasūtra, the Smṛti and Subsequent Periods*

The Dharmasūtras and the Smṛtis add little to the ritualistic side of this Saṁskāra. Rather they lay down rules regulating the performance, e.g. when the conception should take place; recommended and prohibited nights; astrological considerations; how a polygamous man should approach his wives; conception a compulsory duty and its exceptions; the right of performing the Saṁskāra etc. Only a few Smṛtis like the Yājñavalkya, the Āpastaṁba and the Śātātapa prescribe bathing for husband after coition,[16] though the wife is exempted from this purification. The last named authority says, "In the bed the husband and the wife both become impure. But after they get up, only the former becomes impure while the latter remains pure."

The Prayogas and the Paddhatis add a few new features to this Saṁskāra. They introduce the worship of Puranic gods and prescribe Saṅkalpa (determination), Mātṛpūjā and Nāndiśraddha, and worship of Gaṇeśa or Vināyaka in the beginning of it.[17] Presents and feasts are also enjoined at the end of the Saṁskāra.[18] These features, however, are common to almost all the Saṁskāras.

(v) *The Time of Performance*

The first question that was raised in connection with the Garbhādhāna ceremony was about the time of its performance. The Dharmaśāstras are unanimous at the point that it should be performed when the wife was physically prepared to conceive, that is, in her Ṛtu. The proper time for conception was from the fourth to the sixteenth night after the monthly course of the wife.[19] The majority of the Gṛhyasūtras and the Smṛtis consider the fourth night ceremoniously pure for conception. But the Bobhila Gṛhyasūtra[20] takes a more rational view. According to it, conception

---

16. ऋतौ तु गर्भशंकित्वात्स्नानं मैथुनिनः स्मृतम्। याज्ञवल्क्य and आपस्तम्ब
उभावप्यशुची स्यातां दम्पती शयनं गतौ।
शयनादुत्थिता नारी शुचिः स्यादशुचिः पुमान्॥ शातातप
Quoted by Gadādhara on P.G.S. i. 11.

17. The **Daṭakarma**-Paddhatis.

18. **Ibid.**

19. **M.S. iii. 2; yāj. S. I. 79.**

20. चि जा यास्तस्मिन्नेव दिवा।

should take place after the stoppage of the flow of impure blood. The woman, before the fourth night, was regarded untouchable and a man approaching her was pollutted and also taken to be guilty of abortion, because his semen was scattered in vain.[21]

Only nights were prescribed for conception and day time was prohibited.[22] The reason given for it was that the vital airs of one, who cohabts with his wife in the day time, leap out; one approaching his wife in the night time is still a Brahmachāri; one should avoid coition in the day time, because from it unlucky, weak end short-lived children are born.[23] Exceptions to this rule however, were recognized. But they were meant for only those who generally lived abroad, separated form their wives, or when their wives were intensely desirous of cohabitation.[24] The idea underlying the second exception was that women should be satisfied and protected by every means, so that they should not go astray.[25]

Among the nights later ones were preferred. Baudhāyana says that "one should approach his wife from the fourth to the sixteenth night, specially the later ones."[26] Āpastamba and others endorsed the same view.[27] Children conceived on later nights were reegarded more lucky and meritorious: "A son conceived on the fourth night becomes short-lived and without wealth; a girl conceived on the fifth generally gives birth to female children; a son conceived on the sixth becomes mediocre; a girl conceived on the seventh would become barren; a son conceived on the eighth night becomes a lord or prosperous; if the conception takes place on the ninth

---

21. व्यर्थीकारेण शुक्रस्य ब्रह्महत्याभवाप्नुयात् ।आश्वलायन quoted in the V.M.S. vol. I.

22. Yāj. S. I. 79. The Aśvalāyana Smṛti, उपेयान्मध्यरात्रान्ते । quoted in V.M.S. vol. 1.

23. प्राणां वा एते स्कन्दन्ति ये दिवा रत्या संयुज्यन्ते ।
ब्रह्मचर्यमेव तद्यद्रात्रौ रत्त्या संयुज्यन्ते ॥ The Praśnopaniṣad. i. 13.
नार्तवे दिवा मैथुनमर्जयेदल्पभाग्याः अल्पवीर्याश्च दिवा प्रसूयन्तेऽल्पायुश्चेति । आर्थवणिक श्रुतिः । quoted in V.M.S. vol. I.

24. अनृतावृतु काले वा दिवा रात्रावथापि वा । प्रोषितस्तु स्त्रियं गच्छेत्प्रायश्त्ती भवेन्न च ॥ व्यासः ibid.

25. यस्मात्तस्मास्त्रियः सेव्याः कर्तव्याश्च सुरक्षिता M.S. Ibid.

26. B.G.S. i. 7. 46.

27. तत्राप्युत्तरोत्तराःप्रशस्ताः । Áp. D.S. ii. 1.

night an auspicious womaṅ is born and a son conceived on the tenth becomes wise; a girl conceived on the eleventh night becomes an irreligious woman and a son conceived on the twelfth becomes the best man; on the thirteenth an adultress woman is born and on the fourteenth a religious, grateful, self-realized and firm in his vow, son is born; on the fifteenth a mother of many sons and devoted to her husband; and on the sixteenth a learned, auspicious, truthful, selfcontrolled and a refuge of all creatures is born."[28] The rationale of this belief was that conception, farther removed from the contact of monthly impurity, was purer and more meritorious.

The sex of the would-be child was believed to be determined by the number of night on which the conception took place. Even nights were selected for the birth of a male child and odd ones for a female child.[29] It was thought that quantity of semen and menstrual discharge was responsible for the sex of the child.[30] Parents were guided by their desire of possessing the child of a particular sex.

Certain dates of the month were prohibited for conception. The eighth, the fourteenth, the fifteenth and the thirtieth, and all the Parvans were specially avoided.[31] A twice-born householder observing the above rule was regarded to be ever a Brahmachāri. The Viṣṇupurāṇa,[32] stigmatizes these nights and damns the persons guilty of approaching their wives on them to hell. Manu[33] taboos the eleventh and the thirteenth days also. These days were meant for religious observances, and therefore any sexual act was eschewed on them. But there may be other reasons why these nights were forbidden. The ancient Hindus were well conversant with astrology and astronomy.

---

28. व्यास, quoted. in V.M.S. vol. I.

29. युग्मासु पुत्रा जायन्ते स्त्रियोऽयुग्मासु रात्रिषु। M.S. iii. 48.

30. पुमान्पुंसोऽधिके शुक्रे स्त्री भवत्यधिके स्त्रियाः।
समेऽपुमान्पुंस्त्रियौ वा क्षीणेऽल्पे च विपर्ययः॥ Ibid. iii. 49.

31. पर्ववर्जं व्रजेच्चैनां तद्व्रतो रतिकाम्यया। M.S. iii. 45; yāj. S.I. 79.

32. पर्वाण्येतानि राजेन्द्र रविसंक्रान्ति रेव च।
तैलस्त्रीमांसभोगी पर्वस्वेतेषु यः पुमान्।
विन्मूत्रभोजनंनाम नरकं प्रतिपद्यते॥ The Visnupurāna, quoted in the V.M.S. vol. I.

33. तासामाद्याश्चतस्रस्तु निन्दितैकादशी च या।
त्रयोदशी च शेषास्तु प्रशस्ताः दश रात्रयः॥ M.S. iii. 47.

When they could fix the paths of the sun and the moon, they would have observed that their conjunction on different dates produced different effects on the earth. It is a common-place knowledge of physical geography that, owing to the attraction of the moon and increase of the watery substance, the physical condition of the earth becomes abnormal on the Parvan dates and consequently the health of the animal world is not sound. So it was thought advisable that such an important act as the Garbhādhāna should not be performed on these dates. Most probably, this experience of the astronomers found its place in the Dharmaśāstra, when astrology developed

(vi) *A Polygamous Householder*

The next question connected with the Garbhādhāna was: How should a polygamous man approach his wives when they were all in theyr monthly course at once? This question is not raised in the Gṛhyasūtras, the Dharmasūtras and the majority of the Smṛtis. In very early times polygamy could not have been very common. When the Aryans became well-settled in India and began to lead a luxurious life, keeping many wives together became a fashion and a sign of greatness. During the mediaeval period polygamy was very popular, specially among the ruling families. So, when this condition obtained, the Śāstrakāras thought it necessary to lay down some provisions in order to avoid the clash of conflicting interest of co-wives. Devala,[34] a mediaeval Smṛti-writer, opines that in such a case the husband should approach the wives according to their caste-status, or if they were without any issue, according to the priority of their marriage.

(vii) *The Performer*

Another problem was: Who should perform the Garbhādhāna Saṁskāra? The later works on the Dharmaśātra do not discuss this problem, as they suppose that none but the husband could perform this Saṁskāra. The early writers, however, raised this question. Usually the husband was the natural performer of this Saṁskāra. But in his absence, substitutes were also allowed. Levirate was current in ancient times, because it was thought necessary to beget children at any cost for the benefit of the family and the dead Fathers. In the Vedic literature we get references where a widow

---

34. यौगपद्ये तु तीर्थानां विप्रादिक्रमशःव्रजेत ।
रक्षणार्थमपुत्राणां ग्रहणक्रमशोऽपि वा ।। Devala, quoted in V.M.S. vol. I.

invites her brother-in-law to raise children for her husband.[35] Manu[36] and many other Smṛtis allow the widow or the wife of an impotent or invalid person to bear children from the brother of her husband, a Sagotra or a Brāhmaṇa, though elsewhere he does not like this idea.[37] In the Mahābhārata[38] Bhīṣma asks Satyavatī to invite a Brāhmana for raising children on her daughters-in-law, and he goes on describing the qualities of a substitute. Yājñavalkya[39] also permits the substitution: "The brother of the dead husband should co-habit with his wife in her Ṛtu with the permission of the elders, having rubbed ghee on his body. In his absence a Sagotra or Sapiṇda should do this." Another Smṛti says, "Father is the best performer of the Saṁskāras, the Garbhādhāna and others but in his absence either a man of his own family or a friend of another family should perform them."[40]

Later on, when the idea of female chastity changed and begetting children was not such an imperative need of the time, substitutes for the husband were discouraged and ultimately disallowed. Protest against substitution is recorded even in Manu, where levirate is called Paśudharma or animality.[41] The later Smṛtis allow substitutes in the Saṁskāras other than Garbhādhāna. According to the Āśvlāyana[42] Smṛti, if the husband is dead, degraded from the caste, retired from the household life or gone abroad, some elder person of the same Gotra should perform the Saṁskāras, the Puṁsavana etc." Raising children on a widow became tabooed under the Kalivarjya. The Āditya[43] and the Brāhma Purāṇas[44] both include livi-

35. को वा शयुत्रा विधवेव देवरं मर्यं न योषा कृणुते सधस्थ आ । R.V. X. 40. 2.

36. देवराद्वा सपिण्डाद्वा स्त्रिया सम्यङ् नियुक्तया ।
जेप्सिताधिगन्तव्या सन्तानस्य परिक्षये ।। M.S. ix. 59.

37. Ibid. ix. 66–68.

38. बीजार्थं ब्राह्मणः कश्चिद्धनेनोपनिमन्त्र्यताम् ।
The Mahābhārata, Ādiparva quoted in the V.M.S. vol. I.p. 165.

39. अपुत्रां गुर्वनुज्ञातो देवरः पुत्रकाम्यया ।
सपिण्डो वा सगोत्रो वा घृताभ्यक्त ऋतावियात् ।। Yaj. S. I. 68.

40. गर्भाधानादिसंस्कर्ता पिता श्रेष्ठतमः स्मृतः ।
अभावे स्वकुलीन स्याद् बान्धवो वाऽन्यगोत्रजः ।। Quoted in V.M.S. vol. I.

41. अयं द्विजैर्हि विद्वद्भिः पशुधर्मो विगर्हितः । M.S. vol. I. ix. 66.

42. पत्यो मृते वा पतिते सन्यस्ते व विदेशगे ।
तदगोत्रन्नजेन श्रेष्ठेन कार्याः पुंसवनादयः ।। Quoted in V.M.S. vol. I. p. 165.

43. विधवायां प्रजोत्पत्तौ देवरस्य नियोजनम् । Quoted in N.S. p. 262.

44. Ibid. p. 261.

rate in the list of usages prohibited in the Kali age. At present none but the husband is authorised to perform the Garbhādhāna Saṁskāra.

(viii) *Whether a Garbha-or a Kṣetra-Saṁskāra*

The mediaeval treatises also discuss the question whether the Garbhādhāna was a Garbha-Saṁskāra or a Kṣetra-Sṁskāra. There were two schools of opinion on this point. The first school held that it was the Saṁskāra of Garbha or embryo and based its arguments on Manū[45] and Yājñavalkya[46], who were of the opinion that "religious rites of the twice-born from the conception to the funeral should be performed." The Gautama Dharmasūtra[47] also says that forty Saṁskāras were meant for Puruṣa or man. According to the second school, Garbhādhāna was a Kṣetra-Saṁskāra or the consecration of the wife. They supported their views by such authorities as follows; "Having once co-habited with the wife ceremoniously one should approach her in future ordinarily (without any ceremony)." One should recite the verse beginning with "Viṣṇuryonim" after touching the genital organ of the wife. A child born in her without the Garbhādhāna attains impurities."[48] They were also of the opinion that this Saṁskāra should be performed only in the first conception,[49] as the Kṣetra once consecrated lends purity to every conception in future. Logically speaking, the Garbhādhāna was a Garbha-Saṁskāra in the beginning, and the second school represents the tendency of simplifying and omitting the Saṁskāras and, certainly, is of a later origin.

(ix) *A Sacred and Compulsory Duty*

Approaching the wife during her Ṛtu was a sacred and compulsory duty of every married man Manu[50] enjoins, "Remaining

---

45. निषेकादिः श्मशातान्तो मंत्रैर्यस्योदितो विधिः। M.S. ii. 16.

46. निषेकाद्याश्मशानान्ता स्तेषां मंत्रतः क्रियाः। yāj. S. I. 10.

47. viii. 24.

48. विष्णुर्योनिं जपेत्सूक्तं योनिं स्पृष्ट्वा त्रिभिर्व्रती।
गर्भाधानस्याकरणादस्यां जातस्तु दुष्यति॥
An anonymous quotation in VMS. vol. 1. p. 157

49. ऋतुमत्यां प्राजापत्यमृतौ प्रथमे।

50. ऋतुकालाभिगामीस्यात्स्वदारनिरतः सदा। M.S. iii. 45.

true to his wife, one should approach her in every Ṛtu." Parāśara[51] not only enjoins this compulsion but threatens the non-conformist with sins; "One who, though in good health, does not go to his wife during her Ṛtu, attains the sin of causing abortion, without any doubt." The duty of approaching the husband was equally binding on the wife, when she became pure after her monthly course. Parāśara[52] says, "A woman, who having bathed does not go to her husband, becomes a swine in her next life." Yama[53] goes still further and prescribes punishment to her. "She should be abandoned after having been declared "as one causing abortion" in the middle of the village."

The above compulsion represents the condition of an early society, when a large number of children was a great help to the family, both economically and politically. The Aryans, at their rise in India, were a community seeking expansion. So they prayed to gods for sons, at least, ten in number. In ancient times there was no anxiety about the expansion of the family. Besides, begetting as many children as possible was regarded religiously meritorious. The larger the number of children the more happy the Fathers would be in heaven, being sumptuously feasted by their descendants. The ancestral debt could be paid only in the form of children, and the existinction of the family was regarded to be a sin. These circumstances were responsible for making the Garbhādhāna a compulsory Saṁskāra.

(x) *Exceptions*

Exceptions, however, on physical, mental and moral grounds were recognized. "A man has no fear of sin, who does not approach a woman who is very old, barren, or corrupt; whose children have all died, who does not pass menses; who is a minor girl or a woman with many sons."[54] The Viṣṇupurāṇa says, "One should not approach

51. ऋतुस्नातां तु यो भार्यां सन्निधौ नोपगच्छति।
घोरायां ब्रह्महत्यायां युज्यते नात्र संशयः ॥ P.S. iv. 15.

52. ऋतुस्नाता तु या नारी भर्तारं नानुमन्यते।
सा मृता तु भवेन्नारी शूकरी च पुनः पुनः ॥ Ibid. iv. 14.

53. ऋतुस्नाता तु या भार्या भर्तारं नोपगच्छति।
तां ग्राममध्ये विख्याप्य भ्रूणाघ्नीं परित्यजेत् ॥
Quoted in the V.M.S. vol. I. p. 162.

54. वृद्धां वन्ध्यामसद्वृत्तां मृतापत्यामपुष्पिणीम्।
कन्यां च बहुपुत्रां च वर्जयन्मुच्यते भयात् ॥
The Madanaratna quoted by Gadādara on P.G.S. i. 11. 7.

a woman who has not bathed, who is afflicted, who is still in her menses, who is not praiseworthy, who is angry, who is thinking ill ......, who is not generous, who is thinking of another man, who has no passion at all......, who is hungry or overeaten."[55]

In course of time the social and religious idealogy of the Hindus changed. When the Aryans spread over the country and became master of the soil, their number increased and there was no need of ten sons either for political or economic purposes for every householder. The facination of heavenly enjoyments also, arising from the offerings of many sons, became less important than salvation dependent on the moral life of the individual. Therefore, the compulsion of approaching the wife in every month was loosened and finally removed. It was binding only in case of those who were childless. After the birth of one son, it became ineffective. "A man should approach his wife in every month until a son is born. The Vedic prayer for ten sons is only a praise."[56] Manu says, "By the birth of the first son alone, man becomes Putrin (Possessing sons) and pays off his ancestral debt. By whose birth one removes the debt of the Fathers, obtains the highest bliss, he alone is the son born of Dharma, or Law. The rest are born of passion."[57] At present there is no craze for a large number of children in the Hindu society.

(xi) Significance

The study of the Garbhādhāna Saṁskāra is very interesting from the cultural point of view. Here we do not find a primitive man

---

55. नास्नातां तां स्त्रियं गच्छेन्नातुरां न रजस्वलाम्।
नाप्रशस्तां न कुपितां नानिष्टां न च गुर्विणीम्॥
नादक्षिणां नान्यकामां नान्ययोषितम्।
क्षुत्क्षामामतिभुक्तां वा स्वयं चैभिर्गुणैः युतः॥
The Visṇuprāṇa quoted by Harihara on P.G.S. i. 11. 7.

56. ऋतुकालाभिगामी स्याद्यावत्पुत्रोऽभिजायते।
दशास्यां पुत्रानाधेहि इति प्रशंसार्था श्रुतिः॥
The Kūrmapurāna, quoted in the S. C. Áhnika, Prakarana I.

57. ज्येष्ठेन जातमात्रेण पुत्री भवति मानवः।
पितॄणामनृणश्चैव स तस्मात्सर्वमर्हति।
यस्मिन्नृणं सन्नयति येन चानन्त्यमश्नुते।
स एव धर्मजः पुत्रः कामजानितरान्विदुः॥
M.S. ix. 106, 107, cf. V S xviii. 1-3.

expressing wonder at the prospects of a child and only seeking the help of gods to secure it, nor conception here is a haphazard accident without any desire for the progeny. Here we come across a people who approached their wives with a definite purpose of procreating children, in a definite manner calculated to produce the best possible progeny and with the religious serenity which, they believed, would censecrate the would be child.

2. THE PUṀSAVANA (QUICKENING A MALE CHILD)

(*i*) *The Meaning of the term*

After the conception was ascertained, the child in the womb was consecrated by the Saṁskāra named Puṁsavana. By Puṁsavana was generally understood "that rite through which a male child was produced."[1] Vedic hymns recited on this occasion mention Pumān or Putra (a male) and favour the birth of a son.[2] The word Puṁsavana is rendered into English by "a rite quickening a male child."

(*ii*) *The Vedic period*

In the Atharvaveda and the Sāmveda-Mantra-Brāhmaṇa[3] we get prayers for male children. The husband prays by the wife. "Unto thy womb let a foetus come, a male one, as an arrow to a quiver; let a hero be born unto thee here, a ten-months' son. Give birth to a male, a son; after him let a male be born; mayest thou be mother of sons, of those born and whom thou shall bear etc."[4] We do not know what exact kind of rite was performed. But the above verses bear testimony to the fact that some kind of celebration was made with these prayers. The ceremony is called Prājāpatya in these hymns. "I perform the Prājāpatya (the ceremony of Prajāpati) etc."[5] Some sort of medicinal herb was also given to the pregnant woman with the verse, "The plants of which heaven has been the father, earth the mother, ocean the root, let those herbs of the gods favour thee, in order to acquire a son."[6] Thus the main features of the later day Saṁskāra are found in the Vedic period. But the rules

---

1. पुमान् प्रसूयते येन कर्मणा तत्पुंसवनमीरितम् ।
   Śaunaka quoted in V.M.S. vol. I. p. 166.
2. पुमांसं पुत्रं जनय तं पुमाननुजायताम् ।
   भवासि पुत्राणां माता जातायां जनयाश्चयान् ॥ A.V. iii. 23. 3. 3.
3. i. 4. 8-9.
4. आते योनिं गर्भ एतु पुमान् बाणइवेषुधिम् ।
   आवीरोऽत्र जायताम् पुत्रस्ते दशमासस्य ॥ ibid iii. 23.
5. कृणोमि ते प्राजापत्यम् । Ibid.
6. यासां द्यौ पिता पृथ्वी माता समुद्रो मूलं विरुधां बभूव ।
   तास्त्वा पुत्रविद्याय दैवी प्रावन्त्योषधः ॥ ibid iii. 23. 6.

regulating the various aspects of the Saṁskāra cannot be traced in the Vedas.

(*iii*) *The Sūtra Period*

During the Gṛhyasūtra period the Puṁsavana Sāṁskāra was performed in the third or the fourth month of pregnancy or even later, on the day when the moon was on a male constellation, on Tiṣya particularly.[7] The pregnant woman was required to fast on that day. After bath she put on new clothes. Then in the night the prouts of the banyan tree were pounded and the juice was inserted into the right nostril of the woman with verses beginning with 'Hiraṇyagarbha etc."[8] According to some Gṛhyasūtras Kuśakantaka and Somalatā were also to be pounded with the above.[9] If the father desired that his son should be Vīryavān or virile, he should place a dish of water on the lap of the mother and touching her stomach recited the verse "Suparṇosi."[10]

(*iv*) *The Later Rules and Considerations*

The Dharmasūtras and the Smṛtis do not add anything to the ritual proper. The Prayogas and the Paddhtis solely draw upon the Gṛhyasūtras of the Vedic School they follow with the only addition of the Mātṛipūja and Ābhyudayika Śrāddha.[11]

(*v*) *The Proper Time*

The Smṛtis deal with the proper time when the Saṁskāra should be performed. According to Manu[12] and Yājñavalkya[13] it should be performed before the foetus begins to move in the womb. Śaṅkha[14] followed them. Bṛhaspati[15] prescribes the time after the movement. Jātūkarṇya[16] and Śaunaka[17] say that it should be per-

---

7. P.G.S. i. 14. 2; B.G.S. i. 1.

8. P.G.S. i. 14. 3.

9. Ibid, i. 14. 4

10. Ibid. i. 14. 5.

11. Almost all the Paddhatis.

12-13. गर्भाधानमृतौ पुंसः सवनं स्पन्दनात्पुरा । Yāj. S. I. 11.

14. The S. S. ii. 1.

15. सवनं स्पन्दते शिशौ । quoted in V.M.S. vol. I. p. 166.

16. Ibid.

17. Ibid.

formed in the third month of pregnancy after conception becomes manifest.

The time of performance ranged from the second to the eighth month of pregnancy. It was due to the fact that the symptoms of conception became visible in the case of different woman in different months. The Kulācāra or family custom was also responsible for this variation. Bṛhaspati differentiates between these periods." In the first pregnancy, the Saṁskāra should be performed in the third month. In the case of women who have already given birth to children it should be performed in the fourth, sixth or even in the eighth month of pregnancy."[18] In the first conception, the symptoms show themselves earlier than in the others. That is why later periods are prescribed in the second case.

(vi) Whether performed in every pregnancy

The Smṛtis also discuss the question whether this Saṁskāra should be performed in every pregnancy or not. According to Śaunaka this rite should be repeated in every conception, because by touching and feeding, the foetus becomes purified; moreover by the force of the verses recited in this Saṁskāra, one obtains the memory of the past lives. So, it is prescribed in every conception."[19] In the Mitākṣarā on the Yajñavalkya, we find an eliminating tendency where Vijñāneśvara says, "These Puṁsavana and Sīmanta being Kṣetra Saṁskāras should be performed only once."[20]

(vii) The Ritual and its Significance

The significance of the Saṁskāra consisted in its main features. It should be performed when the moon was on a male constellation. This time was regarded as favourable for producing a male issue. Inserting the juice of the banyan tree was a device meant for preventing abortion and ensuring the birth of a male child. In the opinion of Suśruta the banyan tree has got the properties of removing all kinds of troubles during pregnancy, e.g., excess of bile, burning etc.[21] He says, "Having pounded with milk any of these herbs,

18. तृतीये मासि कर्तव्यं गृष्टेरन्यत्रशोभनम् ।
गृष्टेश्चतुर्थे मासे तु षष्ठे मासेऽथवाऽष्टमे ।। Quoted in V.M.S. vol. I. p. 168.

19. Ibid.

20. एते च पुंसवनसीमन्तोन्नयने क्षेत्रसंस्कारकर्मत्वात्सकृदेव कार्ये न प्रतिगर्भम् । On Yāj. S. 1. 11.

21. Suśruta, Sūtrasthāna, ch. 38.

Sulakṣmaṇā Baṭaśuṅga, Sahadevī and Viśvadeva, one should insert three or four drops of juice in the (right) nostril of the pregnant woman for the birth of a son. She should not spit the juice out."[22] Insertion of medicine into nostrils is a common thing in the Hindu system of treatment. Therefore, it is evident that the ritual prescribing it was undoubtedly founded on the medical experience of the people. Putting a dish of water on the lap was a symbolical performance. A pot full of water denoted life and spirit in the would be child. Touching the womb emphasized the necessity of taking every care by the expectant mother, so that the foetus should be healthy and strong in the womb and abortion may not take place. The hymn "Suparṇa etc." or "of beautiful wings" expresed the wish that a handsome child should be born.

22. लब्धगर्भाश्चैतेष्वहः सुलक्ष्मणा वटशुंगसहदेवीविश्वदेवानामन्यतमं क्षीरेणाभिकुट्य त्रींश्चतुरो वा बिन्दून् दद्याद्दक्षिणे नाशापुटे पुत्रकामायैन्नच तंन्निष्ठीवेत्।
ibid. Śarirasthāna, ch. 2.

3. THE SĪMANTONNAYANA (HAIR-PARTING)

(i) *The Definition of the term*

The third Saṁskāra of the embryo was Sīmantonnayana. That rite was called Sīmanta, in which the hairs of a pregnant woman were parted.[1]

(ii) *The Purpose*

The purpose of this Saṁskāra was partly superstitious and partly practical. People believed that a woman in her pregnancy was subject to attacks of evil spirits and some rite should be performed to ward them off. The Āśvalāyana-Smṛti has preserved this belief. It says, "Evil demons bent on sucking the blood, come to woman in the first pregnancy to devour the foetus. In order to remove them, the husband should invoke the goddess Śrī, as the lurking spirit leave the woman protected by Her. These invisible cruel flesh-eaters catch hold of the woman in her first pregnancy and trouble her. Therefore, the ceremony named Sīmantonnayana is prescribed."[2] The religious intention of the Saṁskāra was to bring about prosperity to the mother and long life to the unborn child, as it is indicated by the verses recited. Physiological knowledge of the Hindu was also responsible for instituting this rite. From the fifth month of pregnancy the formation of the mind of the would-be child begins.[3] So the pregnant woman was required to take utmost care to facilitate this process, avoiding any physical shock to the foetus. This fact was symbolically emphasized by parting her hair. Another purpose of the Saṁskāra was to keep the pregnant woman in good cheer. To address her as Rākā or "full-moon night," Supeśā, or "of beautiful limbs" and parting and dressing the hair by the husband himself were methods used for it.[4]

---

1. सीमन्तः उन्नीयते यस्मिन्कर्मणि तत्सीमन्तोन्नयनमिति कर्मनामधेयम् ।
V.M.S. vol. I. p. 172.

2. पत्न्याः प्रथमजं गर्भमत्तुकामाः सुदुर्भगाः ।
आयान्ति काश्चिद्राक्षस्यो रुधिराशनतत्पराः ॥
तासां निरसनार्थाय श्रियमावाहयेत्पतिः ।
सीमन्तकरणी लक्ष्मीस्तामावहति मंत्रत ॥
Aśvalāyanāchārya quoted in V. M.S. vol. I. p. 172.

3. पञ्चमे मनः प्रतिबुद्धतरं भवति, षष्ठे बुद्धिः । Suśruta, Śarirasthāna ch. 33.

4. B.G.S. i. 10. 7.

(iii) *Early History*

The only pre-Sūtra reference to this ceremony is found in the Mantra-Brāhmaṇa; "As Prajāpati establishes the boundary of Aditi for great prosperity, so I part the hair of this woman and make her progeny live to a old age."[5] In the same Brāhmaṇa reference is also made to the simile between the Udumbara tree and a fertile woman. "This tree is fertile. Like it be fruitful etc."[6] In the Gṛhyasūtras the Saṁskāra is described at length and all the features are fully developed.

(iv) *The Time of Performance*

The Gṛhyasūtras, the Smṛtis and the astrological works discuss the proper time of performing this Saṁskāra. The Gṛhyasūtras favour the fourth or the fifth month of pregnancy.[6a] The Smṛtis and the astrological books extend the period up to eighth month or up to the birth of the child.[7] Some writers are even more liberal. According to them, if delivery took place before this Saṁskāra was performed, it was celebrated after the birth of the child, placing it on the lap of the mother or putting it into a box.[8] The later periods indicate that the original sense of the Saṁskāra was being lost and it was becoming a farce

(v) *The Object of Purification*

The authorities are divided in their opinion whether this Saṁskāra should be performed in every pergnancy or it should be performed only in the first conception. According to Āśvalāyana, Baudhāyana, Āpastamba and Pāraskara, it is a Kṣetra Saṁskāra and should be performed only once.[9] Hārīta and Devala followed them.

5. ओं येनादितेः सीमानं नयति प्रजापतिर्महते सौभागाय। तेनाहमस्यै सीमानं नयामि प्रजामस्यै जरदष्टिं कृणोमि ॥ The S.V.M. Br. i. 5. 2.

6. Ibid. P.G.S. i. 15. 6.

6a. प्रथम गर्भायाश्चतुर्थे मासि सीमन्तोन्नयनम्।
B.G.S. i. 10. 1; A.G.S. i. 14. 1; Āp. G.S. *xiv*. 1

7. षष्ठे अष्टमे वा सीमन्तः। Yāj. S. I. 11.

8. स्त्री यद्यकृतसीमन्ता प्रसूयते कदाचन। गृहीतपुत्रा विधिवत्पुनः संस्कारमर्हति ॥ Satyavrata तदानीं पेटके गर्भं स्थाप्य संस्कारमाचरेत्।
Gārgya quoted in V.M.S. vol. I. p. 177.

9. A.G.S. i. 14; B.G.S. i. 10; P.G.S. i. 15. 1.

"A woman once purified by the Sīmantonnayana, every child produced by her becomes consecrated."[10] But in the opinion of others it was a Garbha-Saṁskāra and should be performed in every conception. The difference of opinion was due to the fact the child in the womb was consecrated through the mother, so the first school thought it enough that the idea of protecting the unborn child was impressed even once on her mind, or protection aganist evil spirits was once ensured for her.

(vi) The Ceremonies

The constellation under which the Saṁskāra was performed, was a male one. The mother was required to fast on that day. The ritual proper began with preliminary rites, e.g. the Mātṛpūjā, the Nāndiśrāddha and oblations to Prajāpati.[12] Then the wife was seated on a soft chair on the western side of the fire and the husband parted the hair of the wife upwards (e.g. beginning from the front) with a bunch containing an even number of unripe Udumbara fruits, and with three bunches of Darbha-grass, with a porcupines quill that had three white spots, with a stick of the Vīratara wood and with a full spindle, with the mantra "Bhūr Bhuvaḥ Svaḥ" or with each of the three Mahāvyāhṛtis.[13] Baudhāyana prescribes two other verses at this point.

A later practice of making a red mark on the person of the wife to frighten demons was also prevalent.[15] After the partion of hair the husband tied the Udumbara branch round the neck of the wife with a string of three twisted threads with the words. "Rich in sap is this tree; like the tree rich in sap, be thou fruitful."[16] Baudhāyana recommends barley-sprouts instead of the Udumbara branch.[17] This ceremony was symbolical of fertility of the woman. This idea was suggested by numerous fruits of the Udumbara branch and the barley-sprouts. The next step in the Saṁskāra was asking the wife by the husband to look at the mess of rice, sesame

10. Quoted in V.M.S. vol. I. p. 176.

11. केचिद् गर्भस्य संस्कारा त्प्रति गर्भं प्रयुज्यते । Viṣṇu, Ibid.

12. The Pāraskara-gṛhyapaddhati.

13. P.G.S. i. 15 4.

14. i. 10. 7-8.

15. V.G.S. xvi.

16. अयमूर्ज्जावतो वृक्ष उर्ज्जीव फलिनी भवेति । P.G.S. i. 15. 6.

17. i. 10. 8.

and ghee and see into it offsprings, cattle, prosperity and long life for the husband.[18] Some authorities provide that Brahman ladies sitting beside the pregnant woman should utter the following phrases: "Be mother of heroic sons, be mother of living sons etc."[19] Then the husband asked the two lute players, "S ng ye the King, or if anybody else is still more valiant."[20] The following stanza was prescribed to be sung. "Soma alone is our King. May this human tribe, dwell on thy bank, O (river) whose dominion is unbroken."[21] The Aryans were still a militant race, aiming at further conquest and praying for heroic sons to achieve it. The above stanza was a kind of heroic ballad meant to create a heroic atmosphere and thereby to influence the unborn child. The ceremony closed with the feasting of the Brahmans. The mother kept silent after the ceremony until the stars appeared in the sky. Then she touched a calf, a performance suggestive of a male issue, uttered the Vyāhṛtis, Bhūr Bhuvaḥ Svaḥ and broke her silence.[22]

(vii) The Duties of a Pregnant Woman

The Smṛti-writers realized that every conduct of an expectant mother influenced the unborn child. So, after laying down rules and regulations about the pre-natal Saṁskāras, they prescribed the duties of a pregnant woman and her husband. These duties can be grouped into three classes. The first class is based on the superstitious belief that evil spirits try to injure the pregnant woman and, therefore, she should be protected from them. The second class containing rules aiming at the preventing of physical overexertion, and the third class was calculated to preserve the physical and mental health of the mother.

To begin with the first class, we find in the Mārkaṇḍeya-Purāṇa the following observation: "There are terr ble fiends and witches bent on devouring the foetus of a pregnant woman. Therefore, she should be always protected from them by ever observing purity, writing sacred mantras and wearing beautiful garland. O Brāhmaṇa, Virūpa and Vikṛti generally dwell in trees, trenches, ramparts and seas. They are always in search of pregnant women. Hence,

18. किं पश्यसि। प्रजां प्रशून्त्सौभाग्यं मह्यं दीर्घायुष्टं पत्युः।
S.V.M. Br. i. 5. 1-5; G.G.S. ii. 7. 10–12. ibid.

19. वीरसूर्ज्जीवपत्नीति ब्राह्मण्यो मङ्गल्यानि वाग्भिरुपासीरन् सूर्जीव पत्नीति ii. 7.

20. P.G.S. i. 15. 7.

21. Ibid. 1. 15. 7.

22. G. G. S. ii. 7.

they should not visit these places. The son of Garbhahantā is Vighna, and Mehinī is his daughter. The first enters the womb and eats away the foetus. The second having entered it causes abortion. From the mischief of Mehinī are born snakes, frogs, tortoises from the womb of a woman."[23]

Again, there is a long conversation between Kaśyapa and Aditi in the Padmapurāṇa about the duties of a pregnant woman in which the former said to the latter, "She should not sit on ordure, a mace or pestle and a mortar; she should not bathe in a river..., nor she should go to a deserted house; she should not sit on an anthill and never be mentally disturbed; she should not scratch the earth with her nails, charcoal and ashes; she should not always be sleeping and dorment; she should avoid exerc se; she should not touch husk, coal, ashes and skull; she should avoid quarrel in the family and mutilation of her limbs; she should not leave her hair dishevelled and never remain impure: while sleeping she should not keep her head towards north and downwards and remain naked, disturbed and wetfooted; she should not utter inauspicious words and laugh too much; always busy with good work, she should worship her father-in-law and mother-in-law, and wishing welfare of her husband remain happy."[24] In the Matsya-purāṇa Kaśyapa says to Diti, his second wife, "O of beautiful colour, a pregnant woman should not take her meals during twilights; she should not go and remain under a tree; she should not be always sleeping; she should avo d the shade of a tree, bathe with warm water mixed with medicinal herbs, remain protected and decorated, worship gods, and give alms; she should observe Pārvati-vratas on the third day of a month; she should avoid mounting an elephant, horse, mountain and many-storeyed buildings; she should give up exercise, swift-walking, journey in a bullock-cart, sorrows, blood-letting, sitting like a cock, exertion, sleeping in the day, keeping awake in the night, highly saline, sour, hot, stale and heavy food. The son of a woman observing the above rules becomes long-lived and talented; otherwise abortion takes place without doubt."[25]

The Smṛtis, the Kārikās and the Prayogas give nothing more but a summary of the above rules. The Vāraha-Smṛti-prohibits the taking of meat during pregnancy.[26]

---

23. The Mārkandeya-Purāna, quoted in V.M.S. vol. I. p. 180.

24. The Padma-purāṇa, V. 7. 41–47.

25. The Matsya-purāna quoted in V.M.S. vol. I p. 180.

26. सामिषमशनं यत्नात्प्रमदा परिवर्जयेदतः प्रभृति।
Vārāha quoted by Harihara on P.G.S.

(viii) *The Duties of the Husband*

The first and foremost duty of the husband was to fulfil the wishes of his pregnant wife. According to Yājñavalkya, "By not meeting the wishes of a pregnant woman, foetus becomes unhealthy; it is either deformed or it falls down. Therefore, one should do as desired by her."[27] The Āśvalāyana-Smṛti lays down other duties of the husband: "After the sixth month of her pregnancy, he should avoid cropping hair, coition, pilgrimage and performing Śrāddha."[28] The Kālavidhāna prohibits "....going in a funeral procession, pairing nails, joining war, building a new house, going abroad, marriage in the family and bathing in the sea, as it would shorten the life of the husband of a pregnant woman."[29] Another Smṛti forbids the hewing of a tree also.[30]

(ix) *The Medical Basis*

The rules laid down for the health of the pregnant woman are based on the medical knowledge of the Hindus. Suśruta[31] prescribes similar precautions. "From the time of pregnancy she should avoid coition, over-exertion, sleeping in the day, keeping awake in the night, mounting a carriage, fear, sitting like a cock, purgative, phlepotomy and untimely postponement of natural flow of excretion, urine etc." Thus every possible care was taken to preserve the physical and mental health of the pregnant woman.

---

27. दोहृदस्याप्रदानेन गर्भो दोषमवाप्नुयात् ।
    वैरूप्यं निधनं वाऽपि तस्मात्कार्यं प्रियं स्त्रियः ॥ Yaj. S. III. 79.
28. वपनं मैथुनं तीर्थं वर्जयेद्गर्भिणी पतिः ।
    श्राद्धं च सप्तमान्मासादूर्ध्वं चान्यत्रवेदवित् ॥
    Áśvalayana quoted by Harihara P.G.S. i. 15.
29. क्षौरं शवानुगमनं नरवकृन्तनं च युद्धं च वास्तुकरणं त्वतिदूरयानम् ।
    उद्वाहमम्बुधिजलं स्पृशनोपयोगमायुः क्षयो भवति गर्भिणिकापतीनाम् ॥
30. सिन्धुस्नानं द्रुमच्छेदं वपनं प्रेतवाहनम् । Quoted in V.M.S. vol. I. p. 184.
31. Suśruta, śarirathāna, Ch. II.

CHAPTER VI

THE SAMSKĀRAS OF CHILDHOOD

1. THE JĀTAKARMA (BIRTH CEREMONIES)

(i) *The Origin*

The birth of a child was a very impressing scene for the early man. Owing to its wonderfulness, he attributed this event to some superhuman agency. He also apprehended many dangers on this occasions, for the avoidance of which various taboos and observances arose.[1] The helplessness of the mother and the new born during her confinement required natural care, from which ceremonies connected with the birth of a child originated. Even in very ancient times ordinary human feelings must have been moved at the sight of a mother, who had just given birth to a child. The man, who shared the pleasures in the company of his mate, sought to protect her and the babe, during the critical time, from natural and supernatural dangers. Thus the birth ceremonies had a natural basis in the physical conditions of child-birth. The primitive wonder, supernatural fear and natural care were, in course of time, combined with the cultural devices and aspirations to protect the mother and the child and to consecrate the babe.

(ii) *The History*

The word "Janman" or "birth" occurs thrice in the Ṛgveda.[2] But it is used there in the sense of relations.[3] Besides, the context in which it is used shows that the passages where the word occurs have nothing to do with any ceremony like it. In the Atharvaveda, however, there is one full hymn containing prayers and spells for easy and safe delivery. The hymn runs as follows: "At this birth, O Pūṣan, let Aryaman (as efficient Vedhas) invoke utter Vaṣat for thee; let the woman rightly engender, be relaxed; let her joints go apart in order to give birth. Four are the directions of sky, four

1. Cf. Gardner and Jewans, Greek Antiquitus, p. 299.

2. iii. 15. 2; ii. 26. 3.

3. जनेन विण; जन्मना पुत्रैः।
अग्निरस्मि जन्मना जातवेदाः। iii. 26. 7.

also of the earth; the gods sent together the foetus; let them unclose her in order to give birth. Let Pūṣan unclose her; we make the Yoni go apart; do thou Sūṣaṇa loosen; do thou Viṣkala, let go. Not as it were stuck in the flesh, not in the fat, not as it were in the marrow, let the spotted slimy afterbirth come down for the dog to eat; let the afterbirth descend. I split apart thy urinator, apart the Yoni apart the two groins, apart both the mother and the child, apart the boy from the afterbirth; let the afterbirth descend. As the wind, as the mind as fly the birds, so do thou O ten months' child, fly along with the afterbirth; let the afterbirth descend."[4] This hyman is both a piece of prayer and of magic. The husband was moved at the labour-pain of the wife. He wished that she should be free as soon as possible. The help of gods and the will of magicians were requisitioned to ease the mother undergoing the throes of childbirth. The Gṛhyasūtras employ the third verse of the above hymn in the rite, Soṣyantīkarma, for speedy delivery. But besides the prayers and spells no details of the ceremonies associated with them can be gathered.

In the Gṛhyasūtras this Saṁskāra is fully described. But here, too, the ritual is purely religious and popular and superstitious elements are hardly given their proper scope. The Dharmasūtras and the Smṛtis do not give any descriptive details. The mediaeval treatises, however, introduce many preliminary items e.g. the arrangement of the maternity house, ceremony accompanying entery into it, presence of desirable persons near the expectant mother, and some other superstitious observances which are otherwise unknown to earlier sources.

(iii) Preliminary Precautions and Ceremonies

We know from the later sources that preparations for delivery began one month before the birth of the child. "On the eve of the month of delivery special arrangement should be made."[5] The first thing done in this connection was the selection of a suitable room in the house. "On an auspicious day when the sun is in an auspicious zodiacal mansion, a room selected in the convenient direction is called the Sūtikā-bhavana or maternity house by the learned."[6]

---

4. A. V. I. 11; Kauśika quotes it at the beginning of a long and intricate ceremony for safe delivery.

5. आसन्नप्रसवे मासि कुर्याच्चैव विशेषतः ।
Ratnākara quoted in the V.M.S. vol. I. p. 184.

6 वारेऽनुकूले राशौ तु दिने दोषविवर्जिते ।
स्वानुकूलदिशं प्रोक्तं सूतिकाभवनं बुधैः ।। Garga quoted in V.M.S. vol. I. p. 184,

Vasiṣṭha does not leave the selection to option but prescribes the room situated in the south-west corner of the house.[7] "The house should be elegantly built on an even ground by expert architects; it should face either the east or the north and look auspicious and strong."[8]

A day or two before the delivery, the expectant mother entered the Sūtikā-gṛha which was well protected from all sides, having worshipped the gods, the Brahmans and the cows, amidst sounds of conchshells and other musical instruments and the recital of auspicious verses. Many other women also, who had given birth to children, who were capable of bearing hardships, of leasing manners and reliable, accompanied the mother. They cheered up the woman, and prepared her for safe delivery by means of useful ointment and regulations about diet and living. When the time for actual delivery came, they made the mother lie on her back.[9] Some rites were then performed for the protection of the house from evil spirits. The place was anointed to ward off demons. A Brahman loosened all the knots in the house.[10] It symbolized the loosening of the foetus in the womb of the mother. Fire, water, staff, lamp, weapons, mace and mustard seeds were kept in the house.[11] Tūryanti plants were also placed before the mother.[12] It was believed that in their absence, terrible bloodsucking demons would kill the new-born.[13]

Before the Jātakarma proper, a ceremony named Soṣyantī-karma was performed to expedite the delivery by force of the Atharvan verse, "Not as it were stuck in the flesh, not in the fat, not as it were in the marrow, let the spotted slimy afterbirth come down, for the dog to eat." Special rites were prescribed if the child died

---

7. नैऋत्यां सूतिकागृहम् । ibid.

8. सुभूमौ निर्मितं रम्यं वास्तुविद्याविशारदैः ।
प्राग्द्वारमुत्तरद्वारमथवा सुदृढं शुभम् ॥ The Viṣṇudharmottara, Ibid.

9. Ibid.

10. A coresponding custom is found in Germany where people open all the doors and locks of the house.

11. The Mārkandeya-purāṇa quoted in V.M.S. vol. I. p. 185.

12. Áp. G.S. xiv. 14; H.G.S. ii. 2–8.

13. सा जातहारिणी नाम सुघोरा पिशिताशना ।
तस्मात्संरक्षणं कार्यं यत्नतः सूतिकागृहे ॥
The Mārakaṇdeya-puraṇa, V.M.S. vol. I. p. 185.

in the birth. If the delivery was safe and the child was born alive a fire was lighted in the room to warm utensils and to smoke the child and the mother.[14] This fire was kept burning for the days. Grains of rice and seeds of mustard were thrown into it with appropriate formulas to, drive away various kinds of evil spirits. The Sūtikā fire was regarded impure and it disappeared on the tenth day when the domestic fire came into use after the purification of the mother and the child was performed.

(iv) *The Time of Performance*

The Jātakarma ceremony was performed before the severing of the navel cord.[15] This seems to have been the original time, but later writers state that if the time expired it was performed at the end of the ceremonial impurity of ten days, or, if the birth took place during the impurity caused by a death in the family, the ceremony was postponed until its expiry.[16] In later times the moment of birth was noted with meticulous care for preparing horroscope, as it was thought to be a determining factor in the life of the child. Then the good news was brought to the father. Different sentiments were expressed at the birth of a boy and a girl, as different prospects were depending on them. The first born was liked to be a boy, as he freed the father from all ancestral debts. But for a sensible man a girl was not less meritorious, because her gift in marriage brought merits to the father. After this, the father went to the mother in order to see the face of the son, because by looking at the face of the newborn son the father is absolved from all debts and attains immortality.[17] Having seen the face of child, he bathed with his clothes on, invited the elders

---

14. S.G.S. i. 25. 4; P.G.S. i. 16. 23. g.b.s. i. 8. The purifying influence of fire is recognized in the Greek ritual also. Here the child is swiftly caried round the fire in an awphiobornia for strength and speed.

15. प्राङ्नाभिवर्धनात्पुंसो जातकर्म विधीयते।
मंत्रतः प्राशनं चास्य हिरण्यमधुसर्पिषाम् ।।
Saṁvyarta quoted in V.M.S. vol. I. p. 187.

16. मृताशौचस्य मध्ये तु पुत्रजन्म यदा भवेत् ।
अशौचापगमे कार्यं जातकर्म यथाविधि ।।
The Smṛti-Saṁgraha quoted by Gadādhara on P.G.S.

17. ऋणमस्मिन्सन्नयति अमृतत्वं च गच्छति।
पितापुत्रस्य जातस्य पश्येच्चेज्जीवितो मुखम् ।। V.S. xvii. 1

and performed the Nāndi-Śrāddha[18] and the Jātakarma ceremonies.[19] Generally speaking, Śrāddha is an inauspicious ceremony. But the one performed here was an auspicious Śraddha. It was meant for entertaining the Fathers. Hārita says, "Merits arise form the happiness of the Fathers at the birth of a son. Therefore, one should offer Śrāddha to them with pots full of sesame and gold, after having invited the Brāhmanas."[20] The Brāhma-purāṇa also enjoins to perform the Nāndī Śrāddha at the birth of a son.[21]

(v) *The Ceremonies and their Significance*

(a) Medh-janana. Now the Jātakarma ceremonies proper commenced.[22] The first ceremony was the Medhājanana or production of intelligence. It was performed in the following way. The father with his fourth finger and an instrument of gold gave to the child honey and ghee or ghee alone. Others add to it sour milk, rice, barley and even whitish black and red hairs of a black bull. The formula employed was, "Bhūḥ I put into thee: Bhuvah I put into thee; Svaḥ I put into thee: Bhūr bhuvaḥ svaḥ every thing I put into thee." The Medhājanana ceremony speaks of the high concern of the Hindus about the intellectual well-being of the child, which they thought their first business with it. The Vyāhṛtis uttered on this occasion were symbolical of intelligence; they were recited with the great Gāyatrī mantra which contains prayer for stimulating talent. The substances, with which the child was fed, were also conducive to mental growth. According to Suśruta, the following are the properties of ghee: "It is producer of beauty; it is greasy and sweet; it is remover of hysteria, headache, epilepsy, fever, indigestion, excess of bile; it is increaser of digestion, memory intellect, talent, lustre, good sound, semen and life."[23] The properties of honey and gold are equally favourable to the mental progress of the child. According to the Gobhila Gṛhyasūtra,[24] at this time, a name was given to the child, while the phrase, "Thou

18-1 जातं कुमारं स्वं दृष्ट्वा स्नात्वाऽऽनीयगुरून्पिता।
नान्दीश्राद्धावसाने तु जातकर्म समाचरेत्॥
The Brahma-purāṇa quoted in the V.M.S. vol. I. p. 188.

20. जाते कुमारे पितृगामामोदात्पुण्यम् etc. हारीत ibid.

21. Ibid. p. 191.

22. P.G.S. i. 16; G.G.S. 1. 7. A.G.S. i. 15. S.G.S. i. 24; M.G.S. i. 17; H.K.G.S. ii. 3; Bh. G.S. i. 24; B.G.S. ii. 1.

23. Sarirasthna, Ch. 45.

24. i. 7.

are the Veda," was being uttered in its ear. This was the secret name known to the parents only. It was not made public, as they were afraid that enemies might practise magic on it and thus injure the child.

(b) Āyuṣya. The next item of the Jātakarma ceremonies was the Āyuṣya or the rite for ensuring a long life for the child. Near the navel or the right ear of the babe the father murmurred, "Agni is longlived; through the trees he is longlived. By that long life I make thee longlived. Soma is long-lived; through the herbs etc. The Brahman is long-lived; through ambrosia etc. The Ṛṣis are longlived; through observances etc. Sacrifice is longlived; through sacrificial fire etc. The Ocean is longlived; through the rivers etc."[25] Thus all the possible instances of long life were cited before the child, and by the association of ideas it was believed that through the utterance the life of the babe would be also lengthened. Other rites were also performed for long life. The father thrice recited the verse, "The threefold age," thinking that it would three times lengthen the span of child's life. If the father desired that the son may live the full term of his life, he touched him with Vātsapra hymn. Not satisfied with the single will of his own, the father invited five Brahmans, placed them towards five regions and requested them to breathe upon the child. The Brahmans helped the infusion of life into the child in the following way. The one in the south said, "Back-breathing; the one to the west, "Downbreathing!" the one to the north, "Out-breathing!" and the fifth one looking upwards said "On-breathing!"[26] If the help of the five Brahmans could not be secured the father himself recited the above phrases, going round the child. The breathing was thought to be productive of life. Therefore, this magical ceremony was performed to strengthen the breath of the child and prolong its life.

The earth, where the child was born, was naturally believed by the simple folk to be instrumental in the safe delivery of the child, and therefore reverenced. So the father offered his grateful thanks to it: "I know, O Earth, thy heart, thy heart that dwells in heaven, in the moon. That I know; may it know me." He further prayed to it: "May we see a hundred autumns; may hear a hundred autumns."[27]

25. P.G.S. i. 16. 6.

26. P.G.S. i. 16, 10–12

277 P.G.S. i. 16. 13.

(c) Strength. The father next performed another rite for the hardy, martial and pure life of the child. He asked the babe, "Be a stone, be an axe, be an imperishable gold. Thou indeed art the self called son; thus live a hundred autumns."[28]

After this the mother was praised for bearing a son, the hope of the family. The husband recited the following verse in her honour: "Thou art Idā, the daughter of Mitra and Vaıuṇa; thou strong woman hast borne a strong son. Be thou blessed with strong children, thou who hast blessed us with a strong son."[29]

Then the navel-cord was severed and the child washed and given the breasts of the mother. The father put down a pot of water near the head of the mother with the verse, "O waters, you watch with the gods. As you watch with the gods, thus watch our this mother, who is confined, and her child." The waters were supposed to ward off demons. Hence the mother was commended to theiı protection. Having ceremoniously established near the door of the maternity house the fire that had been kept burning from the time of the wife's confinement, the husband offered into that fire mustard seeds mixed with rice-chaff, every morning and evening until the mother got up from the child-bed, in order to scatter away goblins and demons. The following magical formula was used. "May Śuṇḍa and Marka. Upavīra and Śauṇdikeya, Ulūkhala and Malimlucha, Droṇāsa and Chyavana, vanish, hence. Svāhā! May Ālikhata, Animiṣa Kimbadanta, Upaśruti, Haryakṣa, Kumbhina Śatru, Pātrapāṇi. Nṛmaṇi, Hantṛmukha, Sarṣapāruṇa, Chyavan Vanish, hence Svāhā!"[30] The above are the names of diseases and deformities that attack an infant. They were conceived and addressed as goblins and demons by early people. Here, as their conception is fantastic but picturesque, so their remedies were magical but useful.

If the disease-bringing demon Kumāra attached the child, the father covered it with a net or with an upper garment, took him on his lap and murmurred. "Kurkura, Sukurkura, Kurkura, who holds fast children. Chet ! Chet ! doggy ! let him loose. Reverence be to thee,

28. अङ्गगद् अङ्गगद् संभवसि हृदयादधिजायसे।
आत्मा वै पुत्रानाभासि स जीव शरदः शतम्॥
अश्मा भव परशुर्भव हिरण्यमसृतं भव। ibid. i. 16. 14.

29. इडासि मै ावरुणी वीरे वीरमजीजनथः।
सात्वं वीरवती भव याऽस्मान्वीरवतोऽकरदिति॥ ibid. i. 16. 15.

30. Ibid. 16. 19.

the Sīsra, barker, bender etc."[31] It was an euphamism to placate the supposed demon. The father at the ceremonies expressed his last wish with the words. "He does not suffer, he does not cry, he is not stiff, he is not sick when we speak to him and when we touch him."[32] It was the expression of the heartfelt solicitude of the father for the child.

When the ceremonies were over, presents were offered to the Brahmans and gifts and alms distributed. The Brāhma and the Āditya-purāṇa say, "On the birth of a son the gods and the Fathers come to witness the ceremonies at the house of a twice-born. Therefore, that day is auspicious and important On that day should be given gold, earth, cows, horses, umbrella, goats, garlands, bedding seats etc."[33] According to Vyāsa the merits of alms given on the day of a son's birth are eternal.[34]

31. Ibid. i. 16. 20.

32. Ibid. i. 16. 21.

33. Quoted in V.M.S. vol. I. p. 199.

34. पुत्रजन्मनि यात्रायां शर्बर्यां दत्तमक्षयम् । व्यास, ibid.

2. THE NĀMAKARAṆA (NAME-GIVING)

(i) *The Importance of Naming*

Ever since men evolved a language, they have tried to give names to things of daily use in their life. With the progress of social consciousness men were also named, because without particular names of individuals it was impossible to carry on the business of a cultured society. The Hindus very early realized the importance of naming persons and converted the system of naming into a religious ceremony. Bṛhaspati with a poetic exaggeration remarks about the desirability of naming: "Name is the primary means of social intercourse, it brings about merits and it is the root of fortune. From name man attains fame. Therefore, naming ceremony is very praiseworthy."[1]

(ii) *The Origin*

The origin of name-giving is a linguistic problem beyond the scope of the present work. We are here concerned with ceremonial naming of persons only. It is generally found that the choice of a name for the child is often connected with religious ideas. The child is frequently named after a god who seems to be regarded its protector or it is named after a saint whose blessings are sought for it. Secular ideas are also responsible for determining names. They denote a particular quality in the person named. New names are also given to a novitiate when he enters a secret society.[2] The adoption of the father's name is prevalent, which is based on the family attachment and pride. The assuming of a secret name is also found. It involves the personality of a man and is, therefore, withheld from enemies. Thus, there are so many factors working behind the system of giving name to a person.

(iii) *The Vedic Period*

'Nāman' or name is a word of common occurrence in the Sanskrit literature and is found even in the earliest work of the Indo-

---

1. नामाखिलस्य व्यवहारहेतुः शुभावहं कर्मसु भाग्यहेतुः ।
नाम्नैव कीर्तिं लभते मनुष्यस्ततः प्रशस्तं खलु नामकर्म ।।
Bṛhaspati, quoted in V.M.S. vol. I. p. 241.

2. H. Webster, Primitive Sacred Societies, pp. 40 ff.

Aryans, the Ṛgveda.[3] Names of objects and persons are found in the Vedic literature. Other peculiar names suggested in the Sūtras and the Smṛtis are also found in the Vedic and the Brāhmaṇa literatures. The Ṛgveda[4] recognizes a secret name, and the Aitareya[5] and the Satapatha[6] Brāhmaṇas refer to it. But the practice, as given in the Sūtras, of giving a secret name after the Nakṣatra-name is nowhere instanced in the Vedic literature. The adoption of a second name is assumed for success and distinction in life. The common fashion was to adopt two names. The one name was the popular one, the other being a patronymic or matronymic. For example, in Kākṣivanta Auśija,[8] the first is the popular name and the second is the name derived from Uśijā (the name of mother); in Bṛhaduktha Vāmneya[9] the second name is derived form Vāmanī. In such cases, however, it should be noted that parentage was not necessarily direct. A person could be named even after a remote ancestor. Some local names, although not prescribed by scriptures, are found in the Brāhmaṇas, e.g., Kauśāmbeya (named after Kośāmbi) and Gāṅgeya (named after Gaṅgā).[10] Besides the incidental references, one positive rule is also found in the Śatapatha Brāhmaṇa[11] for performing the naming ceremony of a newborn child: "One should give a name to the newborn son."

(iv) *The Sūtra and later Periods*

From the study of the Brāhmaṇas it is evident that there was a system of naming in the pre-Sūtra period. But we do not precisely know what ceremonies were associated with it. Even the Gṛhyasūtras, except the Gobhila, do not quote Vedic verses to be recited on this occasion, though they lay down rules for the composition of the name. It seems that the Nāmakaraṇa was more a custom than a ceremoney in the beginning. But being the occasion of a great social importance, it was later on included in the Saṁskāras. It is only

3. X. 55. 2; 71. 1.
4. Ibid.
5. i. 3. 3.
6. vi. 6. 1. 3, 9; iii. 6. 2. 24; v. 4. 3. 7; Br. U. vi. 4. 5.
7 Ś. Br. iii. 6. 24; V. 3. 3. 14.
8. The P. Br. xiv. 11 17
9. Ibid. xiv. 9. 38.
10. Ibid. viii. 6. 8.
11. तस्मात्पुत्रस्य जातस्य नाम कुर्यात्। vi. 1. 3. 9.

in the Paddhatis that the common preliminary ceremonies are prescribed, and the Vedic verse "Aṅgāt (form body)" is quoted for re cital.

(a) The Composition of the Name. The first question which has been discussed from the time of the Gṛhyasūtras onwards is the composition of the name. According to the Pāraskara Gṛhyasūtra,[12] the name should be of two syllables or of four syllables, beginning with a sonant, with a semivowel in it, with the long vowel or the Visarga at its end, with a Kṛt suffix, not with a Taddhita. In the opinion of Baijavāpa[13] there is no restriction of syllables. "The father should give a name to the child containing one syllable, two syllables, three syllabes, or an indefinite number of syllables." But Vasiṣṭha[14] restricts the number to two or four syllables and asks to avoid names ending in l and r. The Āśvalāyana Gṛhyasūtra[15] attaches different kinds of merits to different nmuber of syllables: "One who is desirous of fame, his name should consists of two syllables, one who desires holy lustre, his name should contain four syllables." For boys even number of syllables were prescribed.

(b) Naming a Girl. The naming of a girl had a different basis. The name of a girl should contain an uneven number of syllables, it should end in a and should have a Taddhita.[16] Baijavāpa[17] says, "The name of a girl should contain three syllables and end in ī." Manu[18] gives further qualifications of the name of a girl: "It should be easy to pronounce, not hard to hear, of clear meaning, charming, auspicious, ending in a long vowel and containing some blessing." She should not be given an awkward name indicating "a constellation, a tree, a river, a mountain, a bird, a servant, and a terror."[19] Manu forbids to marry girls who were named after these objects. The most probable reason seems to be that such

---

12. i. 17. 1.

13. पिता नाम करोति एकाक्षरं द्वयक्षरं त्र्यक्षरम् अपरिमिताक्षरं वा।
Quoted in V.M.S. vol. I. P. 241.

14. तद्द्वयक्षरं वा चतुरक्षरं वा विवर्जयेदन्त्य लकाररेफम् V.D.S. iv.

15. द्वयक्षरं प्रतिष्ठाकामश्चतुराक्षरं ब्रह्मवर्चसकामः । i. 15. 5.

16. अयुजाक्षरमाकारान्तं स्त्रियै तद्धितम्। P.G.S. i. 17. 3.

17. त्र्यक्षरमीकारान्तं स्त्रियाः। Quoted in V.M.S. vol. I. P. 2. 43.

18. स्त्रीणां च सुखमक्रूरं विस्पष्टार्थं मनोहरम्।
माङ्गल्यं दीर्घवर्णान्तमाशीर्वादाभिधानवत्॥ M.S. ii. 33.

19. Ibid. iii. 9.

names were current in the non-Aryan peoples with whom the Aryans were not willing to form matrimonial relations.

(c) Status a Determining Factor. The social status of the person to be named was also a determining factor in the composition of the name. "The name of a Brāhmaṇa should be auspicious, that of a Kṣattriya should denote power, that of a Vaiṣya, wealth and that of a Śūdra contempt."[20] For example, a Brahman should be named Lakṣmīdhara, a Kṣatriya Yudhiṣṭhira, a Vaiśya Mahādhana and a Śūdra Naradāsa." Further, "the name of a Brāhmaṇa should contain the idea of happiness and delight, the name of a Kṣattriya should denote strength and ruling capacity, the name of a Vaiśya wealth and ease and that of a Śūdra should contain the idea of obedience and servitude."[21] Diferent castes should have different surnames. "Śarman was added to the name of a Brāhmaṇ, Varman to that of a Kṣattriya, Gupta to that of a Vaiśya and Dāsa to that of a Śūdra."[22] The idea of caste was deeprooted in the Hindu mind, and the birth in a family determined the future career of a child. What a man would be in the world was a foregone conclusion and, accordingly, he was provided with privileges of social significance. But this caste complex was not peculiar to the Ancient Hindus alone. It was prevalent, and is still common, in other Indo-European peoples also.[23]

(d) Fourfold Naming. There was current fourfold naming, according to asterism under which the child was born, the deity of the month, the family deity, and the popular calling. This system was not fully developed in the pre-Sūtra or the Sūtra period. The Gṛhyasūtras knew the Nakṣatra name and the popular name. The rest were unknown to them. The system was fully worked out by the later Smṛtis and the astrological works. This development was due to the rise of religious sects and astrology. The sectarian religions gave birth to the family deities. Astrology brought the people under the influence of astral world, and every period of time was believed to be presided over by a deity or a spirit. The gods of days, months etc., arose out of this belief.

---

20. माङ्गल्यं ब्राह्मणस्य स्यात्क्षत्रियस्य बलान्वितम् ।
वैशयस्य धनसंयुक्तं शूद्रस्य तु जुगुप्सितम् ॥ M.S. ii. 31.

21. Ibid. ii. 32.

22. शर्मेति ब्राह्मणस्योक्तं वर्मेति क्षत्रियस्य तु ।
गुप्तदासात्मकं नाम प्रशस्तं वैश्यशूद्रयोः ॥ Vyāsa.

23. Kultur der Indo-german, pp. 302. ff.

(1) *Nakṣatra-name*

To begin with the Nakṣatra name, it was a name derived from the name of a Nakṣatra (a lunar asterism) under which the child was born, or from its presiding deity.[24] Śaṅkha and Likhita prescribed that "the father or an elderly member of the family should give the child a name connected with the constellation under which the child is born."[25] The following are the names of the constellations and their deities: Aśvinī—Aśvi, Bharaṇī—Yama, Kṛttikā—Agni, Rohiṇī—Prajāpati, Mṛgaśirā—Soma, Ārdrā—Rudra, Punarvasu—Aditi, Puṣya—Bṛhaspati, Aśleṣā—Sarpa, Maghā—Pitṛnī Pūrvāphālguṇī—Bhaga, Uttarāphālguṇī—Aryaman, Hasta—Savitṛ, Chittrā—Tvaṣtrā, Svāti—Vāyu, Viśākhā—Indrāgni, Anurādhā—Mitra, Jyeṣṭhā—Indra, Mūlā—Nirti, Purvāṣādhā—Āp, Uttarāṣāḍhā—Viśvedevā, Śravaṇa—Viṣṇu, Dhaniṣṭhā—Vasu, Śatabhik—Varuṇa, Pūrvabhādrapada—Ajaikapāda, Uttrabhādrapada—Ahirbudhnya and Revati—Pūṣan. If a child was born under the constellation Aśvinī, he was named Aśvinikūmara, if under Rohiṇī, Rohiṇīkumāra etc. Another method of naming the child after the constellation was also current. The letters of the Sanskrit alphabets are believed to be presided over by different constellations. But as there are fifty two letters and only twenty-seven constellations, each constellation has more than one letter under its influence. The first letter of the child's name should begin with one of the letters ruled over by a particular asterism. A child who was born under Aśvinī, which presides over the latters Chu-Che-Cho-la was named Chūḍāmani, Chedīśa Choleśa or Lakṣmaṇa according to the different steps of the constellations.

According to Baudhāyana, the name derived from the constellation was kept secret.[26] It was the second name for greeting the elders and was known to the parents only up to the time of the Upanayana. In the opinion of some authorities the secret name was given on the birth day. About the greeting name Āśvalāyana also says that it should be selected on the naming day and should be known to the parents only.[27] Śaunaka is of the same opinion, "The name by which he should greet the elders after being initiat-

24. A.G.S. i. 15. 4.

25. नक्षत्रनामसम्बद्धं पिता वा कुर्यादन्यो कुलवृद्ध इति ।
Quoted in V.M.S. vol. I. p. 237.

26. नक्षत्रनामधेयेन द्वितीतं नामधेयम् गुह्यम् ।
B.G.S. quoted in V.M.S. vol. I. p. 238.

27. अभिवादनीयं च समीक्षेत तन्मातापितरौ विद्यातामुपनयनात् । A.G.S. i. 15. 9.

ed, should be given to him. Having thought over it, the father should pronounce it closely to the child so that others may not know it. The parents should recollect this name at the time of initiation."[28] The name derived from the Nakṣatra was vitally connected with the life of the individual. So it was kept secret less enemies may do mischief to the man through it.

(2) Name after month-deity

The second mode of naming was based on the deity of the month in which the child was born. According to Gārgya, the names of the deities of months beginning from Mārgaśīrṣa are Kṛṇna Ananta, Achyuta, Chakrī, Vaikuṇṭha, Janārdana, Upendra, Yajña-puruṣa Vāsudeva, Hari, Yogīśa and Puṇḍarīkakṣa.[29] The child was given a second name connected with the deity of the month. The above names are all of Vaiṣṇava sect and they originated much later than the Sūtra period

(3) Name after family-deity

The third name was given according to the family deity.[30] A family deity was a god or goddess worshipped in a family or tribe from very early times.[31] The people naming a child after it thought that the child would enjoy special protection of the deity. The deity may be Vedic e.g. Indra, Soma, Varuṇa, Mitra, Prajāpati, or Puranic e.g., Kṛṣṇa, Rāma, Śankara, Gaṇeśa etc. While naming the child, the word Dāsa or Bhakta "a devotee" was added to the name of the deity.

(4) Popular Name

The last mode of naming was popular. The popular name was meant for general use in the society and was very important from the practical point of view. The rules of the composition given above were consulted in framing this name. The formation

28. Quoted in V.M.S. vol. I. p. 238.

29. कृष्णोऽनन्तोऽच्युतश्चक्री वैकुण्ठोऽथवा जनार्दनः ।
उपेन्द्रो यज्ञ पुरुषो वासुदेवस्तथा हरिः ।
योगीशः पुण्डरीकाक्षो मासनामान्यनुक्रमात् ।। ibid. p. 237.

30. कुलदेवतासम्वद्धं पिता नाम कुर्यादिति । Śaṅkha, Ibid.

31. कुल देवता कुलपूज्या देवता तया सम्बन्धं तत्प्रतिपादकमित्यर्थः ।
अस्मिंश्च व्याख्याने अनादिरवच्छिन्नः शिष्टाचारो मूलम् । V.M.S. vol. I. p. 237.

of this name mainly depended on the culture and education of the family. This name was desired to be auspicious and significant.[32]

The principles followed in naming were the following. First of all, the name should be easy to pronounce and sweet to hear. Particular letters and syllables were chosen for this purpose. Secondly, the name should indicate the sexual difference. Nature has differentiated sexes by physical formation. Men are hardy and robust; women are tender and lovely. Therefore, the names of men and women were to be so selected as to be indicative of their natural built and disposition. It is why female names end in feminine ā and ī. The uneven number of letters in the name of a female was also meant for the same purpose. The third principle was that the name should be significant of fame, wealth, power etc. Lastly, the name was suggestive of one's own caste. It made quite clear the social status of the person bearing it without any other inquiry. The system of naming shown above is a sensible one, and cannot be profitably neglected, even if superstitious and religious aspects of the Saṁskāra may be ignored. The meticulous attention paid to the naming of a child was due to the fact that it was a life-long suggestion to the man. It was a constant reminder of an ideal to which the man was asked to be true.

(5) Repulsive Name

This is so far as the scriptural methods of naming were concerned. But the common people must have taken many other things into consideration, as they do even now. The unfortunate parents who had lost their previous issues gave the child an awkward name, repulsive and disgusting, to frighten away demons, diseases and death.

(v) Ceremonies and their Significance

According to the general rule of the Gṛhyasūtras,[33] the Nāmakaraṇa ceremony was performed on the tenth or the twelfth day after the birth of the child with the single exception of the secret name which was given, in the opinion of some, on the birth-day. But the later options range from the tenth up to the first day of the second year. One authority says, "The naming ceremony should be performed on the tenth, twelfth, hundredth day or at the ex-

32. बृहस्पति। ibid. p. 241.

33. Ś.G.S. i. 24. 4; A.G.S. i. 15. 4. P.G.S. i. 17. G.G. ii. 7 15. Kh. G.S. ii. 2. 30; H.G.S. ii. 4. 10. Āp. G.S. 152.

piry of the first year".[34] This wide option was due to the convenience of the family and health of the mother and the child. But the option from the tenth up to thirty second day was due to the different periods of ceremonial impurities prescribed for different castes. In the opinion of Bṛhaspati, "The naming ceremonies should be performed on the tenth, twelfth, thirteenth, sixteenth, ninetneenth or thirty-second day after the birth of the child". [35] But according to astrological works even these dates were to be postponed if there was any natural abnormality or lack of religious propriety. "If there be a Saṁkrānti (the passage of the sun from one zodiac to another), and eclipse or Śrāddha, the ceremony cannot be auspicious".[36] There were other prohibited days also which should be avoided.

At the expiry of impurity caused by birth, the house was washed and purified, and the child and mother bathed. Before the proper ceremony, the preliminary rites were performed. Then the mother, having covered the child with pure cloth and wetted its head with water, handed it over to the father.[37] After this, offerings were made to Prajapati, date, constellation, their deities, Agni and Soma.[38] The father touched the breaths of the child, most probably, to awaken its consciousness and to draw its attention towards the ceremony. Then the name was given, How it was done is not described in the Gṛhyasūtras, but the Paddhatis[39] contain the following procedure. The father, leaning towards the right ear of the child, addressed it, "O child! thou art the devotee of the family deity, so thy name is . . . . . .; thou art born in such and such month, so thy name is . . . . .; thou art born under such and such constellation, so thy name is . . . . . and thy popular name is . . . . ." The Brahmans assembled there said, "May the name be established". After it the father formally made the child salute the Brahmans who blessed it, repeating its name every time, "Be long-lived, beautiful child." They also recited the verse. "Thou art Veda etc." The name for greeting was given last. The ceremonies terminated with feasting the Brahmans and respectfully dismissing the gods and the Fathers to their respective places.

34. The Gobhila-gṛhyasūtra-pariśi ṭa.

35. द्वादशहे दशाहें वा जन्मतोऽपि त्रयोदशे।
षोडशैकोनविंशे वा द्वात्रिंशे वर्णतः क्रमात् ॥ Quoted in V.M.S. vol. I. p. 234.

36. An anonymous authority, quoted. in V.M.S. vol. I. p. 234.

37. G.G.S. ii. 7. 15.

38. The Saṁskāra-vidhi by Svami Dayānanda Sarasvati.

39. Sodaśa-saṁskāra-vidhi by Pt. Bhīmasena Śarmā.

3 THE NIṢKARMAṆA (FIRST OUTING)

(i) *The Origin*

Every important step in the progressive life of the child was a festive occasion for the parents and the family, and it was celebrated with appropriate religious ceremonies. When the taboos of the maternity house were withdrawn, the mother came out of the small room and began to take part in the family life agan. The child's world also widened. It could be carried to any part of the house. The parents and senior members of the family fondled it and the small children played with it. The curious little eyes of the babe gazed at the inmates of the house very closely and never let any thing pass without being observed. But within a month or two the universe of the child was found too small. The curiosities of the child and the movements of its limbs required wider scope to satisfy themselves. So it was thought proper that it should be introduced to the outer world. Indeed, it was a land-mark in the life of the child and the parents gave expressions to the sense of joy on this occasion. Life outside the house, however, was not free from natural and supernatural dangers. Therefore, for the protection of the child, gods were worshipped and their help was sought.

(ii) *Its History*

The custom of taking the child out ceremoniously may be very old, but we do not get any reference to it in the Vedic literature. Even the Vedic verse, "That eye etc."[1] recited in this Saṁskāra is of general applicability and is used every where, when one has to look at the sun. Hence, it has no specific significance here. The procedure given in the Gṛhyasūtras is very simple. It consisted in taking the child out by the father and making it look at the sun with the verse. "That eye."[2]

The later Smṛtis and the Nibandhas elaborate the rituals and customs relating to it.

(iii) *The Time of Performance*

The time for performing the Niṣkarmaṇa Saṁskāra varied from the twelfth day after the birth to the fourth month.[3] The twelfth

1. P.G.S. i. 17. 5. 6.
2. Ibid.
3. Ibid.; M.S. ii. 134.

day is recommended by the Bhaviṣya-pūrāṇa and the Bṛhapti-Smṛti only.[3a] Perhaps it was only possible when this Saṁskāra was performed with the Nāmakaraṇa, when the child was brought out of the Sūtikā-gṛha for giving it a name . The general rule, however, according to the Gṛhyasūtras and the Smṛtis was that this Saṁskāra took place either in the third or in the fourth month after the birth. The rationale of the option between the third and the fourth month is supplied by Yama, who says, "The ceremony of looking at the sun should be performed in the third, and that of looking at the moon in the fourth month".[4] For taking out the child in the night a longer period was required. In course of time when the ceremony could be performed even later the two ceremonies blended together. If the above prescribed dates expired, the Niṣkramaṇa was performed with the First Feeding in the opinion of Āśvalāyana.[5] There are many astrologically objectionable dates when the ceremony should be postponed. The above options were based on the convenience of the parents, the health of the child and suitability of the weather.

(iv) The Performer

According to the Gṛhyasūtras, the father and the mother performed the ceremony. But the Purāṇas and the astrological works extend this privilege to others also. In the opinion of the Muhūrtasaṁgraha it was desirable that the maternal uncle should be invited to perform the ceremony.[6] It was due to the affectionate feelings that he cherished for the children of his sister. The Viṣṇudharmottara recommends that the solicitous nurse should take the child out.[7] This custom probably arose when the respectable ladies could not come out of the house owing to the Purdah system. But in practice it was confined to the rich families only. These customs are non-Vedic and popular. When the Saṁskāra was regarded

3a. Quoted in the V.M.S. vol. I. p. 250.

4. ततस्तृतीये कर्त्तव्यं मासि सूर्यस्य दर्शनम् ।
चतुर्थमासि कर्तव्यं शिशोश्चन्द्रस्य दर्शनम् ॥
Yama, quoted in the V.M.S. vol. I. p. 250.

5. Ibid. p. 251.

6. उपनिष्क्रमणे शास्ता मातुलो वाहयेच्छिशुम ।
The Muhūrta-Saṁgraha, quoted in the V.M.S. vol. I. p. 253.

7. ततस्त्वलंकृता धात्री बालमादाय पूजितम् ।
बहिर्निष्काशयेद् गेहात् शंखपुण्याहनिस्वनैः ॥ The Viṣṇu-dharmottara ibid.

a domestic sacrifice, only the father could properly perform it. But when it ceased to be so, the right of performance was transfered even to persons other than him.

(v) *The Ceremonies and Significance*

On the day of performing the Saṁskāra, a square portion of the court-yard, from where the sun could be s een was plastered with cowdung and clay, the sign of Svastika was made on it and grains of rice scattered by the mother. In the Sūtra period the ceremony ended when the father made the child look at the sun. But more details are available from later sources.[8] The child was fully decorated and brought to the family deity in the house. Then the deity was worshipped with instrumental music. The guardians of eight directions, the sun, the moon, Vāsudeva and sky were also propitiated. The Brahmans were fed and auspicious verses recited. The child was carried out with sounds of conchshell and recital of Vedic hymns. As the time of outing, the father repeated the Śakunta hymn or the following verse, "Whether the child is conscious or unconscious, whether it is day or night, let all the gods led by Indra protect the child."[9] Then the child was brought to the temple of a god, who was worshipped with insense, flowers, garlands etc. The child bowed to the deity and the Brahmans gave blessings to it. After this the child was taken out of the temple to the lap of the maternal uncle who brought it home. In the end the child was given presents, e.g., toys, gifts etc. and blessings.

Bṛhaspati[10] gives different procedure. According to him, having properly decorated the child, the father should take it out on a carriage, or the maternal uncle should carry the child himself. The friends and relations accompanied the child amidst sounds of musical instruments. Then the child was placed on a pure plot of ground plastered with cowdung and bestrewn with grains of rice. After performing the Rakṣā (Protection) ceremony the father repeated the Mṛtasañjīvana (reviving even the dead) mantra, "Tryaṁbakaṁ yajāmahe." In the last Śiva and Gaṇeśa were worshipped and the child was given fruits and other eatables.

8. Āśvalāyanāchārya and the Viṣṇu-dharmottara, Ibid.

9. अप्रमत्तं प्रमत्तं वा दिवा रात्रावथापि वा।
रक्षन्तु सततं सर्वे देवाः शक्रपुरोगमाः॥ The Viṣṇu-dharmottara, Ibid.

10. Quoted in the V.M.S. vol. I. p. 254.

The significance of the whole ceremony lay in the physical necessity of the child and impressing on it the sublime grandeur of the universe. The Saṁskāra implied that after a certain period of time the child must be taken out in the fresh air and from thence the practice should be continued. It also emphasized on the budding mind of the child that this universe is a sublime creation of God and it should be respected duly.

4. THE ANNAPRĀŚANA (FIRST FEEDING)

(i) The Origin

Feeding the child with solid food was the next important stage in the life of the child. So long it was fed on the mother's milk. But after six or seven months its body developed and required greater amount and different types of food, while the quantity of the mother's milk diminished. So, for the benefit of the child and the mother both, it was thought necessary that the child should be weaned away from the mother and some substitute for her milk should be given to the babe. Thus this Saṁskāra was connected with the satisfaction of the physical need of the child. This fact is endorsed by Suśruta,[1] who prescribes the weaning of a child in the sixth month and describes the types of food to be given. It was only later on that this system of feeding the child for the first time assumed a religious shape. Food was a lifegiving substance. People thought that there was something mysterious about it from which life emanated. The source of energy was to be infused into the child with the help of gods.

(ii) Its History

The corresponding Parsi custom of feeding the child ceremoniously indicates that the Annaprāśana was a common Indo-Iranian ceremony and it originated when both the peoples were living together. Praises of food are found in the Vedas[2] and the Upaniṣads,[3] but whether they were sung at an ordinary dinner or on the occasion of the first feeding of the child is doubtful. It seems that the ceremony of feeding the child for the first time put on its proper ritualistic garb during the Sūtra period. The Sūtras contain prescriptions about the time of performance, the types of food and the verses to be recited. The later Smṛtis, the Purāṇas and the treatises supply a few changes in regulations which took place in subsequent times, while the Paddhatis follow the same ritual.

---

1. षण्मासं चैनमन्नं प्राशयेल्लघुहितं च । The Suśruta, śarīrasthāna, Ch. 10. 64.
2. Y.V. xvii. 33.
3 The T.U. iii. 7. 9.

(iii) The Time of Performance

According tot the Gṛhyasūtras,[4] the ceremony was performed in the sixth month after the birth of the child. Early Smṛtis like Manu[5] and Yājñavalkya[6] are also of the same opinion. Laugākṣī,[7] however, differs from the mathematical determination of the time and prescribes an individual test when the child could digest solid food. He gives the option, "Or after teeth come out." Teeth were visible signs that the child was able to take solid food. Giving food before the fourth month was strictly prohibited. For weak children further extention of time was allowed. "The feeding ceremony should be performed in the sixth solar month after the birth; if postponed, in the eighth, ninth or tenth month; but some learned people are of the view that it might be performed even at the expiry of one year."[8] The last limit was one year, because further postponement would have told on the physidal well-being of the mother and the digestive capacity of the child. The even months for boys and odd ones for girls were prescribed. This difference based on sex was sentimental that even in ceremonies some sort of discrimination should be made about different sexes.

(iv) Different kinds of Food

The types of food were also determined by the scriptures. The simple prescription was that food of all kinds and of different sorts of flavours should be mixed together and given to the child to eat.[9] Some prescribe a mixture of curd, honey and ghee. Different kinds of food, including meat, were recommended for different ends. The father fed the child with the flesh of the bird Bhāradvāja, if he wished to the child fluency of speech, with flesh of Kapiñjala and ghee if abundance of nourishment, with fish if swiftness, with the

---

4. A.G.S. i. 16; P.G.S. i. 19. 2; Ś.G.S. i. 27 B.G. S. ii. 3; M.G. S. i. 20; Bh. G.S. i. 27.

5. M.S. ii. 34.

6. Yaj. S.I. 12.

7. षष्ठे अन्नप्राशनं जातेषु दन्तेषु वा। Quoted in the V.M.S. vol. I. P. 267.

8. जन्मतो मासि षष्ठे वा सौरेणोत्तममन्नदम्।
तदभावेऽष्टमे मासे नवमे दशमेऽपि वा॥
द्वादशे वाऽपि कुर्वीत प्रथमान्नाशनं परम्।
सम्वत्सरे वा सम्पूर्णे केचिदिच्छन्ति पण्डिताः॥ Narada. ibid.

9. P.G.S. i. 19. 4.

flesh of the bird Kṛkasā or rice mixed with honey if long life, with the flesh of the bird Ati and partridge if he desired holy lustre, with ghee and rice if brilliance, with curd and rice if strong senses, and with all if he desired every thing for the child.[10] From the above it is evident that the Hindus were no Jains in the Gṛhyasūtra period. They would not refrain from taking meat if it brought physical and mental strength to them. The Gṛhyasūtras were still saturated with the Vedic idea of animal sacrifice and animal food, so they did not feel any hitch in recommending meat and flesh. The later-day tendency, however was towards vegetarianism. It was due to the cults of non-violence which influenced the Hindu diet to a great extent. But animal products like curd, ghee and milk were still retained and regarded as the choicest articles of food for the child. The Mārkaṇḍeya-Purāṇ[11] recommends a mess of milk and rice with honey and ghee. The popular practice that at last became current was of giving milk and rice. Books on ritual, however, still insist on animal food. Many of the Paddhatis contain the prescriptions given in the Gṛhyasūras. The reason is that though the higher religion of the Hindus forbids animal food and they have general regard for animal life, the lower customs are not particular about it.

Whatever the type of food may be, one thing was kept in mind that it should be light and conducive to the health of the child. Suśruta says, "One should feed the child in the sixth month with light and suitable food."[12]

(v) *The Ritual and its Significance*

On the day of the feeding ceremony the materials of sacrificial food were first of all cleansed and then cooked with appropriate Vedic verses. When food was prepared, one oblation was offered to Speech with the words, "The gods have generated the goddess, Speech; manifold animals speak her forth. May she, the sweet-sounding, the highly praised one, come to us. Svāhā!"[13] The next oblation was offered to vigour, "May vigour come to us to-day." Having made the above sacrifices, the father offered further four oblations with the following phrases: "Through up-breathing may

---

10. Ibid; Ś.G.S.; i. 27; Āp. G.S. i. 16. 1 A.G.S. i. 10; H.G.S. ii. 5.

11. मध्वाज्यं कनकोपेतं प्राशयेत्पायसं तु तम्। Quoted in the V.M.S. vol. I. p. 275.

12. षण्मासं चैतमन्नं प्राशयेल्लघुहितं च। Śarīrasthāna, Ch. 10. 64.

13. P.G.S. i. 19. 2.

I enjoy food, Svāhā! Through downbreathing may I enjoy food. Svāhā! Through my eye, may I enjoy, visible things. Svāhā! Through my ear, may I enjoy fame. Svāhā!"[14] Here the word "food" is used in a wide sense. The prayer was offered that all the senses of the child should be gratified so that he may live a happy and contented life. But one thing was kept in mind. One in search of gratification should not violate the rules of health and morality, because it would spoil the fame of the man. In the end the father set apart food of all kinds and flavours for feeding the child and fed it silently or with the syllable "Hant (well !)." The ceremony terminated with the feasting of the Brahmans.

The significance of the Annaprāśana-Saṁskāra was this that children were weaned away from their mothers at proper time. They were not left at the caprice of their parents who often injure their children by overfeeding them without taking into consideration their digestive capacity. The feeding ceremony also warned the mother that at a certain time she should stop suckling the child. The ignorant mother, out of love for her child, goes on suckling it up to a year or more. But she little realizes that thereby she allows her own energy to be sapped away without doing real good to the child. A timely caution was given by the ceremony for the benefit of both the child and the mother.

---

14. Ibid. i. 19. 3.

5. THE CHŪḌĀKARAṆA (TONSURE)

(i) *The Origin*

It was after a long stride in the march of civilization when men came to realize the necessity of keeping short hair for health and beauty. Ring-worms were a great trouble to primitive people. To keep the head clean some device was bound to be invented. Cutting the hair was meant to meet this end. But being a novel thing, it was regarded an important event in the life of an individual. Chopping the hair by means of an iron instrument was a new and exciting scene. People knew that it would clean the head, but at the same time they were afraid that it might injure the person whose hair was cut. Necessity and fear both mingled together and gave rise to the Chūḍākaraṇa ceremonies. The practical and beneficient aspects found their expression in the accompanying verses. The sharp razor coming into contact with the child naturally inspired terror in the father of the child, who requested the sharp and hard iron razor to be mild and harmless to it. These sentiments were responsible for giving the Chūḍākaraṇa a religious shape.

(ii) *The Purpose of the Saṁskāra*

The purpose of the Saṁskāra as given in the scripture was the achievement of long life for the recipient.[1] "Life is prolonged by tonsure; without it, it is shortened. Therefore, it should be performed by all means."[2] The scriptural object of the Chūḍākaraṇa is supported also by medical books of the Hindus. According to Suśruta,[3] shaving and cutting the hair and nails remove impurities and give delight, lightness, prosperity, courage and happiness, Charaka[4] opines, "Cutting and dressing of hair, beard and nails give

---

1. तेन ते आयुषे वपामि सुश्लोकाय स्वस्तये। Ā. G. S. i. 17. 12.
2. Vasiṣtha, quoted in the V.M.S. vol. I. P. 296.
3. पापोपशमनं केशनखरोमापमार्जनम्।
   हर्षलाघवसौभाग्यकरमुत्साहवर्धनम्। Cikitsāsthāna, Ch. 24. 72.
4. पौष्टिकं वृष्यमायुष्यं शुचिरूपं विराजनम्।
   केशश्मश्रुनखादीनां कर्तनं सम्प्रसाधनम्॥

strength, vigour, life, purity and beauty." At the basis of the tonsure ceremony the idea of health and beauty was prominent. In the opinion of some anthropologists,[5] however, this ceremony had a dedicative purpose in its origin, that is, hair was cut off and offered as a gift to some deity. But this supposition is not correct, at least so far as the Hindu tonsure is concerned. The dedicative purpose was unknown to the Gṛhyasūtras and the Smṛtis. No doubt, at present, the tonsure ceremony is sometimes performed at the temple of a deity, but so are some other Saṁskāras e.g. the Upanayana. The Saṁskāras of only those children are performed at the place of a deity who are born after a long disappointment or the death of pdevious children. Moreover, this practice is not universal. Thus, there is not an innate connection between the tonsure ceremony and its dedication to a deity.

(*iii*) *The Vedic Period*

Almost all the verses that are used in the Gṛhyasūtras at the tonsure ceremony are found in the Vedic literature and they are all of specific character which shows that they were composed for the purpose of cutting the hair only. Wetting the head for tonsure is mentioned in the Atharvaveda.[6] The shaving razor is praised and requested to be harmless: "Thou art friendly by name. Thy father is hard iron. I salute thee; do not injure the child."[7] Cutting the hair by the father himself for abundance of food, progeny, wealth and strength is also referred to.[8] The barber, an impersonification of Savitā or the sun, is also welcomed.[9] Many other mythological allusions to hair-cutting are given in the Vedas.[10] So it is quite clear that the Chūḍākaraṇa was a religious ceremony as early as in the Vedic period, consisting of wetting the head, prayer to the razor, invitation to the barber, cutting the hair with Vedic verses and wishes for long life, prosperity, valour and even progeny for the child.

---

5. Crawford Howell Toy, Introduction to the History of Religions, p. 81.
6. vi. 68. 1.
7. ओं शिवो नामासि स्वधितिस्ते पिता नमस्ते मा मा हिंसीः। Y.V. iii. 63.
8. ओं निवर्तयाम्यायुषेऽन्नाद्याय प्रजननाय रायष्पोषाय सुप्रजास्त्वाय सुवीर्याय। Y. V. iii. 33.
9. A.V. vi. 68. 2.
10. Ibid. vi. 68. 3; viii. 4. 17.

(iv) *The Sūtra and the Subsequent Periods*

The tonsure ceremonies assumed a systematic form in the Sūtra period. The Gṛhyasūtras[10a] give the procedure and lay down rules for particular performances. In the subsequent period many Puranic elements entered the ceremony. It is evidenced by the Smṛtis, commentaries and the mediaeval treatises. They represent a new phase of the Saṁskāra and supply many social and astrological details, though still later Paddhatis followed the ritual procedure as given in the Gṛhyasūtras.

(v) *The Age*

In the opinion of the Gṛhyasūtras the Chūḍākaraṇa ceremony took place at the end of the first year or before the expiry of the third year.[11] The earliest Smṛti, Manu, also prescribes the same: "According to the rules of the Vedas, the Chūḍākaraṇa of all the twice-born should be performed either in the first or the third year of the child."[12] The later authorities extend the age up-to the fifth and the seventh year. Some say that it could be performed with the Upanayana which might take place even later. "Chūḍākaraṇa is praiseworthy in the third or the fifth year; but it can be performed even in the seventh year or with the Upanayana."[13] The tendency of prescribing later periods for performing the ceremony was due to the fact that in times subsequent to the Sūtras, its purpose became ceremonial instead of real. In practice, hair was cropped early in the life of the child, but its ceremonial performance was postponed up to the time of the Upanayana when it was performed a few minutes before the initiation with all the formulas of the scripture. This is the custom which is generally followed at present. However it is not liked and an early age is regarded more meritorious. "Chūḍākaraṇa performed in the first year prolongs life and increases holy lustre. In the third year it fulfils all the desires. One who desires cattle should perform it in the

---

10a. Ś.G.S. i. 28; Ā.G.S. i. 17; P.G.S. ii. 1; G.G.S. ii. 9; Kh. G.S. ii. 3–16; the B.G.S. ii. 6; Āp. G.S. 16. 3; B.G.S. ii. 4.

11. P.G.S. ii. 1. 1-2.

12. M.S. ii. 35.

13. तृतीये पञ्चमे वाऽब्दे चौलकर्म प्रशस्यते।
प्राग्वाऽसमे सप्तमे वा सहोपनयनेन वा॥ Āśvalāyana, quoted in the V.M.S. vol. I. 296.

fifth year. Its performance in the even year is prohibited."[14] "Chūḍākaraṇa performed in the third year is regarded as the best by the learned; in the sixth or the seventh year it is ordinary; but in the tenth and eleventh year it is worst."[15]

(vi) The Time of Performance

Astrological and other factors, though unknown to the Gṛhyasūtras, were also taken into consideration in fixing the time of the Chūḍākaraṇa in the later Smṛti period. It was performed when the sun was in the Uttarāyaṇa. According to the Rājamārtaṇḍa, Chaitra and Pauṣa, but according to the Sārasaṁgraha Jyeṣṭa and Mārgaśīrṣa were prohibited for the Saṁskāra.[16] It was performed only in the day time. The obvious reason was that hair-cutting in the night was dangerous. The Chūḍākaraṇa was prohibited during the pregnancy of the child's mother,[17] as she could not take part in the ceremony. But this rule was applicable after the fifth month of pregnancy.[18] Moreover, it was not binding in the case when the ceremony took place after the fifth year of the child.[19] When the mother of the child was in the monthly course the ceremony was postponed until she became pure. Bad results were apprehended if the Saṁskāras were performed during this period. "If the marriage, the initiation and the tonsure were performed during the monthly course of the mother, the girl became widow, the student dunce and the child dead...."[19a] The above statement, no doubt, contains threats for ignorant half-civilized people, but the underlying idea of this prohibition was that the mother was half sick during her monthly course and therefore she could not participate in the ceremony 'without' which half its mirth and

14. तृतीये वर्षे चौले तु सर्वकामार्थसाधनम् ।
संवत्सरे तु चौलेन आयुष्यं ब्रह्मवर्चसम् ॥
पञ्चमे पशुकामस्य युग्मे वर्षे तु गर्हितम् ॥ Atri Ibid., p. 298.

15. N. S. quoted in the V.M.S. vol. I. p. 296.

16. Ibid. p. 300.

17. गर्भिण्यां मातरि शिशो क्षौरकर्म न कारयेत् । Bhrhaspati Ibid. p. 312.

18. Vasiṣṭha. Ibid. p. 312.

19. N. S. Ibid.

19a. विवाहे विधवा नारी जडत्वं व्रतबन्धने ।
चौले चैव शिशोर्मृत्युस्तस्मादेतत्त्रयं त्यजेत् ॥ Vṛddha-gārgya, quoted in the V. M. S. vol. I. p. 312.

joyousness would have been lost. This question is not raised in the case of the Saṁskāras preceding the tonsure. The reason is that this question did not arise at all, because the monthly course stops during pregnancy and a few months after delivery.

(vii) The Choice of the Place

Another development not found in the Gṛhyasūtras and evolved only from later customs is the choice of the place where the ceremony should be performed. During the Vedic and the Sūtra periods, home was the theatre of all domestic sacrifices including the Saṁskāras. But in subsequent times sacrifices fell into disuse and the domestic fire was not always kept burning in every house. So the householder could transfer the stage of performing the ceremonies to the outside of the home also. When the ritualistic religion declined and devotional cult embracing idol worship developed, the temple of gods became the centre of religious activities. After disappointments and deaths of children the parents prayed to gods for progeny. If they were blessed with children they believed that the child was a gift from them. They also regarded it obligatory to perform some of its Saṁskāras in the honour of the deity prayed to. Every family has at present its favourite deity where the Chūḍākaraṇa and the Upanayana Saṁskāras are performed.[19b]

(viii) The Arrangement of the Top-hair

The arrangement of the top-hair or Śikhā was the most important feature of the Chūḍākaraṇa, as the very name of the Saṁskara suggests. The hair on the top was arranged according to the family custom: "One should arrange the hair in accordance with one's family tradition."[20] The number of tufts was determined by the number of the Pravara in the family, as it may be three or five. Laugākṣi[21] gives examples of different families following different fashions: "The descendants of Vasiṣṭha keep only one tuft in the middle of the head; the descendants of Atri and Kaśyapa two on either sides, the descendants of Bhṛgu remain without any tuft (Muṇḍita); the descendants of Añgiras keep five. Some keep one line of hair and others but one Śikhā." Later on keeping of only one tuft became universal in northern India, probably due to its

19b. This custom, however, is not universal.

20. यथाकुलधर्मं केशवेशान्कारयेत् । A.G.S. i. 17.

21. Quoted in the V.M.Ś. vol. I. p. 315.

simplicity and decency, though in the Deccan and the South the ancient traditions are kept alive to some extent. The fashion of the Bhārgavas is followed at present by the Bengalis who are not very particular about keeping tufts.

This system of keeping special number of tufts was a tribal fashion and the insignia of the family.

Keeping the top-hair, in its course of evolution, became an indispensable sign of the Hindus.[21a] The tuft and the sacred thread are the compulsory out-ward signs of the twice-born. A man not keeping the tuft does not get the full merit of religious ceremonies. "One should always remain with the sacred thread and the tuft; without them performance of religious ceremonies is tantamount to non-performance."[22] Atonement is prescribed for chopping off the tuft: "The twice-born, who out of infatuation, ignorance or hatred cut off the top-hair, become purified by undergoing the Taptakṛcchra vrata."[23] The fashion of keeping sacred top-hair is passing through a very critical period of its life at present. A large number of English-educated young men of to-day have dispensed with it. But even in their zeal for fashion they are still walking in the footsteps of their ancestors, the Bhārgavas.

(ix) *The Ceremonies*

An auspicious day was fixed for the performance of the Chūḍākaraṇa.[24] In the beginning, preliminary ceremonies e.g. Saṁkalpa, worship of Gaṇeśa, Mangala-Śrāddha etc. were performed. Then food was distributed among the Brahmans. After this the mother took the child, bathed it, put on it a new garment which had not yet been washed, put it (child) on her lap and sat down to the west of the sacrificial fire. The father, taking hold of her, sacrificed Ājya oblations, and after he had partaken of the sacrificial food,

21a. It may be a reaction against Buddhism and Sannyāsa.

22. विशिखो व्युपवीतश्च यत्करोति न तत्कृतम् । Devala, quoted in the V.M.S. vol. I p. 315.

23. शिखां छिन्दन्ति ये मोहाद् द्वेषादज्ञानतोऽपि वा ।
तप्तकृच्छ्रेण शुध्यन्ति त्रयो वर्णा द्विजातयः ॥ Laghu-Hārīta 4. ibid.

24. पापग्रहाणां वारादौ विप्राणां शुभदं रवेः ।
क्षत्रियाणां क्षमासूनोर्विट्शूद्राणां शनौ शुभम् ॥ Bṛhaspati quoted, by Gadādhara on the P.G.S. ii. 1. 4. .

looking at the barber he poured down warm water into cold one with the words, "With warm water come hither, Vāyu! Aditi, cut the hair." He mixed a piece of fresh butter or ghee or some curd with the water and taking some of it he moistened the hair near the right ear with, "On the impulse of Savitṛ may the divine waters moisten the body in order that long life and splendour may be thine." Having dishevelled the hair with a porcupine's quill that had three white spots he put three young kuśa shoots into it with the formula, "Herb, protect this child. Do not inflict pain on it." The father then took an iron razor with the formula, "Thou art friendly by name. Thy father is iron; Salutation be to thee. Do not hurt the child," and cut the hair with the words, "I cut off the hair for long life, properly digesting food, productivity, prosperity, good progeny and valour. The razor with which Savitṛ, the knowing one, has shaven the beard of the kings Soma and Varuṇa, with that ye Brahman, shave his head, in order that he may be blessed with long-life and may reach old age."

Cutting of the Kuṣa shoots together with the hair, he threw them on a lump of bull's dung which they kept northward of the fire. In the same way two other tufts were chopped off silently. He cut the hair behind with the verse, "The threefold age." Then on the left side with the verse, "By that prayer by which mayest thou, a mighty one, go to heaven, and long mayest thou see the sun: With that prayer I shave thee for the sake of life, existence, glory and welfare."

The head was three times shaved round from left to right with the verse, "when the shaver shaves its head with the razor, wounding, the well shaped, purify his head, but do not take away his life." With that water the father moistened the head again and gave the razor to the barber with the words, "Without wounding him, shave him. The locks of hair that were left over were arranged according to the family tradition. In the end the lump of the dung with hair was hidden in a cowstall, or thrown into a small pond or covered in the vicinity of water. The ceremonies ended with giving of presents to the teacher and the barber.

(x) *The Main Features of the Ceremonies*

In the Cūḍākaraṇa ceremonies the following main features can be distinguished. The first is the moistening of the head. It was done for facilitating the shaving. The second feature is actually cutting the hair with prayers for non-injury to the child. An iron razor on the tender head of the child inspired fear in the father, who praised the instrument and requested it not to harm the babe.

The third feature is hiding or throwing away the severed hair with cow-dung. The hair was regarded as a part of the body and was therefore subject to magic and spell by enemies. So it was kept away from their reach. The fourth feature is the keeping of top-hair. It was a racial fashion and widely differed in different families. Many ancient peoples kept tuft of hair on their head and some Asiatic peoples even now follow this custom.[25]

(*xi*) *The Association of Top-hair with long life*

The most striking characteristic of the prayers cited in this ceremony is that they were meant for long life of the child. The question may be asked why did the Hindu sages suppose that the Chūḍākaraṇa would prolong one's life? Is there any connection between longevity and the top-hair? Suśruta,[26] again, helps us in tracing the connection between the two. According to him, "Inside the head, near the top, is the joint of a Śirā (artery) and Sandhi (a critical juncture). There in the eddy of hairs is the vital spot called Adhipati (Overlord). Any injury to this part causes sudden death." The protection of this vital part was thought necessary and keeping a tuft of hairs just over the vital part served this purpose

25. The people, who migrated from Asia to Alaska, shaved their heads except one lock called a scalplock.... (The Book of knowledge, Part I. pp. 15, 16). The Chinese and the Tibetans still keep tufts of hair on their heads.

26. मस्तकाभ्यन्तरोपरिष्टात् शिरासन्धिसन्निपातो रोमावर्तोऽधिपतिस्तत्रापि सद्यो मरणम् । Śarīrasthāna, Ch. 6. 83.

6. THE KARṆAVEDHA (BORING THE EARS)

(i) *The Origin and Early History*

Boring of different limbs for wearing ornaments is current among savage peoples all over the world. So its origin is very ancient. But even when civilization progressed, ornamentation continued, though it was refined. In the case of boring ears, it was undoubtedly ornamental in its origin, but later on it proved to be useful, and for emphasizing its necessity, it was given a religious colouring. Suśruta says, "Ears of a child should be bored for protection (from diseases in his opinion) and decoration."[1] He, again, explicitly prescribes the boring of ears for preventing hydrocele and hernia.[2] Thus it was a precaution taken early in life, so that the chances of the above diseases may be minimised.

The recognition of the Karṇavedha as a Saṁskāra and the ceremonies attached to it are of a late origin. Almost all the Gṛhyasūtras omit it. It is described only in the Kātyāyana-Sūtras incorporated in the Pariśiṣṭa of the Pāraskara Gṛhyasūtras. The later-day Paddhatis describing this Saṁskāra quote their authorities, "The Yājñikas say so," which suggests it had no scriptural authority in the origin. The cause of the late inclusion of this ceremony in the list of the Saṁskāras is that its original purpose was decorative and there was the absence of any religious idea associated with it. It was only in a very wide sense that it entered the holy precincts of the Saṁskāras.

But there is one hymn in the Atharvaveda[3] which refers to ear-boring. This hymn is, however utilized by Kauśika[4] in the ceremony of marking the ears of cattle, and it is never quoted on the occasion of the Karṇavedha ceremony by any later authority.

(ii) *The Age and Time of Performance*

This ceremony was performed on the tenth, the twelfth or the sixteenth day after the birth of the child according to Bṛhaspati.[5]

---

1. रक्षाभूषणनिमित्तं बालस्य कर्णौ विध्येत् । Śarīrasthāna, Ch. 16. 1.
2. शङ्खोपरि च कर्णान्ते त्यक्ता यत्नेन सेवनीम् ।
   व्यत्यासाद्वा शिरां विध्येदन्त्रवृद्धिनिवृत्तये ॥ ibid, Cikitsāsthāna, Ch. 19. 21.
3. vi. 141.
4. K. S.
5. जन्मतो दशमे वाह्नि द्वादशे वाऽथ षोडशे । Bṛhaspati quoted in the V.M.S vol. I. p. 258.

Garga regards the sixth, the seventh, the eighth or the twelfth month as suitable periods. In the opinion of Śrīpati,[6] the Karṇavedha ceremony should be performed before teeth of the child come out, and while it is still creeping on the lap of the mother. The Kātyāyana Sūtra,[7] however, prescribes the proper time of performing the ceremony in the third or fifth year of the child. The idea underlying the early age was that the boring would be easier and less troublesome to the child. Taking physical facility into consideration Suśruta prefers the sixth or the seventh month. The Gṛhyapariśiṣta of Pāraskara is certainly of a later day when the Saṁskāra became a ceremony and it must be performed without paying any heed to the comfort of the child. The third and the fifth years coincided with the periods of the Cūḍākaraṇa ceremony. In this case both the Saṁskāras would save been performed together. At present, in many cases both the Chūḍākaraṇa and the Karṇavedha are performed with the Upanayana.

(*iii*) *The Performer*

In the opinion of the Kātyāyana-Sūtra father performed the ceremony, but it is silent as to who should bore the ears. According to Suśruta a surgeon should pierce the ears.[9] But Śrīpati, a mediaeval writer, allows this privilege to a professional needle-maker,[10] more often a goldsmith. Suśruta was more reasonable in his prescription than Śrīpati. The goldsmith, however, has acquired a hereditary experience and in the majority of cases it is he who is invited to bore the ears.

(*iv*) *The Types of Needle*

The types of needle with which the ears were bored are also determined by writers on ritual. "Gold needle lends elegance, but one can use silver or even iron needle according to his means."[11]

---

6. शिशोरजातदन्तस्य मातुरुत्संगसर्पिणः।
सौचिको वेधयेत्कर्णौ सूच्या द्विगुणसूत्रया॥ Quoted in the V.M.S. vol I. p. 261.

7. The P.G.S. Pariśiṣṭa 1.

8. Suśruta, Sūtrasthāna, Ch. 16 1.

9. भिषग्वामहस्तेन . . . . विध्येत्। Ibid. Ch. 16. 2.

10. सौचिको वेधयेत्कर्णौ सूच्या द्विगुगसूत्रया। Śrīpati.

11. शातकुम्भमयी सूचीवेधने शोभनप्रदा।
राजती वाऽयसी वाऽपि यथा विभवतः शुभाः॥ Bṛhaspati quoted in V.M.S.

The Smṛti-Mahārṇava[12] prescribes copper needle for all, "One should pierce the ears with copper needle covered with white yarns." Descrimination was made according to the caste of the child. "The needle for a prince should be made of gold, that of a Brāhmaṇa and a Vaiśya made of silver and that of a Śūdra made of iron."[13] The basis of this differential treatment was economic.

(v) A Compulsory Ceremony

When the Karṇavedha assumed a religious garb, its performance became compulsory and its omission was regarded a sin. The defaulter was thought to be fallen from his status. Devala, a mediaeval Smṛtiwriter, says, "All the accumulated merits disappear at the sight of a Brāhmaṇa, through whose ear-holes do not pass the rays of the Sun. No gift should be given to him in the Śrāddha ceremonies. If one gives, he becomes an Asura or demon."[14]

(vi) The Ceremonies

The Karṇavedha ceremony described in the Kātyāyana-Sūtra is very simple. On an auspicious day the ceremony was performed in the first half of the day. The child was seated facing towards the east and given some sweet-meats. Then the right ear was bored with the verse "May we hear auspicious things through ears etc." and the left ear with the verse, "Vakṣyanti etc." The ceremony closed with the feasting of the Brahmans.[15]

(vii) Suśruta on the Boring of Ears

Suśruta gives a very cautious procedure of the ceremony. He says that the ceremony should be performed in the sixth or seventh month, in the bright half and on an auspicious day. After the preliminaries the child should be put on the lap of the mother or

---

12. The Smṛti mahārṇava, Ibid.

13. सौवर्णी राजपुत्रस्य राजती विप्रवैश्ययोः।
शूद्रस्य चायसी सूची मध्यमाष्टांगुलात्मिका॥ Quoted in the V.M.S. vol. 1. p. 261.

14. कर्णरन्ध्रे रवेश्छाया न विशेदग्रजन्मनः।
तं दृष्ट्वा विलयं यान्ति पुण्यौघाश्च पुरातनाः॥
तस्मै श्राद्धं न दातव्यं यदि चेदासुरं भवेत्॥ Devala, ibid.

15. The P.G.S. pariśiṣṭa, Karnavedhasūtras 1, 2.

the nurse. Then the child should be fondled and persuaded by means of toys. Now the surgeon should pull the ears with his left hand and bore them slowly at the natural holes which are visible in the sunlight. If the ears are tender they should be pierced with a needle, if stiff with a probe. After boring oil should be applied to the ears by means of a cotton thread or bougie.[16]

(viii) Later Phases

The later writers on the Saṁskāra introduced more religious elements and social mirth in the ceremony. On the day of performance Keśava (Lord Viṣṇu) Hara (Śiva), Brahmā, the sun, the moon, deities of quarters, Nāsatyas, Sarasvatī the Brāhmaṇas and cows were worshipped. The teacher of the family was decorated and offered a seat. Then the nurse, wearing white garment, brought the child well-adorned, with its ears painted with red powder. The child was persuaded and kept still. The surgeon pierced the ears in one stroke but very lightly. The right ear of the boy and the left of the girl was bored first. In the end, presents were given to the Brahmans, astrologers and the surgeon. Ladies, friends, the Brahmans and relatives were paid respect and entertained.[17]

16. Suśruta Sūtrasthāna, Ch. 161.

17. The Viṣṇudharmottara, quoted in V.M.S. vol. I. p. 262.

CHAPTER VII

THE EDUCATIONAL SAMSKĀRAS

1. THE VIDYĀRAMBHA (LEARNING OF ALPHABETS)

(i) *Names, Meaning and Purpose of the Saṁskāra*

When the mind of the child was prepared to receive education, the Vidyārambha Saṁskāra was performed to mark its beginning, and alphabets were taught. The Saṁskāra is variously named. It is called Vidyārambha,[1] Akṣarārambha,[2] Akṣarasvīkaraṇa[3] and Akṣarālekhana[4] by different writers. As its very name suggests, it was more cultural than natural. It originated at a very high stage of civilization, when alphabets were evolved and utilised for writing purposes.

(ii) *The Sources of Information*

Though the Vidyārambha precedes the Upanayana in order, the origin of the former is far posterior to that of the latter. The Gṛhyasūtras, the Dharmasūtras and the early Smṛtis do not mention it. Even the mediaeval and the modern Paddhatis that describe the Saṁskāras do not contain it. Our authorities for information about this Saṁskāra are a few treatises, namely, the Vīramitrodaya (Saṁskāraprakāśa, Vol. I, pages 321 ff.), the Smṛti-chandrikā (Saṁskārakāṇda pages 67 ff.), the Saṁskāra-ratnamālā of Gopīnātha Bhaṭṭa and the commentary of Aparārka on the Yājñavalkya-Smṛti. All these sources are very recent in the history of the ritual literature in India and they can be placed subsequent to the eleventh century.[5] Even the original authorities, Viśvāmitra,[6] Bṛhaspati[7] and Mārkaṇḍeya[8]

1. V.M.S. vol. I. p. 321; Viśvāmitra, ibid.
2. Gopīnātha Bhaṭṭa: Saṁskāra-ratnamālā I.
3. Vasiṣṭha, quoted in V.M.S. vol. I. p. 321.
4. The Mārkaṇḍeya-purāṇa, ibid.
5. Cf. P.V. Kane. History of Dharmaśāstra, pp. 440; 343; 328.
6. Ibid., p. 236.
7. Ibid., p. 207.
8. Ibid.

quoted by them cannot be much earlier. As the astronomical details given by the writers named above cannot be traced back anterior to the seventh or the eighth century A.D., we conclude that they flourished after these centuries.[9]

(*iii*) *The Later Origin and its Cause*

It seems very strange that the Gṛhyasūtras and the Dharmasūtras that deal with even insignificant ceremonies like the First outing and the First Feeding of a child, pass over the Vidyārambha, which marked the beginning of the primary education and was thus a very important occasion in the life of the child. The omission could not be by mistake. It can be only explained by the fact that while many of the Saṁskāras originated in the pre-sūtra period, the Vidyārambha did not come into existence till very late. Sanskrit was then a spoken language, and the Upanayana marked the beginning of primary education. Learning of Sanskrit did not require a preparatory training in reading and writing. The education of children began with the memorizing of the sacred hymns without any help of writing. Moreover, writing was unknown in early times,[10] or at least not used for educational purposes. Therefore there was no need of instituting another Saṁskāra besides the Upanayana for celebrating the learning of alphabets.

Later on, Sanskrit ceased to be the spoken language of the people. The literature of the Hindus progressed and became complicated. The sciences of grammar and exegesis evolved and different branches of learning came into existence. The mass of literature was increasing and becoming too unwieldy for memory. Hence, to preserve the treasure of learning, alphabets were invented and the art of writing became known. At this time, for studying the Sanskrit literature, a preliminary instruction in reading and writing became necessary. Thus, in course of time the Upanayana could not mark the beginning of primary education. Rather it was performed at the commencement of secondary education. So a new Saṁskāra was needed to solemnise

9. Ibid., Dr. A. S. Altekar, Education in Ancient India, p. 2.

10. Dr. Bühler (Indian Antiquary, 1904) says that the introduction of Alphabets in India was subsequent to 800 B.C., but his opinion has been given up in the light of the Indus valley discoveries, M. M. Rai Bahadur Pandit Gaurī Shankar Hiracand Ojha, in his Prāchīna Lipimāla, has proved, on literary evidences, that the art of writing was known in India in the later Saṁhitā period (c. 1600—1200 B.C.). There is however, no evidence, to show that letters were introduced earlier.

the start of the primary education. It was to meet this need that the Vidyārambha Saṁskāra came into existence.

The Saṁskāra originated earlier than its mention in the Smṛtis. This late recognition of "The Learning of Alphabets" as a Saṁskāra was, probably, due to the fact that for a very long time this Saṁskāra was performed with the Chaula or tonsure ceremony.[11] This supposition is supported by the Arthaśāstra,[12] according to which the education of a prince began at the time of the Chaula Saṁskāra. It is evidenced by the Uttara-Rāmacharita also, where the sage Vālmiki started the education of Kuśa and Lava after their tonsure ceremonies and they had learnt many sciences before they commenced their Vedic Studies after the Upanayana.[13] There was one more factor which facilitated the preformance of the Vidyārambha with the Chūḍākaraṇa. The latter was performed between the fourth and the seventh year of the child. This was the proper time for commencing the primary education also. So both the Saṁskāras were combined and performed together. The number of tufts of hair to be kept at the time of the tonsure ceremony was determined by the number of celebrated sages (Pravaras) in the family.[14] This was a convenient suggestion that the primary education of the child should commence at the time when its tonsure ceremony was performed.

(*iv*) *The Age*

The Vidyārambha Saṁskāra was performed in the fifth year of the child according to Viśvāmitra.[15] In the opinion of an anonymous Smṛti writer quoted in the Ṣoḍaśa-Saṁskāravidhi, it could be performed even in the seventh year.[16] But, if owing to some unavoidable circumstances it was postponed, it must be performed some times before the Upanayana ceremony. "The wise should begin the learn-

---

11. Cf. Dr. A. S. Altekar, Education, in Ancient India, p. 2.

12. वृतचौलकर्मा लिपिं संख्यानं चोपयुञ्जीत। 1. 2; Rag. V. iii. 28.

13. निवृत्तचौलकर्मणोश्च तयोस्त्रयीवर्जमितरास्तिस्रो विद्याः सावधानेन मनसा परिनिष्ठापिताः। The Uttararāmacarita Act. II.

14. यथर्षि शिखां निदधाति। A.G.S. xvi. 6; V.G.S. iv.

15. Quoted in the V.M.S. vol. I. p. 321.

16. पञ्चमे सप्तमे वाऽब्दे। The Ṣoḍaśa-Saṁskāravidhi by Pandit Bhīmasena Śarma.

ing of alphabets before the second birth."[17] The proper time of performance was from the month of Mārgaśīrṣa to Jyeṣṭha. The months form Āṣāḍha to Kārtika, when Lord Viṣṇu was supposed to be sleeping, were prohibited for this Saṁskāra.[18] Here one thing is remarkable. During the Sūtra and the pre-Śutra periods, the educational session began particularly during the rainy season. But according to the above authority this very season was avoided.

(*v*) *The Ceremonies*

When the sun was in the northern hemisphere, an auspicious day was fixed for performing the Saṁskāra.[19] In the beginning, the child was required to bathe and to be scented and decorated. Then Vināyaka, Sarasvatī, family goddess and Bṛhaspati were worshipped. Narāyaṇa and Lakṣmī were also propitiated, and one's own Veda and the Sūtrakāras of one's own Vedic School were paid respects. After this a Homa was offered. The teacher, facing towards the east, performed the Akṣarārambha of the crild who was facing towards the west. The Saṁskāra consisted of writing and reading both. Saffron and other substance were scattered on a silver plank and letters were written with a gold pen. But as it was possible in the case of only the rich, letters may be written on rice with any pen specially made for this occasion. The following phrases were written. 'Salutation to Gaṇeśa, Salutation to Sarasvatī, salutation to family gods and goddesses and salutation to Narāyaṇa and Lakṣmī.' After this "Om namaḥ Siddhāya or salutation to Siddha."[20] Then the child worshiped the teacher, and the latter made the child read thrice what was written. Having read, the child presented clothes and ornaments to the teacher and made three circumambulations round the gods. The Brahmans were entertained and propitiated with sacrificial fee. In return, they blessed the child. The ladies whose husbands and children were alive, waved lamps. In the end the teacher was pre-

---

17. द्वितीयजन्मतः पूर्वमारभेताक्षरान्सुधीः ।
Bṛhaspati quoted in the V.M.S. Vol. I. p. 32.

18. अप्रसुप्ते जनार्दने। विश्वामित्रः ibid.
आषाढ़शुक्लद्वादश्यां शयनं कुरुते हरिः ।
निद्रां त्यजति कार्तिक्यां तयोः संयुज्यते हरिः । Viṣṇudharmottara, ibid.

19. उदग्गते भास्वति । Vasiṣṭha ibid.

20. It indicates the Jain influence on the Hindu Saṁskāras.

sented a turban. The ceremonies closed with the dismissal of gods to their respective places.[21]

21. For description of the ceremonies see the Mārkaṇḍeyapurāṇa and the Ṣoḍaśa-Saṁskāravidhi by Pandit Bhimasena Śarma.

The ceremony associated with the learning of alphabets was performed by the Mohammadans also. We are informed that Humayun, the moghul emperor, was admitted into a Maktab when he was four years, four months and four days old, and the occasion was solemnized with due ceremonies (Tazkiratul Sacatin, Ms. in Boh. Coll. vol. I. p. 169; Shah-i- Jahan Nāmah, Ms. in ASB. p. 45).

2. THE UPANAYANA (INITIATION)

(i) *The Origin*

Ceremonies performed in connection with the arrival of youth are universally prevalent. The youth is welcomed into the tribe with proper ceremonies. The Parsis, the Christians, the Mohammadans etc. all have rites specially meant for this purpose. Even the savage tribes of the world perform some kind of ceremonies for greeting the youth into their fold. These ceremonies are as important as any other class of social procedure. Their basis is civil. Their object is to prepare the young men for entering on the active duties of citizenship. The importance of the clan is realized and the people are anxious to preserve the life of their community unimpaired. To meet this end the flowers of the race are disciplined to shoulder the burden of the elders. Thus the ceremony in question arose out of the civil needs of the community. But in course of time it received a religious colouring, as every phase of early life was saturated with the idea of religion, and every communal function was in the need of religious sanction for its validity.

(ii) *Forms of Initiation*

Initiation of young men takes place in different ways in different tribes and religions. Some savage tribes initiate their youths by tests of endurance.[1] In certain communities girls are initiated by observing a temporary seclusion.[2] A few tribes re-arrange the taboos for a young man when he enters the life. Mutilation of the body is another method of initiation in some wild tribes.[3] The Mohammadans still initiate their young men by means of circumcision.

(iii) *The Hindu Initiation*

The scheme of education framed by the ancient Hindus to initiate the young men for preparing them for full citizenship of the community marked a great advance over the primitive idea of initia-

---

1. Frobenius, Childhood of Man, Chap. iii. Frazer, Golden Bough, 2nd. ed. iii. pp. 442. ff.

2. Frazer, Golden Bough i. pp. 826. ff; iii. 204. ff.

3. H. Spencer, Principles of Sociology, i. 189. 290.

tion. Here we find that the conception of race was cultural, and it was on the basis of cultural fitness that one could seek admission into, and claim the full rights and privileges of, the community. Without the Upanayana none could call himself a twice-born. One who would not undergo this Saṁskāra was excommunicated and debarred from all the privileges of the race. The initiation was a passport to the literary treasures of the Hindus. It was also a means of communion with the society, because without it none could marry an Aryan girl. Thus the Hindu ideal made universal education the indispensable test and insignia of their community. The most striking fact in connection with the Upanayana is that by virtue of its performance the initiated ranked as a Dvija or twice-born. This transformation of man's personality by means of religious ceremonies compares well with the Christian rite of baptism, which is regarded as a sacrament and carries with it a spiritual effect to reform the life of man. If we look beneath the surface of the ceremonies, we cannot but recognize in it the expression of a deep human conviction that man, due to his contact with the world, loses his native purity, and that he must be born again to enter the spiritual kingdom again.

(*iv*) *The Antiquity of the Upanayana*

The Upanayana ceremonies are of a hoary antiquity. The corresponding Parsi rite called Naujat (The New Birth[4]), by which Parsi children, both boys and girls, receive religious initiation after they have attained the age of six years and three months, indicates that the Upanayana or the initiation of the child originated in the period when both the Indo-Aryans and the Iranians were living together.

(*v*) *The Vedic Period*

The word "Brahmacharya" is twice mentioned in the Ṛgveda in the sense of the life of a religious student.[5] We also get a reference to a student who has just performed his Upanayana Saṁskāra.[6] In the Atharvaveda[7] the Vedic student is extolled in two hymns which give many details of the Upanayana Saṁskāra found in the later day ceremonies. The Vedic student was called "Brahmachāri" and the

4. It closely corresponds with द्वितीय जन्म or the Second Birth of the Hindus.

5. x. 109. 5.

6. Ibid., iii. 8. 4, 5.

7. xi. 5; xv,

teacher "Āchārya." The initiation of the student was regarded a second birth: "The teacher, taking him in charge, makes the Vedic student an embryo within; he bears him in his belly three nights; the gods gather unto him to see him when born."[8] The student wore sacred girdle, put on the deerskin, kept long beard, practised austerity, collected fuel and offered them in the sacred fire: "The Vedic student fills the worlds with fuel, girdle, toil and fervor. The Vedic student goes....clothing himself in the black antelopeskin, consecrated and long-bearded."[9] The student also begged alms: "This broad earth, and the sky, the Vedic student first brought as alms."[10] All these characteristics of a student re-appear in the post-Vedic literature on the ritual.

During the Brāhmaṇa period the Upanayana assumed almost a ceremonious shape and its procedure was going to be fixed.[11] The student be-took himself to the teacher and announced his intention to become a student: "I have come for Brahmacharya; let me be a Brahmachārī." The teacher, then, asked the name of the student and took him in charge. After this he grasped the hands of the student with appropriate verses and commended him to the protection of deities and beings. He also delivered the five commandments to him for guidance of his conduct. Then the student was taught the sacred Gāyatrī mantra and the teacher observed continence for three days: "When one has admitted a Brāhmaṇa to a term of studentship, he should not carry sexual intercourse etc." The procedure given above is the prototype from which the laterday procedure[12] evolved.

In the Upaniṣadic period the theory of the four Āśramas seems to have been established and "Brahmacharya" or a student's life became a respected institution. The importance of the teacher was recognized even for Brahmavidyā and the Āchārya was the final resort.[13] Upanayana was no more than going to a teacher and being

---

8. आचार्यो उपनयमानो ब्रह्मचारिणं कृणुते गर्भमन्तः।
तं रात्रीस्तिस्र उदरे बिभर्ति तं जातं द्रष्टुमभिसंयन्ति देवाः॥ A.V. xi. 5. 3.

9. Ibid., xi. 5, 6.

10. Ibid., xi. 5. 9.

11. Ś. Br. i. 2. 1–8.

12. cf. P.G.S. ii. 2.5

13. आचार्यस्तु ते गतिवक्ता। Ch. U.

admitted as a pupil.[14] But admission was not open to all. Students were admitted when they had satisfied the conditions laid down by the teacher: "This knowledge should not be imparted to the sceptic, to the wicked and the vicious etc."[15]

The Brahmachārins resided and boarded at the house of their gurus[16] and in return rendered many personal services, such as tending his cows and looking after the sacrificial fire. From the story of Satyakāma Jābāla we learn that he was asked to stay with the cows of the guru and return only when they had increased to a thousand. Moreover, the student helped his guru by begging alms also.[17] The usual period of studentship was from the twelfth to twenty-fourth year of a man.[18] But longer periods are also mentioned. The age at which studentship began and the period spent at the house of the guru varied according to the individual inclination and capacity. To give an instance, Śvetaketu commenced his studentship at twelve and studied for twelve years. The Upaniṣads also inform us that every time a man approached a new teacher, he had to perform his Upanayana anew.[19] The story of Āruṇi tells that even old man could become a pupil for a time.[20] The teacher was held in high respect. It is preached that devotion to the teacher is necessary for the highest kind of knowledge.[21] At the end of the student life many practical instructions were given which are of very high value, such as "Speak the truth. Lead a pious life etc."[22]

(vi) *The Sūtra and later Periods*

The Upanayana Saṁskāra became fully established in the time of the Gṛhyasūtras. All the Gṛhyasūtras presuppose that Upanayana was universal and encumbent on every twice-born. They lay

---

14. उप त्वा अयानि। ibid., iv. 4.
15. एतद्गुह्यतमं नापुत्राय नाशिष्याय कीर्तयेदनन्यभक्ताय सर्वगुणसम्पन्नाय दद्यात्। T. U.
16. आचार्यकुलवासिन् or अन्तेवासिन्। Ch. U. iii. 2. 5; iv. 10 1.
17. Ch. U. iv. 3. 5.
18. Ch. U. vi. 1. 2.
19. Ibid.
20. Br. U. vi. 1. 6.
21. Ś. U. vi. 23.
22. T. U. I. 11.

down all the regulations and every possible detail of the ceremony. The development of the ritualistic side of the Saṁskāra was complete by the time of the Sūtras. The Dharmasūtras and Smṛtis do not contribute anything to the ritual proper. They take up the link supplied by the Gṛhyasūtras about the social side of the Saṁskāra and develop it. They give full information and discussions about the age of the child to be initiated, the lawful recipients, the duties of a student and his conduct. In these rules and regulations many changes were introduced at different times which will be shown in their respective places. The Paddhatis, that were written still later, follow the ritual of their particular Vedic school in general, but at the same time admit many local customs prevalent in their times.

(*vii*) *The Meaning of the term Upanayana*

The conception of Upanayana has undergone many changes in course of time. In the Atharvaveda the word "Upanayana" is used in the sense of "taking charge of a student."[23] Here it meant the initiation of the child by a teacher into sacred lore. "Upanayana" connoted the same thing during the Brāhmaṇa period, as it is evident by the initiation of a student in the Śatapatha-Brāhmaṇa.[24] Even in the Sūtra period the proposal of the student for studentship and its acceptance by the teacher is the central point in the Saṁskāra. But later on when the mystic significance of the Upanayana increased, the idea of the second birth through the Gāyatrī mantra overshadowed the original idea of initiation for education. Manu says, "In the Vedic birth of the student, symbolized by wearing girdle made of Muñja-grass, Sāvitrī is the mother and the teacher the father."[25] By many writers the Saṁskāra itself is called "The Teaching of Sāvitrī" (Sāvitrīvadanam) Aparārka remarks on the word "Upanayana" used by Yājñavalkya, "By Upanayana is understood the establishment of connection between the pupil and Sāvitrī, which is performed by the teacher."[26] In still later times the word "Upanayana" was used only in the physical sense, that is, taking the pupil near the teacher by his guardians. By the Upanayana-Saṁskāra was meant that rite through which the child was taken to the teacher.[27] One authority extends

23. उपनयमानो ब्रह्मचारिणम् । A.V. xi. 5. 3.

24. xi. 5. 4.

25. तत्र यद् ब्रह्मजन्मास्य मोञ्जीबन्धनचिह्नितम् ।
तत्रास्य माता सावित्री पिता त्वाचार्य उच्यते ॥ M.S. ii. 170.

26. Apararka on Yāj. S. I. 14.

27. उप समीपे आचार्यादीनां वटोर्नीतिर्नयनं प्रापणमुपनयनम् । Bhāruchi, quoted in V.M.S. vol. I. p. 334.

the meaning of the word "Upanayana" and does not restrict it to the educational sense alone: "The rite through which a man is initiated into the vows of the guru, the Vedas, the restraints, observances and the vicinity of a god, is called Upanayana."[28] In the latest development of the Saṁskāra its educational sense has departed altogether. The word "Upanayana" is used in sense of a ceremonial farce which is performed sometimes before the marriage of a twice-born. In this sense it is called "Janeoo,"[29] that is, a ceremony in which a boy is invested with the Sacred Thread. What a mockery of fate! The Sacred Thread as such is not mentioned in the Gṛhyasūtras. It was a later substitute for the upper garment which was put on at the time of a sacrifice.[30] One did not know that this insignificant decorative substitute would outweigh the original elements of the Saṁskāra. But when not education but a badge became the sign of regeneration, the Sacred Thread reigned supreme.

(viii) *The Purpose of the Saṁskāra*

The purpose of the Saṁskāra has also suffered various vicissitudes. Originally education was the main purpose and ritual or ceremoniously taking the initiate to the teacher an ancillary item. It was not only at the first initiation of a boy but at the beginning of every branch of the Veda, that the Upanayana was performed.[31] Evidence is available to show that such was the case. In the Upaniṣads we come across a number of cases where a man underwent the rite of Upanayana when approaching a guru for learning a new branch of philosophy.[32] Yājñavalkya regards the reading of the Vedas the highest object of the Upanayna: "The teacher, having initiated the pupil with the Mahāvyāhṛtis, should teach him Vedas and the rules of conduct.[33] According to Āpastamba and Bhārad-

---

28. गुरोर्व्रतानां वेदस्य यमस्य नियमस्य च।
देवतानां समीपं वा येनासौ नीयतेऽसौ॥ Abhiyukta, ibid.

29. This word is current in Northern India.

30. Cf. यज्ञोपवीतं कुरुते सूत्रं वस्त्रं कुशरज्जुं वेति। G.G.S. ii. 10.
तृतीयमुत्तरीयार्थो वस्त्राऽलाभे तदिष्यते॥ Devala, quoted in V.M.S. vol. I. p. 415.

31. यच्छाखीयैस्तु संस्कारैः संस्कृतो ब्राह्मणो भवेत्।
तच्छाखाध्ययनं कार्यमेवं न पतितो भवेत्॥ Vasiṣṭha, Ibid. p. 337.

32. Ch. U. V. ii. 7.

33. उपनीय गुरुः शिष्यं महाव्याहृतिपूर्वकम्।
वेदमध्यापयेदेनं शौचाचारांश्च शिक्षयेत्॥ Yāj. S. I. 15.

vāja, the Upanayana was meant for learning: "Upanayana is the sacrament of a person desirous of learning."[34] But in course of time the performance of the ritual and the Vratādeśa or the commandments for observing vows became the chief object and education a secondary one. Gautama was the first exponent of this school: "Being consecrated by forty-eight Saṁskāras a man goes to the vicinity of Brahman and Ṛṣis."[35] According to Manu also the ritual purifies this life as well as the other.[36] Aṅgirā also thinks that the Saṁskāra properly performed produces Brahmanhood.[37] When the Upanayana was an educational Saṁskāra, the Vratādeśa or the delivery of commandments by the initiator was a secondary performance, but when it became a bodily Saṁskāra the ritualistic significance rose into importance. In the latest of its development, the Upanayana became a religious achievement (Puruṣārtha) bereft of any educational intention. Even the mad, the dumb, the deaf or otherwise disabled persons who were originally excluded[38] from the right of performing this Saṁskāra were required to undergo the ceremony.[39]

(ix) *The Age*

The first problem to be considered in connection with the Upanayana Saṁskāra was: At what age of the initiate should it be performed? The general rule given in the Gṛhyasasūtras and endorsed by the later authorities was that the Upanayana ceremony of a Brahman boy should be performed in the eighth year, that of a Kṣatriya in the eleventh and that of a Vaiśya in the twelfth.[40] As regards the basis of this differentiation many speculations have been offered.

---

34. उपनयनं विद्यार्थस्य श्रुतितः संस्कार इति। Ap. D. S. I.

35. G.D.S. viii. 14. 24.

36. M.S. ii. 26.

37. Quoted in V.M.S. vol. I. p. 137.

38. Śaṅkha and Likhita quoted by Harihara on. P.G.S. ii. 2.

39. तस्माच्च षण्ढबधिरकुब्जवामनपङ्गुषु।
जडगद्‌गदरोगार्तशुष्कांग विकलाङ्गेषु॥
मत्तोन्मत्तेषु मूकेषु शयनस्थे निरिन्द्रये।
ध्वस्तपुंस्त्वेषु चैतेषु संस्काराः स्युर्यथोचितम्। The Brahma-purāṇa, quoted in V.M.S. vol. I. p. 399.

40. P.G.S. ii. 2; A.G.S. i. 19; Ś.G.S. ii. 1; Ṭ.G.S. ii. 5; Ap. G.S. xi; G.G.S. ii. 10; M.S. ii. 36; Yāj. S. I. 11.

Some writers[41] regard it as a fancy and self-conceit of the Brahmans. As the number of letters in the Sāvitrī mantras of the Brahmans, Kṣattriyas and the Vaiśyas happened to be eight, eleven and twelve,[42] the Brahmans took fancy to them and determined the respective ages of the boys of the upper three classes for initiation at eight, eleven and twelve. They quote Medhātithi[43] and the Vīramitrodaya[44] to support their views. According to another set of scholars[45] the differentiation was based on the intellectual superiority of the Brahmans; the Brahman child was more intelligent than the Kṣattriya and the Vaiśya children. In connection with the first speculation it should be noted that the observations of Medhātithi and the Vīramitrodaya, far removed from the time of the Sūtras, may be fanciful, but relation between the Sāvitrī mantra and the age of the initiate cannot be traced in the Gṛhyasūtras. Equality of letters is accidental which gave rise to the fancy of later-day writers, to whom Upanayana was a farce and not a real necessity. Moreover, there is no sanctity attached to these numbers in Hindu religion. So, it is difficult to believe that the difference in age for the performance of the Saṁskāra, a ceremony full of consequences in the beginning, originated from mere fancy. The second speculation also cannot be supported. Baudhāyana recommends any year between eight and sixteen for a Brahman boy.[46] So, it seems quite improbable that earlier age for their children was due to the superior intellect or the superiority complex of the Brahmans.

The more plausible basis of differentiation seems to be that, in early times, the father was the teacher in case of the Brahman Brahmachārins. Therefore, it was inconvenient to them if they were initiated at an early age, because they had not to leave their homes for education. But quite different was the case with the Kṣattriya and the Vaiśya children. They had to part with their parents for receiving education. Therefore, they would have been put to troubles, had they been separated form their parents in a very young age. Thus paternal feelings were responsible, to a great extent, for the higher age at which the initiation should be performed. There

41. Keay, Ancient Indian Education, p. 29.

42. ब्राह्मणादिवर्णसम्बन्धिनां छन्दसां पाद्यक्षरसख्यैरुपनयनस्य विधिः। Medhātithi on M.S. ii. 36.

43. Ibid.

44. V.M.S. vol. I. p. 344.

45. S.K. Das; The Educational systems of the Ancient Hindus, p. 72.

46. B.G.S. ii. 5. 5.

was one more operative factor in fixing the age of the Kṣattriya and the Vaiśya children. The Brahmanical education that began after the Upanayana was mostly religious and priestly and consisted of Vedic and allied studies. The Brahmans had to busy themselves earlier with this kind of education, because their further prospects depended on the knowledge of the Vedic lore. But the professions of the Kṣattriyas and the Vaiśyas were different. No doubt, they had to maintain a racial standard of culture by undergoing a literary education, but they had to specialize in the military art and administration, and commerce and agriculture respectively. So, these two classes joined the Brahmanical education later, as they were not required to pass the same course of studies as the Brahman students. Thus, caste differentiation originated form practical necessity and not out of fancy and superiority-complex of the Brahmans.[47]

Optional ages were prescribed for securing special merits. In the opinion of Baudhāyana "One desirous of holy lustre should perform the Upanayana in the seventh year, of long life in the eighth year, of glory in the ninth year, of food in the tenth, of cattle in the twelfth, of talent in the thirteenth, of strength in the fourteenth, of brothers in the fifteenth and of all in the sixteenth."[48] Manu also says, "The Upanayana of a Brāhmaṇa child desirous of holy lustre should be performed in the fifth year, that of a Kṣattriya child desirous of power, in the sixth year and that of a Vaiśya child desirous of wealth in the eighth year."[49]

At the first, sight the wide options meant for different merits look fanciful. But when we take into consideration the change which the conception of Upanayana underwent in course of time, their rationale becomes evident. In the beginning the Upanayana marked the commencement of the primary education. Therefore, an early age was preferred and the earliest possible age for the Upanayana was fixed at five. But when the Upanayana ceased to signalize the primary education and was performed at the beginning of the secondary education, higher age was prescribed for this purpose, though it was always within the period of educational suitability. The age should be such that the mind of the student be still receptive and he may get sufficient time to study. The same age, however, would

---

47. Cf. Dr. A. S. Altekar, Education In Ancient India, Chap. I. p. 18.

48. B.G.S. ii. 5. 5.

49. ब्रह्मवर्चसकामस्य कार्यं विप्रस्य पञ्चमे ।
राज्ञो बलार्थिनः षष्ठे वैश्यस्यचार्थिनोऽष्टमे ॥ M.S. ii. 37.

not suit every child. So, intermediate options were allowed to meet the need of every type of children. But at whatever time it may be performed, it was regarded always meritorious, because it was considered to be a sacrament full of religious significance.

The last limit for the performance of the Upanayana Saṁskāra in the case of a Brahman student was sixteen, of the Kṣattriya twenty-two and of the Vaiśya twenty-four.[50] When the Upanayana became a compulsory bodily Saṁskāra, it had got to be performed howsoever late it may be. The underlying purpose was to enlist all the possible young men of the community and stamp them with the peculiar culture of the race. For the Brahman the age was still earlier, as he was the custodian of the Aryan religion and the teacher of the Aryan race. The Kṣattriyas and the Vaiśyas, who were less enthusiastic about priestly education could be initiated later. Twenty four was the last age, because it was the time about which marriage generally took place. The Upanayana must be performed some times before the marriage of a twice-born. Mitramiśra, a seventeenth century writer, permits Upanayana up to twenty-four years of a Brahman, thirty-three of a Kṣattriya and thirty-six of a Vaiśya.[51] This was the time when India was under the full hold of the Muslims. The performance of religious ceremonies was not a certain and safe thing. So, even wider scope was allowed for contingency. Probably it would have helped the reconversion of the new Muslims into the Hindu fold also.

(x) *The Vrātya*

One, who inspite of the wide option allowed by the scriptures would not abide by the rules, was regarded fallen from the status of a twice-born and exammunicated from the community. According to Manu, "If after the last prescribed time people remain uninitiated, they become Vrātyas, fallen from Sāvitrī, discarded by the Aryans."[52] These non-conformists were debarred from all religious and social privileges of the Aryans. Non-abidance to the rule, in some cases, may have been due to carelessness, or adverse circumstances. But in the majority of cases it was deliberate. Hence, the severe punish-

50. P.G.S. ii. 5. 36–38.

51. V.M.S. vol. I. p. 347.

52. अत ऊर्ध्वं त्रयोऽप्येते यथाकालमसंस्कृताः ।
सावित्रीपतिता व्रात्या भवन्त्यार्यविगर्हिताः ॥ M.S. ii. 39.

ment was inflicted upon them and they were classed with a non-Aryan tribe, the Vrātyas, and classed with the Śūdras.[53]

It would not be out of place to trace briefly the history of the word "Vrātya" to make the connection between the Vrātyas and the non-conformance with the Vedic initiation more clear. In the Atharvaveda the word Vrātya is used not in the sense of "one who has not performed his Upanayana" but it is employed in the sense of the Highest Brahman; "The Highest Brahman is conceived and exalted as the Vrātya-both as the heavenly Vrātya, identified with the Great God (Mahādeva), the Lord Īśana or Rudra, and his prototype, the earthly Vrātya. The Vrātyas were certain, probably Eastern tribes, whether Aryan or non-Aryan, but certainly living outside the pale of Brahmanism, roving about in lands on rough waggon covered with boards in a rather warlike fashion, owners of cattle, having their own peculiar customs and religious cults."[54] According to some scholars the word "Vrātya" is used in the sense of a non-Aryan tribe,[54a] while others hold that it denotes the earliest worshippers of Rudra and Śiva. Mr. J. W. Haver[54b] regards "Vrātya" as the ecstatics of the Kṣattriya class and the forerunners of the later-day Yogins.

The Vrātyas were Aryan in race, though they were not Vedic in religion. This inference is supported by the fact that the door of Aryandom was always open for them if they sought admission,[55] while it was closed against the Śūdras. Thus, though the exact sense of the term is not certain, it is clear that it was not used in the Smārta sense, that is, in the sense of a person who has not performed the Upanayana. But because the Vrātya dissented form the Vedic religion, those, who did not perform their Saṁskāra, in later times, were classed with them. They were called "'Vrātyas" because after observing certain vratas (sacrificial ceremonies) they could be admitted into the Aryan community.[56] According to the scriptures, persons outcasted for nonperformance were eligible to re-admission into the Aryan fold after performing the Vrātyastoma sacrifice.

53. शूद्राणाञ्च सधर्माणः। Ibid. x. 41.

54. Winternitz, History of Indian Literature, vol. I. ?

54a. Rājārāma Rāmakrisna Bhāgavata, I. B. R. A. S. 19, 1896.

54b. Die Anfä-ugeder Yogapraxis, Berlin, 1922, pp. 11 H.

55. तेषां संस्कारेप्सुर्व्रात्यस्तोमेनेष्ट्वा काममधीयीरन्। P.G.S. ii. 5. 44.

56. व्यवहार्या भवन्तीति वचनात्। Ibid.

(*xi*) *The Upanayana not Compulsory in the beginning*

Though the Gṛhyasūtras and the later literature on the rituals presuppose that the Upanayana was a compulsory Saṁskāra, such does not seem to be the case before the Sūtra period. It may be argued that during the Atharvavedic times, the Upanayana was regarded as a second birth[57] and, most probably, all the twice-born received their status from this rite. But the idea of the second birth was not peculiar to the Upanayana only. It was also associated with the initiation which was performed before a sacrifice.[58] So the significance of the second birth in the Vedic time was religious and not social; and not all the persons of the upper three classes were compulsorily required to perform the Upanayana Saṁskāra. For a very long time before the rules laid down in the Gṛhyasūtras crystallized, the Upanayana was a voluntary ceremony. Whosoever desired to learn, approached his guru and performed the initiation ceremony, while his cousins, not willing to do so, remained without any initiation. The Upanayana was confined to literary and priestly families only. This is borne out by Āruṇi's advice to his son Śvetaketu that he should pass through the life of a student, because members of his family did not claim Brahmanhood by birth.[59] It should be also noted that the Āśrama theory, though recognized, was not universally observed. The word "Vrātya," as already pointed out, did not denote a person who had not performed his Upanayana, but it was used in the sense of a person who did not offer Soma sacrifice or keep the sacred fire.[60] In the Smṛti and subsequent times many disabilities were imposed for not performing the Upanayana ceremony. But no such punishment was inflicted on the defaulter in the Vedic times. The social status of the Vrātyas suffered in no way, as it is evident from their exaltation in the Atharvaveda.[61] It is, therefore, quite clear that the Upanayana Saṁskāra was not regarded compulsory, rather it was a privilege to be availed of by a willing person for entry into the sacred library of the race.

---

57. आचार्य उपनयमानो ब्रह्मचारिणं कृणुते गर्भमन्तः।
तं रात्रीस्तिस्र उदरे बिभर्ति तं जातं द्रष्टुमभिसंयन्ति देवाः॥ A.V. xi. 5. 3.

58. अजातो ह वै तावत्पुरुषो यावन्न यजते। Ś. Br. ii. 3. 4.

59. Ch. U. vi. 1. 1.

60. यस्य पिता पितामहो वा न सोमं पिबेत्स व्रात्यः। A Vedic text quoted in the Parāśara-mādhavīya, 1. 1. p. 165.

61. A.V. X. V.

(xii) The Upanayana becomes Compulsory

The Upanayana Saṁskāra became compulsory somewhere towards the close of the Upaniṣadic period. There were many factors that led to it. First of all there was the cultural factor. For any advancing civilization education is essential. In order to make education universal, the Upanayana was made compulsory. Every Aryan was compelled to spend at least some years at the house of a teacher or in some educational institution. The next but the allied factor was that the mass of literature and learning was increasing. Different branches of learning evolved. Therefore, in order to preserve the sacred literature the services of the entire community were conscripted by making the Upanayana a compulsory Saṁskāra.[62] The third factor was a purely religious one. The Upanayana came to be believed to have possessed sanctifying power. One may or may not receive education but he must consecrate his person. This undue importance attached to the sanctity of the Saṁskāra was also instrumental in making it compulsory for all. The last factor was racial. The Indo-Aryans had to distinguish themselves from the non-Aryan population round them. In the first contact with the non-Aryans they were superior to, and distinct from them by their colour and culture both. But in course of time these characteristics dwindled, and there arose the danger of fusion with them and thus of lowering the standard of their civilization. The Upanayana which was already prevalent in the society, served a good means for differentiation. The Aryans, who may not devote the period of youth to education, but underwent the ceremony and put on the Sacred Thread, were called the regenerate and distinguished from the Śūdras, the later-day non-Aryan population. The Upanayana was called a second birth in the sense that it heightened the social status of the recipients. All the Aryans became twice-born. A non-Aryan having only one physical birth was certainly regarded inferior to an Aryan.

(xiii) Ridiculous Consequences of Compulsion

When the Upanayana became a compulsory Saṁskāra people gradually forgot its real purpose and many ridiculous consequences followed. Formerly when it was purely an educational Saṁskāra, persons inherently incompetent for education were excluded from the right of performance.[63] But when it became a bodily Saṁskāra, the opinion

62. Cf. Dr. A. S. Altekar, Education in Ancient India, Chap. I. pp. 11, 12.

63. नोन्मत्तमूकान्संस्कुर्यात् । Śaṅkha and Likhita, quoted by Harihara on P.G.S.

was advocated that the Upanayana should be performed in the case of the dumb, deaf, blind etc. also.[64] A few Smṛti-writers dissented from this view.[65] But the majority accepted this absurd procedure in order to enable even disabled persons to marry, by providing them with a badge of superior castes. Another consequence of the Upanayana being a bodily Saṁskāra was that a fresh Upanayana was prescribed for a person, when he happened to be defiled by drinking wine, eating onion etc.[66] This repetition presents a sad contrast to the fact that in the Vedic times it was repeated when the student began a new branch of the Vedas. The most absurd consequence that followed the degradation of the Upanayana from its original purpose was that even the Upanayana of trees came to be performed. A fourteenth century Carnatic inscription records that a Brahman performed the Upanayana ceremony of four peepal trees.[67]

(xiv) *The Upanayana Partly neglected during the mediaeval period*

So long as the Brahmanical culture had a strong hold over the Hindus, the compulsion was followed regularly. But during the Muslim period of Indian history, Hinduism received a rude shock. The religious life of the people was endangered and many high and prosperous families of the Kṣattriyas and the Vaiśyas were reduced to agriculturists. The theory became current that there are no Kṣattriyas and the Vaiśyas in the Kali Age.[68] Though it was not universally accepted, the majority of the Vaiśyas and the Kṣattriyas of many localities dispensed with the Upanayana Saṁskāra. From the ninteenth century, however, owing to cultural revival by orthodox associations,[69] they are again becoming particular about performing the Upanayana Saṁskāra.

(xv) *Who look the child to the Teacher?*

Another problem was: Who should take the child to the Āchārya? In early times, in the Brahman families, it was the father

64. The Brâhma-purāṇa, quoted in V.M.S. vol. I. p. 399.

65. Śaṅkha and Likhita, quoted by Harihara on P.G.S.

66. Śatātapa and Yama, quoted in V.M.S. vol. I. p. 545.

67. Epigraphica Carnatica, III. Malavalli Inscriptai no. 23.

68. कलौ आद्यन्तयोः स्थितिः।

69. The Āryasamājas and the Sanatanadharma Societies.

who taught the boy.[70] So, there was no need of discussing the problem. But the non-Brahman children were taken to the Brahman teachers. Moreover, when education developed and the art of teaching was specialized, the Brahman children also went to efficient teachers for study. Therefore, for proper initiation the question of taking the student to the Āchārya came to be discussed. In the opinion of Pitāmaha, the father, the grand-father, an uncle and an elder brother were rightful guardians of a boy, and, in the absence of the former the latter took the student to the teacher.[71] In the absence of the above natural guardians an elderly member of the same caste was also authorized to conduct the child to the Āchārya.[72] But when there was none to do so, or none would care to take the child to the teacher, the pupil himself went to the Āchārya for initiation.[73]

(xvi) *The Selection of the Teacher*

The selection of a teacher was determined by certain considera tions. The best possible teacher was sought for, because the main object of the Upanayana was the acquisition of knowledge and the building of character. If the teacher himself was lacking in knowledge or virtue, he could not elevate the life of the student. "From darkness to darkness he goes, whom an ignorant person initiates. Therefore, one should desire an initiator, who comes of a good family who is learned and who is self-controlled."[74] "A Brāhmaṇa who is well-read, of good family, of good character, purified by penance, should initiate a child."[75] A man was asked not to make a person his teacher who was not firm in his character, for "hands besmeared with fat cannot be purified with blood."[76] Vyāsa recommends a per-

---

70. For example, Śvetaketu was taught by his father Āruṇi (Ch. U. vi. 1.); Br. U. vi. 2. 1; The Ch. U. iv. 5. 5; M. U. i. 2. 12.

71. पितैव उपनयेत्पुत्रं तदभावे पितुः पिता।
तदभावे पितुर्भ्राता तदभावे तु सोदरः । Pitāmaha.

72. ज्ञातयो गोत्राग्रजाः। Vṛddhagarga.

73. Such cases are very common in the Upaniṣads.

74. तमसो वा एष तमः प्रविशति यमविद्वानुपनयते यश्चाविद्वानिति हि ब्राह्मणम्। तस्मिन्नभिजनविद्यासमुदेतं समाहितं संस्कर्तारमीप्सेत्। तस्मिंश्चैव विद्या कर्मान्तमविप्रतिपन्ने धर्मेभ्यः। आप० ध० सू० I. I. I. 11–13.

75. कुमारस्योपनयनं श्रुताभिजनवृत्तवान्।
तपसा धूतनिःशेषपाप्मा कुर्याद्द्विजोत्तमः॥ Śaunaka, ibid.

76. न याजयेद् वृत्तिहीनं वृणुयाच्च न तं गुरुम्।
नहि मज्जाकरौ दिग्धौ रुधिरेण विशुध्यतः॥ Hāritā, Ibid.

son for teachership "who is a Brāhmaṇa, entirely devoted to the Vedas, who comes of a good family, whose profession is the performance of Vedic sacrifices, who is pure who is particular about the study of his own Vedic Śākhā and who has no lethargy."[77] Some further qualifications of an Āchārya are given by Yama[78] as follows: "An Āchārya should be truthful, courageous, capable, merciful towards all creatures, believer in God, firm in the study of the Vedas and pure in character." These considerations were binding or respected when the Upanayana was an educational Saṁskāra. When it ceased to be so, they could be dispensed with. Later on, it was not meant for education but consecration. The Āchārya was not expected to teach the initiate. His only business was to perform the ceremony with the recital of the Vedic verses. So, any-body who could do so was approached for this purpose. At present, in many cases, the Āchārya is dispensed with altogether. To save expenses and botherations, people go to a sacred place, dip the Sacred Thread into the water poured on the deity and put it round the neck of a boy. It is due to the appalling ignorance of the real purpose of the Saṁskāra on the one side and the non-religious character of the modern life on the other.

(xvii) The Ceremonies and their Significance

In the beginning the Upanayana Saṁskāra must have been very simple. In early times when the sacred Vedic lore was handed down from generation to generation in priestly families, the father himself was the guru. In this case, the formalities observed with him naturally should have been limited. The very ancient teachership of the father is proved by the parable of gods, men and demons all spending their student life under the guidance of their common father Prajāpati.[79] During the Upaniṣadic period also there are instances of students studying with their fathers.[80] Original parental simplicity is re-echoed in the Upaniṣads, where in many cases the Upanayana is

---

77. वेदैकनिष्ठं धर्मज्ञं कुलीनं श्रोत्रियं शुचिम् ।
स्वशाखायामनालस्यं विप्रं कर्तारमीप्सितम् ॥ Vyās.a

78. सत्यवाक् धृतिमान् दक्षः सर्वभूतदयापरः ।
आस्तिको वेदनिरतः शुचिराचार्य उच्यते ॥
वेदाध्यापनसम्पन्नो वृत्तिमान् विजितेन्द्रियः ।
दक्षोत्साही यथावृतः जीवनेहस्तु वृत्तिमान् ॥ Yama, ibid.

79. Br. Br. U. V. 2. 1.

80. Br. U. vi. 2. 1; Ch. U. V. 3; iv. 5. 5; v. 11. 7; M. U. i. 2. 12.

very simple. The student approached his teacher with sacrificial fuel in his hands, thereby showing that he intended to be his pupil and that he was ready to serve the teacher.[81] There are other instances where an oral request on the part of the student and its acceptance on the part of the Āchārya was all that constituted an Upanayana.[82] But these are sporadic cases of simplicity. Even before the close of the Vedic period, the ceremony was assuming a complicated character. The Upanayana of the Atharvavedic time included many items of the later-day ritual. During the Brāhmana period noted for sacrificial elaboration, the Upanayana Saṁskāra was developed and its ceremonious character is evident from the details available in them.[83] The Gṛhyasūtras[83a] describe a full-fledged ritual with well-developed details. The Saṁskāra in its onward march also gathered many non-Vedic and popular materials under its auspices.

(a) The Time. An auspicious time was selected for the performance of the Saṁskāra. Generally the Upanayana took place when the sun was in the northern hemisphere,[84] but in the case of the Vaiśya children, its southern course was also prescribed.[85] Different seasons were meant for different castes.[86] The Upanayana of a Brahman was performed in spring, of a Kṣattriya in summer, of a Vaiśya in autumn and of a Rathakāra in the rainy season. These different seasons were symbolical of the temperament and occupation of different castes. The moderation of spring symbolized the moderate life of a Brahman; the heat of summer represented the fervour of a Kṣattriya; autumn, when the commercial life of ancient India re-opened after the rainy season, suggested the wealth and prosperity of a Vaiśya; and the easy time of rains indicated facility for a chariot-maker. The later astrological works associated different kinds of merits with different months from Māgha to Āṣāḍha: "A boy whose Upanyana is performed in the month of Māgha becomes wealthy, in the month of Phālguna intelligent, in Chaitra talented and well-versed

81. Ibid.

82. Cf. वाचाह स्मैव पूर्व उपयन्ति। Bṛ u. VI. 2. 7.

83. Br. xi. 5. 4.

83a. Ś.G.S. ii. 1; AG.S. i. 19. iii. 5; P.G.S. ii. 2; G.G.S. ii. 10 Kh. G.S. ii. 4; iii. 1; H.G.S. i. 1. ii. 18. A.G.S. 10.

84. P.G.S. ii. 2; A.G.S. 1. 19.

85. दक्षिणे तु विशां कुर्यात्। Bṛhaspati quoted in V.M.S. vol. I. p. 354.

86. वसन्ते ब्राह्मणमुपनयति ग्रीष्मे राजन्यं शरदि वैश्यं वर्षासु रथकारमिति। B.G.S. 11. 5. 6.

in the Vedas, in Vaiśākha provided with all kinds of enjoyments, in Jyeṣṭha wise and great, and in Āṣāḍha a great conqueror of enemies and famous Pandit."[87] The bright half of the month was preferred, as it was delightful time for any social function and its brightness was symbolical of knowledge and learning. Holidays, Parvans, inauspicious times and the days of natural abnormality were avoided.

(b) Preparations. Before the actual ceremony took place, a canopy was set up under which the Saṁskāra would be performed.[88] A day before the ceremony, many pauranic Performances took place. The most auspicious god Gaṇeśa, was propitiated and several other goddesses, Śri, Lakṣmi, Dhṛti, Medhā, Puṣṭi Śraddhā, and Sarasvatī were worshipped.[89] On the previous night, the candidate was smeared all over with a yellow substance, and a silver ring was tucked to his top-knot.[90] After that, he was commanded to spend the whole night in absolute silence. It was a mystic rite which prepared the candidate for the second birth. The yellowish power gave a show of embryonic atmosphere and absolute silence made the boy a speechless child anew.

(c) The Joint Meal. The next morning the mother and the child ate totgether for the last time. It was rather an unusual procedure in a Hindu Saṁskāra. According to Dr. Altekar[91] it marked the end of an irregular life of a child and reminded the boy that he was no longer an irresponsible child and that he had to lead a systematic life thence onward. But it might have been the parting feast of the mother and the child also. It was a sad touching ceremony. It expressed the deep affection of the mother for her child. After his Upanayana the mother no more could take food with him as a rule. The very idea moved the mother to show her last affectionate feeling. Both the ideas may have operated in the above

---

87. माघे मासि महाधनो धनपतिः प्रज्ञायुतः फाल्गुने
मेधावी भवति व्रतोपनयने चैत्रे च वेदान्वितः।
वैशाखे निखिलोपभोगसहितो ज्येष्ठे वरिष्ठो बुध–
स्त्वाषाढे सुमहाविपक्षविजयी ख्यातो महापण्डितः॥ The Rājamārtaṇda quoted in V.M.S. vol. I. p. 355.

88. पञ्चसु बहिः शालाया विवाहे चूडाकरणोपनयने केशान्ते सीमन्तोन्नयने इति। P.G.S. i. 4. 2.

89. It was a later development not found in the Gṛhyasūtras.

90. It is a local custom in many provinces.

91. Education in Ancient India, I. P. 19.

ceremony. But there seem to be some more factors that gave rise to it. The boy not only could not take food with his mother, but also was going to be separated from her for a long time. The mother could not enjoy his company during this period. So her heart was heavy on the occasion and the most impressive act of love that she could do was to eat with the child. There was perhaps, one practical necessity of feeding the child in the morning. The ceremony was a protracted one. In order that he may not get hungry during the ceremony, he was fed before it began. After the mother's feast, a number of young men were entertained. It was a party which was given to the playmates of the candidate at the departure of their friend to the teacher's house.

(d) The Bath. After the feast was over the father and the mother took the child to the canopy, where the sacrificial fire was burning in the alter. The first scriptural item of the ceremony was the feeding of the Brahmans, an act always meritorious and in this case symbolical of Brahmayajña and Brahmacharya. which the life of the student was going to be after his Upanayana. Then the boy was shaved. If the Chūḍākaraṇa had been performed, he was simply shaved in the ordinary way by the barber. But sometimes to economize the expenses, though not sanctioned by the scriptures, the haircutting ceremony was postponed till now and it was performed before the thread-giving. When the shaving was finished, the boy was bathed. It was a ceremony essential to every Saṁskāra. Washing purified both, the mind and the body of the recipient.

(e) The Kaupīna. The bath being over, the boy was given a Kaupīna to cover his private parts. The social consciousness had already dawned upon the mind of the boy, but from now he had particularly to observe the social decorum and to maintain his own dignity and self-respect. Then the boy went near the Āchārya and announced his intention to become a Brahmachārī: "I have come hither for the sake of studentship. I will be a student."[92] Having accepted his request the Āchārya offered him clothes with the verse, "In the way in which Bṛhaspati put the garment of immortality on Indra, thus I put this garment on thee, for the sake of long life, of old age, of strength, of splendour."[93] The Hindu idea of decorum required that, when engaged in a religious ceremony, the upper part of the body should be covered with a piece of cloth. On the occasion of the Upanayana, therefore, the young scholar was offered

92. P.G.S. ii. 2. 9.

93. Ibid. ii. 2. 10.

an upper garment, because from this time his proper religious life began. From the ancient literature we know that the original piece of the upper garment offered at this occasion was the deer-skin. We are informed by the Gopatha Brāhmaṇa that the deer-skin was symbolical of spiritual and intellectual pre-eminence.[94] By putting it on, the student was constantly asked to become a youth of ideal character and deep scholarship. In the early pastoral life of the Aryans the use of the deer-skin was a need. Its hoary antiquity lent it a sanctity and, in course of time it became a religious luxury. Its use, however, was limited to bedding. When the Aryans became agriculturists and spinning and weaving came into existence, a cotton cloth was offered to the student. According to the Āpastamba and the Baudhāyana Gṛhyasūtras, this piece of cloth should have been woven in the house of the Brahmachārin just before the ceremony.[95] The Gṛhyasūtras prescribe clothes made of different stuffs for different castes. The clothes of a Brahman student should be made of śaṇa (hemp), that a Kśattriya of Kṣauma (silk) and that of Vaiśya of Kutapa (the kuśagrass).[96] But, optionally, clothes made of cotton were prescribed for all.[97] Formerly on purely religious grounds, white and unwashed clothes were offered, no doubt symbolizing the purity of life.[98] But, later on, practical sense prevailed on the religious motive, though it was still tinged with symbolism. The clothes of a Brahman should be Kāṣāya. (reddish) that of a Kṣattriya Māñjiṣṭha (dyed with madder) and that of a Vaiśya Hāridra (yellow).[99] The clothes were dyed because thereby they would not get shabby very soon. Different colours preserved the distinction of castes. The deep-rooted fascination for white clothes, however, did not die away and many Smṛtis insist that the colour of the clothes of a Brahmachārī should be white.[100] At present the above distinc-

---

94. G. Br. i. 2. 1–8.

95. वासः सद्यक्त्तोत्तम् । B.G.S. ii. 5. 11; Áp. G.S. 11. 16.

96. शाणक्षौमचीरकुतपा । G.D.S. i. 17. 18.

97. सर्वेषां कार्पासं वाऽविकृतम् । Ibid.

98. अहतेन वाससा संवीतमिति । A.G.S. i. 19. 10.
ईषद्धौतं नवश्वेतं सदशं यन्न धारितम् ।
अहतं तद्विजानीयात् सर्वकर्मसु पावनम् ।। Pracettā quoted in V.M.S. vol. I. p. 410.

99. यदि वासांसि वसीरन् रक्तानि वसीरन् काषायं ब्राह्मणो माञ्जिष्ठं क्षत्रियो हारिद्रं वैश्य इति । A.G. S. i. 19. 10.

100. सर्वं तु धारयेच्छुक्लं वासस्तत्परिधानकम् ।Manu quoted in V.M.S. vol. I. p. 410.

tions have vanished away and clothes dyed in Haridrā (yellow) are offered to all the twice-born.

(f) The Girdle. Next, the Āchārya tied round the waist of the youth the girdle with the verse, "Here has come to me, keeping away evil words, purifying mankind as a purifier, clothing herself by power of inhalation and exhalation, with strength, this sisterly goddess, the blessed girdle"[101] or with, "A youth well attired, dressed, come hither. He, being born, becomes glorious. Wise sages extol him, devout ones, turning their minds to gods." Or silently.[101a] The girdle was originally meant to support the Kaupīna. But, later on, it was turned to serve as a religious symbolism. It was made of triple cord, which symbolised that the student was always encircled by the three Vedas.[102] The girdle also informed the student that his belt was "a daughter of Faith and a sister of the sages, possessed the power of protecting his purity and chastity and would keep him away from evil."[102a] Like the upper garment, the girdle was also made of different stuffs for different castes, and even for one single caste options were allowed according to different Vedic schools. The girdle of a Brahman was made of Muñja grass, that of a Kṣattriya of a bow-string and that of a Vaiśya of wool. It must be even and good-looking. Its use at present is momentary, and soon after the Upanayana it is substituted by a cotton girdle.

(g) The Sacred Thread. After the tying of the girdle came the most important item of the Saṁskāra, according to the later authority, the investing the student with the Sacred Thread. It should be, however, observed that it was unknown to the early writers on ritual. None of the Gṛhyasūtras contains the prescription of wearing the Sacred Thread. It seems that the upper garment which was offered to the youth was the prototype from which the sacred thread descended, though both the prototype (but not for sacrificial purpose) and the imitation were retained by the later authorities. The very

101. P.G.S. ii. 2. 11.

101a. Ibid. ii. 2. 12-13.

102. वेदत्रयेणावृतोऽहमिति मन्येत् स द्विजः। Āśvalāyana, quoted in V.M.S. vol. I. p. 432.

102a. श्रद्धाया दुहिता तपसोऽधिजाता स्वसा ऋषीणां भूतकृता बभूव। A.V. vi. 133. 4.
ऋतस्य गोप्त्री तपश्चरित्री घ्नती रक्षः सहमाताः अरातीः।
सा मा समन्तम् अभिपर्येहि भद्रे धर्तारस्ते सुभगे मा रिषाम॥ V.G.S. 5.

name of the Sacred Thread, "Yajñopavīta" supplies a clue to its original nature.[103]

The scriptures prescribe that cotton cords should be worn by the Brahmana, woollen by the Kṣattriyas and linen by the Vaiśyas.[104] But the option of cotton cords is found for all.[105] It seems that it was due to the convenience of getting cotton threads. The Sacred Thread was of different colour according to different castes; the Brahmans wore white, the Kṣattriyas red and the Vaiśyas yellow. It is said that it corresponded with the colour of the mind of the above castes. But the differentiation was afterwards removed and at present the Vaiśya colour, yellow, has been adopted universally.

The Sacred Thread is spun by a virgin Brahman girl and twisted by a Brahman. In it as many knots are made as there are Pravaras amongst the ancestors of the wearer. The composition of the Sacred Thread is full of symbolism and significance. Its length is ninetysix times as the breadth of the four fingers of a man, which is equal to his height. Each of the four fingers represents one of the four states the soul of a man experiences from time to time, namely, waking, dreaming, dreamless sleep and absolute Brahmanhood. The three folds of the cord are also symbolical. They represent the three Guṇas, reality, passion and darkness, out of which the whole universe is evolved. The care is taken that the twist of the thread must be upward. It was done, so that the Sattvaguṇa or the good quality of reality may predominate in a man, and so he may attain spiritual merits. The three cords remind the wearer that he has to pay off the Three Debts he owes to the ancient seers, the ancestors and the gods. The three cords are tied together by a knot called Brahmagranthi, which symbolises Brahmā, Viṣṇu and Śiva. Besides, extra knots are made in the cords to indicate the various Pravaras of a particular family.

The Āchārya, while investing the student with the Sacred Thread repeated an appropriate Mantra, asking for strength, long-life and illumination for the boy,[106] the boy looking, in the meanwhile,

---

103. Cf. Dr. A.S. Altekar, Education in Ancient India, Appendix, A.

104. कार्पासमुपवीतं स्याद्विप्रस्योर्ध्वं वृतं त्रिवृत् ।
शाणसूत्रमयं राज्ञो वैश्यस्याविकसूत्रजम् ॥ M.S. ii. 44.

105. कार्पासं चोपवीतं सर्वेषामिति । Paiṭhīnasi, quoted in V.M.S. vol. I. p. 415.

106. यज्ञोपवीतं परमं पवित्रं प्रजापतेर्यत्सहजं पुरस्तात् ।
आयुष्यमग्रं प्रतिमुञ्च शुभ्रं यज्ञोपवीतं बलमस्तु तेजः ॥ P.G.S. ii. 2. 13a.

towards the sun. A Brahmachārī can put on only one set of the Sacred Thread. A householder is given privilege to wear two, one for himself and one for his wife. There are different methods of wearing the Sacred Thread at different occasions. While performing an auspicious ceremony one should be Upavītī, that is, the Sacred Thread should hang from his left shoulder, at the performance of some inauspicious ceremony a man should be Prāchīnāvīti, that is, the Sacred Thread should hang from the right shoulder; and at times he is called Nivīti when the Sacred Thread is worn round the neck like a garland.[107]

(h) The Ajina. Then the Ajina or deer-skin was presented to the pupil. The word "Ajina" denotes generally the skin of an animal e.g. a gazelle,[108] as well as that of a goat.[109] The use of skins as cloth in ancient times is shown by the adjective "Clothed in skins."[110] (Ajina-vāsin), and the farriers' trade is mentioned.[111] The Maruts were also noted for wearing deer-skins.[112] The wild ascetics of a late Ṛgvedic hymn seem to be clad in skin.[113] The Ajina was first used as an upper garment. But, later on, when cotton cloth was supplied in its place, it was utilized for a seat. In early times the country was covered with forest and skins were found in abundance. But when forests were cleared, there became paucity of hide, and blanket was prescribed.[114] The ancient tradition was adhered to, though the skin was reduced to threads which is now represented by three strands fastened to the Sacred Thread at the time of the Upanayana Saṁskāra. Different kinds of skins were prescribed for different castes. The Pāraskara Gṛhyasūtra says, "The upper garment of a Brāhmaṇa should be an antelope skin; that of a Rājanya the skin of a spotted deer; that of a Vaiśya goats' or cows' skin; or if the prescribed sort of garment is not to be had, a cows' hide should be worn by all, because to that belongs the first place among all kinds of garments".[115] The cow's skin was

107. A परिशिष्ट quoted in V.M.S. vol. I. p. 423.

108. A.V. v. 21. 7.

109. Ś. Br. V. 2. 1. 21.

110. Ibid. iii. 9. 1. 12.

111. The Vājasaneya-Saṁhitā xxx. 15.

112. R.V. i. 166. 10.

113. Ibid. x. 136. 2.

114. सार्ववर्णिकः कम्बलश्च Āp. D.S. I.

115. P.G.S. ii. 5. 2.

easily available; that is why it was a general option for all. According to Viṣṇu tiger-skin was also worn by the Vedic student.[116] But it was a rarity. The skin was of a practical use in the forest life of early times. Because it was generally used by hermits and ascetics, it began to gather sanctity round it. When it became connected with the religious ceremony the writers on Dharma invested it with symbolism. The Gopatha-Brāhmaṇa says that the lovely deerskin was symbolical of holy lustre and intellectual and spiritual pre-eminence.[117] The student, while putting it on, was reminded that he should attain the spiritual and intellectual position of a Ṛṣi.

(i) The Staff. A staff[118] was given by the Āchārya to the student, who accepted with the verse, "My staff which fell down to the ground in the open air, that I take up again for the sake of long life, of holy lustre and of holiness." According to some authorities the scholar should grasp the staff with the verse that was recited while taking a staff at the time of entering on a long sacrifice. The latter prescription was based on the fact that studentship was regarded as a long sacrifice.[119] The Mānava-Gṛhyasūtra observes that really speaking, the student is a traveller on the long road of knowledge.[120] The staff was the symbol of a traveller and while accepting it, the student prayed that he may reach safely the end of his long and arduous journey.[121] One authority, however, remarks that the staff was the symbol of a watchman.[122] The student was armed with the staff and charged with the duty of protecting the sacred Vedas. According to some, the purpose of the staff was to protect the student not only from the human foes but from the demons and evil spirits as well.[123] Aparārka on the Yājñavalkya Smṛti[124] points out that the staff could also serve the purpose of making the student self-confident and self-reliant, when he went

116. मार्गवैयाघ्रवास्तानि चर्माणि। Viṣṇu quoted in V.M.S. vol. I. p. 413.

117. See ante p. 185. footnote 11.

118. P.G.S. ii. 2. 14.

119. दीर्घसत्रं वा एष उपैति यो ब्रह्मचर्यमुपैति। quoted by Harihara on P.G.S. ii. 2–14.

120. M.G.S. i. 22. 11.

121. Cf. Dr. A. S. Altekar, Education In Ancient India, Chap. I. pp. 25. 26.

122. V. G. S. 6.

123. P.G.S. ii. 6. 26.

124. Yāj. S. I. 29.

out in the forest for collecting sacred fuels, for tending the cattle of his guru or when he travelled in darkeness.

The type of the staff was determined by the caste of the student. The staff of a Brahman was of Palāśa wood, that of a Kṣattriya was of Udumbara wood and that of a Vaiśya was of Vilva wood.[125] Options, however, were allowed which were based on local fashion or the availability of a particular wood in the locality. But as the wood of a staff was not of a great consequence, so all could use all kinds of wood.[126] But some limit the staff to the sacrificial trees only.[127] The length of the staff was also fixed according to the Varṇa of the student. "The staff of the Brāhmaṇa measured up to his hair, that of the Kṣattriya up to his forehead and that of a Vaiśya up-to his nose."[128] Vaśiṣṭha[129] prescribes quite the reverse which shows that there was no real significance in the above distinction except the caste difference. Elegance of the staff was also taken into consideration. According to Gautama and Paithīnasi the staff should be unbroken, unscratched and with bark.[130] Manu says that it should be straight, without any scratch, fine-looking not causing uneasiness and not burnt by fire.[131] In some cases, even at present, all these rules relating the staff are respected, but in the majority of cases a very poor or nominal substitute for the staff is presented to the student. The reason is that, now-a-days, it has no practical utility, the initiate not being expected to go outside his home to a hermitage in the forest.

(j) Symbolical Performances. After the student was fully equipped with the necessities of a student life in ancient times, a series of symbolical acts followed before the Āchārya properly took the student in his charge. The first of them was that the teacher, with his joined hands, filled the students' joined hands with water

125. A.G.S. i. 19. 10.

126. सर्वे वा सर्वेषाम् । P.G.S. ii. 5. 28.

127. यज्ञियो वा सर्वेषाम् । G.D.S.

128. Ā.G.S. i. 19. 10.

129. V.D.S. quoted in V.M.S. vol. I. p. 436.

130. अपीडिता यूपवक्तास्सल्का इति । G.D.S.

131. ऋजवस्ते तु सर्वे स्युरव्रणाः सौम्यदर्शनाः ।
अनुद्वेगकराः नॄणां सत्वचोऽनग्निदूषिताः ॥ M.S. ii. 47.

with the verse, "Ye water." This was symbolical of purification.[131a] The student required sanctification before he could legitimatively learn the Gāyatrī mantra. Āśvalāyana says, "The teacher having uttered mantras pours water in the joined hands of the student, so that he may be purified to receive the Sāvitrī mantra."[132] Next, the teacher made the student look at the sun with "That eye etc."[133] The life of a student was a perfect discipline regulated to the minutest details. The sun represents the Cosmic Law which governs the whole universe. The student was asked to learn from the sun the observance of unswerving duty and discipline. Āśvalāyana, again observes; "The sun is a witness to all actions; he is the Lord of all vows, time, action and virtues; therefore he should be properly worshipped."[134]

(k) Touching the Heart. After this, the teacher touched the heart of the pupil reaching over his right shoulder with the words, "Into my will I take thy heart etc."[135] The same verse wás recited at the time of the marriage ceremonies also, with the only change of the deity, in that case being Prajāpati, while here it is Bṛhaspati. The "Lord of Prayers" or the "Presiding deity of Learning" was requested to unite the hearts of the Āchārya and the pupil. This prayer was intended to emphasize that relation between the teacher and the taught was not formal and mercenary but real and sacred. Realization of this fact was necessary. No progress in education was possible unless there was a complete harmony, a deep sympathy and a wholehearted communion between the guru and the initiate.

(l) Mounting the Stone. Then the student was asked to mount a stone with the words, "Tread on this stone; like a stone be firm. Tread the foes down; turn away the enemies."[136] According to the Mānava Gṛhyasūtra,[137] the student, by mounting a stone, was

---

131a. शुचित्वसिद्धये तस्य सावित्रीग्रहणो गुरुः।
अभिमंत्र्य यथावारि सिञ्चत्येव तदञ्जलौ॥ Áśvalāyanācārya quoted in V.M.S. vol. I. p. 426.

132. Ibid.

133. P.G.S. ii. 2. 17.

134. कर्मसाक्षिणमादित्यं तर्पयेत्तं यथोक्तवत्।
सर्वव्रतानां भगवान् सूर्योऽधिपतिरीश्वरः॥ Áśvalāyanācārya, quoted in V.M.S. vol. I. p. 427.

135. P.G.S. ii. 2. 18.

136. M.G.S. i. 22. 10.

137. Ibid. i. 22. 12.

asked to be steadfast in the pursuit of his studies. In the opinion of the Bhāradvāja Gṛhyasūtra,[138] however, stone was also symbolical of strength. The purpose of the rite was to make the student ada mantine in his physique and character. The stone delivered a good sermon to the student that the firmness of determination and strength of character are the most essential needs of a successful student career.

(m) Taking the Charge. Now the proper taking the charge of the student began.[139] The teacher seized the student's right hand and asked his name. The pupil replied, "I am N. N. Sir!" The teacher, again, enquired whose pupil he was, whereupon the student replied "Yours." The Āchārya correcting his answer said, "Indra's pupil art thou; Agni is thy teacher; I am thy teacher, N. N. !" Thus the teacher took the boy in his charge for education and protection. But thinking himself not omnipresent and all-powerful, he commended the student to the protection of gods and all creatures, that were requested to guard him every where. "To Prajāpati I give thee in charge. To the god Savitṛ I give thee in charge. To Heaven and Earth I give thee in charge. To all beings I give thee in charge for the sake of freedom from harm."[140]

(n) The Commandments. Then after a circumambulation of the fire, and offerings to it, the teacher, taking hold of the student, delivered the following commandments: "A student art thou. Take water. Keep silence. Put fuel on the fire. Take water."[141] This commandment is found as early as in the Śatapatha Brāhmaṇa[142] which, besides, offers some explanation of the text also. "Sip water. Water doubtless means ambrosia: Sip ambrosia is thus he tells him; do thy work: work doubtless means vigour; exert vigour is what he tells him; put on fuel: enkindle thy mind with fire, with holy lustre is what he thereby tells him; do not sleep: "do not die" is what he thereby says to him etc." The commandment was a practical advice as well as a symbolical performance.

(o) The Sāvitrī Mantra. Next, the most sacred Sāvitrī mantra was taught to the student.[143] If he could not follow it just on that

---

138. Bh. G.S. i. 8.

139. P.G.S. ii. 2. 19–22.

140. Ibid. ii. 2. 23.

141. ब्रह्मचार्यस्यपोशान कर्म कुरु मा दिवा सुषुप्था वाचं यच्छ समिधमाधे- ह्यपोशानेति । Ibid. ii. 3. 2.

142. xi. 5. 4.

143. P.G.S. ii. 3. 3; Ś.G.S. i. 21. 5.

day, it could be recited to the boy after one year, six months, twenty-four days, twelve days or three days.[144] The teacher, looking at the face of the child, uttered the Sāvitrī mantra, "Let us meditate on the most excellent light of the Creator (the Sun); May he gide our intellect."[145] The mantra was recited Pāda by Pāda, then hemistich by hemistich, and the third time the whole verse. To a Brahman the Āchārya recited the Sāvitrī mantra in the Gāyatrī metre, to a Rājanya in Triṣṭubha, and to a Vaiśya in Jagatī, or to persons of all castes in the Gāyatrī metre. The last option has now obtained universality. The teaching of the sacred mantra signalized the second birth of the child, as the teacher was regarded the father and Sāvitrī the mother of the child.[146] In early times the teacher himself was supposed to have conceived the child: "By laying his right hand on the pupil, the teacher becomes pregnant with him; In the third night he is born as a Brahman with the Sāvitrī."[147] The prayer was simple but significant. It was very appropriate to students whose prime business was to stimulate and develop their mind.

(p) The Sacred Fire. The rite of first enkindling and feeding of the sacred fire[148] was performed after the teaching of the Gāyatrī mantra. The verses uttered here were full of educational significance. The student wiped with his hand the ground round the fire with the formula. "Agni, glorious one, make me glorious. As thou glorious Agni, art glorious, thus, O glorious one, bring me to glory. As thou Agni are the preserver of the treasure of sacrifice for the gods, thus may I become the preserver of the treasure of the Vedas for men."[149] Then he put fuels on the fire with the prayer. "To Agni I have brought a piece of wood, to the great Jātavedas. As thou, Agni, are inflamed by wood, thus I am inflamed by life, insight, vigour. offspring, cattle, holy lustre....May my teacher be the father of living sons; May I be full of insight, not forgetful of what I have learnt; may I become full of glory and splendour, of holy lustre and enjoyer of food. Svāhā?"[150] The sacred fire was the symbol of Life and Light, for which the student strove. It was

144 Ibid.

145. तत्सवितुर्वरेण्यं भर्गो देवस्य धीमहि। धियो यो नः प्रचोदयात् ॥

146. तत्रास्य माता सावित्री पिता त्वाचार्य उच्यते। M.S. ii. 170.

147. Ś. Br. xi. 5. 4. 12.

148. P.G.S ii. 1–8.

149. Ibid. ii. 4. 2.

150. P.G.S. ii. 4 3

the centre of all religious activities of the Indo-Aryans. Its worship began in the student career and continued throughout his life.

(q) The Rounds for Alms. Then followed the student's going the rounds for alms.[151] This was the ceremonious beginning of what was going to be the chief means of his maintenance throughout his student career. On the day of the Upanayana he begged from only those who would not refuse, e.g., his mother and other relatives. The decorum required that a Brāhmaṇa student should beg addressing the woman whom he asks for alms with the word, "Lady" put at the beginning of his request; a Rājanya with the word "Lady" inserted in the middle; a Vaiśya with the word put at the end." It cannot be said how far the custom of begging was universal in ancient India. But the ceremony of begging emphasized on the student's mind the fact that, being a non-economic entity, he was dependent on the public charity and he should discharge his duties to society when he would become its earning member. Begging of alms, in early times if not universal, must have been common, at least, in the case of Brahman and other poor students, as it is still practised by poor Brahman students. But in later times, excepting some rare cases, it fell into disuse.

(r) Late Features. At present a few new features, unknown to the scriptures, have been introduced in the Upanayana Saṁskāra, which are located after the ceremonial begging. The student undertakes a mimic performance.[152] He enacts a comedy of going on educational mission to Benares or Kashmir. But he is persuaded by his maternal uncle or brother-in-law who allures him by promising a bride. What a tragedy of the educational ideal of the Upanayana Saṁskāra. The Samāvartan that was performed at completion of the studies, is now staged on the same day, simply for the emergency of child-marriage.

(s) Trirātra-vrata. After the initiation ceremonies were over, the student was required to observe three days' continence, which was called "Trirātra Vrata."[153] This continence might extend to twelve days or one year. It was the beginning of a rigorous training. He was not to eat saline food, he had to sleep on the ground, and he was forbidden to take meet and wine and to sleep in the day

151. Ibid. ii. 5. 1–8.

152. In ancient times educational journey of the student was a real one. See the Ś.G.S. ii. 8; A.G.S. iii. 10.

153. A.G.S. i. 22. 12. H.G.S. i. 8. 16.

time. At the end of the vow, the Medhājanana ritual was performed in order to evoke divine help in the sharpening of the intellect, memory and retaining power.[154] It was called Medhājanana, because by performing it one could get intellect fit to grasp the Vedic knowledge. Śaunaka says, "The Sun-born Goddess, the preserver of this world, Herself is Medhā. One who desires success in learning should worship her with a view to stimulate talent."[155] At present, the Upanayana having no educational purpose, these ancillary rites of educational significance have been dropped.

(t) The Dawn of a new Era. When the Upanayana was a living Saṁskāra performed at the beginning of the student career, it must have created a very impressive atmosphere. It marked the dawn of a new era in the life of the initiate. He was no more a child and was introduced to the life of perfect and stern discipline. The ceremony symbolized the fact that the student was a traveller, starting for the boundless realm of knowledge. To reach his destination, he was asked to be firm and steadfast, like a stone, in his determination. A complete harmony between him and his Āchārya was also essential. In his mission, the student was assured the help of all gods and creatures. The ideals before him were Indra, the lord of all gods, and Agni, the most brilliant element in the world, the one suggestive of power and position and the other indicative of life and light. If the student acted up to the symbolisms and suggestions of the Saṁskāra, he was bound to be a successful scholar and a fulfledged man, fit to share the responsibilities of the world.

---

154 Bh. G.S. i. 10.

155. या सावित्री जगद्धात्री सैव मेधा स्वरूपिणी।
मेधा प्रसिद्धये पूज्या विद्यासिद्धिमभीप्सिता॥ Śaunaka quoted in V.M.S. vol. I. p. 440.

3. THE VEDĀRAMBHA (THE BEGINNING OF THE VEDIC STUDY)

(i) *Introductory*

In the earliest enumeration of the Saṁskāras by Gautama,[1] the Vedārambha and the Godāna are not mentioned. Instead, he gives the four Vedic Vratas, "Catvāri Vedavratāni," which according to Āśvalāyana, were Mahānāmni, Mahāvratam, Upaniṣad and Godāna.[2] Besides, special rites were prescribed before the reading of a Veda or its branch.[3] Though these vratas were originally intended for all the twice-born, they were probably observed in the priestly families alone, because it were they who used to specialize in all the branches of the Vedas and the Vedic rituals. The non-Brahmans gradually gave up the practice of performing the Vedic vratas or vows. In course of time, the non-Vedic literature grew in extent and importance and came to be studied extensively by the Brahmans. The Vedic literature was less and less studied. So with the decline of the Vedic study these vratas began to pass out of vogue. They are not mentioned in the majority of the Gṛhyasūtras and the Dharmasūtras and are altogether passed over by the Smṛtis. But respect for the old tradition required that there should be one Saṁskāra that could take the place of the Vedic vows and mark the beginning of higher education. Thus the Vedārambha sprang on the ruins of the ancient Vedic vratas. This is the reason why the Vedārambha appeared so late in the list of the Saṁskāras. Vyāsa mentions it for the first time.[4]

(ii) *The Origin*

There was one more change in the history of the Saṁskāras which necessitated the existence of the Vedārambha as a separate Saṁskāra. In the beginning the Upanayana and the study of the

1. G.D.S. viii. 24.
2. प्रथमं स्यात्महानाम्नी द्वितीयं स्यान्महाव्रतम् ।
तृतीयं स्यादुपनिषद् गोदानाख्यं ततः परम् ॥ Āśvalāyana quoted in S.M. p. 63.
3. यच्छाखीयैस्तु संस्कारैः संस्कृतो ब्राह्मणो भवेत्
तच्छाखाध्ययनं कार्यमेवं न पतितो भवेत् ॥ Vasiṣṭha quoted in V.M.S. vol. I. p. 338.
4. Vy. S. i. 14.

Vedas began almost together. The former was a real going of the child to the house of the teacher and was immediately followed by studentship. The Vedic study was supposed to begin with the most sacred Gāyatrī mantra. But in later times, when Saṁskrit ceased to be a spoken language or a widely understood one the Upanayana became merely a bodily Saṁskāra. Then it was performed when the student had already begun the study of his vernacular, and the nominal Āchārya by whom the Saṁskāra was performed had no intention to take the student in his own charge. Therefore it was thought necessary to perform another Saṁskāra, besides the Upanayana, to mark the beginning of the Vedic Study.

(*iii*) *A New Saṁskāra*

The Saṁskāra, as already pointed out, is first mentioned in the Vyāsa Smṛti.[5] It differentiates the Vratādeśa (a new name of the Upanayana) from the Vedārambha. During the time of the author, the first had nothing to do with study, but the second was purely an educational Saṁskāra performed at the time when the student actually began his Vedic study. The later Paddhati-writers have recognized the distinction between the Upanayana and the Vedārambha and they insert the latter between the Upanayana and the Samāvartana.

(*iv*) *The Ceremonies*

For the performance of the Vedārambha Saṁskāra an auspicious day was fixed after the Upanayana. In the beginning, the Mātṛpūjā the Ābhyudayika Śrāddha and other preliminary ceremonies were performed. Then the teacher established the Laukika-Agni, invited the student and seated him on the Western side of the fire. After this, general offerings were made. If the Ṛigveda was to be begun, two āhutis of ghee were offered to the earth and Agni; if the Yajurveda, to Antarikṣa (the sky) and Vāyu; if the Sāmaveda, to Dyau and the sun; and if the Atharvaveda, to the quarters and the moon. If the study of all the Vedas began together, the above offerings were made together. Besides, Homa were offered to Brahman, Chhandas and Prajāpati. In the end, the teacher, having made gift of the Pūrṇapātra and Dakṣiṇā to the officiating Brahman, began the teaching of the Veda.[6]

---

5. Ibid.

6. The Gargapaddhati.

4. THE KEŚĀNTA OR THE GODĀNA (THE SHAVING OF BEARD)

(i) *Different Names and their Significance*

The Keśānta or the first shaving was one of the four Vedic Vratas.[1] When the first three vratas, that were closely connected with the Vedic Study, disappeared, the Keśānta separated and assumed an independent position, though it retained the ancient ceremonies. The existence of the Keśānta as a separate Saṁskāra seems to be older than that of the Vedārambha. The Gṛhyasūtras[2] describe the Keśānta with the Chūḍākaraṇa, but they nowhere mention the Vedārambha. Jātūkarṇya, an older writer than Vyāsa, enumerates the former but does not mention the latter.[3] It was regarded as a major Saṁskāra by Vyāsa who includes it in the list of the famous sixteen Saṁskāras.[4] The question may rise in one's mind why the Keśānta did not meet the same fate as the other Vedic Vratas met. The reason appears thus. This Saṁskāra had an advantage over its colleagues. While the first three Vratas were dependent, for their life, on the Vedic study, it was essentially connected with the body and conduct of the student. When the Vedic literature ceased to form the general curriculum of studies, the first three Vratas fell into discuse. But the Keśānta still signalized the natural change that took place in the life of the student. Even when the Saṁskāras became mere ceremonies bereft of their original purpose, the Keśānta did not suffer very much.

(ii) *The Origin and Early History*

The Keśānta, as its very name suggests, was a Sáṁskāra which consecrated the first shaving of the student's beard. It was called Godāna also, because it was characterized by the gift of a cow to the teacher and gifts to the barber. This Saṁskāra was performed at the age of sixteen and marked the arrival of youth when the student was no more a boy, and beard and moustaches appeared

---

1. Āśvalāyana quoted in S.M. p. 63.
2. A.G.S. i. 18; P.G.S. ii. 1–3;. Ś.G.S. i. 28. 18; G.G.S. iii. 1; H.G.S. ii. 6. 16; Āp. G.S. 12; Kh. G.S. ii. 5. 1.
3. मौञ्जीव्रतानि गोदानसमावर्तविवाहकाः । quoted in V.M.S. vol I. संस्कारोद्देश.
4. Vy. S. i. 14.

on his face.[5] The consciousness of manhood dawned upon the young man. He required a greater watchfulness over his youthful impulses. Hence it was thought necessary that the student should be reminded once more of his vows of Brahmacharya. He was, after shaving the beard and moustaches, required to take the vow of Brahmacharya anew and to live the life of strict continence for one year.

(iii) *Later History and Confusion*

During the mediaeval and subsequent times confusion entered the Hindu religion and degeneration set in every department of life. When early marriage became common, the Keśānta began to be considered as marking the end of Brahmacharya. In the Sūtra period the shortest period of Brahmacharya was twelve years. According to this calculation, the student career ended at the age of eighteen. But this was not the general custom. Only those students, who were in sure need of the family, took leave of their gurus at this early age. Later on, however, owing to the emergency of child-marriage, it became a common practice to close the Brahmacharya period with the Keśānta or Godāna. The Bhāradvāja and the Vārāha Gṛhyasūtras, which were written subsequent to the beginning of the Christian era. had already begun to prescribe the general option that "in the opinion of some, one could close his Brahmacharya with the Godāna ceremony."[6] The supporters of early marriage began to argue that the termination of Brahmacharya at sixteen was in no way against the Śāstric rule, as if the Upanayana was performed at the age of five, one could get twelve years for the study of the Vedas.[7] Thus what was in the beginning a concession, later on became privilege and right of the people, but certainly for the worse.

As a matter of fact, the Keśānta or Godāna had nothing to do with the termination of Brahmacharya. The Samāvartana was to mark the close of the student life. Both the Saṁskāras were confounded deliberately in order to enable the boy to marry without finishing his complete course of studies. Confusion became more confounded for ordinary men owing to the fact that shaving formed the common element in both the Saṁskāras.

---

5. A.G.S. i. 18; M.S. ii. 65.

6. आगोदानकर्मणः (ब्रह्मचर्यम्) इत्येके। Bh. G.S. i. 9; V.G.S. 9.

7. Śrīnivāsa on J.G.S. i. 18.

(iv) Ceremonies

As already said, the ceremony was performed at the age of sixteen. The procedure followed and the mantras recited at this Saṁskāra were quite the same as adopted in the chauḍaSaṁskāra. The only diflerence was that in it beard and moustaches were shaved instead of head. Just as in the Chūḍākaraṇa, hair of the beard, head, nails were thrown into water. The student, then, offered a cow to the teacher. At the end of the ceremony he observed a vow of silence and led a life of austere discipline for full one year.

5. THE SAMĀVARTANA OR SNĀNA (END OF STUDENTSHIP)

(i) Introductory

This Saṁskāra was performed at the close of the Brahmacharya period and it marked the termination of the student life. Samāvartana means "returning home from the house of the guru."[1] It was called Snāna also because bathing formed the most prominent item of the Saṁskāra. According to some anthropologists, bathing was meant for washing away divinity from the student.[2] During his Brahmacharya period. he was living in divine contact and he himself had some divine halo round him. So, before he returned to the ordinary world, he had to put off divine influence, otherwise he would pollute divine attributes and thereby incur divine displeasure. The early Indian writers also regarded Brahmacharya as a long sacrifice.[3] Therefore, just as at the end of a sacrifice the sacrificial bath or Avabhṛtha was taken by the sacrificer, so the long sacrifice of Brahmacharya also required that the student should have a bath at its end. But there was one more idea associated with bathing in the Samāvartana Saṁskāra, which later on became the most prominent. In the Sanskrit literature learning was compared to an ocean, and one who possessed great learning was supposed to have crossed that ocean. Naturally, a student, who had completed his course of studies, was regarded as a person who had crossed the ocean of learning. He was called a Vidyāsnātaka (one who has bathed in learning) and a Vratasnātaka (one who has bathed in vows).[4] Thus the ceremonial bath at the end of the student career symbolized the crossing of the ocean of learning by the student.

(ii) Importance

The close of one's student career was a very momentus period in one's life. One had to make a choice between the two paths of life. One of them was to get oneself married and plunge into the busy

---

1. तत्र समावर्तनं नाम वेदाध्ययनानन्तरं गुरुकुलात् स्वगृहागमनम्।
V.M.S. vol. I. p. 564.

2. R. H. Nassau, Feticshism in West Africa, p. 212.

3. दीर्घसत्रं वा एष उपैति यो ब्रह्मचर्यमुपैति। Quoted by Gadādhara on the P.G.S. ii. 2. 15.

4. P.G.S. ii. 5. 32. 36.

life of the world, sharing its full responsiblities. The other was that of retirement, that is, to keep off from the turmoil of the world and to lead a life of detachment, both physical and mental. Those students who chose the first path were called "Upakurvāṇa", and those who selected the second path were known as "Naiṣṭhika."[5] The Upakurvāṇas returned from their gurukulas and became householders. The Naiṣṭhikas did not leave their teacher and lived in the service of their masters in quest of supreme knowledge.[6] According to Viṣṇu, some people were compulsorily required to lead the life of a Brahmachāri on physical grounds. They were the hump-backed, the blind by birth, the impotent, the lame and the diseased.[7] They did not perform their Samāvartana, because Vivāha was not possible in their case.

(iii) *The Normal Course*

But the majority of students followed the normal course of life and preferred the life of a householder to that of a celebate one. All the authorities on Dharmaśāstra recommend that one should pass through all the four Āśramas in order. Manu says, "The different orders, Brahmacharya, Gārhasthya, Vānaprastha and Sannyāsa spring from the life of a householder. The four Āśramas followed in order, according to the rules of the Śāstras, bring a man to the supreme state of life."[8]

(iv) *Three Types of Snātakas*

This Saṁskāra was originally performed in the case of those, who had finished their entire course of studies and observed all the Vratas. Those, who simply memorized the texts of the Vedas, without understanding the meaning and without following the rules of conduct prescribed for a Brahmachāri, were excluded from the right of performance.[9] Thus in the beginning the Samāvartana was a ceremony corresponding to modern convocation function. Only those who have

---

5. Yāj. S. I. 49.

6. यदि त्वात्यन्तिको वासो रोचेतास्य गुरोः कुले।
युक्तः परिचरेदेनमाशरीरविमोक्षणात् ॥ M.S. ii. 243.

7. कुब्जवामनजात्यन्धक्लीबपङ्गवार्तरोगिणाम् ।
व्रतचर्या भवेत्तेषां यावज्जीवमनंशतः ॥ Viṣṇu quoted in S.M. p. 62.

8. M.S. Ibid.

9. अन्यो वेदपाठी न तस्य स्नानम् । M.G.S. i. 2. 3.

passed their examinations are at present admitted to the convocation: only those who had finished their education were allowed to take their bath. But in course of time this rule seems to be relaxed. In the opinion of a large number of the Gṛhyasūtras there were three types of Snātakas.[10] The first type was that of the Vidyāsnātakas, who had completed their entire course of studies but not the full term of Brahmacharya. The second type consisted of the Vratasnātakas, who had observed all the vows and spent the full period of Brahmacharya at the house of the guru but had not finished the full course of studies. The third type was constituted by the best students, who had finished their full course of studies and observed all the vows. They were called the Ubhaya-Snātakas.

(v) A pass-port to Marriage

Later on, when the Upanayana lost its educational significance, the original purpose of this Saṁskāra was also lost sight of and it came to be regarded, more or less, a bodily Saṁskāra, a sort of license for marriage. This condition obtained when early marriage became prevalent in the country. Because marriage could not take place before the Samāvartana, it must be performed some time before that. First, the convenient time found for it was that of the Keśānta ceremony, which also resembled it in some details, e.g., in shaving and bathing.[11] But subsequently, the Keśānta too became an insignificant Saṁskāra; so the Samāvartana came to be combined with the Upanayana. At present, in the majority of cases, both the Saṁskāras are performed together. What a mockery of fate! The education of a child was supposed to be complete before it commenced. Another ridiculous result also followed from the ignorance about the real nature of the Samāvartana. In the beginning, it was performed when the education of the youth was over; mariage usually followed but by no means immediately. In later times, the theory became current that one should not remain without an Āśrama even for a single moment.[12] If a Snataka was not immediately married, he would incur sin by spending some days without any particular Āśrama. In mediaeval times it came to be advocated that the Samāvartana should be performed when the marriage of the youth was already settled. So it takes place one day before the marriage, possibly with the Haridrā ceremony.

---

10. त्रयः स्नातका भवन्ति विद्यास्नातको व्रतस्नातको विद्याव्रतस्नातक इति।
P.G.S. ii. 5. 33.

11. See ante p. 247.

12. अनाश्रमी न तिष्ठेत्तु क्षणमेकमपि द्विजः।
आश्रमेण विना तिष्ठन्प्रायश्चित्तीयते हि सः॥ D.S. i. 10.

(vi) *The Age*

At what period after the Upanayana, the Samāvartana-Saṁskāra should be performed was a problem to be considered.[13] The longest period of Brahmacharya was forty-eight years, allowing twelve years for the study of each Veda. The smaller periods stopped at thirty-six, Twenty-four and eighteen according to the circumstances of the student and his parents. The last but one period was the most common type of Brahmacharya and in the majority of cases education finished at twentyfour. The mediaeval writers, however, began to favour the last period in order to enable a boy to marry earlier. But at present there is no time limit. The Vedas have become a sealed book, there is no fixed course of education and even ordinary literacy has become a luxury. The Samāvartana Saṁskāra is now drowned into insignificance and is incorporated either in the Upanayana or the Vivāha ceremonies.

(vii) *The Permission of the Teacher*

Before the student took his bath, he had to discharge a very important duty. He asked the permission of his master to end his student career and satisfied him with the guru-dakṣiṇā or tuition fees.[14] Anujñā or permission was regarded necessary, because it certified the Snātaka that he was a fit person in learning, habit and character for a married life. Manu says, "Being permitted by the guru, one should perform his Samāvartana and marry a woman etc."[15] Up to this time the student did not pay any thing to the Āchārya.[16] So, when he was going to leave him, he was expected in all propriety, to pay him according to his means, in the form of fees. The teacher should be given earth, gold, cow, horse, umbrella, shoes, clothes, fruits and vegetables.[17] According to Vyāsa, only cows should be given in fees.[18] The services rendered by the teacher to the student were highly respected and none could pay too much for them. "Even the earth contain-

13. P.G.S. ii. 6. 2-3.

14. विद्यान्ते गुरुमर्थेन निमन्त्र्य कृतानुज्ञानस्य वा स्नानमिति। A.G.S. iii. 8.

15. गुरुणानुमतः स्नात्वा समावृत्तो यथाविधि।
उद्वहेत द्विजो भार्यां सवर्णां लक्षणान्विताम्। M.S. iii. 4.

16. Ibid. ii. 245.

17. Ibid. ii. 246.

18. स्नायीत गुर्वनुज्ञातो दत्वाऽस्मै दक्षिणां हि गाम्। Quoted in V.M.S. vol. I. p 565.

ing seven continents was not sufficient for the guru-dakṣiṇā."[19] "There is no object on this earth by giving which one can free himself from the debt of even a teacher who teaches a single letter."[20] If one could not pay anything in the form of money or land etc. he should at least, go to the teacher and formally take his permission. In such cases the teacher used to say, "My child, enough with money! I am satisfied with thy merits."[21]

(*viii*) *The Ceremonies and their Significance*

When the preliminary considerations were disposed of, an auspicious day was fixed for the performance of the Saṁskāra. The ceremonies opened with a very strange procedure. The student was required to shut himself up in a room throughout the morning. According to the Bhāradvāja Gṛhyasūtra, it was done, so that the sun may not be insulted by the superior lustre of the Snātaka, as the former shines only with the light borrowed from the latter.[22] At the midday the student came out of the room, embraced the feet of his teacher and paid his last tribute to the Vedic fire by putting some fuel on it. Eight vessels full of water were kept there. The number eight indicated the eight quarters of the earth and suggested the idea of honour and praise being showered on the student from all over the earth. Then the student drew water out of one vessel with the words, "The fires that dwell in the waters, the fire that must be hidden, the fire which must be covered, the ray of light, the fire which kills the mind, the unbearing one, the pain causing one, the destroyer of the body, the fire which kills the organs, these I leave behind. The shining one that I seize here.... Therewith I besprinkle for the sake of prosperity, of glory, of holiness, of holy luster."[23] With other appropriate verses he bathed from other vessels. The body of a student was heated with the fire of austerity and penance, hence for the comfortable life of a householder it required a cooling influence, which was symbolised by bathing and indicated by the verses associated with it.

---

19. सप्तद्वीपवती भूमिर्दक्षिणार्थं न कल्पते। तापनीय श्रुति, Ibid.
20. एकमप्यक्षरं यस्तु गुरुः शिष्ये निवेदयेत्।
    पृथिव्यां नास्ति तद्द्रव्यं यद्दत्त्वा त्वनृणो भवेत्॥ लघुहारीत ibid.
21. अलमर्थेन मे वत्स त्वद्गुणैरस्मि तोषितः। संग्रह ibid.
22. एतदहः स्नातानां ह वा एष एतत्तेजसा तपति तस्मादेनमेतदहर्नाभितप्रेत्।
    Bh. G.S. ii. 1. 8.
23. P.G.S. ii. 6. 8–10.

After the grand bath the student cast off his entire out-fit, e.g. the mekhalā, the deerskin, the staff etc. into water and put on a new loin cloth. Having eaten some curd and sesame he cut off his beard, lock of hair, nails, and cleansed his teeth with an Udumbara tree branch with the verse," Array yourself for food. Here has come King Soma; he will purify my mouth with glory and fortune."[24] The student had practised continence both in food and speech. Now he was going to prepare for a fuller and more active life of the world. At the time of the Samāvartana, the austere life of a student was over, and many comforts and luxuries of life denied to him during his Brahmacharya, were presented to him by the Āchārya. First, he gave the student a bath with fragrant water.[25] Then ointment was applied to different organs of the student and a wish was expressed for the gratification of senses, "Satiate my up-breathing and down breathing; satiate my eyes; satiate my ears."[26] The student, then, put on new garments which had not yet been washed or soaked in dye and received flowers and garlands. Ornaments, collyrium, earrings, turban, umbrella, shoes and mirror, the use of which was forbidden to the student, were officially offered to him. A bamboo staff was also given to the scholar for safety in life. Well-to-do guardians were expected to furnish a double set of the above articles, one for the teacher and the other for the student.[27]

In the case of a Brahman student, according to some, a Homa was performed and the hope was expressed that the Snātaka would get plenty of students to teach.[27a] The teacher, then, offered to the student the Madhupark, indicating a great respect, for it was reserved for a few, e.g., a king, a teacher, a son-in-law etc.[28]

Dressed in his new attires, the Snātaka would proceed to the nearest assembly of the learned in a chariot or on an elephant.[29] There he was introduced as a competent scholar by his teacher. But according to other authorities, after the ceremony was over, all day

24. P.G.S. ii. 6. 12.

25. Ibid. ii. 6. 13; G.G.S. iii. 4. 11; Kh. G.S. iii. 1. 9.

26. Ibid.

27. A.G.S. iii. 8.

27a. B.G.S. ii. 6

28. षडर्घ्या भवन्ति। आचार्य ऋत्विग्वैवाह्यो राजा प्रियः स्नातक इति।
P.G.S. i. 3. 1-2.

29 Ap. G.S. i. 11. 5; D.G.S. iii. 1. 26.

the Snātaka kept away from the sun-shine and remained silent till the stars appeared. Then he went east or northwards, paid reverence to the quarters, and the stars and the moon, conversed with friends and went to where he expected argha gift which was regarded appropriate to a Snātaka immediately after the bath.[30]

(ix) *The Respect paid to the Snātaka*

A survey of the Samāvartana ceremonies shows how high was the respect in which scholars, who had completed their education, were held by society in ancient India. A Brāhmaṇa passage quoted in the Gṛhyasūtras asserts that the Snātaka was a powerful personality.[31]

(x) *An Absurd Simplification*

At present, the whole caremonies have been reduced to an absurd simplicity. The Samāvartana is performed either with the Upanayana or the Vivāha in hurry and the only remnants of the detailed procedure are the bath and the decoration of the person, and these also without proper Vedic mantras.

30. G.G.S. iii. 5. 21.

31. महद्वै एतद्भूतं यः स्नातकः। A.G.S. iii. 9. 8.

CHAPTER VIII

THE VIVĀHA (MARRIAGE CEREMONIES)

(i) *The Importance of Marriage*

The Vivāha is the most important of all the Hindu Saṁskāras. The Gṛhyasūtras generally begin with it, because it is the origin and centre of all domestic sacrifices. They presuppose that every man, in his normal conditions, is expected to marry and run a home. Even before them, in the Vedic period, to which only a few of the Saṁskāras can be traced back in their ceremonial form, the marriage ceremonies were developed and they have found literary expression in the Ṛgveda[1] and the Atharvaveda.[2] A sweet home, a lady love and fondlings in the house—these were coveted objects for the Vedic Aryans. Therefore, marriage received great importance even in early times. When religious consciousness developed, marriage was not only a social necessity but became a religious duty encumbent upon every individual. Marriage was regarded as a sacrifice[3] and one who did not enter the married life was called "one without sacrifice," a contemptible term, indeed, for the Vedic Hindus. The Taittirīya Brāhmaṇa says, "He, indeed, is without sacrifice who has got no wife." It again adds,[4] "He is himself a half man, the second half is wife." When the theory of Three Debts[5] evolved, marriage gained even greater importance and sanctity, as it was through marriage that one could pay off one's ancestral debt, by producing children.

During the Upaniṣadic times, the Āśrama theory was established. The advocates of this theory maintained that one should proceed Āśrama by Āśrama, that is, a man should first live the life of a student, then he should enter the married life, after this he should lead a retired life and in the last Āśrama he should give up all worldly attachments and become a religious wanderer. The married life was regarded essential for the growth of personality and no time of antipathy was attached to it.

---

1. x. 85.
2. xiv. 1. 2.
3. अयज्ञो वा एष योऽपत्नीकः । T. Br. ii. 2. 2. 6.
4. अथो अर्द्धो वा एव आत्मनः यत्पत्नीः । ibid. ii. 9. 4. 7.
5. जायमानो वै ब्राह्मणस्त्रिभिर्ऋणवान् जायते ब्रह्मचर्येण ऋषिभ्यो यज्ञेन देवेभ्यः प्रजया पितृभ्यः। T.S. vi. 3. 10. 5,

In the time of the Smṛtis the Āśrama system was believed to be divinely ordained, and it was thought to be the sacred duty of every person to respect it. From the Gṛhyasūtras and the Dharmasūtras we learn that the number of Naiṣṭhika Brahmachāris was very much limited and majority of young men accepted the life of the householder. The Smṛtis entirely endorse the Āśrama system and emphatically prescribe that a man should marry after his student life. Manu[6] enjoins, "Having spent the first fourth part of his life in the house of his guru, the second fourth in his own house with his wife, the third part in forests, one should take Sanyāsa in the fourth part, casting away every worldly tie." Hārīta[7] is of the same opinion: "One who spends his life in the said manner, having conquered all the worlds, attains the world of Brahmā." According to Dakṣa,[8] the order of the first three Āśramas cannot be changed. None is more sinful than one who trangresses this rule. The Smṛtis highly praise the life of a householder. They call it the best Āśrama and regard it as the centre and prop of the whole social structure. "Just as all creatures exist depending on air, so do all he Āśramas depend upon the householder. Because the householder supports the three orders by means of knowledge and food, so his order is the highest. One who longs for imperishable heaven and happiness in this world, should uphold the Gṛhastha-Āśrama. . . ."[9] Quite in keeping with these ideas, a man who did not marry was held in low scale. An anonymous quotation by Aparārka on Yajñavalkya[10] says, "O, King, a man, he may be a Brāhmaṇa, Kṣattriya, a Vaiśya or a Śūdra, who is without a wife, is not fit for religious act."

---

6. चतुर्थमायुषो भागं वसित्वाद्यं गुरोः कुले।
द्वितीयमायुषो भागं कृतदारो गृहे वसेत् ॥
वनेषु च विहृत्यैवं तृतीयं भागमायुषः।
चतुर्थमायुषो भागं त्यक्त्वा सङ्गान्परिव्रजेत् ॥ M.S. iv. 1, 2.

7. अनेन विधिना यो हि आश्रमानुपसेवते।
स सर्वलोकान्निर्जित्य ब्रह्मलोकाय कल्पते ॥ Quoted in S.M. p. 64.

8. त्रयाणामानुलोम्यं स्यात्प्रातिलोम्यं न विद्यते।
प्रातिलोम्येन यो याति न तस्मात्पापकृत्तरः ॥ D.S. i. 12.

9. यथा वायुं समाश्रित्य वर्तन्ते सर्वजन्तवः।
तथा गृहस्थमाश्रित्य वर्त्तन्ते सर्वआश्रमाः ॥ etc. M.S. iii. 77–79.

10. पत्नीधमर्थिकामानां कारणं प्रवरं स्मृतम्।
अपत्नीको नरो भूप कर्मयोग्यो न जायते।
ब्राह्मणः क्षत्रियो वाऽपि वैश्यः शूद्रोऽपि वा नृपः ॥ 1. 51.

For several reasons marriage was held in high esteem among ancient peoples. Doubtless, in rude pastoral, and even agricultural times, economic and social causes were at the basis of this esteem. Large family was a blessing. Marriage was a family affair rather than a personal one; indeed the generation of offspring was the supreme motive of every union to the end that a man's house or family might not die out. Then religious motives were equally operative in assigning such a great regard to marriage. Worship of ancestors and gods was dependent on progeny, which could be obtained only through marriage. In later development of Hinduism, the last idea became more prominent than the social and economic ones.

Other ancient peoples also held marriage in high esteem. Among the people of Israel it was respected for the same reasons as among the Hindus.[11] "Later on in the age of the Messianic prophesies, marriage gained an added sanctity from the precious possibility that the fruit of the union might be the promised messiah of the Jews, its long desired saviour from oppression." In Greece also marriage was highly respected and looked upon as a sacred ceremony.[12] "By means of such union family was perpetuated, the inheritance of property provided for and the worship of ancestral gods continued. Therefore, celebacy was regarded a serious offence, a crime against the household gods. So strong was the feeling in Athens that a law was enacted enjoining the first magistrate of the City to see to it that no family became extinct."[13] And in Sparta Plutarch tells us that a man who did not marry lost certain rights and was not treated by younger men with that respect so scrupulously accorded by Spartan youths to their elders.[14] Like ancient peoples the Romans looked upon marriage as a sacred and important act and stamped celebacy with public disapproval, since it was disadvantageous alike to the state, which needed supporters, and to the family which needed sons to continue its domestic worship.

But a contrast is presented by the Christian views regarding marriage. There can be no reasonable doubt that the view of the early Christian Fathers concerning the marriage bond was profoundly influenced by the opinions of St. Paul. The doctrines of this

11. Willystine Goodsell, Ph.D., A History of The Family As A Social And Educational Institution, pp. 58. ff.

12. Ibid. pp. 86 ff.

13. Ibid.

14. Life of Lycurgus, Bohn's Classical Library, vol. 1. p. 81.

great leader are so familiar that only a brief reference need be made to a few of the more influential of them. He writes: "Nevertheless, to avoid fornication let every man have his own wife, and every woman have her own husband."[15] But this doubtful sanction is promptly followed by the words: "But I speak this by permission and not of commandment.... For I would that all men were as myself.... I say therefore to the unmarried and widows, it is good for them if they abide even as I. But if they cannot content, let them marry; for it is better to marry than to burn."[16] There is no tint in Paul's writing, nor does it clearly appear in the works of the later Church Fathers that marriage is a spiritual as well as a physical union and that the latter should be impossible without the former. "Obviously these pronouncements show scant appreciation of the uplifting and strengthening influence of a true marriage, of its power to quicken and deepen all worthy emotions. Thus it is that the reading of the marital views of the later Church Fathers is a distasteful task from which the student willingly turns."[16a] But it should be noted that this was a reaction against the corrupt Roman society where sexual relations were very loose and which led to the physical as well as spiritual downfall of the Romans.

(ii) *The Origin*

Such an important occasion as marriage naturally attracted much attention of the people and many and various ceremonies gathered round it. But for fully understanding the development of the marriage ceremonies it is necessary to know how and under what circumstances they arose. The circumstances, in which the institution of marriage originated, conditioned the nature of marriage rituals. The word "marriage" has a reference to "a union of the male and female which does not cease with the act of procreation but persists after the birth of offspring until the young are capable of supplying their own needs."[17] It is evident that sexual instinct itself could not have brought about permanent relationship between man and woman. Nor that the aboriginal man had that glimmering conception of that ideal love which to-day binds a pair together in

15. 1. Cor. vii. 2.

16. Ibid. vii. 7-8.

16a. Willystine Goodsell. A History of the Family as A Social and Educational Institution, pp. 80. ff.

17. Ibid. p. 6.

the strongest of human ties. The weakness of the savage female also was not responsible for marriage tie, because she was as strong and capable of self-defence as the male. The source of marriage is to be sought for elsewhere. We can look for it in the utter helplessness of the new-born offspring and the need of both the mother and the young for protection and food during a varying period of time. So it appears that marriage has its source in the family, rather than the family in marriage, and the very roots of the permanent union of the sexes are found in parental duties. It was the natural desire of woman for sufficient protection during the critical period of her confinement and for adequate protection of the child in its helpless state of infancy that drove her to select a permanent companion in life. In this selection she was very cautious, as she fully considered the fitness of the man and arrived at a mutual undestanding before she gave herself away to him. The love making and other means of enticement were there that helped in effecting the union.[17a] The desire for a son, the protection of wife and children, the need of running a home and the ideal of domestic felicity are duly reflected in the marriage ceremonies.

(iii) Pre-marital Stage

Now we have to consider the evolution of marirage in ancient periods of Indian history, though the marriage ceremonies of the Hindus presuppose a monogamous union. The Ṛgvedic society emerges with a well established home which could not have been possible in the pre-marital stage of sexual relation. There is no instance of promiscuity proper in the Vedic literature. The only reference to it is found in the Mahābhārata.[18] There it is stated that women were free in early primitive times and they could have sexual relation with any body they liked, even though they were married. This revolting custom, however, was abolished by Śvetaketu, son of Uddālaka. This story, at most, proves that the Aryans had passed through a stage of society when such intercourse was tolerated in society. Temporary sexual relations also are not to be found either in the Vedas or in the Gṛhyasūtras. The marriage as described in them was meant to be regular and permanent. The only instance of marriage by periodical contract is supplied in the story of Urvaśī and Purūravas in the Ṛgveda.[19] This form of marriage, however,

17a. A. C. Das Ṛgvedic Culture.

18. अनावृताः किल पुरा स्त्रिय आसन्वराननेे।
कामाचारविहारिण्यः स्वतन्त्राश्चारुहासिनि ।। i. 128.

19. X. 59.

was not current in the Ṛgvedic times and must have been a recollection of ancient times, when temporary marriages were in vogue.

(iv) Marriage Proper.

It is a mistake to suppose that sexual relation in the early society was promiscuous. The great anthropologists with their vast and intimate knowledge of primitive culture have arrived at the conclusion that the sexual relation between man and woman in ancient times was not promiscuous, Westermarck remarks: 'It is not of course impossible that among some peoples intercourse between the sexes may have been almost promiscuous. But there is not a shred of genuine evidence for the notion that promiscuity even formed a general stage in the history of mankind.... Although polygamy occurs among most existing peoples, and polyandry among some, monogamy is by far the most common from of human marriage. It was so among the ancient peoples of whom we have any direct knowledge. Monogamy is the form which is generally recognized and permitted. The great majority of peoples are, as a rule, monogamus, and other forms of marriages are usually modified in a monogamous direction."[20] Almost the same observations are made by Howard[21] on the topic: "In a progressive society monogamy is the natural and usual form of marriage. Other forms of marriage are degradation or retrogression to the primitive conditions. Promiscuity never creates the home, nor engenders those noble sentiments of self-sacrifice and self-denial that have helped to uplift the human race.' The Vedic hymns and the Gṛhyasūtras celebrate a regular marriage for a life-long companionship. The Hindu Saṁskāras recognize the fulfiedged marriage bereft of savage waywardness on the part of man and woman.

(v) The Forms of Marriage

After we have considered the general state of sexual relation, we have to see how a young man and a young woman were united to lead the life of a householder. The Smṛtis[22] have recognized eight methods through which it was done. These are Brāhma, Daiva, Ārṣa, Prājāpatya, Āsura, Gāndharva, Rākṣasa and Paiśācha. Though

20. History of Human Marriage, pp. 133. 149.

21. History of Matrimonial Institution, pp. 90, 91.

22. ब्राह्मो दैवस्तथा आर्षः प्राजापत्यस्तथासुरः ।
गान्धर्वो राक्षसश्चैव पैशाचस्त्वष्टमोऽधमः ॥ M.S. iii. 21; Yaj. S. I. 58–61.

many of these methods can be traced back to the Vedic period, they have not been mentiond as such in the per-Sūtra literature. To the majority of the Gṛhyasūtras the eight methods are unknown. The Mānava Gṛhyasūtra[23] refers to the Brāhma and Śulka (Āsura) only. So does the Vārāha. The Āśvalāyana[24] is the only Gṛhyasūtra that mentions all the eight methods. The omission, however, does not mean that these methods were not current before, or even during, the composition of the Gṛhyasūtras. They were, more or less, a social problem beyond the proper scope of the ritual literature When every thing was settled about marriage, the particular rite was required to solemnize it.

The Smṛtis have divided the eight methods into two groups, Praśasta or approved and Apraśasta or disapproved.[25] The first four are Praśasta, the rest are Apraśasta. The first four methods were regarded praiseworthy, among which the first was the best, the fifth and the sixth were tolerated and the last two were forbidden. But all of them were legalized. At present the only two forms, Brāhma and Āsura are recognized. The more objectionable the method the more primitive it was though some of them were current side by side. They will be dealt with in their ascending order.

(vi) The Historical Growth of Eight Forms

(a) Paiśācha. The least approved method was Paiśācha.[26] According to it the bridegroom fraudulently got possession of the person of the girl, and it was, therefore, characterized as the basest of all methods. In the opinion of the Āśvalāyana-Gṛhyasūtra, carrying off a girl, who was either sleepy, intoxicated or unconscious was called Paiśācha. The capture of the girl was common with the Rākṣasa method, but unconsciousness on the part of the girl and her guardians gave it a different form. Gautama and Viṣṇu define it as "Cohabiting with a girl who is unconscious, sleepy or intoxicated." Manu[26'] defines: "When a man cohabits with a girl in loneliness when she is sleepy, mad or intoxicated, it is called the Paiśācha method." Yājñavalkya calls a marriage Paiśācha

23. M.G.S. i. 7. 12.

24. A.G.S. i. 6.

25. M.S. iii. 24. 25.

26. पैशाचश्चाष्टमोऽधमः । M.S. iii. 21.

26. सुप्तां मत्तां प्रमत्तां वा रहो यत्रोपगच्छति ।
स पापिष्ठो विवाहानां पैशाचश्चाष्टमोऽधमः ।। ibid. iii. 34.

when a girl is married through fraud. Devala gives a similar definition. The Paiśācha was the most uncivilized and barbarous method through which marriage could be effected. In it the bride was ravished then and there, a revolting event indeed. It was prevalent in primitive savage tribes, later on very rarely repeated and ultimately disapproved altogether.

(b) Rākṣasa. The next method in ascending order was Rākṣasa[27] According to Manu[27a] "Capture of a girl by force while she is crying and weeping, having killed, scattered and injured her relatives is called Rākṣasa-Vivāha." In this method the bridegroom did not wait for the consent of the father or of the girl herself, but took her away by force. This method was prevalent in ancient warring tribes and the captive women were enjoyed as war booties. The definition given by Manu pictures a scene of battle. Viṣṇu[28] and Yājñavalkya[29] actually say that it arose from war.

In the opinion of some scholars it is the oldest method of marriage, which was prevalent among all the primitive peoples. They see the semblance of the original war in the marriage procession of the present time. They say that this is proved by many procedures adopted in the marriage ceremonies among savage and half-civilized tribes of to-day. For example, in India also, many simulated farces of fights and capture are performed at the time of marriage in the jungle tribes. Among the Gonds, the bridegroom pursues the bride who poses to run away before the nuptials. In Bihar, among the Birhols, the bridegroom captures the running bride.

The above view presupposes a regular marriage from outside. It is very doubtful, however, whether any people habitually secured wives from without their tribe. The supposition that conflicts of wedding ceremonials are derived from war is also not well founded and can be explained on other grounds. Most probably the procession is due to the festivity of marriage and the assemblage of people is derived from the custom of marrying relatives which gave certain persons a vested interest in the women of their own com-

---

27. A.G.S. i. 6. M.S. ii. 21; Yaj. S. I. 61.

27a. हत्वा छित्त्वा च भित्वा च क्रोशन्तीं रुदतीं गृहात् ।
प्रसह्य कन्यां हरतो राक्षसो विधिरुच्यते ।। M.S. iii. 33.

28. युद्धहरणेन राक्षसः ।

29. राक्षसो युद्धहरणादिति ।

munity. Moreover, capture cannot be the only original method of securing a wife. Even in the primitive sexual relation, willingness of the parties concerned must have been very common, as it is found in animals also. There is a pre-arranged natural harmony between opposite sexes which unites them without any external force. So, even in the very primitive times, the Gāndharva form of marriage must have been more common than the Rākṣasa one.

The Indo-Aryans, during the Vedic times, were not always warring, and the old savage customs were disappearing from amongst them. The capture of a girl against her wishes was falling into disuse and in the majority of cases the girl was carried away with her own consent, though against the consent of her parents. Such kinds of capture were sometimes prearranged by the bride and the bridegroom. Sometimes the lovers came into conflict with their guardians, and the marriage had to be accomplished by capture and elopement, which was regarded as a commendable step for the knight and the lady alike; thus in the case of Vimada and Purumitra's daughter,[30] it appears that there was no violence pure and simple, but that the affair was prearranged with the consent of the bride who refused to be directed by her parents. This previous consent is a fact which distinguishes such instances of capture and elopement of the bride from Rākṣasa method of marriage. In the epic instances of Rukmiṇī and Subhadrā also the consent of the bride was obtained.[31]

In course of time when people became settled, marriage by capture generally disappeared from the society. It continued, however, among the Kṣattriyas, the military caste of India. The simple reason for this is, that it were they who mostly participated in war and obtained wives as war booties. This original war booty grew into a knightly fashion later on. Manu[32] regards the Rākṣasa form the main form commendable for the Kṣattriyas. In the Mahābhārata Bhīṣma also calls it the best form for the ruling caste,[33] and he actually captured wives for the Kuru princes. Hārīta[34] calls it the Kṣāttra marriage and Devala[35] regards it as a sign of power and

30. R.V. i. 112–19; 116–1; 117–2; x. 39.7; 65, 65, 65, 12.

31. M.B. viii. 37. 34.

32. राक्षसं क्षत्रियस्यैकम् । M.S. iii. 24.

33. क्षत्रियाणां तु वीर्येण प्रशस्त हरणं बलात् । M.B. I. 245. 6.

34. अलंकृतामभिजयतः क्षात्रः ।

35. वीर्यहेतुः विवाहः सप्तमः समुदाहृतः ।

prestige. This custom was current up to the Rajput period of Indian History, though in the majority of cases the captured wife was a willing one, for instance, the capture of Saṁyuktā by Pṛthvīrāja was prearranged.[36] Subsequent to the twelfth century of the Christian era this custom disappeared, as the political power of the Rajputs dwindled away and the Hindus became, more and more, an agricultural people.

(c) Gāndharva. The next method of obtaining a wife was Gāndharva.[37] According to Āśvalāyana "that form of marriage is called Gāndharva where a man and a woman having entered a contract, approach each other." In the opinion of Gautama and Hārīta that form is called Gāndharva where a girl selects her own husband. Manu[38] gives the most comprehensive definition: "Where the bride and the bridegroom meet each other of their own accord and the meeting is consummated in copulation born of passion, that form is called Gāndharva." In this form, it were not the parents of the girl who settled the marriage, but the bride and the bridegroom arranged it among themselves out of sensual inclination.

The Gāndharva form of marriage is as old as, or even older than, the Paiśācha and the Rākṣasa ones, because it is more natural than any other form. In the childhood of humanity, men and women, becoming of age, must have attracted each other without any force or fraud. In the Ṛgvedic[39] opinions "that "vadhū" alone was "bhadrā," who, brilliantly attired, herself selected her mate, even in the midst of an assembly." The most usual type of marriage seems to have been that in which the bride and the bridegroom had previously come to enjoy one another's company in their ordinary village life or in various other places of festivals and fairs where their free choice and mutual attachment were generally approved by their kinsmen. A passage in the Atharvaveda[40] shows that parents usually left the daughter free in selection of her lover and directly encouraged her in being forward in love-affairs. The mother of the girl thought of the time when the daughter's developed youth (Pative-

---

36 The Pṛthvirājarāso.

37. A.G.S. i. 6.

38. इच्छयाऽन्योन्यसंयोगः कन्यायाश्च वरस्य च।
गान्धर्वस्स तु विज्ञेयो मैथुन्यः कामसंभवः ॥ M.S. iiii. 32.

39. X. 27. 17.

40. आ नो अग्ने सुमतिं संभलो गमेदिमां कुमारीं सह नो भगेन।
जुष्टा वरेषु समनेषु वल्गुरोषं पत्या सौभगमस्त्वस्यै ॥ ii. 36.

danaṁ) would win a husband for her. It was a smooth and happy sort of affair with nothing scandalous and unnatural about it.[41] In the Atharvaveda there are other references to this form of marriage.[41a] At one place in the same work Gāndharva husbands are actually mentioned.[42] Instances of Gāndharva marriage can be multiplied from Sanskrit epics.

This method was called Gāndharva, because it was mostly current in a tribe called Gandharva, living on the slopes of the Himalayas. It was more prevalent among the Kṣattriyas than among any other section of the Hindu community, as they represented the freest element in the society.

According to some authorities[43] this method was praiseworthy, as it proceeded from mutual attraction and love. Kaṇva, the foster-father of Śakuntalā, says in the Mahābhārata.[44] "The marriage of a desiring woman with a desiring man, though without religious ceremonies, is the best marriage." But in the opinion of the majority of law-givers it was not regarded so; on the other hand they discouraged it on religious and moral grounds.[45] It was inferior to the first five forms of marriage, because it was performed without sacred rituals and originated from lust. There was some fear also as regards the stability of the marriage tie. Because cupidity was the determining factor in such a marriage, the relation may or may not be lasting.

It seems that, from the time of the Sūtras, this form of marriage was falling into disuse. The Gṛhyasūtras[46] speak of "Dattā" or "Prattā", "the given one," bride, whose hand was to be grasped by the husband. In course of time when the sense of property increased, the children were regarded as possessions and the parents began to exercise greater control over their sons and daughters. There fore, the independence of the bride and the bridegroom in selecting their mates diminished. The marriages, in ninety percent cases, began to be settled by the guardians. The child-marriage system

41. R.V. vi. 30. 6.

41a. vi. 3. 6.

42. जाया इद् वो अप्सरसो गन्धर्वाः पतयो यूयम्। iv. 37. 12.

43. गान्धर्वमित्येके प्रशंसन्ति स्नेहानुगत्वात्। G.D.S. ii, 1. 31.

44. सकामायाः सकामेन निर्मन्त्रः श्रेष्ठ उच्यते। IV. 94. 60.

45. गान्धर्वस्तु क्रियाहीनः रागादेव प्रवर्तते। Quoted in V.M.S. vol II. p. 357.

46. P.G.S. i. 4. 16.

rendered a death–blow to the Gāndharva form of marriage, because children have no proper idea of marriage and they cannot exercise their discretion and rights in marriage affairs. Ultimately this form of marriage diasppeared from the Hindu society and at present it is not legally recognized.

(d) Āsura. Then a bit superior to Gāndharva was the Āsura[47] method of marriage. "Where the husband, after having paid money to the relations of the bride and the bride herself, accepts her out of free will, it is called the Āsura type of marriage."[48] The main consideration in this kind of marriage was money and it was, more or less, a purchase. By some writers it is called Mānuṣa or human. There is no doubt that it was a great improvement, in early times, on the Paiśācha and the Rākṣasa from of marriages where fraud and force were applied.

In the patriarchal system of family children were regarded as family property and the girls could be given away in marriage for money. We find in the Vedic period that sometimes bargains were struck, and the bride was practically sold for a heavy price.[49] Sometimes, out of greed, girls themselves selected wealthy, though otherwise unfit, husband for money.[50] In one passage a Ṛṣi invokes Aśvins to be generous like a Bijāmātṛ.[51] Yāska explains Vijāmātṛ as Kritāpati (husband of a purchased girl). The Maitrāyaṇī-Saṁhitā[52] condemns the faithlessnes of a purchased wife.

In the beginning, there seems to be no stigma attached to this custom. Later on, it became distasteful. From the Mahābhārata[53] we know that Bhīṣma procured wives for some Kuru princes by purchase. When he approached Śalya for this purpose, the latter felt the awkwardness of the situation, but had no courage to stop the custom of demanding price for a girl. In the case of royal families,

47. A.G.S. i. 6.

48. ज्ञातिभ्यो द्रविणं दत्वा कन्यायै चैव शक्तितः।
कन्याप्रदानं स्वाच्छान्द्यादासुरो धर्म उच्यते। M.S. iii. 31.

49. R.V. i. 107. 2.

50 कियती योषा मर्यतो वधूयोः परिप्रीता पन्यसा वार्येण। Ibid. x. 27. 12.

51. अश्रवं हि भूरिदावत्तरा वां विजामातुरुत वा घा स्यालात्। Ibid. i. 109. 2.

52. अनृतं वा एषा करोति या पत्युः क्रीता सती अन्यैः सञ्चरति। i. 10. 11.

53. पूर्वैः प्रवर्तितं किञ्चित्कुलेऽस्मिन्नृपसत्तमैः।
साधु वा यदि वासाधु तन्नातिक्रान्तुमुत्सहे।। etc. M.B. I. 122. 9. ff.

however, it was a custom rather than a sale. Bhīṣma admitted that there was no sin in the transaction. But Śalya's hitch in demanding money shows that the public opinion was not in its favour.

In course of time the sale of girls began to savour too much of worldliness with the growing conception of the religious character of marriage, where the bride was regarded a meritorious gift by the father to the bridegroom. The Smṛtiwriters describe the Āsura marriage only either as a traditional custom or as a necessary evil. In their free opinion, however, they condemn it and call it a sale in the guise of marriage. Manu says, "The learned father of the girl should not accept even the least amount of price. Accepting the price out of greed, he becomes the seller of children."[54] According to Āpastamba-Smṛti, "not even a Śūdra should accept money while giving away his daughter. Taking money is a sale in disguise".[55] Not only this much. In the opinion of some writers, "a purchased wife cannot attain the full status of a wife and is not entitled to share the worship of gods and the Fathers. She should be regarded as a maid servant."[56] More and more sin was being attached to the sale of a daughter. "Those who blinded with greed give their daughters in marriage for money, are sellers of their own selves and the sinners of the first water. They fall into hell and kill the merits of seven previous generations."[57]

But in spite of its unqualified condemnation this custom lingered in india, and is still found, though restricted to very poor families. The presence of this custom in the North-West frontier is attested by Greek writers[58] At present in India, in low castes and in some poor families of upper castes also, this custom is followed. But it is not done with a clean conscience and an attempt is made to hide the sale.

---

54. न कन्यायाः पिता विद्वान् गृह्णीयाच्छुल्कमण्वपि।
गृह्णन्हि शुल्कं लोभेन स्यान्नरोऽपत्यविक्रयी। iii. 51.

55. आददीत न शूद्रोऽपि शुल्कं दुहितरं ददत्।
शुल्कं हि गृह्णन्कुरुते छन्नं दुहितृविक्रयम्॥ ix. M.S. ix. 98.

56. क्रीता द्रव्येण या नारी न सा पत्नी विधीयते।
न सा दैवे न सा पित्र्ये दासीं तां कवयो विदुः॥ B.D.S. i. 11. 20.

57. शुल्केन ये प्रयच्छन्ति स्वसुतां लोभमोहिताः।
आत्मविक्रयिणः पापा महाकिल्बिषकारकाः॥
पतन्ति निरये घोरे घ्नन्ति चासप्तमीकुलम्। Ibid. i. 11. 21.

58. Megasthenes, quoted in Oxford History of India, vol. I p. 60

The similar custom of dowry to be offered by the father of the bride to the bridegroom is not to be found in ancient literature of the Hindus. There are however, some references where the guardians of the girl had to offer dowry to the bridegroom. A daughter who had some physical defects was to be disposed of with money.[59] In the marriage hymn "Vahatu" or dowry is mentioned.[60] In the Atharvaveda a king is cursed that his queen may not fetch dowry for him.[61] In the Aitareya-Brāhmaṇa[62] a bargain marriage is called "Paśuvivāha", "animal marriage" but it is not clear as to which party exacted money.

In times when the Āsura and the Ārṣa forms of marriages were common, it was absurd for the bridegroom to demand money from the relations of the bride. Equity of the time required that the father of the girl should demand her price. But in course of time circumstances changed. In early times advanced maidenhood was tolerated; later on, the marriage of a girl became compulsory and pre-puberty marriage came into existence. Now the father of the girl became very anxious to dispose of the girl within a limited time. On religious grounds he wanted to get rid of the girl even with an offer of money which the father of the bridegroom demanded. The religious conception of marriage as a sacrifice also helped the rise of this custom. Dowry was regarded as Dakṣiṇā attending the main gift of a girl, and to this extent it was offered willingly. The right of daughter's inheritance was also instrumental in making this custom rigid in the propertied class of people. In the form of dowry, the daughter got her share from the property of her father. In modern times, in the educated circle, education of sons is costly. The father of the boy thinks that the cost of education should be shared by the father of the girl, who reaps all the advantages of his son's education. At present it is felt that the demand of dowry is a great impediment in the selection of a proper bride or bridegroom, and the public opinion is being prepared to do away with the rigidity and absurdity of the dowry system.

(e) Prājāpatya. Next comes the Prājāpatya[62a] method of marriage. According to it the father gave away his daughter to a suitor on the distinct understanding that they should both perform

59. R.V. x. 23. 11.

60. Ibid. x. 85.

61. नाअस्य जाया शतवाही कल्याणी तल्पमा शये। V. 7. 12.

62. A. Br. I. 16.

62a. A.G.S. i. 6.

their civic and religious duties together.[63] The father, here, obtained some sort of bond from the bridegroom who himself came forward as the suitor for marriage. Āśvalāyana[64] defines it in this way: "That form of marriage where the commandment-You both should perform your duties together-is given, is called Prājāpatya." Gautama[65] and Manu[66] almost repeat the same words. The very name Prājāpatya suggests that the pair entered the solemn bond for discharging their debts to Prajāpati, that is, for procreating and bringing up children. The most practical side of this method is brought out by Devala,[67] who regards it "a marriage by fixing conditions." The modern people will regard it the most satisfactory and up-to-date form of marriage, because here the rights of the husband and the wife are equally well secured. But according to the Hindu point of view, it is inferior to the first three methods. The reason is that, here, the gift is not free but it is bent low under conditions, which should not have been according to the religious conception of a gift. This form is still Praśasta or commendable.

This form could not have been current in very early times. Only in the advanced stage of the society, educated men and women would have resorted to it. It also required a free society where there was no seclusion of women, and the bridegroom came forward to ask the hand of the bride. This form declined at the introduction of child-marriage, because for it only grown-up parties were eligible, who could understand the implications of the bond they were going to enter. In course of time marriage became a pure gift by the father to the bridegroom and any condition, howsoever prudent it might be, became offending to the religious sense of the Hindus.

(f) Ārṣa. The Ārṣa[68] method of marriage excelled the Prājāpatya in order of merit. According to this method the father of the bride received from the bridegroom a pair of kine or two for the uses prescribed by law, e.g., the performance of some sacrifice.[69]

63. Yāj. S. I. 60.

64. सहधर्मं चरत इति प्राजापत्यः। i. 6.

65. संयोगमंत्रः प्राजापत्ये सहधर्मं चर्यतामिति।

66. सहोभौ चरतां धर्ममिति वाचानुभाष्य च।
कन्याप्रदानमभ्यर्च्य प्रजापत्यो विधिः स्मृतः॥ iii. 30.

67. सहधर्मं क्रियाहेतोर्दानं समयबन्धनात्।
अलंकृत्यैव कन्याया विवाहः स प्रजापतेः॥ Quoted in V.M.S. vol. II. p. 851.

68. A.G.S. i. 6; M.S. iii. 29; Yāj. S. I. 61.

69. एकं गोमिथुनं द्वे वा वरादादाय धर्मतः।
कन्याप्रदानं विधिवदार्षो धर्मः स उच्यते॥ M.S. iii. 29.

Evidently it was not the bride's price, but there was some consideration for the gift, though the father of the bride did not want to make a bargain out of it. Āśvalāyana, Baudhāyana and Āpastamba all agree that when a youth married a girl, after having offered a pair of kine to her father, it was called the Ārṣa form of marriage. A condition, however, was imposed on the offer, in that it was exclusively meant for a sacrifice. Thus it was distinguished from the Āsura. Manu.[70] observes, "Where the relatives do not accept price for the girl, it is not a sale; what is taken is only in name". In the opinion of the Vīramitrodaya,[71] it was not a price, because its quantity was limited. Moreover, it was given away with the bride herself. This method was called Ārṣa, because it was current mostly in priestly families, as its very name suggests. A. C. Das in his Ṛgvedic Culture.[72] however, gives a different interpretation of the word Ārṣa. He writes, "Then there was a form of marriage called Ārṣa, when a daughter was married to a Ṛṣi for his vast knowledge and spiritual culture." But in this way we cannot explain the origin of the custom of demanding a pair of kine. Reverence and demand both would go ill together. With the decline of sacrifices, this method of marriage became out of fashion. Formerly it was a commendable type of marriage, but later on even the nominal acceptance of a pair of kine became repulsive to the idea of Kanyādāna. (the gift of a girl). As early as in the time of the Manu-Smṛti, the opinion was voiced: "Some prescribe the acceptance of one pair of kine in the Ārṣa Vivāha, but it is improper. It is a sale; it matters little whether one accepts a large sum or a small one".[73] In course of time the very word "take" on the part of the bride's father was eschewed from the auspices of marriage.

(g) Daiva. The next form superior to Ārṣa was Daiva.[74] In this form the decorated girl was given away by the father to a priest, who officiated at a sacrifice commenced by him. According to Baudhāyana,[75] the girl was given as a Dakṣiṇā or sacrificial fees. It

---

70. यासां नाददते शुल्कं ज्ञातयो न स विक्रयः ।
अर्हणं तत्कुमारीणामानृशंस्यं च केवलम् ।। iii. 54.

71. धर्मनिमित्तो ह्यसौ सम्बन्धो न लोभनिमित्तकः । गोमिथुनग्रहणं च स्वयं कन्योपकरणदानासमर्थस्य तद्दानार्थं वेदितव्यम् । V.M.S. vol. II. p. 852.

72. P. 253.

73. आर्षे गोमिथुनं शुल्कं केचिदाहुर्मृषैव तत् ।
अल्पोऽप्येवं महान्वापि विक्रयस्तावदेव सः ।। M.S. iii. 53.

74. ऋत्विजे वितते कर्मणि दद्यादलंकृत्य स दैवः । A.G.S. i. 6.

75. दक्षिणासु दीयमानास्वन्तर्वेदि यदृत्विजे स दैवः B.D.S,

was called Daiva, because in it the gift was made on the occasion of a Daiva sacrifice. The gift of a maiden in marriage for services rendered is illustrated even in the Vedic literature. But sometimes its bareness was clothed by other elements. Thus in the case of Rathavīti, Dālbha's daughter, Syāvāśva was at the same time an ardent suitor for the maiden subsequently given to him.[76] Priests very often received from their princely patrons, noble maidens or slave girls for services at sacrifices who were called "Vadhūs";[77] but this appears to have involved no proper, marriage, and is to be re garded as concubinage associated with polygamy developing among rich and powerful classes. This method was mainly prevalent among the upper three classes of the Hindus. People thought it meritorious to give their daughters away in marriage to a priest. Later on, with the merits of sacrifices, this custom also fell into disuse, and it was thought not proper to offer a girl to a priest without considering his other conditions. Moreover, the conception of marriage came to involve that it was not merely a gift but it was the settlement of the girl in life and therefore, it should be well arranged. This form of marriage was regarded inferior to Brāhma, because, here, the father, of the girl took the services of the bridegroom into consideration, whereas in the Brāhma method, marriage was a pure gift.

(h) Brāhma. The purest and the most evolved method of marriage was Brāhma.[78] It was called so, because it was thought fit for the Brahmans. In it the girl was given by the father, with such ornaments as he could afford, to a man of character and learning, whom he invited voluntarily and received respectfully without taking any thing in return.[78a] The Smṛtis regard it the most honourable type of marriage, as it was free from physical force, carnal appetite, imposition of conditions and lure of money. Here the social decency was fully observed and religious considerations taken into account. In its very nature, this method could not have been very primitive, as it presupposes a long culture of social habits. But this form can be traced back up to the Vedic times. The marriage of Sūryā with Soma, as described in the Ṛgveda, is the prototype of

76. R. V. V. 61. 17–19.

77. Ibid.

78. A.G.S. i. 6; M.S. iii. 27; Yāj. S.I. 58; V.S. ii. 5; Ś.S. iv. 2.

78a. आच्छाद्य चार्चयित्वा च श्रुतिशीलवते स्वयम् ।
आहूय दानं कन्याया ब्राह्मो धर्मः प्रकीर्तितः ॥ M.S. iii. 27.

the Brāhma marriage.[78b] This form is still current and the most popular in India, though it has been prostituted with the morbid stipulation of dowry.

(vii) *Some other Forms*

Besides, there were other forms of marriage of which the scriptures do not take cognizance. For example, marriages by exchange and service etc. The first of the above is still current in the Hindu society. But only poor parents whose children do not attract the notice of match-makers, arrange the marriages of their sons and daughters by exchange. It is not a voluntary custom but a procedure forced by circumstances. In other respects it resembles the Brāhma type of marriage.

(viii) *Popular Forms*

At present the only two methods of marriage in use are the Brāhma and the Āsura. In the first, the father of the girl gives her away to a person whom he invites for the purpose, without accepting anything from him in any shape. In the second, the father accepts money from the bridegroom as the price of his daughter. It will be noticed that our law-givers do not contemplate a third contingency in which the intending bridegroom may put pressure upon the father of the girl to pay him handsomely for favour of marrying her, no matter whether his means allows him to do so or not. The present system of fixing dowry and to make it the main consideration in settling the marriage does not seem to have existed in ancient times.

(ix) *Religious Ceremonies Essential*

Whatever may be the method through which marriage was effected, the religious ceremonies were essential to make it valid.[78c] Vasiṣtha and Baudhāyana declare: "Where a damsel is taken by force but is not solemnly married according to the religious rites, she may be duly given in marriage to another, for then she remains a virgin as before."[79] Devala says, "In the forms of marriages,

78b. x. 85.

78c. नोदकेन विना चायं कन्यायाः पतिरुच्यते।
पाणिग्रहणसंस्कारात् पतित्वं सप्तमे पदे॥ Y.S. I. 76.

79. बलादपहृता कन्या यदि मंत्रैर्न संस्कृता।
अन्यस्मै विधिवद्देया यथा कन्या तथैव सा। Vasiṣtha and Baudhāyana quoted in V.M.S. vol. II. p. 860.

beginning with the Gāndharva to the Paiśācha the marital rites have again to be performed in the presence of fire".[80] In the Gāndharva marriage, consummation of the union preceded the nuptials. According to Manu[81] rituals should be performed only in the case of a virgin. But the later Smṛtis, as cited above, prescribe the rites even after consummations. Manu[82] modifies his previous injunction by emphasizing the need of ritual. It was done so for legalizing the marriage, legitimatizing the children and avoiding the public scandal. Mādhavāchārya also realizes the necessity of performing the religious ceremonies in every form of marriage: "It must not be supposed that in these disapproved forms of marriages, beginning with the Gāndharva, the relationship of husband and wife does not arise for the want of the ceremonies of marriage including the taking of seven steps, because although they do not take place at the outset before acceptance, afterwards they are invariably performed".[83]

The religious idea was supreme in the Hindu life. It was of less consequence how the pair was united, but if once united, the tie should be consecrated and thus union made lasting. The nuptials were supposed to impart sanctity to the marital relation. Hence it was thought necessary that they should be performed in every case. At present, however, such cases do not arise owing to the custom of child-marriage and Purdah system. Only in low-caste peoples rare cases of irregular marriage are noticed.

(x) Limitations of Marriage

Another problem regarding marriage was the examination of the family of the bride and that of the bridegroom. "According to Senart the Aryan people practised in affairs of marriage both a rule of exogamy and endogamy. A man must marry a woman of equal birth, but not of the same gens, according to the Roman law as interpreted by Senart and Kovalevsky, and an Athenian must marry an Athenian woman, but not of the same genos. In India these rules are reproduced in the form that one must not marry within the Gotra, but not without the Caste".[83a]

80. गान्धर्वादिविवाहेषु पुनर्वैवाहिको विधिः ।
कर्तव्यश्च त्रिभिर्वर्णैः समयेनाग्निसाक्षिकः ॥ Devala, Ibid.

81. M.S. Ibid.

82. M.S. Ibid.

83. Quoted by P. N. Sen, Hindu Jurisprudence, p. 270.

83a. Vedic Index, ii. 268.

(a) Exogamy. The bar of exogamy is not peculiar to India, but it is prevalent in other parts of the world also. It is current in barbarous, half-civilized and civilized tribes. In tribes where there is no Gotra system, totem serves the purpose, and it separates one group from the other. The origin of this bar is shrouded in mystery. Various scholars have propounded divergent theories to explain its rise.

We can briefly refer to these theories as follows. According to one school of opinion the custom of exogamy arose owing to the paucity of women in early times.[84] Another school of opinion holds that exogamy was introduced to prevent the early sexual promiscuity within the clan.[85] Then, there are scholars who are of the opinion that the origin of exogamy was due to the absence of sexual attraction between persons who are brought up together.[86] The fourth school is of opinion that in primitive times the patriarch of the family himself wanted to keep the young girls of the family for himself. So his jealousy drove the youngmen of the clan to seek their wives outside: What was at first necessity, subsequently became a voluntary custom.[87] The fifth school holds that the totem was responsible for evolving the custom of exogamy. The clan blood was regarded sacred and to spare the divinity of the totem one had to refrain from its appropriation for sexual purpose.[88]

These theories do not seem to be conclusive in themselves. To take the first theory even if granted that the female population was less than the male one, in ancient times, the paucity of women would not stand in the way of every young man for taking his wife from within his own clan. As regards the second theory, we are quite familiar with the fact that the savages are not credited with such a thoughtful scheme of improving morality of the clan. The third theory does not take the facts in order; the absence of sexual attraction is a result rather than the cause of prohibition; for example, animals do not betray such repulsion, and in many religious orgies of India, even at present, no scruples are felt in sexual intercourse within the same clan. The fourth theory of patriarchal coercion is

84. I.F. Mac Lennan, Studies in Ancient History, I. p. 90.

85. L. H. Morgan, Ancient Society, p. 24; Frazer, Totemism and Exogamy, i. 164 ff.

86. Westermark, Human Marriage, xiv-xvi; Crawley, The Mystic Rose, p. 222.

87. J. J. Atkinson, Primal Law.

88. Durkheim, Annee Sosiolegique, i. 1–70.

borrowed from the beast-herds, where the strongest animal drives the younger ones away from the females. But will not the patriarch appropriate the new-comers also? So the origin of exogamy must be sought for somewhere else. The theory of totemic sanctity also is not supported by facts. It is not probable that the totem was regarded as divine in the period when the custom of exogamy arose. Moreover, the members of the clan were regarded as friends and equal and not as gods. In this case the clan blood was not too sacred for sexual intercourse.

More plausible suppositions regarding the origin of exogamy appear to be these. The young men of a clan or tribe went off to seek food and thus came into contact with a new clan. Being compelled to seek wives in their new surroundings, they might thus initiate a habit of outside marriage that would in time become general usage and 'therefore' sacred. Marriage by capture also seems to have been instrumental, to some extent, in evolution of exogamy. In ancient times warring people captured women in wars and made them their wives. This habit was hardened into instinct and even after the dawn of civilization, the fashion of marrying outside was retained, though war was replaced by mutual negotiation and the tribal army by a marriage party. Exogamy might have been introduced to avoid the jealousy and quarrel in the family also. When marriage was allowed in the family, the same girl was desired by a number of cousins, who sometimes quarreled among themselves. To prevent this trouble, the head of the family might have thought it wise to arrange the marriage of young men outside the family. Experience also taught that the marriage within the same family or clan was not desirable, as it led to the degeneration of the race. Darwin says. "The consequence of close inter-breeding carried on for too long a time are, as is generally believed, loss of size, constitutional vigour, and fertility, sometimes accompanied by a tendency of malformation."[89] This racial eugenics required that marriages should take place outside the clan. But we cannot assert that there was only one cause at the root of the custom of exogamy. In different localities, under different circumstances, the causes must have varied considerably, and at such a distance of time we cannot be very positive in our speculations.

It cannot be said how far the above causes were applicable in case of the Indo-Aryans, who at the dawn of history were sufficiently advanced in civilization. It is also a great wonder how this institu-

89. Variation of Animals and Plants under Domestication, London, 1868.

tion sprang up into existence all of a sudden in the Indo-Aryans. Among other Indo-Germanic races, the bar is nowhere prevalent at present. The probable source of this custom seems to be the con tact with, and the assimilation of, the Dravidians among whom like many other tribes this custom was strictly observed.

The word "Gotra" in its modern sense is not known in the Vedas, though it occurs in the sense of a cowpen.[90] The earliest mention of this word in its technical sense is to be found in the Chāndogya-Upaniṣad where the teacher of Satyakāma Jābāli asks his Gotra.[91] We find frequent use of Gotras in the Buddhist and Jain literature, for example, Mānava, Vasiṣṭha Gautama etc. It seems that by the time of the Buddha, the Gotra system was an established institution.

But the idea of "Kula" or family was there even in Vedic times. So far as prohibition of marriage with near relatives is concerned, we come across the lively discussion between Yama and Yamī in the Ṛgveda,[92] which shows that, though marriage with a near relative may have been common in early times, it was falling into disuse in the later Vedic period. The moral, however, given by Yama against such marriages does not speak any horror. But the family prohibition did not go too far. There is a passage in the Śatapatha Brāhmaṇa[93] that refers to the union of brothers and sisters in the third or the fourth generation. Harisvāmin, the commentator on the above Brāhmaṇa says, in the way of illustration, that one Kaṇva married a girl in the third generation. In Surāṣṭra, there are instances of marriage in the fourth generation. The prohibition of marriage in one's Piṇḍa also does not seem to be in force in the Vedic period. In the Khailika hymn (VIII) Indra is invoked in the way which shows that daughters of maternal uncle and paternal aunt could be married.[94]

In the Brāhmaṇas, all sorts of speculations were a pace, but there is not a single reference to the institution of Gotra. Though it is a negative evidence, but coupled with other facts it is of a

90. Roth, quoted in the Vedic Index, i. pp. 235, 236, 240.

91. iv. 4. 1.

92. x. 10.

93. इदं हि चतुर्थे पुरुषे तृतीये संगच्छामहे। i. 8. 3. 6.

94. आयाहीन्द्र पथिभिरीलितोऽभि यज्ञमिमं नो भागधेयं जुषस्व।
तृप्तां जहुर्मातुलस्येव योषा भागस्ते पैतृष्वसेयी वपामिव॥

great significance. Vedic rituals are not connected with Gotra Sacrificers have not to choose only those hymns that were composed by their own Gotra-Kṛts. The Āpri hymns are the only exceptions; but this is the view of the Śrauta Sūtras only and the Yajurveda does not lay any such restriction. Thus Gotra was not as yet much consulted in the matter of religious ceremonies.

Prohibition of marriage within the Pravara is first found in the Gṛhyasūtras, but there is no similar prohibition of Sagotra marriage. Āpastamba, Kauśika, Baudhāyana and Pāraskara, all avoid Pravara but not Gotra.[95] From the time of the Dharmasūtras, however, Sagotra and Sapiṇḍa marriages are being prohibited. Vasiṣṭha prohibits Sagotra marriage.[96] But the range of Gotra was still very limited and marriage was possible beyond the seventh generation of the father and the fifth of the mother. According to the Āpastamba Gṛhyasūtra,[97] however, the limits of Gotra were extended. It could go too far and was not co-extensive with the seventh generation of the father.

The institution of exogamy seems to have been established subsequent to the beginning of the Christian era. Almost all the metrical Smṛtis declare the marriages within the Gotra, ipso facto, invalid. Such marriages could not be legalized, nor the children born of such wedlocks.[98] But there seems to be still some leniency about marrying a girl within the Gotra. One Smṛti[99] prescribes only an ordinary atonement for marrying a girl within the Gotra, while later on the marriage is nullified and the punishment is very severe.

The later writers on Dharmaśāstra are dead against Sagotra and Sapiṇḍa marriages. They prohibit not only such marriages but try to explain away ancient statements that might go against them. For example, they say that the invocation to Indra in the Khailika hymn is not a Vidhi (rule) but an Arthavāda (praise); if it were a rule, incest would become permissible. Again they declare that the pas-

95. The Gotrapravaramañjarī by Keśava.

96. V.D.S.

97. iii. 10.

98. असपिण्डा च या मातुरसगोत्रा च या पितुः।
सा प्रशस्ता द्विजातीनां दारकर्मणि मैथुने ।। M.S. iii. 5.

99. परिणीय सगोत्रां तु समानप्रवरां तथा।
त्यागं कुर्याद द्विजस्तस्यास्ततश्चान्द्रायणं चरेत् ।। Quoted by Gadādhara on P.G.S. i. 4–8.

sage in question refers to children born from Asajātīya marriages. Some ingeniously explain that "of the maternal uncle" and "of the sister of the father" do not mean the daughters of the maternal uncle and the paternal aunt but they mean Mātṛsadṛśamukhī and Pitṛsadṛśamukhi, that is, girls whose face is like that of the mother and the father. The Vīramitrodaya[100] and the Smṛtichandrikā[101] take a bolder step and say that the above passage contains "an example not to be followed", "Dṛṣṭodharmavyatikramaḥ." These writers flourished in a time when Sagotra and Sapiṇḍa marriages became extinct. In order to give this institution a hoary antiquity they attempted to explain away the passage which might prove stumbling-blocks in their way. Aparārka followed quite a different line of argument. He offers an altogether different meaning of the above invocation. "O Indra, invited by your devotees come to the sacrifice and enjoy your share. We offer vapā, fat, as disinterestedly as the Mātulayoṣā (daughter of the maternal uncle) and the Paitṛṣvaseyī (daughter of the paternal aunt) are offered in marriage without the least desire of self-appropriation."[102] He quotes the Brahma-Purāna, prohibiting Sagotra marriage, with cow-slaughter, as Kalivarjya, "prohibited in the Kali age". These facts show that the prohibition of Sagotra marriage was an accomplished fact during the time of the commentators and the Nibandhakāras. Since then it has been followed in the Hindu society with every care.

(b) Just as exogamy is strictly observed among the Hindus so is endogamy an established institution of theirs. All the Smṛtis enjoin that a twice-born should marry a girl of his own caste.[103] This is but natural and may have been the general rule even in early times, but it could not have been strictly observed, as the caste system was not firmly established.

(c) Hypergamy. During the Vedic times, inter-marriages between several castes were much easier. It is difficult to believe how the freedom of social intercourse was given to young men and women, in popular gatherings and private company, if there were any real bars to intercaste marriages. Intercaste marriages generally took the form of hypergamy. Men of the Ṛgvedic priestly class are often stated to have married into royal families, as Chyavan

---

100. V.M.S. vol. II.

101. S. C. Ānlika, Vivāhaprakaraṇa.

102. On Yaj. S.I. 55.

103. उद्वहेत द्विजो भार्यां सवर्णां लक्षणान्विताम् । M.S. iii. 4.

Śyāvāśva or Vimada did.[104] Perhaps, the greater prominence of hypergamy is due to the records preserved by the Brahmans, who generally passed over the Kṣattriyas, marrying Brahman girls. Still, there are some instances of such marriages. For example, king Svanaya Bhāvayavya's beloved wife was an Āṅgirasī.[105] The Atharvaveda[106] glorifies the Brahman as the best husband for women of all other classes, though from the same text it can be inferred that the Brahman women, sometimes, held opposite views and they had to the reclaimed from the persons of other classes, with the help of king.[107] Vaiśiputras are known to the early Brāhmaṇas.[108] The connexion of an Arya with a Śūdrā girl is made the subject of joke in courts and priestly circles, as is known from the Yajurveda.[109] Such marriages must have been legal and frequent, and respectable Vedic personages, like Auśija, Kavaṣa, Vatsa etc. were sons of Dāsī, or Śūdrā mothers.[110] The frequent use of the word Dāsī, as compared with that of Dāsa, in Vedic texts, shows that Dāsīs came into contract with their Aryan masters as a result of the conquest and subjugation of neighbouring tribesmen; so Dāsīputras became very common in the Aryan society.

(d) Pratiloma. A few cases of Śūdra-Āryā connexion are also recorded in the Vedic texts. A Yajurveda Saṁhitā[111] mentions the word "Ayogu," which, if it is connected with the later Āyogava, may mean the Arya woman (a Vaiśyā) married to a Śūdra.[112] This interpretation of the Vedic text is supported by the evidently old tradition recorded in the Āśvalāyana Gṛhyasūtra,[113] that the family slave, equally with the brother-in-law of the widow, could lawfully marry the widow of his master. Other Yajurvedic texts refer frequently to such cases which points to the beginning of such inter-

104. R.V. i. 112–19; 116. 1; 117. 20; x. 39.

105. Ibid. i. 126.

106. A. V. V. 17. 8. 9.

107. Ibid.

108. T. Br. iii. 9. 7. 3; Ś. Br. xiii. 2.

109. V. Sans xxiii. 30. 31; T.S. vii, 4. 19. 2-3.

110. R.V. i. 18. 1; i. 112. 11; P. Br. xiv. 11. 16.

111. Vaj. S. xxx. 5.

112. शूद्रादायोगवः क्षत्ता चण्डालश्चाधमो नृणाम्।
वैश्यराजन्यविप्रासु जायन्ते वर्णसंकराः॥ M.S. x. 12.

113. iv. 2. 18.

mixture in the earlier period. In the Atharvaveda[114] a charm is directed against a rival lover or one's wife's paramour who is referred to as a Dāsa, winning her love by sheer physical strength.

Thus the above instances evidently show that Anuloma as well as Pratiloma connexions were known and permissible in the Vedic times, though they may not have been very common.

(e) Later History of Inter-caste Marriage. Later on inter-caste marriage though tolerated was not encouraged. During the Gṛhyasūtra period the general rule was to marry a girl of the same caste. Hypergamy, however, was recognized, though a Śūdra wife was not liked. Parāshara[115] says, "A Brāhmaṇa can have three wives, a Rājanya two and a Vaiśya one. According to some, all can have one Śūdra wife also, without recital of the Vedic verses." The Dharmàsūtras and the early Smṛtis all allow to marry a girl from the lower castes, though such cases were not many, and generally they were not esteemed. Manu[116] declares, "Among the twice-born, a girl of the same caste is commendable for wifehood. But for those who are given to lust, girls from other castes can also be had in order." Al these scriptures are against the marriage of a low-caste man with the girl of a higher class.

An indirect light is also thrown on the problem of the inter-caste marriage from the Smṛti literature. The Dharmasūtras and the Smṛtis make provision, for Āśauca caused by the death of the relatives of different castes, which indirectly proves the existence of intercaste marriages. In the partition of properties, sons born of mother belonging to different castes, receive their shares. Here, too, Dharmaśāstra contemplates the possibility of an inter-caste marriage. A student is enjoined to salute the wives of his teacher, coming from lower castes, from a distance and not to touch their feet. It is presupposed that the gurus could have wives from different castes and it was, in no way, derogative to their position. In adoption a Vijātīya child could be adopted. All these side-lights prove the existence of inter-caste marriages.

That the inter-caste marriages were current as late as in the mediaeval period of Indian History is evident from the concrete

114. A.V. ii. 5. 6.

115. i. 4. 9–12.

116. सवर्णाग्रे द्विजातीनां प्रशस्ता दारकर्मणि ।
कामतस्तु प्रवृत्तानामिमाः स्युः क्रमशोऽवराः ।। M.S. iii. 12.

cases recorded in the Sanskrit literature. Bāṇa had two Pārāśava brothers born of a Śūdra step-mother.[117] The wife of Rājaśekhara, Avantisundarī was a Kṣattriya girl.[118] Kalhaṇa in his Rajataraṅgiṇī[119] describes the marriage of the sister of Saṁgrāmarāja with a Brāhmaṇa. In the Kathā-Śaritsāgara,[120] we have a number of instances of inter-caste marriages. A king asks his commander-in-chief to search a husband for his daughter, who must be either a Brahman or a Kṣattriya. At the Svayaṁvara of Anaṅgamtaī, suitors of all the castes assembled together, which shows the possibility of a marriage between different castes. Again, we get a Brahman marrying a Kṣattriya girl and the sentiments of the pact leave no doubt that such marriages were regarded still desirable. "The marriage between the princess and the Brahman youth was for the glory of each other like the union of the Goddess of Learning and Discipline."[121] In the Bank inscription of Jodhapur, the founder of the Pratihāra dynasty is described to have married two wives, one Kṣatriya, the other Brāhmaṇī. According to the inscription of Vākāṭaka Hastibhoja, a Brāhmaṇa Somadeva married a Kṣatriya wife in accordance with Śruti and Smṛti.[122] Such was the state of affairs during the first millennium of the Christian era. The custom was regarded as "sanctioned by the Śruti and the Smṛti." These instances are very valuable, as they are incidental. Even the Purāṇas, while dealing with the Kalivarjyas, do not include the intercaste marriage in the list. The Mitākṣarā on the Yājñavalkya Smṛti[123] and the Dāyabhāga, both recognize the validity of intercaste marriage. The cases of Pratiloma marriage are very rare and they do not find literary mention.

(f) Intercaste Marriage forbidden. But a time came when inter-caste marriages were not only discouraged but totally forbidden. Even in the time of the Manu-Smṛti,[124] marriage with a Śūdra wife

117. The Harṣacharita. I.

118. The Kāvyamīmāṁsā. I.

119. vii. 10–12.

120. xviii. 2. 65.

121. तयोस्तु सोऽभूद्राजेन्द्रपुत्री विप्रेन्द्रपुत्रयोः ।
सङ्गमोऽन्योन्यशोभायै विद्याविनययोरिव ॥ The Kathāsaritsāgara xxv, 171.

122. Epigraphia Indica.

123. II. 122.

124. हीनजातिस्त्रियं मोहादुद्वहन्ते द्विजातयः ।
कुलान्येव नयन्त्याशु ससन्तानानि शूद्रताम् ॥ iii. 15.
शूद्रां शयनमारोप्य ब्राह्मणो यात्यधोगतिम् ।
जनयित्वा सुतं तस्यां ब्राह्मण्यादेव हीयते ॥ iii. 17.

was scandalous. The later Smṛtis unanimously forbid marriage with Śūdrā, and excommunicate a man marrying her. The sinner was threatened with the fire of hell. In course of time, the same abhorrence was shown to the marriage between the upper three classes also. Manu[125] calls intercaste marriages lustful and later on develops the fictitious theory of the Varṇasaṁkaras, giving low social status to the children born of intercaste unions.[126] The logical consequence of this tendency was that none was allowed to marry beyond his own caste, and this process at present is complete. Now, among the Vaiśyas and the Śūdras, not only the Varṇa distinction but even sub-caste distinction is respected in a marriage alliance. The same tendency has also manifested in the prohibition of inter-provincial marriages.

There were different causes responsible for the confinement of marriage within one's own caste. First of all there was the race-complex. Owing to the difference of culture and colour, men and women desisted from choosing a wife or husband from a lower race. This was at the root of prohibition of marriage between an Arya and a Śūdra. With the development of the rigidity of the caste system, marriage between the twice-born also declined, as the standards of their life were different. But besides the standard of living, caste superiority, born of attaching too much importance to the birth of a person, was also instrumental in discouraging the system of inter-caste marriage.[126a]

(g) Examination of the Family. In addition to the consideration of the Varṇa, the particular family to be related was also thoroughly examined. According to the Āśvalāyana Gṛhyasūtra,[127] "first of all the family should be examined, both from the mother's and the father's side." Manu[128] says, "A man of a noble family, in order to increase the excellence of his own, should always make relation with men of noble families, and should shun the ignoble ones." In later times the importance of the family so increased that the theory was being advocated that the girl, in marriage was given

125. iii. 12.

126. M.S. x.

126a. Under the impact of modern education inter-caste and inter-religious marriages are again being revived.

127. कुलमग्रे परीक्षेत मातृतः पितृतश्चेति। i. 5.

128. उत्तमैरुत्तमो नित्यं सम्बन्धानाचरेत्सदा।
निनीषुः कुलमुत्कर्षमधमानधमांस्त्यजेत्। Quoted in V.M.S. II. p. 5. 87.

to the family and not to an individual. In the case of the Brahmans at least, family was the only consideration. In comparison with the family, even the learning was dispensed with. In the opinion of Viṣṇu[129] "of a Brāhmaṇa, only his family is to be considered, not his Vedas or learning. In the gift of a girl and Śrāddha, learning does not count." Yājñavalkya[130] explains Kulīnatā or family-reputation as follows: "Families of the Śrotriyas famous from ten generations (are called good ones)." The commentary on this runs. "The family of those is to be taken as good, who are famous from five generations, both from mother's and father's side, and are reputed for their learning and character."[131]

The most esteemed families were those noted for their good deeds, learning and morality. "Those should be always made relatives, who are pure from their deeds done in accordance with the injunction of the Śruti and the Smṛti; who are born in good families and observe unbroken Brahmacarya; who are related to noble families and have risen to eminence; who are contented, gentlemen, agreeable, saintly and equitable; who are deviod of greed, attachment, envy, pride and infatuation; and those who are not given to anger and are always tranquil in their minds."[132]

On moral and physical grounds many families were prohibited. In the opinion of Manu,[133] these ten families, howsoever rich they might be, should be avoided. They are–one without good deeds; without great men; without Vedas; hairy; and suffering from pile, consumption, dysentery, epilepsy, white leprosy and leprosy proper. Families suffering from, or infected by, contagious disease were also to be shunned. Yama[134] prohibits the fourteen kinds of families on almost the same grounds, adding a few new details. The new objectionable families are those, whose members are either very tall or very short; either very white or very black; possess either

---

129. ब्राह्मणस्य कुलं ग्राह्यं न वेदाः सपदक्रमाः।
कन्यादाने तथा श्राद्धे न विद्या तत्र कारणम् Viṣṇu, quoted in V.M.S. vol. II. p. 585.

130. दशपूरुषविख्याताच्छ्रोत्रियाणां महाकुलात्। 1. 54.

131. पुरुषा एव पूरुषाः दशभिः पुरुषैः मातृतः पञ्चभिः पितृतः पञ्चभिर्विख्यातं यत्कुलं तस्मात्। विज्ञानेश्वर, Ibid.

132. M.S. iii. 6; iii. 17.

133. Ibid. iii. 6.

134. Quoted in V.M.S. vol. II. p. 58.

less or extra number of limbs; who are very passionate and suffer from jaundice etc.

The moral objections were the following: "Those families should be avoided with care, the members of which are thieves, cheats, impotent, atheists, living on objectionable means, deformed, always bringing enmity with brave persons, enemies of the state, always dining at funeral feasts, cowards and ill-reputed; the women of which are either barren or produce only female issues and try to kill their husbands."[135]

The reason for the utmost care spent on the examination of the family was primarily eugenic. The best possible progeny was desired and for it physically, mentally and morally fit matches were necessary, as the children inherit the good or bad qualities of their parents. Hārīta says on the point. "Offsprings are born according to the families'..[136] Manu[137] opines in the same strain. "The children follow the character of either the father or the mother, or the both. An issue of bad origin cannot attain the proper condition." In order to save the family from degeneration, one had to be very cautious in selecting a match. "The good families fall to ill fame etc. from bad marriages, disappearance of the religious duties and the non-study of the Vedas."[138] Domestic felicity was another object in view while selecting the particular family for marriage, as the culture of a family counts much in such affairs.

(xi) The Marriageable Age

After the consideration of the Varṇa and the family, the bride herself was examined. The first consideration was her age. In the Vedic times, as it is evident from the marriage hymns[139] in the Ṛgveda and the Atharvaveda, the parties to marriage were grown up persons

135. Manu, Ibid.

136. कुलानुरूपाः प्रजा सम्भवन्ति। Ibid.
पितुर्वा भजते शीलं मातुर्वोभयमेव वा।

137. न कथञ्चन दुर्योनिः प्रकृतिं स्वां नियच्छति॥ Manu, Ibid.

cf. मातुलान् भजते पुत्रः कन्यका भजते पितॄन्।
यथाशीला भवेन्माता तथाशीला भवेन्नृप॥ Vyāsa, Ibid.

138. कुविवाहैः क्रियालोपैर्वेदानध्ययनेन च।
कुलान्यकुलतां यान्ति ब्राह्मणातिक्रमेण च॥ M.S. iii, 63.

139. R.V. x. 85; A.V. xiv. i. 2.

competent to woo and be wooed, qualified to give consent and make choice. The bridegroom was supposed to have a house where his wife could be mistress, even in case his parents, brothers and sisters, for some reasons, happend to live with him, thus giving her position of a supremacy in the household.[140] This could not have been possible in the case of a child-wife. The Vedic rituals presuppose that the married pair were grown up enough to be lovers, man and wife, and parents of children.[141] Almost at every step, formula are repeated showing their immediate fitness for procreation; and hand-grasping and consummation are the essential parts of the Vedic marriage. These all go to show that marriage took place when the girl had attained her puberty.

We have many references in the Vedas to unmarried girls who grew old in the house of their fathers.[142] The maidens growing up in their father's home mixed with the youth of the village.[143] In Ṛgvedic times no girl was married before she had reached the womanhood. She must be fully developed physically in her father's house (Pitṛpadaṁ Vyaktā) before her marriage could be thought of.[144] Sūryā, the daughter of Sūrya (the Sun), was given away to Soma (the Moon) in marriage, only when she became youthful and yearned for a husband.[145] Ghoṣā, the lady Ṛṣi, married when she had nearly passed her youth. The virile young man (marya) is normally a lover, constantly in the company of youthful maidens (Yuvatī), embracing (Kanyā), and flattering (Yoṣā).[146] On the other hand the young maiden is also engaged in the midst of a number of suitors trying her best to please and attract them. Ladies were competent to arrange their own marriages. We get various charms and spells in the Ṛgveda and the Atharvaveda compelling the love of a man or a woman.[147] A lover seeks to send the entire household to sleep when he visits his beloved.[148] In the

140. सम्राज्ञ्येधि श्वशुरेषु सम्राज्ञ्युत देवृषु ।
ननान्दुः सम्राज्ञ्येधि सम्राज्ञ्युत स्वश्र्वाः ।। A.V. xiv. 1. 44.

141. R.V. viii. 55, 5, 8.

142. R.V. i. 117. 7; ii. 17. 7; x. 39. 3.

143. Vedic Index. ii. p. 485.

144. R.V. x. 85. 21, 22.

145. Ibid. x. 85.

146. Ibid. iii. 31. 7; 33, 10; x, 96. 20.

147. Ibid. x. 145; A.V. iii. 18. ii. 30; iii. 25; vi. 8. etc.

148. A.V. v. 28.

Atharvaveda[149] a Kumāriputra (Kānīna, according to Mahīdhara) is mentioned, which indicates that a girl could bear children before marriage. These evidences hardly leave any doubt about the fact that the bride and the bridegroom both were grown-up before marriage.

There are only a few references of doubtful character to the existence of child-marriage in the Vedic times. "One might adduce in the favour of the existence of child-marriage the Itihāsa (story) related on the obscene verse, Ṛgveda, I 126.6.7. Here Bhāvavya invited to the enjoyment of love, laughs at his spouse Romaśā believing that she is still immature. On this Romaśā invites him to convince himself of the contrary adding that she knew that the intercourse before puberty was forbidden by the law. But apart from the fact that these passages favour the general prevalence of marriage with mature girl the story conveys too much the impression of being a late invention occasioned by an etymological play on the name Romaśā." Another possible reference to an early marriage is in the Chhāndogya-Upaniṣad (I. 10. 1) where a poor Brahman teacher adopts the life of a beggar with his Āṭīkī wife. The mediaeval commentators give Āṭiki a fanciful sense of Ajātapayodharā etc. which evidently reflects their own dislike of the idea that a Brahman teacher's youthful wife should go about freely. It should be noted that Āṭīkī is not a proper name, and it has to be taken as an adjective. Its only rational interpretation would be "fit for or used to wandering life" i.e. hardy and patient.

The Gṛhyasūtra marriage rituals also show that marriage was generally arranged after the girl had attained her puberty. The consummation of marriage could take place immediately after the nuptial ceremonies. According to the Pāraskara-Gṛhyasūtra[150] the married couple "for three days should not eat saline food, should sleep on the ground and should not cohabit for a year, twelve nights, six nights or at least three nights." The last option speaks of the maturity of the bride. Baudhāyana[151] contemplates the possibility of the bride's being in her monthly course at the time of marriage. There was no second marriage system in the Gṛhyasūtra period, which proves the existence of child-marriage. Thus the instructions regarding the period of continence after the removal to the husband's

149. V. 28.

150. i. 8. 21.

151. iv. 1. 16.

house has taken place as also regarding the necessity of consummating after the expiry of time can only refer to a grown-up girl. This was the general rule, but a tendency of lowering the marriageable age can be marked in the later Gṛhyasūtras. Gobhila[152] and the author of the Mānava Gṛhyasūtra[153] declare a Nagnika to be the best. It shows that in their time late marriages, though still customary, had fallen into discredit.

During the periods of the Rāmāyaṇa and the Mahābhārata also, girls were grown up at the time of their marriage. In the first chapter of the Rāmāyaṇa it is described that after the brides came to Ayodhya, they, having paid due respects to the elders, lived merrily with their husbands in seclusion, which presupposes post-puberty marriege.[153a] Sītā, again, says to Anasūyā, in the Rāmāyaṇa, "My father, having seen me of marriageable age, became very anxious and pulled down like a man who has lost his wealth. After a long time, the illustrious Rāghava came here with Viśvāmitra to see Yajña (here Dhanuṣa Yajña)."[153b] The above statement shows a girl could wait for a long time after her puberty for suitable match. In the Vanakāṇḍa, however, it is put in the mouth of Sītā that, when Rāvaṇa went to kidnap her, she was eighteen and her husband twenty-five and that they had spent twelve years at Ayodhyā. Thus, the age of Sītā is brought down to about six years at the time of her marriage. But it should be noted that the epic was recast many times and the verses in question are later interpolations, quite inconsistent with overwhelming evidences to post-puberty marriages. Bhavabhūti, in his Uttara-Rāmacharita,[154] simply reflects the ideas of his age when he bases the description of Sītā as a child-bride on the above text of the Rāmāyaṇa.

The Mahābhārata, equally with the Rāmāyaṇa, offers evidences in favour of the marriages of grown-up girls. On hearing the Gāndharva marriage of Śakuntalā, Kaṇva expresses his sentiments,

---

152. ii. 1.

153. i. 7. 12.

153a. अभिवाद्याभिवाद्यांश्च सर्वा राजसुतास्तथा।
रेमिरे मुदिता सर्वा भर्तृभिः सहिताः रहः॥ I. 77. 14.

153b. पतिसंयोगसुलभं वयो दृष्ट्वा तु मे पिता।
चिन्तामभ्यगमद्दीनो वित्तनाशादिवाधनः॥ etc. I. 119. 34.

154. He describes Sita as a child, playing before her mothers-in-law (Act I. 37; I. 20).

"O pure-smiling one, many menses of yours went in vain. Now, you have become fruitful. You have committed no sin.[154a] In the Umā-Maheśvara dialogue, a girl who has attained her puberty is called fit for marriage. "A girl, who bathes after her menses, is called pure. The father, the brother, the mother, the maternal uncle and the paternal uncle should give her away in marriage."[155] Even in the later classical Sanskrit epics the same tradition is maintained. In the Sanskrit dramas the main theme is a love intrigue or a love-marriage, which could only have been possible in the case of grown-up matches.

In subsequent times, the marriageable age of the bride went down lower and lower. There were many causes that conspired to bring about this state of affairs. After the complete subjugation of India the life of the Aryans became ease-loving and luxurious. They became supreme in the country and began to enjoy life in its full profligacy. This led to an early sexual life. The stoppage of Vedic study and the Upanayana of girls also removed the restrictions of a disciplined and chaste life under teachers. But there were other causes also that helped this process. From the third or the fourth century B. C. the foreign invasions of India began. The Greeks, the Bactrian, the Parthians and the Scythians, who were physically stronger but less civilized than the Indians, occupied the North-West provinces of India. The position of woman was very low among these peoples and she was regarded as an article of enjoyment. The social life of the Hindus was endangered and influenced by these onslaughts. Perhaps, for safety and fashion both, they began an early married life.

The Dharmasūtras that were reduced to writing about 500 B. C. onwards clearly evince the tendency of lowering the marriageable age of the bride. They generally expect that a girl should be married before she attains her womanhood. But they permit her to wait for sometimes if her marriage was not arranged by her guardians at the proper time. Vasiṣṭha[156] and Baudhāyana[157] allow

---

154a. ऋतवो बहवस्ते वै गता व्यर्था शुचिस्मिते।
सार्थकं साम्प्रतं ह्येतन्न च पाप्माऽस्ति तेऽनघे ॥ M.B. i. 94. 65.

155. M.B. Anu. 286, 6.

156. कुमारी ऋतुमती त्रीणि वर्षाण्युदीक्षेत। V.D.S. xvii. 59.

157. त्रीणि वर्षाण्युदीक्षेत कुमारी ऋतुमती सती। B.D.S. iv. I. 14.

three years and Gautama[158] and Viṣṇu[159] three months. Though it was desired that marriage should take place before attaining womanhood, the Dharmasūtras are silent about the sin resulting from the late marriage, and they do not inflict stigma and threats on the guardians of a grown-up girl, which is so common with the later authorities. It seems that marriages were generally arranged before sixteen.

Different stages in the evolution of the custom of child marriage can be traced in the Smṛti literature. In the one and the same law-book we find passages which see no offence in marriage between adult, and others which recommend child marriage. It can be accounted for only when we suppose a gradual transition from the Vedic custom of late marriage to an increasing extent of child-marriage.

In the much-discussed passage in Manu[160] the more importance is attached to the question that a father must give his daughter at all events to a suitor of an equal caste and superior qualities than to the problem whether a girl at marriage should be mature or not: "Let the father give the girl, even if she be not yet marriageable, to a suitor who is high-born, handsome and belonging to an equal caste." According to the regulation "Let a girl, when she has reached maturity, remain till death in the house of her father, rather than that one should ever give her to a husband lacking the high qualifications."[161] We, again find in the Manu-Smṛti:[162] "Let a girl wait for an appropriate suitor for three years after the commencement of first menses, from then onwards let her seek a husband for herself from an equal caste." But although in these verses emphasis is laid on the choice of a suitor from an equal caste, yet also on the one hand marriage before puberty is represented in "Aprāptāmapi" as the exception and on the other hand words "Trīṇi" etc.

---

158. त्रीन्कुमारी ऋतूनतीत्य स्वयं युज्येत etc. G.D.S. xviii. 20.

159. Viṣṇu, D.S. 24. 41.

160. उत्कृष्टायाभिरूपाय वराय सदृशाय च।
अप्राप्तामपि तां तस्मै कन्यां दद्याद्यथाविधि॥ ix. 88.

161. काममामरणात्तिष्ठेद्गृहे कन्यर्तुमत्यपि।
न चैवैनां प्रयच्छेत्तु गुणहीनाय कर्हिचित्॥ ix. 89

162. त्रीणि वर्षाण्युदीक्षेत कुमार्यृतुमती सती।
ऊर्ध्वन्तु कालादेतस्माद्विन्देत सदृशं पतिम्। ix. 90.

'three' expressly admit that if an appropriate suitor be not found, marriage may be postponed until after the commencement of menses and may even take place a long time thereafter. And when Manu[163] shortly afterwords lays down that a man of thirty years shall marry a girl of twelve, and a man of twenty-four a girl of eight years, and quickly too, if law is in danger, perhaps, this verse can be regarded as advocating hastened marriage even with a girl who is under age.

But when we come down from the time of the Manu-Smṛti to the later periods, we find regulations which unconditionally enjoin child-marriages. In the Baudhāyana[164] it is stated that "To a virtuous, pure husband the girl should be given while she is still immature; even from an unworthy man she should not be withheld if she has attained womanhood." The strict rules regarding marriage before the commencement of puberty gained additional force from the fact that disregard of it was represented as accompanied by evil consequences to the guardians of the girl. While Manu[165] is content to characterize the father as blameworthy who does not give his daughter in marriage at the proper time, it is stated in Vasiṣṭha:[166] "For fear of commencement of puberty let the father give his daughter in marriage while she is still going about naked. For if she remains at home after the marriageable age sin falls upon the father."

In still later periods the dread of postpuberty marriage became so terrible that the Smṛtis brought down the marriageable age still lower. They divide the marriageable girls into five classes: (1) Nagnikā or naked, (2) Gaurī, eight years old, (3) Rohiṇī, 9 years old, (4) Kanyā, 10 years old and (5) Rajasvalā, above ten years.[166a] Nagnikā was regarded as the best for marriage. Some authorities give ludicrous prescription. For example, a later interpolation in the Mahābhārata says. "The father should give his daughter at her birth to a suitable husband. Having given her away at the

163. ix. 94.

164. Quoted in V.M.S. vol. II.

165. कालेऽदाता पिता वाच्यो वाच्यश्चानुपयन्पतिः।
मृते भर्तरि पुत्रस्तु वाच्यो मातुररक्षिता ॥ M.S. ix. 4.

166. प्रयच्छेन्नग्निका कन्यामृतुकालभयात्पिता।
ऋतुमत्यां हि तिष्ठन्त्यां दोषः पितरमृच्छति ॥ The V.S. xvii.

166a. The Sarvasaṁgraha quoted by Gadādhara on P.G.S. i. 4. 8. Y.S. i. 22; S.S. i. 67; P.S. vii. 6.

proper time, he attains merits."[167] In the opinion of the Brahmapurāṇa[168] also a girl should be given in marriage while she is quite a child: "The father should give his daughter to a handsome husband while she is a child; there he attains his goal; if not, sin falls on him. By all means he should marry his daughter between four and ten. While she does not know womanly bashfulness and plays with dust, she should be given in marriage, if not, the father falls to an evil state."

The hold of child-marriage became so strong that the commentators, who flourished in the mediaeval and the Muslim periods of Indian history, tried to explain away ancient passages in favour of adult marriages. For instance, they say that the verses like "one should remain unmarried if a suitable husband is not available etc." do not increase the age but they emphasize the suitability of the match.

When did this change occur cannot be precisely ascertained. Most probably it took place about the beginning of the Christian era. First, it did not appeal to all the sections of the Hindu society. In the Manu-Smṛti the Gāndharva and the Rākṣasa forms of marriages are recognized. In the Sanskrit dramas and epics grown-up matches are mentioned. But, as already pointed out, the Hindus were influenced by the foreigners, who conquered the North-western parts of India. During the Gupta period, however, there was a national awakening and the security of life, so adult marriages were revived and they continued up to the advent of the muslims. The conquest of India by the Mohammadans, again, made the life of the Hindus insecure, and the influence of the Muslim culture itself was towards the lowering of the marriageable age of a girl.

But besides the danger and influence of the foreign conquest of India, there was a religious belief also which changed the idealog of the Hindus about marriage. Marriage, in course of time, came to be regarded as a gift by the father to her husband. A gift is given once and should not be replaced; moreover, a thing already enjoyed should not be given in gift; its disregard is sinful. Unfor-

---

167. जातमात्रा तु दातव्या कन्यका सदृशे वरे।
काले दत्तासु कन्यासु पिता धर्मेण युज्यते। अनुशासन, 33.

168. यावल्लज्जां न जानाति यावत्क्रीडति पांशुभिः।
तावत्कन्या प्रदातव्या नो चेत्पित्रोरधोगतिम्॥ Chapter 1. 5.

tunately the mythical gods, Soma, Gāndharva and Agni who were believed to help the physical development of a girl,[168a] came to be held as the enjoyers of her person. So the religious father of a girl became anxious to give her away in marriage before she was enjoyed by these gods. A Nagnikā was preferred for this very reason.

At first the age of the bridegroom was not lowered with that of the bride, as its danger and religious need was not felt. But when like girls they also did away with the Āśrama system, their marriageable age fell down. In course of time, in order to make suitable matches, the age of the boy was brought down with that of the girl.

Although these sacred regulations received ever wider acceptance and finally became essential for an orthodox marriage, marriages at an advanced age must have been common for centuries till about the middle ages. Local differences also must have been there, as they are at present. Otherwise it will be difficult to explain the disregard of this custom in the Sanskrit dramas, epics and the mediaeval Rajput customs of grown-up marriages. The early medical authors among the Hindus, have also rightly recognized that a girl does not reach the full development of her physical capacities, even in India, until she is sixteen. Suśruta[169] says: "A man in his twenty-fifth but a girl in her sixteen have reached the summit of their vigour, an experienced doctor ought to know that." In another passage he confirms this view with these details: "When a man who has not reached his twenty-fifth has intercourse with a girl who is below sixteen, the embryo dies in the womb, or if it is born it cannot live long, or lives with little vigour; therefore, one must not permit any to have intercourse with a woman who is too young.

It is a happy sign that all the progressive opinions in India to-day are advocating the cause of grown-up marriages, and the

168a. सोमस्य जाया प्रथमं गन्धर्वस्ते परः पतिः।
तृतीयोऽग्निष्टे पतिस्तुरीयस्ते मनुष्यजाः ॥ R.V. x. 85. 40. V.S. reproduces the above passage and interprets it as follows.

पूर्वं स्त्रियः सुरैर्भुक्ता सोमगन्धर्ववह्निभिः।
गच्छन्ति मानुषान् पश्चाद् नैता दुष्यन्ति धर्मतः ॥
तासां सोमो ददच्छौचं गंधर्वः शिक्षितां गिरम्।
अग्निश्च सर्वभक्षत्वं तस्माद् निष्कल्मषाः स्त्रियः ॥

169. 35. 8.

mediaeval orthodoxy is passing away with the circumstances under which the custom of child-marriage arose. The Government of India have also thought it wise to enact a law, namely "The Child-marriage Restraint Act," otherwise known as "The Sarda Act" to stop this undersirable custom.

(xii) *Qualifications of the Bride*

After the consideration of the age of the bride, her personal qualifications were taken into account. We have no particular reference to this question in the pre-sūtra literature. In the Śatapatha Brāhmaṇa, however, we get a description in which an altar is being compared to a woman from which we can form an idea about the Standard of a beautiful woman. "They praise that woman whose hips are wide, breasts are developed and loin is thin."[170] Again we find, "That beautiful young woman, sweet and emotional." When we come to the Gṛhyasūtras, greater details are supplied to us. The Āśvalāyana Gṛhyasūtras is content with "a woman with good external signs."[171] According to the Bhāradvāja Gṛhyasūtra,[172] there are four considerations in a marriage—wealth, beauty, intellect and family. The more secularly-minded authorities, says the author of the above Gṛhyasūtra, went very far and put the beauty of the bride above all "A man should marry a girl in whom his mind finds pleasure and towards whom his eyes are attracted. A girl of this type is called of good qualities. What will he do with intellect?"[173] But this was not the most accepted canon. The more religiously-minded writers preferred intellect to other considerations. "How could one put up with a woman without intellect?[174]

External qualifications of a bride are more detailed in the Śmṛtis. Manu[175] says, "Let him wed a woman, who is free from

170. एवमिव हि योषां प्रशंसन्ति पृथुश्रोणिर्विमृष्टान्तरा सा मध्ये संग्राह्येति।
S. Br. i. 2. 5. 16.

171. i. 5.

172. चत्वारि विवाहकरणानि वित्तं रूपं प्रज्ञा बान्धवमिति। i. 6.

173. यस्यां मनोऽनुरमते चक्षुश्च प्रतिपद्यते तां विद्यात्पुण्यलक्ष्मीकां किं ज्ञानेन करिष्यतीति। i. 12.

174. अप्रज्ञेयया हि कथं संवासः। i. 16.

175. अव्यंगांगीं सौम्यनाम्नीं हंसवारणगामिनीम्।
तनुलोमकेशदशनां मृद्वंगीमुद्वहेत्स्त्रियम्॥ M.S. iii. 10.

bodily defects; who has an agreeable name, the graceful gait of a swan or an elephant, a moderate quantity of hair on the body and on the head, small teeth and soft limbs." Yājñavalkya[176] speaks in a general way that the bride should be Kāntā or lovely. Śātātapa supplies further details, "Having married a girl whose voice is like that of a swan, whose colour is like that of a cloud and whose eyes are sweet and reddish, a householder finds happiness."[177]

The following girls were avoided on physical grounds: "Let him not marry a maiden (with) reddish (hair) nor one who has a redundant member, nor one who is sickly, nor one either with no hair (on the body) or too much, nor one who is garrulous or has red eyes."[178] The Viṣṇu-Purāṇa, quoted in the Vīramitrodaya, enumerates some other bodily defects of a bride: "One should not marry a woman who has beard or moustaches on her face, nor one whose appearance is like that of a man, nor one whose voice is hoarse, who speaks always satirically. A wise man should not wed a girl whose eyelids do not fall, nor one whose eyesight is lost, whose thighs are covered with hairs, whose ankles are projected or prominent, whose cheeks are sunken, who has lost her lustre, who is suffering from jaundice, whose eyes are red, and whose hands and feet are very thin. One should not marry a girl who is a dwarf or very tall, who has no eye-brows, whose teeth are very rare and whose mouth is terrible."[179]

Awkward and inauspicious names were also a disqualification in a girl. Manu[180] declares, "one should not marry a girl who is named after a constellation, a tree, a river, a low-caste man, a mountain, a bird, a snake, a slave, nor one whose name inspires terror." The idea underlying this prohibition seems to be this, that these names were originally current among the uncultured, rude aboriginal forest-dwellers whose mode of living and contact, both, were avoided by the civilized Aryans. Afterwards these very names were refined and given to girls of respectable families. Ultimately the prohibition was removed. Āpastamba[181] forbids to marry a girl

176. I. 752.

177. Quoted in V.M.S. vol. II. p. 731.

178. M.S. iii. 8.

179. V.M.S. vol. II. p. 731.

180. M.S. iii. 9.

181. सर्वाश्च रेफलकारान्त्यवर्णा विवर्जयेत्। Quoted in V.M.S. vol. II. p. 732.

whose name ends in "r" or "l," most probably on the ground of phonetic difficulties. Yama[182] taboos even a girl who is named after a Veda or a Gāndharva. Perhaps a Veda was thought too sacred for a secular purpose, and a Gāndhrva was a representative of lust, which should not be always present with a woman in the form of her name.

Some other qualifications were also considered while selecting a bride. According to the Vārāha Gṛhyasūtra "One should marry a girl who has brothers, is virgin and is excellent even when stripped of her clothes (Nagnikā)."[183] A brotherless girl was not desired on religious basis, as her eldest son should be adopted by her father and therefore the Fathers of her husband would starve for want of ancestral worship. This prohibition, later on, was not strictly observed, because religious considerations gave way to economic gain. At present people do not attach any importance to this question. Virginity was required to secure a chaste and unwidowed woman. This rule was more and more strictly followed later on, as the remarriage of a widow was altogether tabooed among the upper caste Hindus. The last qualification of Nagnikā has got different and interesting interpretations. The later Smṛtikāras and commentators interpret Nagnikā, as already pointed out, as "a girl who has not attained her womanhood."[184] The commentator on the Mānava-Gṛhyasūtra,[185] however, while repeating the same interpretation, says "Or (one should marry) a Nagnikā who is the best." He further elucidates his remark: "One should marry a woman who proves to be the best even when she is stripped of her clothes, because even ugly women with ornaments and clothes appear charming; therefore, being naked, not all look beautiful."

In this connection it would be interesting to note the view of Sir Thomas More recorded in his Utopia that before marriage a staid and honest matron "Showed the woman, be she maid or widow,

182. वेदनाम्नीं नदीनाम्नीं शैलगन्धर्वनामिकाम् ।
ऋक्षवृक्षलतानाम्नीं दारार्थे परिवर्जयेत् ॥ Ibid.

183. X. 8.

184. नग्निकां तु वदेत्कन्यां यावन्नर्तुमती भवेत् ।
अव्यभिजाता भवेत्कन्या कुचहीना च नग्निका ॥ गृहसग्रह
Quoted V.M.S. vol. II. p. 767.

185. नग्निकामप्राप्तस्त्रीभावाम् ।... अथवा नग्निकां श्रेष्ठां, विवस्त्रा सती श्रेष्ठा या भवेत्तामुपयच्छेत् । यस्मा कुरूपाऽपि वस्त्रालंकारकृता मनोहारिणी भवति । तस्माद्विवस्त्रा सती न सर्वा शोभते । i. 7. 8.

naked to the wooer . . . At this custom we laughed and disallowed it as foolish. But they on their part, do greatly wonder at the folly of all other nations which, in buying a colt . . . be so chary and circumspect that though he be almost all bare, yet they will not buy him unless the saddle and all the harness be taken off, lest under these coverings he hid some gall or sore. And yet in choosing a wife, they be so reckless that all the residue of the woman's body being covered with clothes, they estimate her scarcely by one hand's breadth (for they can see no more than her face) and so join her to them."[186]

This custom of showing the bride naked to the wooer would not have been very common even when and where there was no seclusion of women. With the introduction of the Purdah system in the Hindus, when women became invisible to outsiders, the very demand of showing a girl became absurd, and more absurd became her naked examination.

Further, the bride should be younger (than the bridegroom). Yavīyasī and "Ananyapūrvikā" (not previously having come into physical contact with a man).[187] A younger girl was matched with a grown-up man, because her physical capacities develop earlier than those of a man. There were two kinds of "Anyapūrvikās" Punarbhū and Svairiṇī. Yājñavalkya[188] explains the former as "one married for the second time whether she has come into physical contact of a man or not." The latter according to the same author is "one who, out of lust, having left her own husband, approaches another man." The very prohibition shows that at one time marriage with these women was permissible under law, though not liked by people, But later on when the standard of female chastity became very high and the widow-remarriage was tabooed, such marriages became out of question.

The last, but not the least, qualification of a bride was, that she should be a "Strī" "a woman" or a potential mother. Vijñāneśvara[189] on Yājñavalkya explains the word "Stri" as

186. Quoted by H. Ellis, Studies in Psychology of Sex. vol. vi. p. 102.

187. Yāj. S. I. 52.

188. अक्षता च क्षता चैव पुनर्भूस्संस्कृता पुनः।
स्वैरिणीं वा पतिं हित्वा सवर्णं कामतः श्रयेत्॥ Ibid.

189. अविलुप्तब्रह्मचर्यो लक्षण्यां स्त्रियमुद्वहेत्। Yāj. S. I. 52.
स्त्रियं नपुंसकत्वनिवृत्तये स्त्रीत्वेन परीक्षिताम्। विज्ञानेश्वर, Ibid.

"one examined in her womanhood in order to remove the doubt of barrenness." The main purpose of marriage , according to the Hindus, was the procreation of children, and a woman was compared to a field where seed could be sown. So, there was no sense in marrying a woman, who could not produce children. This consideration was based on the racial instinct of the people. In course of time, however, the idea that marriage was meant for uniting a man and a woman for social purposes rather than for exclusively racial one, gained ground, though it was not absent in early times too. Therefore, the importance of womanhood was not particularly realized. The system of child-marriage also discouraged the examination of a girl.

The internal qualifications of a bride were believed to be difficult to comprehend, so people resorted to queer superstitious means to know them. The Āśvalāyana Gṛhyasūtra[190] says, "(In ternal) signs (of a girl) are very difficult to know. Therefore having brought eight clods of earth from different places, one should address them with the verse. "Ṛta, the moral order was born first in the very beginning. The Truth is established in the moral order. Let that come to her to which the girl is born. Let that be seen what is true." After the clods were addressed thus, the girl was asked to touch a particular clod she liked. Different clods told different fortunes, according to which the poor girl was either accepted or rejected. Gobhila[191] and Śaunaka[192] repeat the same test. But it seems that the test in question was not very popular as it is mentioned by no other ancient authorities. The Dharmasūtras, and the Smṛtis do not refer to it. The modern Paddhatis do not contain it. Perhaps it was omitted very early as a silly procedure.

Such were the ideal qualifications of a bride. But, if strictly expected, they would have excluded fifty percent of girls from matrimony. The practice, however, must have been milder than the rules. In course of time, family and monetary considerations became so important that they overhadowed all others except the virginity of the girl. When child-marriage became very common, the bridegroom, who must have been very inquisitive about his mate, lost his voice in the matter and automatically the examination of the bride came to be neglected. Only in the Deccan and the South,

190. दुर्विज्ञेयानि लक्षणानीति। अष्टौ पिण्डान्कृत्वा पिण्डानभिमंत्रयते। i. 5.

191. G.G.S. ii. 1.

192. Quoted in, V.M.S. vol. II. p. 732.

ancient Hindu traditions are alive to some extent and a cursory formal test of the bride takes place.

(viii) Qualifications of the Bride-groom

The qualifications of a bride-groom were equally high. Yājña-valkya[193] says that a bride-groom should possess all the good qualities of a bride. So there was no concession or partiality towards the former. The first requirement of a bride-groom was the completion of his Brahmacharya. Manu[194] declares: "A student who has studied, in due order, the three Vedas, or even only one, without breaking the rules of studentship, shall enter order of a householder." He[195] again adds, "Having bathed with the permission of his teacher, and performed the Samāvartana according to the rules, a twice-born should marry a wife." Brahmacharya was a primary condition accepted by almost all the Smṛtis.

The next important qualification of a bridegroom was his age. According to the Liṅga-Purāṇa quoted in the Vīramitrodaya, "Before anything else, the age should be considered and then other signs. What is the use of the signs of a man who has passed his marriageable age?"[196]

In the opinion of the Vārāha-Gṛhyasūtra[197] "a bridegroom should have subdued his anger and be cheerful in his spirits". Other considerations were wealth, beauty, learning, intellect and family status. The latter were more important than the former. Gautama[198] says that the bride should be given to "a man who possesses learning, character, friends, and modesty." Āpastamba[199] gives similar qualifications. Yama lays down the most comprehensive qualifications of a bridegroom: "Having considered the family, character, physique, age, learning, wealth and resourcefulness—these seven quali-

---

193. एतैरेव गुणैर्युक्तः। Yāj. S. I. 55.

194. वेदानधीत्य वेदौ वा वेदं वापि यथाक्रमम्।
अविप्लुतब्रह्मचर्यो गृहस्थाश्रममावसेत्॥ M.S. iii. 2.

195. iii. 4.

196. पूर्वमायुः परीक्षेत पश्चाल्लक्षणमादिशेत्।
आयुर्हीननराणां च लक्षणैः किं प्रयोजनम्॥ V.M.S. vol. II. p. 752.

197. विनीतक्रोधः सहर्षः सहर्षां भार्यां विन्देत। x. 1; x. 6.

198. विद्याचारित्र्यबन्धुशीलसम्पन्नाय कन्यां दद्यात्। G.D.S.

199. बन्धुशीललक्षणसम्पन्नः श्रुतवानरोग इति। Ap. D.S. 1. 3. 20.

fications of a bridgroom—a wise man should give his daughter to him; there is nothing else to be considered."[200]

Just as "Strītva" or womanhood was essential in a bride, so Puṁstva or potency was an indispensable quality in a bridegroom. "Women are created for offsprings; a woman is the field and a man is the possessor of the seed; the field should be given to him who possesses the seed; a man without the seed does not deserve a girl."[201] "If a man is really found potent after his examination in potency by the signs of his own limbs, he deserves a girl."[202] Nārada[203] mentions fourteen kinds of impotent men who were to be avoided.

Ananyapūrvakatva or virginity so necessary in the case of a bride was not essential in a bridegroom, though observance of Brahmacharya was required from him. A Hindu could marry a second time if his first wife was dead, or if she was physically incompetent or morally depraved.[204] In the case of a man his second marriage was imperative on religious grounds. "A man having burnt his dead wife with Agnihotra should marry another woman without delaying the worship of his domestic Fire any further."[205] But giving one's daughter to a bachelor was regarded more meritorious than to a man who married for a second time. "The gift of a girl in the hands of a man, who has not burnt his wife brings infinite merits; in the hands of a man who marries for a second time it brings only half, but the gift is quite fruitless if it is made to a man who has married several times."[206]

---

200. कुलं च शीलं च वपुर्वयश्च विद्यां च वित्तं च सनाथताञ्च ।
एतान्गुणान्सप्त परीक्ष्य देया कन्या बुधैः शेषमचि तनीयम्।। Quoted in V.M.S. vol. II p. 754.

201. अपत्यार्थं स्त्रियः सृष्टाः स्त्रीक्षेत्रं बीजिनो नराः ।
क्षेत्रं बीजवते देयं नाबीजी क्षेत्रमर्हति ।। Nārada quoted by Gadādhara on the P.G.S. i. 8.

202. Ibid.

203. Ibid.

204. Yāj. S. I. 72–74.

205 दाहयित्वाऽग्निहोत्रेण स्त्रियं वृत्तवतीं पतिः ।
आहरेद्विधिवद्दारानग्नींश्चैवाविलम्बयेत् ।। Yāj. S. I. 89.

206. अदग्धहस्ते यद्दत्तं तदनन्तफलं स्मृतम् ।
दग्धहस्ते तदर्द्धं स्यान्निष्फलं बहुगृह्लतः ।। Quoted in V.M.S. vol. II. p. 756.

The disqualifications of a bridegroom were several. The following bridegrooms were to be avoided: "One who is retired from life, one who is hated by his people or left by his friends and relatives, one who belongs to another caste, one who suffers from consumption, one who is a "Liṅgastha" (living in disguise) or an Udarī (having a large belly), lunatic or fallen, who is leper, impotent, or a man of the same Gotra, one who has lost sight and ears or suffers from epilepsy—these all should be disapproved for marriage. If these defects exist before marriage (somehow unknown) or arise after it, in both the cases, the gift of a girl should be regarded invalid."[207] "One should take back his daughter if she is given to a man who has no respectable family and character, who is impotent and excommunicated from his caste, infected with epilepsy, belonging to a different religion, sickly and living in disguise."[208] The same authority enumerates other disqualifications as follows: "A girl should not be given to six kinds of men—one who is very near or very far away, who is either very strong or very weak, who has no means of livelihood and one who is an idiot."[209] Old age and ugliness were also regarded as defects in a bridegroom: "If a man, out of greed for money, gives his daughter to a man who is old, wicked or ugly he is born in his next life as a "Preta" (an evil spirit)."[210]

In early times when girls were married in advanced age and freedom of choice was allowed to them, these qualifications of a bridegroom were more real and valued than in subsequent times when early marriage became the rule and post-puberty marriage came to be stigmatized. The strict Śastric injunction was enforced that "a Nagnikā girl should be given to a meritorious and celebate man, or even to one without merits, but one should not delay the marriage of a marriageable girl."[211] The parents, no doubt, still cherish the pious desire of selecting the most suitable husband, but they do not

---

207. कात्यायन, Ibid. p. 758.

208. कुलशीलविहीनस्य षण्ढादिपतितस्य च।
अपस्मारिविधर्मस्य रोगिणां वेषधारिणाम्॥
दत्तामपि हरेत्कन्यां सगोत्रोढां तथैव च। वसिष्ठ Ibid.

209. Ibid.

210. कन्यां यच्छति वृद्धाय नीचाय धनलिप्सया।
कुरूपायाकुलीनाय स प्रेतो जायते नरः॥ पराशर Ibid.

211. दद्याद्गुणवते कन्यां नग्निकां ब्रह्मचारिणे।
अपि वा गुणहीनाय नोपरुन्ध्याद्रजस्वलाम्। बौधायन, Ibid.

pay full attention to purely religious considerations and the rules of racial eugenics. The greatest determining factors in marriage, at present, are wealth and social status of the bridegroom. Under the present Hindu Law, marriage with those persons who are regarded invalids in early Smṛtis, is recognized as legal.

(xiv) The Ceremonies

(a) Original Simplicity. When the proper selection of the bride and the bridegroom was made, the ceremonies relating to marriage began. In the beginning they must have been very simple. A woman was given to a man by the constituted authority by which they became wife and husband. But as marriage was a very important occasion in the community, many rites, practices and customs arose, which were regulated by the community itself. In course of time the society became complex and many local and chronological differences came into existence.

(b) Gradual complexity. Marriage ceremonies had, primarily, their origin in religious belief of the people, but as marriage was a *festive* event in the communal life, all sorts of mirths and amusements were associated with it in the form of feasts, music, dance etc. *Decoration* of the house and adornment of the bride and the bridegroom expressed aesthetic motives natural to any important event in social life. Besides, we find a number of ceremonies which are suggestive of various features in a marriage. *The assemblage* of the people had its origin in *the vested interest* of the parties concerned. The relatives of the bride had some sort of control or right over her, hence it was necessary that she should be given in their presence, so that there may be no impediment. A large group of ceremonies are *symbolical*. One class of them symbolizes the *union* between the wife and the husband. For example, joining of hands, tying of garments, touching of heart etc. had for their motives the union of the pair. Another group of ceremonies had their origin in desire to promote the *fertility* of the union, or to ensure an *abundance of food* for the household. Some ceremonies are connected with the idea that some *danger* is attendant on every transitional period of life and it should be averted by proper rites. Because marriage inaugurated the most important epoch in one's life, many ceremonies were performed to ward off the evil influences connected with the event. Other features of the marriage ceremonies are essentially *religious* in their origin. The beneficient gods are invoked for boons and blessings and specific appeals are sent to unseen powers with definite

rites of sacrifice and prayer. Divinatory elements are also religious in their character, because they seek to find out whether the higher powers are propitious at a particular time or not.

(c) The Vedic Period. We have no knowledge of the pre-Vedic marriage ceremonies. Most probably they may have been prototypes of those described in the Vedic literature. The marriage rites and ceremonies must have varied in different families even in Ṛgvedic times, but of it we possess no records. We must be content with the information supplied by the marriage hymns of the Ṛgveda[212] and the Atharvaveda.[213] These hymns begin with the allegory of *the marriage of Sūryā,* the daughter of the sun with Soma or the moon. The whole scene is made the basis of a metaphoric description in which the heavens take part. However imaginary the plot may be, it can be safely concluded that the poets largely drew upon the knowledge of the rites they had from the practical life. From these hymns we can make out the main details of the marriage rites prevalent in those times. But we cannot be certain as to in what order they occurred. The procedures given in the Ṛgveda and the Atharvaveda differ at certain points and both the procedures vary from that given in the Gṛhyasūtras. The description given in the Atharvaveda is more detailed. So, noting the differences, we should rely on it for the knowledge of the nuptials in the Vedic period. The following description follows mainly the order, in which the verses are given in the Atharvaveda:

The bride bearing a *beautiful robe* and a coverlet, eyes daubed with unguents, head dressed up in the Opaśa or Kurīra style, started for the house of her intended lord in a canopied chariot accompanied by bridal friends (anudeyī).[214] Her treasure-chest (Kośa) containing her dowry was also placed in her chariot.[215]

When she left her father's house the following *benedictions* were pronounced; "Worship we pay to Aryama, finder of husbands, kindly friends. As from its stalk a cucumber, from here I loose thee, not from there. Hence and not thence I send her free. I make her softly fettered there, that bounteus Indra, she

212. x. 85.

213. xiv. 1, 2.

214. 215. The A.V. xiv. 6—13.

may live blest in her fortune and her sons. Now from the noose of Varuṇa I free thee, wherewith the blessed Savitā has bound thee, In the heaven of righteousness, in the world of virtue, be it pleasant for thee, accompanied by the wooer. Let Bhaga take thy hand and hence conduct thee. Go to the house to be the householder's mistress, and speak as a lady to thy gathered people."[216]

On the day of marriage the bride was bathed in water consecrated with Vedic verses and a yoke was held over her head.[217] She was then dressed with the recital of verses. The mother shed tears on the impending departure of her daughter.[218]

Then the actual wedding rite began. The bride was made to stand on a stone, to represent "the lap of earth."[219] The bridegroom took her hand muttering appropriate verses and promised to cherish her [220]

Then the bridegroom presented to have robes and jewels with which she was invested,[221] and he expressed his rapture at the sight of the newly berobed and bejewelled bride.[222] After saying some prayers to drive away demons and blessing a chariot, they started on a marriage procession.[223] Verses were recited, while the procession was going round, to the effect that the bride was first the wife of Soma, then of Gandharva, then of Agni who lastly bestowed her on her human husband.[224] Then the procession returned to the house of the bridegroom from where demons were exorcised. The bride entered the house, then sat with her husband before the household fire, covered with a wrapper presented to her. She sat on a bull-skin on which was spread the Bulbaja grass and worshipped Agni with her husband.[225]

---

216. Ibid. xiv. i. 17–20.
217. Ibid. xiv. 1. 40.
218. Ibid. xiv. 1. 46.
219. Ibid. xiv. 1. 47.
220. Ibid. xiv. 1. 4–51.
221. Ibid. xiv. 1. 53–57.
222. Ibid. xiv. 1. 59.
223. Ibid. xiv. 1. 60–64.
224. Ibid. xiv. 2. 2–11.
225. Ibid. 12–18, 19, 20, 24.

After this the bride was blessed: "Let there come forth from the lap of this mother animals (children) of various forms, being born; as one of excellent omen, sit thou by this fire, with thy husband be thou serviceable to the gods here. Of excellent omen, extender of houses, very propitious to thy husband, wealful to thy father-in-law, pleasant to thy mother-in-law, pleasant to thy husband and house, pleasant to all their clan; pleasant unto their property be thou. Of excellent omen is this bride; come together, see her, having given her good fortune. What evil-hearted, young women, and likewise, what old ones (are) here, do ye all give splendour to her. They go asunder and away home."[226]

Consummation of the marriage immediately followed the nuptial ceremony.[227] At night the bride was conducted to the bridal bed, where she and the bride-groom anointed each other's eyes. The bride invested her husband with her Manu-born garment and the bride was told by her husband to mount the bridal couch with verses appropriate to the occasion. After this, Viśvāvasu, the Gandharva attached to unmarried girls, was prayed to go away from her[228] and co-habitation followed with the recital of verses. Then valiant sons were prayed for and Agni was supplicated for giving ten sons to the couple.[229]

In the end the nuptial garment was presented to the Brahman priest, so that demons go away with that robe and numerous benedictions were uttered on the newly wedded couple.[230] The husband finally welcomed his wife, "I am the man, that dame art thou; I am the Sāman, thou the Ṛchā; I am the heaven, thou the earth; so will we dwell together, parents of children yet to be."[231]

The marriage customs were almost the same in the Ṛgvedic and the Atharvavedic times, though the Atharvavedic marriage hymns disclose a few changes in the arrangement of the proceedings. Indeed the marriage hymn of the Ṛgveda (X. 85) is taken bodily in the Atharvaveda but with some important changes and

226. Ibid. 25–29.

227. Ibid. vii. 36.

228. Ibid. vii. 37.

229. Ibid. xiv. 2. 33–36.

230. Ibid. 40–50, 51–57.

231. Ibid. 71

is extended up to two long hymns with 64 and 75 verses, forming the whole Kāṇḍa XIV of the Atharvaveda. The taking of the hand of the bride by the bridegroom is the most important ceremony here as it was in the Ṛgveda, and the gift of the bride, as before, rests with her father, the bridegroom going to him to sue for her. But grasping of the bride's hand appears to take place at her house, as generally now is the case, and not at the bridegroom's, because the bridal procession is mentioned again. Curiously enough, the Atharvaveda omits the prayer for ten sons appearing in the Ṛgveda.

Regarding the ceremonies given in the marriage hymns of the Ṛgveda and the Atharvaveda, one thing should be observed that the main outlines of the Hindu marriage rituals of to-day are almost the same as they were some five thousand years ago.

(d) The Sūtra Period. During the Sūtra period the ritualists arranged the floating mass of rituals into a system and every Gṛhyasūtra describes the ceremonies in a set order.[231a] The Gṛhyasūtras, however, differ slightly in the arrangement of their matters and contain a few varying details. It was due to the fact that every Vedic family had its own Sūtras, containing local and tribal differences. But there was no material difference, the religious and the social backgrounds being the same. They quote almost the same Vedic verses and follow the same marriage customs. In addition to the ceremonies developed in the Vedic period, a few new features are found in the Gṛhyasūtras. We can form an idea of the procedure followed in the nuptial ceremonies by the contents given in the two following Gṛhyasūtras:

Pāraskara Gṛhyasūtra	Baudhāyana Gṛhyasūtra
1. Arghya and Madhuparka	1. Vara-prekṣaṇaṁ
2. Vastra paridhānaṁ	2. Brahmaṇa-bhojana.
3. Samañjana	3. Nāndimukha. Vivāha-Homa.
4. Vadhvāsaha Niṣkramaṇa	4. The going of the bride groom to the bride.
5. Samikṣaṇaṁ	5. Samīkṣaṇaṁ

231a. Ś.G.S. i. 5; A.G.S. i. 5; P.G.S. i. 4—8; G.G.S. ii. 1; Kh. G.S. i. 3; H.G.S. i. 19. Āp. G.S. 2. 12. B.G.S. i. 1; Bh. G.S. i. 11—20; M.G.S. i. 7—12; J.G.S. i. 20 ff.

6. Agnipradakṣiṇaṁ	6. Hasta-grahaṇaṁ
7. Vaivāhika Homa Ājyāhuti, Rāṣṭrabhṛta, Jaya and Abhyātana Homas.	7. Saptapadī
8. Lājā-homa	8. Arghya and Madhuparka
9. Pāṇi-grahaṇam	9. Alaṁkaraṇaṁ
10. Aśmārohaṇaṁ	10. Homa to Aditi, Anumati, Sarasvatī, Savitā and Prajāpati.
11. Gāthā-gānaṁ	11. Hṛdaya-sparśa
12. Agni parikramaṇaṁ	12. Karṇe japa
13. Śeṣa-Lājā-Homa	13. Pāṇi-grahaṇaṁ
14. Saptapadī	14. Agni-pradakṣiṇaṁ
15. Mūrdhābhiṣeka	15. Aśmārohaṇaṁ
16. Sūrya-darśanaṁ	16. Lājā-Homa
17. Hṛdaya sparśa	17. Again Agni-pradakṣiṇā
18. Abhimantraṇa	18. Prājāpatya and other offerings.
19. Sitting on a bull-skin	19. Udvāha or departure.
20. Grāma-vachana	20. Gṛha-praveśa.
21. Gift to the Āchārya	21. Sitting on the bull skin
22. Dhurva-darśana	22. Dhruva, Arundhatī and Saptarṣi-darśanaṁ
23. Trirātra-Vrata	23. Trirātra Vrata
24. Āvasathya Homa	24. Chaturthī-karma
25. Udvāhanaṁ	25. Upasaṁveśanaṁ
26. Chaturthī-Karma	
27. Mūrdhābhiṣinchanaṁ	
28. Sthāli-pāka-prāśana	
29. The First Lesson in Conjugal Fidelity.	
30. (Garbhādhānaṁ)	

The above table shows that while mainly following the Vedic rituals, the Gṛhyasūtras elaborated the nuptials and introduced many notable changes, e.g. Madhuparka, Lājā-Homa, Aśmārohaṇaṁ,

Gāthāgānaṁ, Mūrdhābhiṣeka, Hṛdayasparśa, Sūrya-darśana etc. and above all, the great Saptapadī. It would be in vain to try to trace the whole of the Gṛhyasūtra ceremonies in the Vedas. It seems that after the Vedic period, many popular rites and ceremonies were assimilated and given place in the scriptures by the priests, who wanted to enlarge the range of their religion. These later additions did not originally form the part of the Vedic rituals.

(e) Later Innovations. After the Sūtra period, the marriage ceremonies underwent further changes. Many modifications and innovations were introduced. Grāmavachanaṁ of the Pāraskara Gṛhyasūtra[231b] and Janapada-Dharma[231c] of the Āśvalāyana Gṛhyasūtra were potent factors for producing new features in the Saṁskāra. According to the former, many items of the Saṁskāra took their sanction from the old men and women, who were the custodians of ancient and popular rites and ceremonies. The latter recognizes that local customs differed from place to place and they should be consulted in the performance of the Saṁskāra. Nārāyaṇa Bhaṭṭa remarks on the importance of customs. 'The procedure has been given but it should be followed according to one's own Deśācāra."[232] Kamalākara in his Nirṇaya Sindhu says. "The customs prevalent in one's own province and village should be relied upon in the matter of marriage."[232a] The Saṁskāra-Kaustubha informs "Many people overruled the express rules of the scriptures and followed the Deśācāra."[233]

(f) The Present Form. Thus, in course of time, the religious ideology, social customs and rites and ceremonies changed. In the beginning, however, the scriptures were anxious to record only Vedic rituals and did not give the proper place to purely popular rites and customs. Later on, the priests were forced by the circumstance to recognize the latter. The Paddhatis and the Prayogas on the marriage ceremonies, that are more practical than the ancient scriptures, incorporated many new elements under the aus-

231b. ग्रामवचनं च कुर्युः। i. 8. 11.

231c. i. 5.

232. क्रमः उक्तः स च देशाचारवशेनानुसर्तव्यः : The Prayogaratna.

232a. जनपदधर्मा ग्रामधर्माश्च विवाहे प्रतीयान्। पूर्वभाग iii.

233. सकलग्रन्थाननादृत्याचारानुसरणमेवेच्छ.परितोषार्थं यथाचारमपि प्रयोगो लिख्यते।

pices of the Saṁskāra. In different parts of India, different Paddhatis and Prayogas are followed. Consequently, the marriage ceremonies also differ in different localities. But religious and social conservatism is so strong in India that the main outlines of the Saṁskāra are continued from the Vedic period down to the present time, and its general features are universal through the country. Generally speaking, the following procedure is adopted in the Paddhatis and the Prayogas:

Māṇḍalika	Gadādhara
1. Vāgdāna	1. Vāgdāna
2. Maṇḍapakaraṇa	2. Mṛdāharaṇa
3. Puṇyāha-vāchana	3. Haridrālāpana
4. Varagamana	4. Maṇḍapa-nirmāṇa
5. Madhuparka	5. Gaṇapati-pūjana
6. Viṣṭaradāna	6. Saṁkalpa
7. Gaurihara-pūjā	7. Nāndī-Śraddha
8. Kanyādānīya Jalaśuddhi	8. Vara-Varaṇa
9. Kanyādāna	9. Ghaṭi-Sthāpana
10. Akṣataropaṇa	10. Varagamana
11. Kaṅkaṇa-Bandhana	11. Nīrājana
12. Ārdrākṣataropaṇa	12. Madhuparka
13. Tilakakaraṇa	13. Vara-pujā
14. Aṣṭaphalidāna	14. Agni-sthāpana
15. Maṅgala sūtrabandhana	15. Vastra-paridhāpana
16. Gaṇapatipūjana	16. Samañjana
17. Vadhūvaryoruttarīya-prāntabandhana	17. Gotrochchāra
18. Akṣatāropaṇa	18. Kanyādāna
19. Lakṣmi-Pārvati-Śachipūjana	19. Pratigrahaṇa
20. Vāpanadāna	20. Samīkṣaṇa
21. Vivāha-Homa	21. Agni-Pradakṣiṇā
22. Saptapadī	22. Vaivāhika Homa etc.
23. Gṛhapraveśa-Homa	23. Lājā-Homa
24. Arṇidānam	24. Pāṇi-grahaṇa

Māṇḍalika	Gadādhara
25. Svasurāya Kanyārpaṇa	25. Aśmārohaṇa
26. Devakotthāpanaṁ and Maṇḍapodvāsana	26. Gāthāgāna
27. Gṛhapraveśa	27. Śeṣa Lājā-Homa with Parikramā
28. Saptapadī	29. Abhiṣiñchana
30. Sūryāvalokana	31. Hṛdaya-sparśa
32. Abhimantraṇa	33. Sindūra-dāna
34. Sitting on a bull-skin	35. Dakṣiṇā to Ācārya
36. Dhruva-darśana	37. Trirātra-vrata
38. Devakotthāpana and Maṇḍapodvasana	39. Vadhūpraveśa
40. Chaturthīkarma	

(g) Description and Significance.

(1) Betrothal

The preliminary part of the marriage ceremonies consisted in the Vāgdānam (Betrothal) or oral giving away of the bride to the bridegroom. In early times, the selection of the bride and the bridegroom was mutual either from love or other considerations, and in the majority of cases love formed the dominant factor. When the parental control over the children became more rigid, the formal consent of the parents became necessary. Even in the Ṛgvedic times the bridegroom's friends approached the bride's father, to whom the formal proposal was made, as was done in the case of Sūryā by the Aśvins on behalf of Soma.[234] If the bride's father approved the selection, the marriage was settled. The Gṛhyasūtras generally do not begin with the betrothal ceremonies, so we have no information as to how they were performed. One tradition is recorded in the Nārada-Smṛti. Here betrothal is called Kanyāvaraṇa. According to it, not only the friends of the bridegroom, but the bridegroom himself with friends went to the father of the bride for the formal settlement of the marriage. "Within the month of marriage, on an auspicious day, the Kanyāvaraṇa ceremony should be performed.

234. The R.V. x. 85. 9, 15, 33.

The bridegroom, well-dressed and well-adorned, with music and chanting of sacred verses, should go to the bride's home with a loving heart. Then the bride's father should give his consent happily. The bridegroom, having propitiated Śachī, should worship the well-adorned bride and pray to her for good luck, health and progeny."[235] It seems that in the mediaeval times the custom of the bridegroom's himself approaching the bride's father was dropped and he was substituted by his father, who, with a party, went to the bride's father for the oral reception of the bride on behalf of his son. The description of this ceremony as given by Gadāhara is as follows: "In an auspicious time according to astrology, two, four or eight gentlemen, putting on agreeable robes. with the father of the bridegroom, having seen the Śakuna bird should go to the house of the bride's father and request him, "Give your daughter to my son." The bride's father having consulted his wife etc. should say. "On this auspicious moment I give this girl, born in such and such Gotra, daughter of such and such person and namely so and so." After this he should recite the verse, "This girl has been orally given by me for progeny and accepted by you. Be happy in inspecting the girl, having made up your mind." The father of the bridegroom should reply, "The girl has been orally given by you for progeny and accepted by me for progeny. Be happy in seeing the bridegroom, having made up your mind."[236] After the proposal was accepted the father of the bridegroom worshipped the girl with rice, clothes, flowers etc. according to his family custom. The ceremony ended with the blessings of the Brahmans.[237]

This custom is still alive in the Deccan in the form of formally seeing the girl and settling the marriage. In Northern India, however, the Purdah system and the supremacy of dowry have abolished this useful custom. Here, in the majority of cases, betrothal consists in fixing the sum to be paid by the bride's father and presenting the Sacred Thread, money and some fruits to the bridegroom which is called Vararakṣā or Phalādāna. By this ceremony the guardian of the bridegroom is supposed to be morally tied down to the proposal.

The custom of Vara-varaṇa has become more important than that of Kanyā-varaṇa. According to Chaṇḍeśvara "The brother

235. Quoted in V.M.S. vol. II. p. 810.

236. The Vāgdānavidhi, quoted by Gadādhara on P.G.S.

237. ततो ब्राह्मणाश्च आशीर्मन्त्रान्पठेयुः। ibid.

of the bride and Brahmans should go to the house of the bridegroom and offer him Upavīta, fruits, flowers, clothes etc. at the occasion of Vara-varaṇa."[238] At present, this custom is popularly known as Tilaka, and in addition to the articles mentioned above a fixed sum of money is also presented. In the opinion of Gadādhara this ceremoney should take place one day before the marriage, but generally it is performed many days before it.

(2) *Marriage* Day

After the betrothal an auspicious day is fixed for the wedding ceremonies. Astrological considerations do not seem to play an important part in ancient times. As the union of the bride and the bridegroom depended upon mutual attraction of love, there was not much scope for making matches on the actual calculation and determination of the movements of stars. Moreover, though the ancient Hindus were acquainted with astronomy and astrology, the particular branch of astrology that deals with marriage was either not developed or was not much consulted for arranging a marriage. In the Gṛhyasūtras, the astrological considerations are very simple. Marriage was generally performed when the sun was in the northern hemisphere, in the bright half of a month and on an auspicious day. The later Smṛtis, the Purāṇas, the mediaeval astrological works and the Nibandhas are very particular about fixing the proper time for every detail of the marriage ceremony.

(3) *Mṛdāharaṇa*

A few days before the wedding, the ceremony of Mṛdāharaṇa?"[238a] (bringing some earth or clay) ceremony is performed. The origin of this ceremony is popular and it does not find mention in the ancient scriptures of the Hindus. The Jyotirnibandha quoted by Gadādhara says, "In the beginning of every auspicious ceremony sprouts should be used for Maṅgala decoration. On the ninth seventh, fifth or third day before the marriage, in an auspicious moment with music and dancing, one should go in the northern or eastern direction of his house to fetch the earth for growing sprouts in a pot of clay or a basket of bamboo."[239] Another cere-

238. उपनीतं फलं पुष्पं वासांसि विविधानि च।
देयं वराय वरणे कन्याभ्रात्रा द्विजेन च। The Kṛtyacintāmani,

238a. This ceremony is found in the Paddhatis only.

239. Quoted by Gadādhara on P.G.S. 1. 8.

mony performed before marriage is *haridrālepana* or besmearing the bride and the bridegroom with ointment of turmeric root and oil, a day or two before the wedding. The above substances besides being useful to the body are regarded auspicious also.

(4) The Worship of Gaṇeśa

The ceremonies preceding the marriage day are the following: In the beginning the most auspicious god Gaṇeśa is worshipped and his symbol is installed in the nuptial canopy erected according to the rules laid down in the scriptures. The sacrificial altar for the Vaivāhika Homa is also built under the canopy. Then the father of the bride with his wife, in the first half of the day, having bathed, puts on auspicious robes. Next, having seated himself, he sips water and restrains his breaths. After this he prays to place and time, and makes up his mind (Saṁkalpa) to perform Svastivāchana. Maṇḍapa-pratiṣṭhā, Matṛ-pūjana, Vasordhārāpūjana, Āyuṣyajapa and Nāndi-śrāddha as ancillary to marriage.[240] The Saṁkalpa is "a psychological act, the determination to direct and control one's energies in such ways as will secure the attainment of object in view."[241]

(5) Ghaṭikā

On the day of marriage a Ghaṭi or waterclock (Clepsydra) is established with the verse, 'Thou art the mouth of the (universal) machinery, created by Brahman in the beginning; for the Bhāva (good feelings) and Abhāva (lack of good feelings) between the husband and the wife, thou art the measurer."[242] The clock is not only useful carrying the nuptial programme at proper times but it is also symbolical of Time that rules over the entire universe. It should be noted that this custom is not very popular.

(6) The Nuptial Bath

In the morning the bride and the bridgroom, at their respective homes, take the nupital bath with scented water and recital of

240. The गर्गपद्धति।

241. Raghunatha Rao: The Aryan Marriage, p. 20.

242. मुखं त्वमसि यन्त्राणां ब्रह्मणा निर्मितं पुरा।
भावाभावाय दम्पत्योः कालः साधनकारणम् ।। Quoted by Gadādhara on P.G. S. i. 4–8. This item is not found in G.Ss.

Vedic verses indicative of the physical union of the husband and the wife.[243] Then from the side of the bridegroom, the marriage party proceeds to the place of the bride's father. "In the second half of the day, the bridegroom bathes, puts on a pair of white clothes, decorates himself with scent and garlands and prays to the family gods. After this he feeds the Brahmans, who recite the sacred verses.

(7) The Marriage Party

Then many amusements take place and the bridegroom with his friends and relatives, goes to the house of the bride on conveyance suited to his status."[244] At arrival, the bridegroom stands outside the gate of the house facing the east and is welcomed by a company of women bearing lamps and jars full of water," (The marriage procession is mentioned as early as in the Ṛgveda and the Atharvaveda.[245] The Śānkhyāyana and the Āśvalāyana Gṛhyasūtras also describe it, with the marked difference that the conveyance for the bridegrom was either a chariot, an elephant or a horse. There was no system of a palanquin carried by men. Perhaps it was introduced during muslim period.)

(8) The Madhuparka

The first honour that the father-in-law bestows upon the bridegroom is the offering of Madhuparka,[245a] a rare honour, reserved for the distinguished persons of society and the most respected relatives. Having ordered a seat to be got for the guest, the father-in-law says, "Well Sir! Sit down! We will do honour to you, Sir!" They get for him a couch (of grass), to sit down on, another for the feet, water for washing the feet, the Arghya water, water for sipping and the honey mixture in a brass vessel with a brass cover. Another person three times announces to the guest the couch and other things when they are offered to him. The bridegroom accepts the couch and sits down thereon with the verse, "I am the highest one among my peoples as the sun among the thunder bolts. Here I tread on

243. G.G.S. ii. 1. 10; Ś.G.S. i. 11; Kh. G.S. i. 3. 6.

244 कृतकौतुकबन्धश्च मित्रबान्धवसंयुतः ।
यानं यथार्हमारुह्य यातव्यं च वधूगृहम् ॥ Śaunaka quoted in V.M.S. vol. II. p. 819.

245. R.V. x. 85; A.V. xiv. 1, 2.

245a. P.G.S. i. 3. 1–32.

whosoever infests me." When he sits on the couch, the father-in-law washes the left foot and then the right foot of the guest: If the host is a Brahman, the right first. He does so with the formula, "The milk of Virāj art thou. The milk of Virāj may I attain. (May) the milk of Pādya Virāj dwell in me." The bridegroom accepts the Arghya water with the words, "Waters are ye. May I obtain through you all my wishes." Pouring it out he recites over the waters the formula. "To the ocean I send you; go back to your source. Unhurt be our men. May my sap be not shed." He sips water with the formula. "Thou cometh to me with glory. Unite me with lustre. Make me beloved with all creatures, the lord of cattle, unhurtful for the bodies. Then he looks at the Madhuparka with the words, "With Mitra act" and accepts it with the formula, "By the impulse of the god Savitṛ etc." Taking it into his left hand, he stirs it about three times with the fourth finger of his right hand with the formula, "Adoration to the brown-faced one. What has been damaged when the food was eaten, that I cut off from thee." With the fourth finger and the thumb he spirits away some part of it and partakes it three times with the formula, "What is the honeyed, highest form of honey, and by that enjoyment of food may I become highest, honeyed and an enjoyer of food." Having sipped water he touches the bodily organs with the formula, 'May speech dwell in my mouth, breath in my nose, sight in my eyes, hearing in my ears, strength in my arms, vigour in my things. May my limbs be unhurt. May my body be united with my body."[246]

In ancient times, the Argha ceremony was not complete without sacrificing a cow in the honour of the guest.[247] When the guest had sipped water, the host, holding a butcher's knife, said to him three times. "A Cow." To this the guest replied. "The mother of the Rudras, the daughter of the Vasus, the sister of the Ādityas, the navel of immortality. To the people who understand me, I say, "Do not kill the guiltless cow which is Aditi." I kill my sin and N. N.'s sin." This verse was recited if he chose to have it killed. But if he chose to let it loose, he said, "My sin and N. N.'s sin has been killed. Om! let it loose! Let it eat grass!"[248] The cow was the choicest present of the Indo-Aryans.

246. This is the ceremonial reception of the Indo-Aryans. The present practice, however, is a poor apology for it.

247. न त्वेवामांसोऽर्घः स्यात्। P.G.S. i. 3. 30.

248. Ibid. i. 3. 27–29.

An Aryan could not do a higher honour than offering a cow to a guest. But even in the Vedic times the cow was attaining its sacred character, and in course of time it became too sacrosanct to be killed for a guest. This tendency can be marked in the Gṛhyasūtra period when killing of the cow became optional.[249] This tendency may be due to the growing regard for animal life among the Hindus, the close domestic relation between the cow and the householder and, perhaps, to the economic consideration also in killing a cow. In the time of the Smṛtis the cow-slaughter was forbidden altogether. The Purāṇas brought it under the general prohibition of killing a cow in the Kali-Age.[250] At present the living cow is offered to the bridegroom as a gift. Gadādhara in his Paddhati says, "As a rule the cow should be killed in a marriage and a sacrifice. It, however, does not take place in the Kali-Age. In the absence of the slaughter, the word "Cow" is also not announced. Under the universal prohibition, it is simply given away, as it is said in the Kārikā—"In the Kali-Age, in all cases, the cow is offered as a gift owing to the prohibition in cow-slaughter."[250a]

(9) *The Bridgroom Honoured*

After the Madhuparka ceremony the bride is worshipped by the father-in-law with scent, garland, sacred threads and pair of ornaments. The bride seats herself there after having worshipped and meditated on the goddess Gaurī.[251] Then the bridegroom establishes the Laukikāgni. According to the Gṛhyasūtras, this fire was produced by friction. The maternal uncle of the bride brings her near the nuptial fire facing towards the east and a curtain is drawn between the bride and the bridegroom.[252]

(10) *The Presentation of a Garment to the Bride*

Now the bridegroom presents an under-garment to the bride with the verse, "Live to old age; put on the garment! Be the protectress of the human tribes against imprecation. Live a hundred

249. Ibid. i. 3. 29.

250. महाप्रस्थानगमनं गोसंज्ञप्तिश्च गोसवे । Ādityapurāṇa quoted in the Nirṇayasindhu, p. 262.

250a. On P.G.S. i. 3. 30, 31.

251. The Gargapaddnati.

252. Ibid.

years full of vigour. Cloth thyself in wealth and children. Blessed with life put on this garment!" The upper garment was presented with, "The goddesses who spun, who wove, who spread out the threads on both sides, may those goddesses clothe thee for the sake of long life. Blessed with life put on this garment."[253] At present, generally, these presents are not offered in the nuptial canopy. They are sent before the nuptials take place. The custom of presenting clothes to the bridegroom by the father-in-law is also current.

(11) *Anointment*

Next, the bride's father is required to anoint the pair, while the bride-groom should recite the verse, "May the Viśvedevas, may the waters unite our hearts. May Mātariśva, May Dhātṛ, may Deṣṭṛ, join us." The anointment is symbolical of "Sneha" or 'love' and consequently of uniting the pair. This ceremony is called Samañjana. Some authorities explain it as "facing each other." But this explanation cannot be accepted in the light of the fact that the ceremony of Samīkṣaṇa or "looking at each other" is mentioned separately.

(12) *Gotrochchāra*

Before the bride is given away to the bridegroom the names of the ancestors of both the parties with Gotra and Pravara are announced loudly, thrice according to Vāsudeva and Harihara and once according to Gaṅgādhara.[254] This act signifies that the people assembled should know that both, the bride and the bridegroom, come of good families, the pedigree of which can be traced to many generations. The Gṛhyasūtras do not mention this item of the ceremony. It is found in the Paddhatis.

(13) *Kanyādāna*

Then the Kanyādāna[255] or "the ceremony of properly giving away the bride" follows. Only the constituted authorities are entitled to make the gift of a bride. The Gṛhyasūtras[255a] speak of having accepted the girl given by her father." The Smṛtis extend

253. P.G.S. i. 4. 13-14.

254. The Gargapaddhati.

255. Ibid.

255a. पित्रा प्रदत्तामादाय। P.G.S. i. 4. 16.

this right to other relatives also. According to Yājñavalkya "The father, the grand-father, the brother, the caste people and the mother are authorized, in descending order, to give away the girl."[255b] Nārada does not mention the grand-father and includes friends, maternal grand-father and the state in the list.[255c] In ancient times, the last guardian was the patriarchal chief of the tribe or the locality, who had more religious and social considerations than the modern states. But even now according to the Hindu Law, some provision is made for an unmarried girl out of the property of the father.

The guardian of the bride utters the following Saṃkalpa, "determination."[256] "For the obtainment of absolute happiness, as the consequence of Kanyādāna, for our fore-fathers; for purifying my twelve preceding and twelve succeeding generations through the progeny born in this girl; and for the propitiation of Lakṣmī and Nārāyaṇa etc. "I make this gift." He, then, recites the verse, "I give away this girl adorned with gold ornaments to you, Viṣṇu, with the desire of conquering the world of Brahma. The Nourisher of the whole Universe, all creatures and gods are witness to the fact that I make gift of this girl for the salvation of my forefathers." After this the bride is given away to the bridegroom who accepts her formally.

(14) The Conditions

While giving away the girl, the guardian puts forward following condition : "In the attainment of Piety, Wealth and Desire, she is not to be transgressed." To this the bridegroom promises, "Transgress her I will not."[257] The same promise is asked and repeated thrice. Many suitable presents are given with bride, e.g. clothes, ornaments etc. According to the Hindu religion, no sacrifice is complete without its appropriate Dakṣiṇā. So the marriage which is regarded as a kind of sacrifice must be duly finished with a fitting Dakṣiṇā in the form of money and presents.

255b. पिता पितामहो भ्राता सकुल्यो जननी तथा।
कन्याप्रदः पूर्वनाशे प्रकृतिस्थः परः परः ॥ I. 63.

255c. Quoted in V.M.S. vol. II. p. 826.

256. समस्तपितॄणां निरतिशयानन्दब्रह्मलोकावाप्त्यादिकन्यादानकल्पोक्तफलावाप्तये ....द्वादशावरान् द्वादशापरान् पुरुषांश्च पवित्रीकर्तुमात्मनश्च श्रीलक्ष्मीनारायणप्रीतये कन्यादानमहं करिष्ये। The Vivāhapaddhati by Jagannātha.

257. धर्मे चार्थे च कामे च नातिचरितव्या त्वयेयम्।
'नातिचरामि' इति वरः।

(15) *A Significant Question*

After accepting the bride, the bridegroom puts a very significant question to the guardian of the girl: "Who has given this bride to me?" The answer is "Kāma (the God of Love)."[258] Then he leaves the nuptial canopy with the bride and in private utters the following formula to her in order to win her over: "Where thou wanderest far away with thy heart to the regions of the world like the wind, may the gold-winged Vaikarṇa (the Wind) grant that thy heart may dwell with me! N. N!"[259] The Paddhatis call it the Vadhvādeśa or the admonition for the bride. Samīkṣaṇa or looking at each other follows next. The bridegroom while looking at the bride, recites the verse, "With no evil eye, not bringing death to thy husband, bring luck to the cattle, be full of joy and vigour. Give birth to the heroes; be godly and friendly. Bring luck to men and animals."[260]

(16) *Protection Cord*

Then comes the Kañkaṇa-Bandhana ceremony.[261] This ceremony was very important in ancient times, because from this time until the Samāveśa (sexual union) was performed, the bride and the bridegroom could suffer no pollution, as they had Kañkaṇa or Rakṣa (Protective Cord).[262] Now it has only a decorative value. In some provinces it is regarded simply auspicious and is called "Maṅgala-Sūtra." This ceremony is not mentioned in the Gṛhyasūtras and its origin seems to be more popular than scriptural.

(17) *Evolution of the Bride suggested*

Now the bridegroom utters the following verses in which he reminds the bride that she has become of age and they both have to enter the responsible life of a husband and a wife: "First, Soma had thee for his bride; the Gandharva obtained thee next; Agni was thy third husband thy fourth husband am I, born of man. Soma gave

258. कोऽदात् । काम इति।

259. यदेषि मनसा दूरं दिशोऽनुपवमानो वा। हिरण्यपर्णो वैकर्णः स त्वा मन्मनसां करोतु । P.G.S. i. 4. 16.

260. Ibid. i. 4. 17. 1.

261. cf. The paddhati by Maṇdalika.

262. The Aryan Marriage, pp. 24, 25,

thee to the Gandharva, the Gandharva gave thee to Agni, and Agni has given thee to me for wealth and sons."[263] These mystic verses are explained by Sāyaṇa thus: "While yet the desire for sexual intercourse has not arisen, Soma enjoys a girl; when it has just begun, the Gandharva takes her, and at marriage transfers her to Agni, from whom man obtains her (possessing capacity) for producing wealth and sons."[264] The Smṛtis offer a clearer interpretation; "Women are first enjoyed by the gods, Soma, Viśvāvasu and Agni; only then do men enjoy them. But the women are not tainted thereby. When hair has appeared on the pubes, Soma enjoys a maiden; the Gandharva enjoys her when the breasts are developed, and Agni when she had menstrual discharge."[265] Different stages of physical and mental development in a woman are further explained: "Soma is Sasyādhipati, the Lord of the Vegetable world, and presides also over the mind . . . .The physical growth of the girl, including that of the hair, was under the care of the god, Soma. The mind of the girl was also developed under his guidance . . . The Gandharva is the master of graces. It is his function to make the woman's body beautiful and to add richness of tone. Under his care the pelvis develop, the breasts become round and attractive, the eyes begin to speak the language of love, and the whole body acquires a rich hue. His work is advanced and he hands her on to Agni. Who is Agni? He is the Lord of Fire, the Lord of Agni-Tattva. Nature is radiant with colour and joy in Spring and summer; animals breed in Spring......Agni is fructifier. It is he who brings about the menstrual flow, and woman then can bear children. Agni then gives her to man; her fourth Pati or Lord."[266] The Hindus believe that different gods preside over the different stages in the physical development of a girl and these gods are mythologically regarded to be her husbands.

---

263. सोमः प्रथमो विविदे गन्धर्वो विविद उत्तरः ।
तृतीयोऽग्निष्टे पतिस्तुरीयस्ते मनुष्यजः ।।
सोमो ददद् गन्धर्वाय गन्धर्वो ददद् अग्नये ।
रयिं च पुत्रांश्चादादग्निर्मह्यमथो इमाम् ।। R.V. x. 85. 40, 41.

264. सायण on the above verses.

265. पूर्वं स्त्रियः सुरैर्भुक्ताः सोमगन्धर्ववह्निभिः ।
गच्छन्ति मानुषान् पश्चात् नैता दुष्यन्ति धर्मतः ।। V.S.
सोमः शौचं ददौ तासां गन्धर्वाश्च तथा गिराम् ।
पावकः सर्वमेधत्वं मेधत्वं योषितां सदा ।। A.S. 137.

266. The Aryan Marriage pp. 26. 27.

(18) Rāṣṭrabhṛta and other sacrifices

A number of Homas follow, the chief among them being Rāṣṭrabhṛt, Jaya, Abhyātana and Lājā Homa.[267] The first three contain prayers for victory and protection and aim at hostile powers known or unknown to the bridegroom. The last Homa is symbolical of fecundity and prosperity.[267a] The brother of the bride pours out of his joined hands into her joined hands fried grains mixed with Śamī leaves. The bride sacrifices them with firmly joined hands standing, while the bridegroom recites the verses, 'To the god Aryaman the girl has made sacrifice, to Agni. May he, god Aryaman, loosen us from here, and not from the husband's side. Svāhā!' The girl strewing grains prayed thus: "May my husband live long; my relations be prosperous Svāhā! This grain I have thrown into the fire; May this bring prosperity to thee, and may it unite me with thee. May Agni grant us that N. N. Svāhā!"

(19) Pāṇi-grahaṇa

The Pāṇi-grahaṇa or "the Grasping of the Bride's Hand" comes next.[268] The bridegroom seizes the right hand of the bride with, "I seize thy hand for the sake of happiness, that thou mayest live to old age with me, thy husband. Bhaga, Aryamā, Savitṛ, Purandhi, gods have given thee to me, that we may rule over house. This I am. That art thou. That art thou, this am I. The Sāman as I, the Ṛk thou; the Heaven I, the Earth thou: Come let us marry. Let us unite our sperm. Let us beget offsprings. Let us acquire many sons and may they reach old age. Loving, bright with genial minds may we see a hundred autumns, may we live a hundred autumns, may we hear a hundred autumns." This ceremony is symbolical of taking the charge and responsibility of the girl. The responsibility is very sacred, as the girl is supposed to be given not only by his father but also by the above guardian deities who are witnesses to every solemn contract. The prayer in the end is suggestive of a fruitful, prosperous and happy married life.

(20) Mounting the Stone

In order to make the wife firm in her devotion and fidelity to him, the husband makes her tread on a stone,[269] to the north of the

267. cf. P.G.S. i. 6. 1-2.

267a. इमाँल्लाजानावपाम्यग्नौ समृद्धिकरणं तव। ibid.

268. A.V. xiv. 1. 49; Ś.G.S. i. 13. 2; A.G.S. i. 7. 3; G.G. S. ii. 2. 3; Kh. G.S. i. 3. 17, 31; H.G.S. i. 6. 20. 1.

269. Ś.G.S. i. 13. 10; A.G.S. i. 7. 7; P.G.S. i. 7. 1; G.G. S. ii. 2. 3; Kh, G.S. i. 3. 19. H.G.S. i. 19. 18; Āp. G.S. 5. 3.

fire, with her right foot, repeating the verse, "Tread on this stone; like a stone be firm. Tread the foes down; turn away the enemies." Stone, here, is symbolical of firmness and strength in crushing the enemies. This ceremony is known as Aśmārohaṇa or "Mounting the Stone."

(21) The Praise of Woman

The bride thus being confirmed in her duties towards her husband, the latter sings a song in the praise of woman who are here represented by the goddess, Sarasvatī.[270] "Sarasvatī! promote this undertaking, O gracious one, bountiful one, thou whom we sing first of all that is, in whom what is, has been born, in whom this whole world dwells—that song I will sing to-day, which will be the highest glory of women."

(22) Agni-Pradakṣiṇā

The couple, then, go round the fire while the husband recites the following formula: "To thee they have in the beginning carried round Sūryā with the bridal procession. Mayest thou give back, Agni, to the husbands the wife to-gether with offsprings." The rites from the Lājā-Homa are repeated again and the bride pours the remaining fried grains by the net of a basket into the fire with, "To Bhaga Svāhā!"

(23) The Sapta-Padī

Then the great "Sapta-padī[271] or "The Rite of Seven Steps" takes place. The husband makes the wife step forward in a northern direction seven steps with the words, "One step for sap, two for juice, three for the prospering of wealth, four for comforts, five for cattle, six for seasons. Friend! be with seven steps (united to me) So be thou devoted to me." The objects referred to in the above formula are essential for domestic felicities. This ceremony is very important from the legal point of view, as marriage is regarded legally complete after it is performed.[272]

---

270. P.G.S. i. 7. 3.

271. P.G..S. i. 8. 1.

272: स्वगोत्राद् भ्रश्यते नारी विवाहात्सप्तमे पदे। V.S. 78.
पाणिग्रहणमंत्रास्तु नियतं दारलक्षणम्।
तेषां निष्ठा तु विज्ञेया विद्वद्भिः सप्तमे पदे। M.S. ix. 70.
नोदकेन च वाचा वा कन्यायाः पतिरुच्यते।
पाणिग्रहणसंस्कारात्पतित्वं सप्तमे पदे॥ Y.S. 84.

(24) The Bride Sprinkled

After the Saptapadī the bride is sprinkled on her head with the formula. "The blessed, the most blessed waters, the peaceful ones, the most peaceful ones, may they give medicine to thee."[273] Water is famous for possessing medicinal and sanctifying properties among all religions. By this ceremony the bride is supposed to be free from physical troubles and sanctified for the married life.

(25) Touching the Heart

Next, the husband touches the heart of the bride reaching over her right shoulder.[274] with the words, "Into my will I take thy heart; thy mind shall dwell in my mind; in my word thou shall rejoice with all thy heart: May Prajāpati join thee to me." The heart is the centre of feelings. By touching it the husband symbolically tries to rouse them and make them flow out to meet his own heart and thus unite them in the world of love.

(26) The Bride Blessed

Now the bridegroom invites the assembled guests and relatives to bless the bride, reciting the verses over her, "Auspicious ornaments does this woman wear. Come to her and behold her. Having brought luck to her, go away back to your houses."[274a] The Sindūra-dāna or painting of red lead on the head of the bride by the bridegroom takes place on this occasion. It is the most striking feature of the present-day marriage ceremonies, but it is nowhere mentioned in the Gṛhyasūtras. The Paddhatis say, "According to the tradition, Sindūra-dāna etc. are performed."[275] The ceremony is now called Sumaṅgali, the name being suggested by the first word "Sumañgalī" of the above blessing.

(27) Sitting on Bull's Hide

According to the Gṛhyasūtras, after the blessing, a strong man snatched the bride up from the ground and set her down in an eastern or northern direction in an out of the way house, on a red

273. P.G.S. i. 8. 5.

274. Ibid. i. 8. 8.

274a. P.G.S. i. 8. 9.

275. अत्राचारात्स्त्रियः सिन्दूरदानादि कुर्वन्ति । गदाधरपद्धति on the above.

bull's hide, with the words, "Here may the cows sit down, here the horses, here the men. Here may sacrifice with thousand gifts, here may Pūṣan sit down."[276] The bull's hide was symbolical of fertility and prosperity, as it is shown by the prayer associated with this performance. At present, the snatching up of the girl does not take place, nor the bull's hide is requisitioned, as the former is regarded indecent and the latter is religiously objectionable. But after the prayer the pair retire to a room in the house in the company of ladies where many jestive pranks are played with the bridegroom.

(28) Local Customs

At this stage of the marriage ceremonies, a number of rites are performed in conformance with the local customs and traditions. The Pāraskara Gṛhyasūtra says that one should do according to the custom of the village or Grāma-vacanam.[277] Gadādhara explains "Grāmavacana" as follows: "Though not given in the Sūtras, the tying of the auspicious yarns, wearing garlands, tying of the garment of the bride and the bridegroom, touching the cup of a banyan tree, touching the nose at the arrival of the bridegroom, besmearing the chest of the bridegroom with curd etc. and many other things which the women of the place remember, should be done."[278]

(29) Nuptial Fees

In the end, the priest who conducts the nuptials receives his fees. According to the Gṛhyasūtras, the Ācārya should be given a cow by a Brahman, a village by a Rājanya and a horse by a Vaiśya[279] At present, a cow is the ceremonial gift, which is accompanied by some hard cash and clothes.

(30) Looking at the Sun and the Pole Star

Though the nuptials proper end at this point, a number of ceremonies relating to marriage still remain to be performed. The first few are symbolical in their nature. The bride is required to

---

276. P.G.S. i. 8. 10.

277. P.G.S. i. 8. 11.

278. विवाहे श्मशाने च वृद्धानां स्त्रीणां च वचनं कुर्युः। सूत्रे अनुपविद्धमपि वधूवरयोर्मंगलसूत्रं गले मालाधारणं etc. गदाधर on the above.

279. P.G.S. i. 8. 15–17.

look at the sun if the marriage takes place in the day time, with the words, "That eye etc."[280] In the night the bridegroom shows to the bride the firm star (i.e the Pole Star) with, "Firm art thou; I see thee, the firm one. Firm be thou with me, O thriving one! To me Bṛhaspati has given thee; obtaining offsprings through me, thy husband, live with me a hundred autumns."[281] According to other authorities Arundhati star and the Saptarṣi-Maṇḍal should be also shown to the bride.[282] Whether she sees them or not, she is asked to reply when a question is put to her, "I see." These performances were suggestive of firmness in the conjugal life.

(31) Trirātra-vrata

The nuptial rites are followed by the tri-rātravrata[283] or "The Observance of Continence for Three Days." "Through a period of three nights they shall eat no saline food; they shall sleep on the ground; they shall refrain form sexual intercourse, through one year, or through a period of twelve days, or of six nights, or at least of three nights." Such are the religious injunctions to be followed by the husband and the wife. At present, no restraints are put on the couple and they share fully the marriage festivities. In ancient times, a very interesting procedure was adopted at the end of the above observance. The pair had to wear ornaments and lie on the same bed with Viśvāvasu Gandharva occupying the middle position, which consisted of a rod of the Udumbara tree, coated with sandal paste, and covered with cloth. On the fourth night after the performance of the Pakva-Homa, the pair retired to a gaily decorated room, and a verse of great significance was recited: "Rise O Viśvāvasu, from this our bed, rise we pray. Seek thou a girl that is tender in years, and that needs thy assistance. Leave thou this bride, my wife, unto me and let her unite herself to me. O Gandharva, this bride, now united to me, her husband, prostrates to thee, and begs this favour of thee. Depart and find thou an immature girl that still dwells in her father's house. Such a one is verily portion, nay thy birthright."[284] After this the rod was cast away. The exact significance of this rite cannot be explained,

280. P.G.S. i. 8. 7.

281. Ibid. i. 8. 19.

282. A.G.S. i. 7. 22.

283. P.G.S. i. 8. 21.

284. B.G.S. i. 5. 17, 18.

as this custom arose under beliefs that are, at present, foreign to our minds. A. C. Das is of opinion that "This rod was supposed to be inhabited by Viśvāvasu Gandharva, and was the witness of the pairs "Brahmacarya."[285] A. B. Keith, relying on Oldenberg, opines, The exact force of the magic is uncertain; the desire by refraining from consummation to deceive evil demons and cause them to depart is a possible motive. Viśvāvasu as a Gandharva seems to claim his right of connexion with women even after the marriage, and must at first be appeased and then formally banished. But the obvious connexion of the rite with other similar rites over the world down to the trium noctium is a warning against any feeling of security in the interpretation of the custom."[286] The interpretation suggested by Keith seems to be more probable than that offered by Dr. Das. The belief was current in the Vedic times, and it is recorded in the Gṛhyasūtras also, that a maiden in the course of her growth was enjoyed by Soma, Gandharva and Agni and in the last bestowed on the man, her fourth husband.[287] Perhaps the people thought that even after the nuptials the Gandharva was lingering, so it was necessary that he should be formally asked to leave the girl to her husband.

The Purpose of the Tri-rātra-vrata appears to be to give a lesson of moderation to the married couple in the sexual life. Both the husband and the wife were youthful and attracted towards each other by love. It is but natural to suppose that they would be very eager to come into physical contact and wish the rite to be soon over. But no, they had yet to learn and realize that true love was not passionate or passion-born, but was based on perfect self-restraint. They had to lead a life of continence for a period, the minimum being three days and the maximum one year.[287a] The longer the period of continence, the better was the chance of obtaining a superior issue.[287b]

The Tri-Rātra-Vrata was a real necessity when the marriages of grown-up parties took place. After the introduction of early marri-

285. Ṛgvedic Culture, p. 381.

286. Religion and Philosophy of the Vedas, p. 37; Cf. Oldenberg Reli des Veda, pp. 88. 249.

287. A.V. xiv. 2. 3. 4. P.G.S. i. 4. 17.

287a. cf. Ṛgvedic Culture, p. 381.

287b. B.G.S. i. 7. 11.

age however, it became defunct. In the orthodox families it is supposed to terminate with the Caturthī-Karma, which is performed on the fourth-day after marriage. In the majority of cases it is paid no heed at all. The three days' stay at the house of the father of the bride is characterized by feasts, dance and music.

(32) *The Bride carried and blessed*

In ancient times, the marriage ceremonies being over, the married couple started for their home in a car,[288] and as the wife mounted it, she was told by the husband. "Thou shalt be my mistress henceforth and bear me ten sons. Be mistress of thy father-in-law and mother-in-law. Be mistress of these and of the other daughters-in-law of the house, of the children, property and all."[289] In the present Hindu society the bride is not sent to her new home at the time of her marriage, or if sent at all, it is only ceremonial for two or three days. The custom of the second marriage is the general order of the day. Moreover, the child-bride has got neither the capacity to understand the above address nor the privilege to be the mistress of her new home.

(33) *Domestic Fire Established: Chaturthi-karma*

According to the Gṛhyasūtras, in the fourth night after the wedding, towards morning, the husband established the fire within the house, assigned his seat to the south of it, to the Brahman, placed a pot of water to the north, cooked a mess of sacrificial food, sacrificed the two Ājya portions, and made other Ājya oblations with the following verses: "Agni! Expiation! Thou art the expiation of the gods. I, the Brāhmaṇa, entreat thee, desirous of protection. The substance that dwells in her that brings death to her husband, that exterpates in her, Svāhā!" In the same way the husband invoked Vāyu, Sūrya, Chandra and Gandharva for the protection of children, cattle, house and fame. Then he sprinkled the wife with the verse, "The evil substance that dwells in thee, that brings death to thy husband, children cattle, house and fame, that I change into one that brings death to thy paramour. Thus live with me to old age; N. N.!" This rite is called Caturthi-Karma[290]

288. P.G.S. i. 10. 1.

289. According to some, it is a reception address delivered at the arrival of the bride to her new home.

290. P.G.S. i. 11. 13; G.G.S. ii. 5; Ś.G.S. i. 18. 19; Kh. G.S. i. 4. 22: 11. G. S. i. 13. 11; Ap. G.S. 8. 8.

because it is performed on her fourth day after the wedding. At present, it is performed not at the house of the bridegroom but at the house of the bride's father before the marriage party leaves it. The purpose of this rite is to remove evil influence from the person of the bride which may cause harm to the family.

(34) The Common Meal

At the end of the Chaturthī-karma, when it took place at the house of the bridegroom, the husband made the wife eat the mess of cooked food with the words, "I add breath to thy breath, bones to thy bones, flesh to thy flesh, skin to thy skin."[291] Later on, this Prāśana turned into a conjugal feast and now it is performed after the second marriage. On the Pāraskara Gṛhyasūtra,[292] Gadādhara observes, "Here the husband dines with the wife according to the custom." Eating with the wife is prohibited in the Hindu Dharmaśātra. But it is an exceptional case entailing no sin. The ceremony symbolizes the union of the persons of both the husband and the wife.

(35) Removal of the Nuptial Canopy

A ceremony, not recorded in the Gṛhyasūtras, has been prescribed by the Paddhatis, according to which, the gods are dismissed to their respective places and the nuptial canopy is removed.[293] It should be performed on some even day after the marriage. Odd days are prohibited except the fifth and the seventh.

(xv) Symbolism of Hindu Nuptials

(a) The Meaning of a Symbol. A symbol is a thing regarded by general consent as naturally typifying or representing or recalling

---

291. प्राणैस्ते प्राणान्सन्दधामि——अस्थिभिरस्थीनि मांसैर्मांसानि त्वचा त्वचम्।
P.G.S. i. 11. 5.

292. अत्र स्त्रिया सह वरोऽपि समाचाराद् भोजनं करोति। स्त्रिया सह भोजने-
ऽपि न दोष इत्याह हेमाद्रौ प्रायश्चित्तकाण्डे गालवः——
एकयानसमारोहः एकपात्रे च भोजनम्।
विवाहे पथि यात्रायां कृत्वा विप्रो न दोषभाक्॥
अन्यथा दोषमाप्नोति पश्चाच्चान्द्रायणं चरेत्॥

293. समे च दिवसे कुर्याद्वेदिकोत्थापनं बुधः।
षष्ठं च विषमं नेष्टं मुक्त्वा पञ्चमसप्तमौ॥ Quoted in the Gargapaddhati.

something by possession of analogous qualities or by association in fact or thought. A symbol is not important by itself. It has only a vehicular value and conveys something beyond it. It is a mode of expression which vivifies abstract, subtle, unfamiliar or supernatural ideas before common folk. In ancient times, when human fancy was stronger and the human speech was not adequately developed to express every shade of thought, symbols played a very important part. In religions and mythology they were commonly used. But even now they have not lost their value. The most up-to-date political ideology, which recognizes little use of religion, employs symbols for its ends and ideals.

(b) Sacramental Marriage and Symbol. Hindu marriage which the nuptials solemnize is not a social contract in the modern sense of the term, but a religious institution, a sacrament. By it we mean that besides the two human parties, the bride and the bridegroom, there is a third superhuman, spiritual or divine element in marriage. The physical conditions of the two parties are always subject to change and, as such, they cannot form the permanent basis of marriage. It is on the third element that the permanent relationship between the husband and the wife depends. The husband and the wife are responsible not only to each other, but they owe a greater allegiance to this third element. This is the religious or mystic touch in the purely social and material contract between a man and a woman. Without it the conjugal life loses its charm and durability. The mystic aspect of the Hindu marriage necessitates the use of a number of symbols.

(c) Marriage a Union of the Fittest Couple. In the very beginning of the Hindu nuptials there is a ceremony which symbolizes the union of the fittest parties. This ceremony, called Arghya 'Showing Respect'.[294] while conferring great honour on the bridegroom, indicates that he is the best of his sex and equals. Having ordered a seat for the bridegroom, the father-in-law says, "Well Sir, sit down. We will do honour to you, Sir." They get for him a couch of grass, to sit down on, another for feet, water for washing the feet, water for sipping, and the honey-mixture in a brass vessel with a cover of brass. The bridegroom accepts the couch and sitting thereon says, 'I am the highest one among my peoples as the sun is among the shining ones. Here I tread on whosoever infests me."[295] On this

294. The Pāraskara Gṛhyasūtra, I. 3. 1–32.

295. वर्म्मोऽस्मि समानानामुद्यतामिव सूर्यः। etc. Ibid. I. 3. 9.

occasion the guest of honour, accepting his dues from the father-in-law, makes a statement wherein he publicly declares that he is the fittest match for the bride.

(d) Marriage a New Bond. Some of the most important items of the nuptials are those which symbolize that marriage creates a new bond between the bride and the bridegroom. They are united like two young plants, which are uprooted from two different plots and are transplanted into a new one. They have to rear up this union by dedicating their entire energy in the direction of their common interest and ideal. One such item is Samañjana or "Anointment."[296] The father of the bride is required to anoint the pair. While this ceremony is being performed, the bridegroom recites the verse, "May the Viśvedevāḥ, may the Waters unite our hearts. May Mātariśva, may Dhātṛ, may Deṣṭṛ join us."[297] The anointment is symbolical of "Sneha" or love and consequently of the union of the pair. Another ceremony of this type is the Pāṇigrahaṇa or the "Grasping of the Bride's Hand.[298] "The bridegroom seizes the right hand of the bride with the verse, "I seize thy hand for sake of happiness, that thou mayest live to old age with me thy husband. Bhaga, Aryamā, Savitṛ, gods have given thee to me, that we may rule over the house-hold. This I am, That art thou, that art thou, this am I. The Sāman aṁ I, the Ṛk[299] thou; the Heaven I, the Earth thou. Come let us marry. This ceremony is symbolical of physical bond between the husband and the wife. The next ceremony of this kind is the Hṛdayasparśa or "Touching the Heart of the Bride,"[300] The husband touches the heart of the bride reaching over her right shoulder with the words, "Into my will I take thy heart; thy mind shall dwell in my mind; in my word thou shall rejoice with all thy heart: May Prajāpati join thee to me."[301] This performance indicates that marriage is not only the physical union of two persons but also the union of two hearts or souls. The heart is the centre of

296. Ibid. I. 4. 15.

297. समञ्जन्तु विश्वेदेवाः समापो हृदयानि नौ।
सम्मातरिश्वा सन्धाता समु देष्ट्री दधातु नौ॥ Ibid.

298. The Atharvaveda, xiv. i. 49; the Āśvalāyana G.S. I. 7. 3; the Gobhila G.S. II. 2. 16.

299. Ibid.

300. The Pāraskara G.S. I. 8. 8.

301. मम व्रते ते हृदयं दधामि मम चित्तमनुचित्तं ते अस्तु। Ibid.

feelings. By touching it the husband symbolically tries to rouse the soft emotions of the wife and make them flow out to meet his own and thus to create a real union in the psychic world. One more ceremony may be mentioned in this connection. In the Sthālīpāka or the Common Dinner[302] the husband makes the wife eat the mess of cooked food with the words, "I add breath to thy breath, bones to thy bones, flesh to thy flesh, skin to thy skin."[303] Here both the material and the vital selves of the husband and the wife are united.

(e) Marriage a Permanent and Stable Union. Marriage is not a temporary contract to serve the momentary physical demand or to enjoy good company for sometime and then to lapse at the slightest inconvenience. It is a permanent union which stands various vicissitudes in life only to grow stronger and more stable. This fact has been symbolized by a number of ceremonies in the Hindu Nuptials. In the Aśmārohaṇa or "Mounting the Stone"[304] ceremony the husband makes the wife tread on a stone repeating the verse, "Tread on this stone; like a stone be firm."[305] Stone is a symbol of firmness and strength. The wife is exhorted to be adamantine in her conjugal fidelity. Another ceremony of this class is Dhruvadarśana or, "Looking at the Pole Star."[306] In the night the bridegroom shows to the bride the Pole Star with the verse, "Firm art thou; I see thee the firm one. Firm be thou with me, O thriving one. To me Bṛhaspati has given thee obtaining offsprings through me thy husband, live with me a hundred autumns."[307] Here two things are indicated. Firstly, the wife should be as firm and fixed as the Pole Star is amidst innumerable moving bodies in the firmament. Secondly, the union should last for a hundred years which is the normal span of human life. Thus the firm and life-long companionship is the objective in view. This aspect of marriage is highly prized and the husband prays to the goddess Sarasvatī to protect it: "Sarasvati, promote this undertaking, O gracious one, bountiful one, thou whom will sing first of all that is; in whom what is; has been born; in

302. The Pāraskara G.S. I. 11. 5.

303. प्राणैस्ते प्राणान्संदधामि etc. ibid.

304. The Sāmklyāyana G.S. I. 8. 19.

305. आरोहेममश्मानमश्मेव स्थिरा भव। Ibid.

306. The Pāraskara G.S. I. 8. 19.

307. ध्रुवमसि ध्रुवं त्वा पश्यामि etc. ibid.

whom this whole world dwells—that song I will sing to-day, which will be the highest glory of women."[308]

(f) Biological Symbolism of Marriage. The primary function of a marriage is racial, that is, the continuity of the race through the procreation of children. In the Hindu nuptials, there are various ceremonies that point out this fact and intend to make the union fruitful, to avert the dangers associated with the sexual intercourse and to facilitate the various stages of the process of generation. After accepting the bride formally given away by her father, the bridegroom puts a very significant question to the guardian of the girl. Who has given this bride to me? The answer is, "'Kāma or the God of Love."[309] It means that the basic desire to exist through progeny is mainly responsible for marriage. In another place we find a reference to the biological development of the bride, her preparedness for a married life and consequent procreation of children. The bridegroom reminds the bride, "First Soma had thee for his bride, the Gandharva had thee next. Agni was thy third husband; thy fourth husband am I, born of man. Soma gave thee to Gandharva; the Gandharva gave to Agni; and Agni has given thee to me for wealth and sons."[310]

These verses are explained by Sāyaṇa thus, "While yet desire for sexual intercourse has not arisen Soma enjoys the girl; when it has just begun the Gandharva takes her; and at marriage transfers her to Agni, from whom man obtains her (possessing capacity) for producing wealth and sons."[311] The Smṛtis offer a clearer interpretation of the above obscure passage: "Soma gave them (Women) purity; to Gandharva bestowed sweet speech; and Agni Sarvamedhatva or purity. Therefore women are always in possession of Sarvamedhatva or purity."[312] A modern writer further clarifies the suggestion. "Soma is sasyādhipati, the Lord of the Vegetable world; and presides also over the mind . . . The physical growth of the girl, including that of the hair is under the care of the god Soma. The mind of the girl also develops under his guidance. The Gandharva is the master of graces. It is his

308. The Pāraskara G.S. I. 7. 2.

309. कोऽदात् । काम इति ।

310. The Ṛgveda, x. 85. 40, 41.

311. Sāyana on the above verse.

312. The Atrismṛti, 137.

function to make woman's body beautiful and to add richness to her tone. Under his care the pelvis develops, the breasts become round and attractive. The eyes begin to speak the language of love and the whole body acquires rich hue. His work is advanced and he hands her on to Agni. Who is Agni? He is the Lord of Fire, the Lord of Agni-tattva. Nature is radiant with colour and joy in spring and Summer, Animals breed in Spring, Agni is the fructifier. It is he who brings about the menstrual flow and women then can bear children. Agni then gives her to man, her fourth Pati or Lord."[313] In the "Grasping of the Hand" ceremony also the biological aspect of marriage is fully brought out. The bridegroom says to the bride, "The Heaven am I, the Earth thou. Come let us marry. Let us unite our sperm. Let us beget offsprings. Let us acquire many sons and may they reach old age. Loving, bright with genial minds, may we see a hundred autumns, may we live a hundred autumns."[314] Just as in the Vedic pantheon, the Heaven and the Earth (Dyāvā Pṛthivī) are the parents of gods or shining ones, so the husband and the wife are expected to generate a world of their own.

(g) Marriage should be Fruitful and Prosperous. The nuptials symbolize not only the biological function of marriage but also employ a number of symbols which refer to the fertility and prosperity of the married life. There is the Lājā Homa[315] or "offerings of Fried Grains into Fire" ceremony in which the brother of the bride pours out of his joined hands fried grains mixed with Śami leaves. The bride offers them with firmly joined hands standing, while the bridegroom recites the verses, "To the god Aryaman the girl has made sacrifice, to Agni. May he god, Aryaman loosen us from here, and not from the husband's side. Svāhā!" The girl strewing grains prayed thus, "May my husband live long, my relations be prosperous. Svāhā ! This grain I have thrown into the fire, may this bring prosperity to thee, and may it unite me with thee. May Agni grant us N. N. Svāhā !"[316] Here grains and leaves are symbols of fruitfulness and prosperity. There is another ceremony which emphasizes the same thing. According to the Gṛhyasū-

313. The Aryan Marriage, pp. 26, 27.

314. द्यौरहं पृथ्वी त्वं। तावेहि विवहावहै सह रेतो दधावहै etc. The Hiraṇyakeśī G.S. I. I. 6. 20. 1.

315. The Pāraskara. G.S. I. 6. 1.

316. Ibid.

tras, a strong man snatches the bride up from the ground and sets her down in an eastern or northern direction on a red bull's hide with the word, "Here may the cows sit down, here the horses, here the men. Here may sacrifice with thousand gifts, here may Pūṣan sit down.[317] "The bull, the horse, the cows, the men, the sacrifice are all recognized as signs of virility and fecundity. The idea of, and a strong desire for, a prosperous life is better expressed in the ceremony called Saptapadī or the Rite of Taking Seven Steps."[318] The husband makes the wife step forward in a northern direction seven steps with the word, "One step for sap, two for juice, three for the prospering of wealth, four for comforts, five for cattle six for the seasons. Friend, be with seven steps (united to me). So be thou devoted to me."[319]

(h) Marriage a Crisis: Removal of Evil Influences. Marriage is the most critical event in the life of a man and ushers in quite a new era in his life. It establishes a novel relation between two persons, which is attended by many anticipations, hopes and fears. In the nuptials various attempts are made to remove the dangers associated with the crisis of marriage. The father of the bride while making the pair face each other exhorts her in the following words, "Be thou of benign and pleasing eyes; never cherish an evil design against your husband; be kind and well-wishing to cattle and others dependent like them; be always cheerful and prosperous; be the mother of heroic sons; sacrifice to the gods; be happy, be auspicious to us, bipeds and quadrupeds."[320] The first fears and doubts are about the bride who is to form the nucleus of the home and has to deal not only with her hubsand but also with his dependents and cattle. In relation with all these she is expected to be affectionate, kind and generous. In the Rāṣṭrabhṛta sacrifice bridegroom seeks protection from important gods and Fathers against all possible dangers which might be lurking in a married life. He says, "Let Fire, the Iord of creatures protect me, let Indra the Lord of the Great protect me; let Yama, the Lord of the Earth, protect me. . .[321] In the Abhiṣiñchana, "Sprinkling of water"[322] ceremony the waters are re-

---

317. Ibid. I. 8. 10.

318. Ibid. I. 8. 1.

319. Ibid.

320. The Pāraskara G.S. I. 4. 17.

321. Ibid. I. 5. 7–11.

322. Ibid. I. 8. 5.

quested to ensure perfect health and all-round peace: "Let the waters, which are auspicious, the most auspicious, peaceful, the most peaceful, be health-giving medicine to you."[323] Then there is a Sumaṁgate (Auspicious) ceremony in which the bridegroom invites the assembled guests and relatives to bless her with the following words; "Auspicious ornaments does this woman wear, come to her and behold her. Having brought luck to her, go away back to your houses."[324] At the close of the nuptials there is a ceremony, called Caturthī-karma,[325] which is performed on the fourth day after marriage. The husband offers oblations with the verse." Agni! Expiation! Thou art the expiation of the gods. I, the Brāhmaṇa, entreat thee, desirous of protection. The substance that dwells in her, that brings death to her husband, that extirpate in her. Svāhā"[326] Next he sprinkles water on the bride with the words "The evil substances that dwell in thee, that bring death to thy husband, children, cattle, house and fame, that I change into one that brings death to thy paramour.,Thus live with me to an old age."[327] In all these ceremonies the critical nature of marriage and the dangers attendant thereon are realized and attempts are made to remove them. Here one thing particularly is noteworthy. The bride is supposed to be more susceptible to dangers than the bridegroom and, therefore, she is the centre of auspicious ceremonies.

(i) Marriage not a Licence. The fact that marriage is not a passport for sexual indulgence but a human institution aiming at moderation in the conjugal life, has been emphasized at the end of the nuptials, when the Trirātra-vrata or the "Observance of Continence for Three Nights"[328] is undertaken. "Through a period of three nights they shall eat no saline food, they shall sleep on the ground; they shall refrain from the sexual intercourse through one year, or at least three nights."[329] The symbolism of this observance seems to be to give a lesson in moderation to the married couple. It is but natural for a young man and a young woman to be strongly attracted towards each other and to be eager to come into physical

323. Ibid.

324. Ibid. I. 8. 9.

325. The Ápastamba G.S. 8. 8; the Khādira G.S. I. 4. 22.

326. Pāraskara G.S. I. 1. 2.

327. Ibid.

328. The Pāraskara G.S. I. 8. 21.

329. Ibid.

contact as soon as possible. But here the religious ceremonies utter a word of caution by introducing the aforesaid observance. The married couple has as yet to wait and realize that married love should never be controlled by blind passion but should be based on perfect self-restraint The greater the moderation the happier the married life will be.

(j) Marriage a Social Change and a Sacrifice. The nuptials in their utterances, promises, hopes and fears symbolize a great social transition in the life of the bride and the bridegroom. They are no longer irresponsible youths depending for their bread and views on their parents. The seriousness of life dawns upon them. They forsake their old families to form a new one. They have to run an independent home: to earn their own livelihood, to procreate childdren and to discharge their obligations towards gods, Fathers and the creatures of the world. This is the life of responsibilities and cares. It is only in this sense that Hindu marriage or "Vivāha" can properly be understood, which means "to lift, to support, to hold up, to sustain." This involves a great compromise and mutual sacrifice. Those, who regard marriage as the solution of the problem of happiness, suffer from a great misconception. Those, who marry for pleasures are sorely disappointed. The essential difficulties of life are not given send-off under the wedding canopy but, as a matter of fact they are invited. The conscious acceptance of responsibilities in life is to court suffering. We, no doubt, talk of a happy marriage. But the happiness of the married life is not possible in the selfish sense of the personal pleasure. Marriage acquires its true meaning and reaches perfection only when the conjugal relationship is based on the realization that marriage is a willing sacrifice for the good of the partner, the family, the society and the world.

Thus the general function of nuptial symbolism is to cover all the aspects of married life. The biological significance, the critical nature, the physical and mental union of the couple, moderation, the social transition and sacrifice, these are the main features of the Hindu nuptials. They have been symbolically suggested but not described in transparent prose, because conveyed through symbols, they are better emphasized and become more eloquent and telling.

CHAPTER IX

THE ANTYEṢṬI SAṀSKĀRA (THE FUNERAL CEREMONIES)

(1) *Introductory*

The last sacrament in the life of a Hindu is the Antyeṣṭi or the Funeral with which he closes the concluding chapter of his worldly career. While living, a Hindu consecrates his worldly life by performing various rites and ceremonies at the different stages of his progress. At his departure from this world, his survivors consecrate his death for his future felicity in the next world. This Saṁskāra, being post-mortem, is not less important, because for a Hindu the value of the next world is higher than that of the present one. The Baudhāyana Pitṛmedha-Sūtras say, "It is well-known that through the Saṁskāras after the birth one conquers this earth; through the Saṁskāras after the death the heaven."[1] Therefore the ritualists are very anxious to have the funerals performed with meticulous care.

(2) *The Origin*

(i) *The Horror of Death*

The origin of the funeral ceremonies like that of the others is shrouded in mystery. There were many factors that brought into existence the rites and ceremonies attending on the occasion of death. First of all, there was the horror of death. To an early man death was not the natural end of life, but an abnormal event which shocked him to the core. The horror depended not so much upon the physical pain that is caused at the time of death as upon the mystery of it and the result which is produced for its victim and his relatives. All the familiar relations ceased between them, and the body which was the centre of these relations decomposed. This horror has given birth to an obstinate disbelief in the necessity of death. The attempts to escape it are repeated, though with sad failure. Even the most natural and inevitable disease is ascribed to causes not beyond human control. The picture thus presented of the desperate refusal of mankind to accept the necessary end of the

1. जातसंस्कारेणेमं लोकमभिजयति मृतसंस्कारेणामुं लोकम्। iii. 1. 4.

worldly career is one of the most pathetic episodes in the history of human race. In the futile attempts for averting death, many ceremonies of primitive type arose.[2] But the contrast between life and death was so striking that man had ultimately to accept it as the natural end of the human life. He, then, made the proper arrangement for making the death and the life after death easy.[3]

(ii) *The Conception of the Soul after death*

According to the primitive belief, death did not cause the entire annihilation of man. The usual theory of the process of death was the separation of the soul from the body. The soul may separate from the body before death as in dreams. Sickness was frequently held to be such a separation. The distinction between such a separation and that of death was that the latter was final. Thus, the deceased, though disembodied, was supposed to be still living.

(iii) *The mixed Feelings of Dread and Love*

The survivors cherished mixed sentiments towards the dead. First, there was the sentiment of dread. It was believed that the deceased had still some kind of interest in his family property and relations, whom he would not like to quit and, therefore, was lingering about the house. It was also supposed that because he was alienated from the survivors by death, he might cause injury to the family. So attempts were made to avoid his presence and contact. Formal farewell address was given to him;[4] he was asked to depart; and even actual barriers were put between the living and the dead.[5] Besides, he was provided with food and other articles necessary for a traveller, so that he should resume his journey to the next world. The next sentiment was of affection and love towards the deceased. The

---

2. A.G.S.

3. जातस्य वै मनुष्यस्य ध्रुवं मरणमिति विजानीयात्तस्माज्जाते न प्रहृष्येन्मृते च न विषीदेत् ।
अकस्मादागतं भूतमकस्मादेव गच्छति ।
तस्माज्जातं मृतं चैव संपश्यन्ति सुचेतसः ॥
तस्मान्मातरं पितरमाचार्यं पत्नीं पुत्रं शिष्यमन्तेवासिनं पितृव्यं मातुलं सगोत्रमसगोत्रं वा दायमुपयच्छेद्दहनं संस्कारेण संस्कुर्वन्ति ॥ B.P.S. iii.

4. प्रेहि प्रेहि पथिभिः etc. A.V. xviii. 1. 54.
P.G.S. iii. 10. 24.

5. यदाश्रृतं कृणवो जातवेदोऽथेमेनं प्रहिणुतात्पितृभ्यः । Ṛ.V. x. 16. 1.

natural blood-relation still existed between the dead and his relations. The survivors were solicitous about the future welfare of the departed. They thought that it was their duty to help the dead in reaching his destination after death. The corpse was disposed of by means of fire, so that the dead, being purified, may be allowed to enter the holy place of the Fathers.[6] Articles necessary in the journey were supplied to him, so that he may not suffer from want. As the next world was believed to be a replica of this world, every thing necessary for starting a new life was presented to him. For example, the Anustaraṇi or an old cow or a goat was sent with him to serve as a guide in the way; daily food was offered; in later times, and even now the Vaitaraṇi or a cow is given to help the dead in crossing the river lying in the way to Yama.[7] Formerly these things were consumed in fire with the dead. Now they are presented to the Brahmans, who are supposed to send them to the realm of the dead through some mysterious agency.

(*iv*) *Physical Needs*

In addition to the above sentiments, there was the physical need of disposing of the dead body and the subsequent performance of ceremonies and observances. The decomposition of the corpse made it impossible for the relatives to keep it in the house for a long time. So, like other refuses, it was also removed, though with reverence and care denied to them. Moreover disease and death of the dead caused pollution and contagion in the family. In order to remove them many observances and taboos arose.

The main objects of the proper disposal of the corpse and the performance of all the rites and ceremonies connected with it are to free the survivors from the pollution of death and to give rest to the dead. Until these rites and ceremonies are duly performed, the soul of the man is not finally dismissed to its place in the next world; it does not find place in the company of the fathers, it is not elevated to its due position in the cult of ancestral worship and it continues to be Preta, haunting its relatives unpleasantly. This belief was current in all the ancient peoples and is universal in the lower culture even at present. The funeral ceremonies were as significant among the ancient Greeks and Egyptians as among the Hindus.

6. The वैतरणीदानप्रयोग Stein's cat. p. 104.

7. R.V. x. 14. 16, 18.

(3) *Different Kinds of Disposal*

We have no pre-Vedic record of the disposal of the corpse and other funeral ceremonies connected therewith. Recent archaeological discoveries, no doubt, have brought to light some instances of how the dead bodies were disposed of in ancient India. But their chronology is still disputable and we cannot trace them all back to pre-historic times with any appreciable amount of certainty. Moreover, information supplied by them is limited to the burial of the dead and they do not tell anything about the postburial or the cremation ceremonies.

The earliest literary mention of the funeral ceremonies is found in the Ṛgveda[8] and the Atharvaveda.[9] The mode of the disposal of the dead depends on the religious belief of the people concerned and their general culture. The society presented in the Vedic hymns is sufficiently advanced, so the primitive forms of disposal are not to be found in them. Cannibalism or eating away of the dead by the survivors cannot be traced in the Vedas. The sub-aerial deposit or leaving the body on the ground was probably the earliest method of removing the corpse, as it was the simplest. In the funeral there is no description of it, though it is referred to once.[10] In the very primitive times, when people moved from place to place in the search of food and fodder, exposure of the dead and the diceased was very common, as they proved a burden on the wandering family. During the Vedic period, the Indo-Aryans were not a nomadic people but they led a settled and civilized life and the aged were held in love and respect. So no exposure of the aged persons took place. But Kaegie[11] quotes the following remarks of Zimmer to show the treatment accorded by the Germans to the aged, in order to prove the existence of a similar custom among the Ṛgvedic Aryans Among the Germans, when the master of the house was above sixty years old, if the signs of the weakness of age were of such a character that he "no longer had the power to walk or stand, and to ride unassisted and unsupported, with collected mind, free will and good sense, he was obliged to give over his authority to his son and to perform menial service; the old men might be made by hard sons and cruel grand-sons to expiate painfully the love and gentleness they had

8. A.V. xviii. 1. 2. 3. 4.

9. ये निखाता ये परोप्ता ये दग्धा ये चोद्धिताः। A.V. xviii. 2–34.

10. Der Ṛgveda, No. 50.

11. Grimu Deutsche Rechts

neglected in their more powerful days; those who had grown useless and burdensome were even either killed outright, or exposed and abandoned to death by starvation."[12] Kaegie says, "We have to imagine exactly similar conditions among the Indians, when the texts speak of "the divided possessions of an old father" and of "old men exposed."[13]

The above inference is based upon a Ṛigvedic verse, which indicates that the possessions of the old father were divided among his sons in his life-time. But even if we suppose that they were landed-property, provisions had to be first made for his and his wife's maintenance. The passages in the later literature, however, "all negative the idea that the property of the family was legally family property; it is clear that it was the property of the head of the house, usually the father, and that the other members of the family only had moral claims upon it, which the father could ignore, though he might be coerced by his sons if they were physically stronger.........The developed patria potestas of the father, which was marked very early, as shown by the legend of Śunaḥśepa, is inconsistent with the views that the sons were legally co-sharers with the father, unless and until they actually insisted on a division of the property."[14] Then, again, it should be observed that even in the Ṛgvedic[15] times, sons were coveted, because they would offer oblations to the dead parents and their ancestors. This was not only a moral but a religious duty. It cannot, therefore, be conceived by any stretch of imagination that the Ṛgvedic Aryans killed their old and decrepit parents or exposed and abandoned them to die by starvation. The custom found among the ancient Germans must have been a relic of the barbarous times, that prevailed among the prehistoric aborigines of Europe, with whom the half civilized German tribes had amalgamated. There is no distinct trace of the existences of this barbarous custom in the Ṛgveda, the oldest work extant of the Aryan people.

There are a few passages more in the Vedic hymns, from which the existence of exposure is inferred. The Ṛgveda[16] refers to a

12. Zimmer, Act. Laben, 326–328.

13. Vedic Index i. 351, 352.

14. R.V. i. 105. 3.

15. viii. 51. 2.

16. x. 14.

person cast out and the Atharvaveda[17] speaks of the dead man being exposed (Uddhita). But the latter passage may well refer merely to the bodies being exposed after death to the elements as is done by the Parsis. The former passage may refer to the individual case of some person who may have been cast out, and proves absolutely nothing as to a habitual or recognized custom.

We have no record of the cave burial also in the funeral ceremonies of the Hindus. It seems that it was not a recognized form of disposal. Water burial or to fling a dead body into a sea or a river is one of the easiest ways of getting rid of it. That doubtless is the reason for thus disposing of the corpses of slaves or common people in various places. But it does not account for every case of water burial. In some cases the object is not merely to get rid of the body, but to prevent the deceased from returning to plague the survivors,[18] for water is usually regarded a barrier to scare away evil spirits. The practical utility of water burial is recognized in Hinduism in the case of those who have no survivors, to perform their funeral ceremonies. But the sentiment of fear is not so prominent in the Hindu mind. At present water burial is accorded to small children, who are esteemed too innocent to require a purification, or to realize ascetics and mendicants, who have no family ties and do not stand in need of funeral. Married men and women, who die of some epidemics, are given water burial. But in their case, the funeral ceremonies are postponed to a subsequent convenient time when their effigies are properly burnt and the post-cremation ceremonies are duly performed.

Inhumation or burial proper is almost absent in the present day Hindu funerals, except in cases of great saintly personalities and very small children.[19] But the existence of this custom among common people in the Ṛgvedic times is proved by the verses contained in it.[20] Addressing the dead body carried to and lying in the burial ground, the priest says: "Go to this thy mother, Earth, the wide-spread, delightful Earth; this virgin (Earth) is, as soft as wool, to the liberal worshipper; may she protect thee from the proximity of Nirṛti. Earth, rise, above him; oppress him not; be attentive to him

17. xviii. 2. 34.

18. E. S. Hartland, Encyclopaedia of Religion and Ethics, vol. iv. p. 421.

19. अद्विवर्षे प्रेते....शरीरमदग्ध्वा निखनन्ति। P.G.S. iii. 10. 2-5.

20. x. 18. 10–13.

and comfortable; cover him up, Earch as a mother covers her child with the skirt of her garment. May the earth heaped over him lie light; may thousands of particles (of dust) envelop him; may these mansions distil ghee for him; may they every day be an asylum to him in this world. I heap up the earth around thee placing (upon thee) this clod of earth; may I not be injured; let the Piatra sustain this thy monument; may Yama make thee a dwelling here."[21]

Scholars influenced by the later-day custom of cremation and the subsequent burial of the remains hold that the above hymns refer to the Asthi-Sañchaya or the collection of bones. According to Sāyaṇa the above verses were uttered at the time when the bones of the dead were put into an urn and buried into a grave. He bases his opinion on the Āśvalāyana Gṛhyasūtra.[21a] But this was a later custom, and should be regarded as a relic of the ancient custom of burial, which was being replaced by the custom of cremation. It was a compromise between the two customs. The opinion of Sāyana cannot be accepted owing to the following reasons :

(i) At the time of cremation, verses were uttered with the object of sending the dead man to heaven, the dominion of Yama, situated in the highest heaven.[22] If he had already been cremated and gone to heaven, why soon afterwards, at the time of burying his ashes and bones, should he be asked again to go "to this thy mother Earth" the widespread delightful Earth? Such a procedure would be inconsistent and contradictory.

(ii) If it be at all possible for the dead corpse to suffer any pain, it must have suffered extreme agony at the time of cremation, and the burnt bones and ashes would suffer no further pain or agony at the time of their burial in grave, enclosed in an urn provided with a lid, over which earth was heaped up. But the verses become quite intelligible when they are applied to the burial of a corpse. The dead body was still there, as would appear from a perusal of the verses in which the mourners have been described as taking away the bow from the dead man's hand, and it was quite natural for them not to have been able as yet to dissociate themselves from their feelings and belief that the dead man, who had been quite alive a few

21. Ibid.

21a. iv. 5.

22. x. 16. 2.

hours back, could not feel any pain afterwards. It was, therefore, quite natural for them, while performing their last duty towards him, to entertain tender feelings for him, and address him as follows: "Go to this, thy Mother-Earth etc." and the earth was also asked to be kind and soft to him.

There can be no doubt that the foregoing verses refer to the burial of a dead person and not to his ashes or bones after cremation. But it must be admitted that even during the Vedic period this custom was becoming optional and falling into disuse. When the cult of sacrifice was fully established, the funeral came to be regarded as a sacrifice[23] and cremation became the most prevalent custom, replacing the older custom of burial. In the Gṛhyasūtras the burial of the dead bodies is not mentioned, though the ancient tradition was followed in the form of burying the bones and ashes of the dead after cremation. In subsequent times the burial of the dead became quite unknown among the Hindus except in the cases of very small children and ascetics.

Preservation of the dead body in the house with or without previous desiccation or mummification is not mentioned at all in the ritual literature of the Hindus. This custom was prevalent in a rude or archaic society that believed that the soul or spirit of the man was still dwelling in the body after his death. The Indo-Aryans outgrew this stage as early as the Vedic period. According to their faith the spirit departed form the dead body[24] and there was no sense in preserving it.

Cremation or burning of the dead body is the most recognized mode of the disposal of corpse among the Hindus from the time of the Vedas up to the present day. This mode evolved at a high stage of the human civilization, as it is the most scientific and refined. More than one causes might have operated in bringing this custom into existence:

(i) Tribes without a settled abode may have found it convenient, if they desired to carry about the remains of their dead, or to remove such remains beyond the possibility of desecration by their enemies.

---

23. This, however, was a Pitṛyajña as the dead was sent unto the Fathers, cf R.V. x. 16. 1.

24. R.V. x. 14. 7–9.

(ii) Another very powerful motive for cremation may have been the desire to be quit of the ghost. The fortress of the ghost was destroyed by fire and it was frightened away by its flames.

(iii) Fire, consuming forest, grass and refuses might have suggested its utility in burning away the dead also.

(iv) In the beginning the above causes may have been more active, but the most potent factor that gave the custom of cremation a lasting position was the religious belief of the Indo-Aryans that obtained during the Vedic period. Fire was regarded by the Indo-Aryans as the messenger of the gods on earth, and the carrier of the oblations offered to them.[25] The material things that constituted Havya could not be bodily and directly conveyed to the gods in heaven; hence the services of a heavenly messenger and carrier like Agni were requisitioned. This analogy was also extended to human corpses as well as to the carcases of the animals that were sacrificed to the gods. After a man died, it was thought necessary to send his body to heaven. This could be only done by consigning it to Agni. After the body was consumed by it and reduced to ashes, the dead could receive a new body in the world of Yama and join the Pitara and his ancestors.[25a] This seems to be the most powerful idea underlying the custom of cremation, and this idea was essentially a religious one. Before fire was discovered and brought to human use, corpses used to be cast away as a rule, or buried under ground, or exposed to be devoured by carnivorous birds and beasts. The custom of cremation must, therefore, have come into existence in the last. One branch of the ancient Aryans, the Parsis, however, retained the older custom of exposing the corpse to be devoured by birds, even after they had become staunch Fire-worshippers, for they regarded Fire too sacred to be polluted by such an unclean thing as a corpse. But the Vedic Aryans did not agree with them in this view, and anxious as they were to see their beloved dead go to heaven and join his ancestors, they consistently thought it right to consign his dead body to Agni in order to transfer it to heaven, in a subtler and a more resplendent form befitting his new environments.

There was another religious belief also which seems to have been instrumental in introducing the custom of cremation. It was believed that the evil spirits mostly originated from the wicked souls

---

25. वह्निं यशसं विदथस्य केतुं सुप्राव्यं दूतं सद्यो अर्थम्। R.V. i. 60.

25a. R.V. x. 14. 8.

of the dead persons buried in the earth.[26] So the people thought it necessary to restrict their number in the terrestrial region by widely introducing the custom of cremation and thus sending the dead to the regions of Yama or Nirṛti, there to receive the reward or punishment of their actions. The Hindus even now regard cremation as absolutely necessary for the welfare of the souls of the dead, excepting those of the infants who are sinless and pure, and of the holy mendicants or Sādhus who are supposed to have overcome evil tendencies during their life-time, and are, therefore, accorded a burial as perfectly harmless. But in the case of ordinary men and householders, want of cremation is looked upon with horror, retarding the progress of the souls in the other world (Sadgati). The Hindus call the cremation ceremony Aurdhvadaihika-kriyā or the ceremonies that release the soul from the body for its upward journey to heaven. Unless the ceremony is performed, the departed soul is believed to linger about its late habitation and hover without consolation, and in great distress as a Preta.

The rites of cremation are denied to babes and children under the age of (initiation or puberty.[27] Children are gently buried. In some cases at least, and possibly in all, this is done with a view to securing their rebirth. Persons dying of epidemics are generally cast away in water. It is due to the superstition that the evil spirits that bring these diseases will be infuriated if their victims are burnt. Persons held in reverence are also not burnt, as their sacred qualities set them apart from the rest of mankind. Women dying in pregnancy or childhood also are not accorded the rites of cremation.

(4) *The Funerals*

(*i*) *The Vedic Period*

For the full details and descriptions of the funeral ceremonies we should begin with the Vedic period. The details of the rites must, like those of the marriage rites, have differed among different tribes during the time of the Vedas. But we have no record of the different families. Moreover, the verses of the ceremonies are not arranged in the order of their occurrence in the Ṛgveda X. 14–19 and the

26. Vedic Mythology, p. 70. cf. Oldenberg, Die Religion des Veda, 62-2.

27. According to the Gṛhyasūtras, children below two only are denied this rite. See P.G.S. iii. 10. 2.

Atharvaveda XVIII where they are collected. Still we can easily guess the main incidents of the rite:

(i) When a man died, verses were recited to revive him (Atharvaveda VII. 53); when this failed, funeral rites were started.[27a]

(ii) The corpse was washed (Atharvaveda V. 19.4) and the big toes tied together with a bunch of twigs, lest death should walk back to the house after the corpse was sent out (Atharvaveda, V. 19.12).

(iii) The corpse was remo ed on a cart drawn by two bulls (Atharvaveda 2.56; Ta tiriya Āraṇyaka IV. 1.3) accompanied by mourning relatives and professional mourners (Atharvaveda VIII. 1.19, Atharvaveda IX. 2.11).

(iv) The corpse was dressed in the burning ground (Atharvaveda. XVIII. 2.57).

(v) The face of the dead was covered with the omentum of a cow (Atharvaveda. XVIII. 2.58).

(vi) The staff or the bow was taken off from the hand of the dead person (Atharvaveda XVIII. 2. 59. 60).

(vii) The widow lay down on the funeral pile by the side of her husband (The Ṛgveda X. 18.7; Atharvaveda XVIII. 3.1. 2).

(viii) A goat was sacrificed and the pile was lit up. Women expressed their grief (Atharvaveda XVIII. 2. 4. 8).

(ix) The various parts of the dead man's body were directed to go to appropriate places (Ṛgveda X. 16. 3).

(x) The bones were collected and buried and in some cases a funeral monument was erected (Ṛgveda X. 18.11.13).

(xi) A farewell address was presented to the dead. Ṛgveda. X. 14. 7. 8).

(xii) The survivors took their funeral bath to purge the pollution caused by the funeral fire (Atharvaveda XII. 2.40–42).

27a. A Survival of a similar custom is found in Spain. On the death of a pope or a king, a high official of the court calls with a loud voice three times the name of the deceased, and receiving no reply, certifies the death. E. S. Hartland, E, R. E. vol. iv. p. 411.

(xiii) The pure sacrificial fire was lighted up in the house to remove the impure fire. (Atharvaveda. XII. 2.43–45)

(xiv) On the completion of the funeral rites the corpse-eating Fire (Kravyāda) which had been invoked for cremation had to be sent out of the house (Atharvaveda XII. 4.4). The Grāhi Fire was also sent out, who holds fast in his net the house, when a dame's husband dies (Atharvaveda XII. 2.39).

(xv) Then there was feasting and resumption of dancing and laughter (Ṛgveda X. 18.3).

Thus in the above list of the incidents, we find all the four parts of the complete funeral rites, the burning; the Abhiṣiñchana and the Śmaśāna-chiti (the washing of the corpse and piling of the funeral pyre); the Udaka-Karma (water oblations); and the Śāntikarma (pacificatory rites). The details have suffered much alteration during the passage of time, but the fundamental divisions of the rite are still the same.

(ii) *The Sūtra Period*

Coming down from the vedas we find the description of the funeral ceremonies in the sixth Chapter of the Āraṇyaka of the Kṛṣṇa-Yajurveda.[27b] The Āraṇyaka describes the ceremonies under the title of Pitṛmedha, or the rites for the welfare of the manes, and gives all the mantras required for the ceremonial of the first ten days after death, leaving the Śrāddha or the rites meet for the eleventh day altogether unnoticed. The verses are mostly taken from the Ṛgveda, and arranged in consecutive order, but without any clue to the particular rituals for which they are meant. In the few Gṛhya-sūtras, in which the Antyeṣṭi Saṁskāra is described, the ceremonies are further detailed and more systematic. The Baudhāyana and the Bhāradvāja Gṛhyasūtras aphorize the said Āraṇyakas supplying many deficiencies in it. They also give several particulars not to be found in the Āśvalāyana Gṛhyasūtras which also deals with the subject. The Hiraṇyakeśi Gṛhyasūtra also describes the funeral ceremonies and are supposed to be relied upon by laterday writers.

(iii) *Later Additions and Omissions*

The mediaeval and modern Paddhatis and Prayogas generally draw upon these sources, adding new features and omitting obsolete

27b. The Taittirīyāraṇyaka, iii.

items of the Saṁskāra. Besides tradition plays a great part in these ceremonies. The chronological differences will be noticed in their due places while treating a particular item of the funeral rites.

(5) *The Approach of Death*

The scriptures do not fully record all the customs followed and ceremonies observed before death. But from the tradition we know a number of them. When a Hindu feels that his death is near he invites his relatives and friends and holds friendly discourse with them. To promote his future weal he makes presents to the Brahmans and the needy. Among the presents, the gift of a cow is the most valuable. She is called Vaitaraṇī; she is supposed to be the conductor of the dead over the stream of the under-world. In the Sūtra period this cow was called Anustaranī and she was either sacrificed and burnt with the corpse or let loose to run away from the cremation ground.[28] When the slaughter of a cow became prohibited, she was presented to a Brahman and was believed to help the dead in crossing the infernal river through some mysterious power of the receiver. This custom still continues. When the dying hour draws near, the patient is placed on a cleansed spot on sandy soil. The dying couch is prepared in proximity to the three fires or, if he preserves only one, near it, viz., the domestic fire.[29] Here the deceased is laid down with his head turned towards the south. Sacred passages from the Vedas of one's own school are chanted in the ears. If the patient is a Brahman, passages from some Āraṇyaka are repeated in his ears. At present verses from the Bhagvadgītā and the Rāmāyaṇa are recited to a dying person.

(6) *Pre-disposal Ceremonies*

The first mantra given in the Āraṇyaka refers to the performance of a homa just after death. But this rule is binding only on the death of one who, in his life-time, had maintained the sacrificial fires. According to the Baudhāyana, four offerings should be made, while touching the right hand of the dead man, to the Gārhyapatya fire, with a spoon overflowingly full of clarified butter. Bharadvāja, however, prescribes that the offerings should be made to the Āhavanīya fire; he is silent whether they should be fourfold or not. Āśvalāyana[30] recommends that the offerings should be made at a

28. B. P. S. iv. 1.

29. A. G. S. iv. 1.

30. Ibid., iv. 1.

subsequent stage. With the decline of the sacrificial religion among the Hindus, this prescription has lost its force and is followed in a very few orthodox families. New Paurāṇic and popular customs have taken its place. They pour some drops of water with a few leaves of Tulasi in the mouth of the dying person. A very strange custom has evolved in Bengal. According to it, the dying person is carried to the riverside and the lower half of the body is immersed in water at the moment of death.[31] This ceremony is called Antarjalī and forms a very offensive part of the modern ceremonial in Bengal. With a flourish of rhetoric it is called Ghāt murder. That this custom is not ancient will be evident from the following observations. All the scriptures referred to above take it for granted that death has happened within the house, if not near the place where the sacrificial fires are kept.[32] Considering this negative evidence against the custom, its total absence in other parts of India and the oldest authority on the subject being the most recent of the Purāṇas,[33] we can fairly conclude that it is of modern origin. None of the authorities usually quoted, enjoining it as a positive duty, belongs to a time earlier than the sixteenth lentury A.D.[34] It has come into existence probably since the date of Raghunandana and his contemporary writers on ritual.

(7) *The Bier*

According to the Gṛhyasūtras, after the homa, a cot made of udumbara wood (Ficus glemarata) is to be provided, and having spread on it a piece of black antelope skin with the hairy side downwards, and head pointing to the south, the corpse is to be laid thereon with the face upwards.[35] Under the present practices, however, the cot can be made of bamboo and the antelope skin is dispensed with. A son, a brother, or other relative, or in their absence whosoever takes the lead, should next address the corpse to give up its old clothing and dress it in a new suit: "Give up the clothes thou hast hitherto worn; remember the Iṣṭa and the Pūrta sacrifices thou hast performed,

---

31. This custom is not prevalent in other provinces of India.

32. B. P. S. i. 1.

33. The Skandapurāṇa quoted in the Śuddhitattva p. 167; the Agnipurāṇa quoted in the Prāyaścittatattva, p. 292.

34. This is the date of Raghunandana. See P. V. Kane, History of Dharmaśāstra, p. 416.

35. A.G.S. iv. 1.

the fees to Brahmans thou has given, and those gifts thou hast bestowed upon thy friends."[36] The body is then covered with a piece of unbleached uncut cloth, having fringes on both sides, the operation being performed while repeating the mantras, "This cloth comes to thee first." The dead is required to change his or her old shabby clothes and put on pure and new ones for entering the next world. Then the corpse, being wrapped up in its bedding, is to be borne on its cot to the place of cremation.

(8) *The Removal of Corpse*

The removal of the corpse, according to some authorities, should be made by aged slaves, according to others, on a cart drawn by two bullocks.[37] The mantra for the purpose says, "I harness these two bullocks to the cart, for the conveyance of your life, whereby you may repair to the region of Yama, to the place where the virtuous resort." This indicates that the most ancient custom was to employ a cart and not men. The Āśvalāyana Gṛhyasūtra suggests only one bullock to be employed. Any how, the ancient Sūtrakāras evince none of the repugnance to, the employment of the Śūdras for the removal of the corpse of a Brahman, which the modern Smṛtis entertain on the subject. According to the latter, none but the blood relations of the dead should perform this duty and the touch of others than that of one's own caste is pollution, which can be atoned for only by the performance of an expiatory ceremony.[38] This prejudice first manifested itself in the time of Manu.[39] He says, "Let no kinsman, whilst any of his own class are at hand, cause a deceased Brāhmaṇa to be carried out by a Śūdra, because the funeral rite, polluted by the touch of a servile man, obstructs his passage to heaven." The subsequent authorities are equally emphatic on prohibition of a Śūdra's touch.

(9) *The Funeral Procession*

The funeral procession is headed by the chief mourner, generally the eldest son of the dead.[40] In many localities, the man leading

---

36. अपैतदह यदिहाविभः पुरा। इष्टापूर्तमनुसम्पश्य दक्षिणां यथा ते दत्तं बहुधा विबन्धुषु।
37. A.G.S. iv. 1.
38. P.S. iii. 43.
39. M.S. v. 104.
40. The Paddhati by Jayarāma P.G.S. iii. 10.

the procession carries a fire brand in his hand which he has kindled at the domestic fire. The Chief mourner is followed by the funeral bier and the latter is followed by the relatives and the friends of the deceased. The Gṛhyasūtras enjoin that all the Sapiṇḍas should join the funeral procession of the dead who are older than two years.[41] The order of the mourners in the procession is according to age, the elders being in front. In ancient times women also went to the ground of cremation with loose dishevelled hair and their shoulder besprinkled with dust.[42] But now this custom is stopped. The following verse is repeated by the chief mourner at the time of start: "Pūṣā, who knows the road well, has well-trained animals, to carry you, and is the protector of the region, is bearing you away hence; may he translate you hence to the region of the Pitṛs, May Agni, who knows what is meet for you bear you away."

(10) *The Anustaraṇī*

A most important member of the funeral procession, in ancient times, was an animal called Anustaraṇī or Rājagavi.[43] For this purpose a cow of a particular description (which might be substituted by a goat) was chosen. The animal was brought with the following verse : "Protector of regions, this is an offering for thee." According to the Sūtrakāras the cow should be sacrificed, but should any accident happen at the time of the sacrifice, the animal was set free.[44] The mantra for the sacrifice runs : "Companion of the dead, we have removed the sins of the dead by thee; so that no sin or decrepitude may approach us." If it was necessary to let loose the cow, she was to be made to walk thrice round the pyre, while the leader repeated the mantra each time. Then she was sanctified by another verse which runs, "Mayest thou be a source of satisfaction by the milk to those who are living in my family, and those who are dead and those who are just born, as well as those who may be born henceafter," and lastly the cow was set free with, "This cow is the mother of the Rudras, the daughter of the Vasus, the sister of Ādityas, and the pivot of our happiness, therefore, I solemnly say unto all wise

---

41. द्विवर्षप्रभृति प्रेतमाश्मशानात्सर्वेऽनुगच्छेयुः । P.G.S. iii. 10-8.

42. अस्य भार्याः कनिष्ठप्रथमाः प्रकीर्णकेश्यो व्रजेयुः पांसूनंसेष्वावपमानाः ।
B.P.S. i, 4. 3.

43. आनयन्त्येतां कृष्णां कूटां जरतीं तज्जघन्यामनुस्तरणीं पदबद्धाम् ।
B.G.S. i. 4. 1.

44. A.G.S. iv. 1.

men, kill not this sacred harmless cow. Let her drink water and eat grass. Om! I let her loose." At present the cow-sacrifice for any purpose is prohibited altogether and in its place the gift of a cow is made just before the death of the person and at the cremation ground before the corpse is burnt.

In the opinion of Oldenberg,[45] we get the idea of substitution in offering a cow or a goat at the time of burning the dead body. Fire consumes the flesh of the cow or the goat which cover the corpse and spares the dead man. He bases his opinion on the Ṛgvedic verses (X 16.4, 7) that run :

> The he-goat is thy part; with fire consume him;
> Let thy fierce flame, thy glowing heat devour him.
> Shield thee with cows against the flame of Agni,
> Be wholly covered with their fat and richness;
> So may the bold one eager to attack thee
> With fierce glow, fail to girdle and consume.

The German savant is justified in his conclusion so far as the Ṛgvedic ideology is concerned. But during the Sūtra period the ideas changed and the above offerings were regarded as provision during the ethereal journey and for the life in the next world, as is evident from the verses accompanying them.[46] In subsequent periods the same idea continued in the form of gift, though the method of sending the provision to the next world was changed. Formerly the funeral Fire conveyed it there on its up-going flames; now it is done through the mysterious agency of the Brahmans. Moreover the cow or the goat were not only provision but they served as guide and help in the journey of the dead, as their very name, Vaitaraṇī or Anustaraṇī suggests.

The journey from the house of the dead to the cremation ground is divided into three parts, and the funeral procession stops at every halt where special rites are performed.[47] The Yamasūktas are repeated in the way. The general practice at present, however, is to repeat the sacred name of Hari or Rama while carrying the corpse. The majority of population dispense with the ceremonies in the way and the recital of the hymns dedicated to Yama.

---

45. The Ṛgveda, 587-88.

46. A.G.S. iv.

47. Ibid.

(11) *The Cremation*

After the arrival at the cremation ground, the next operation is to select the ground for arranging the pyre and digging a trench.[48] The Āraṇyaka does not allude to the items of the ceremonies preceding the burning of the corpse at the cremation ground which shows that these were formerly performed without the aid of any mantra. But the Gṛhyasūtras contain special regulations, particularly as to its orientation. The rules prescribed for the selection of the ground somewhat resemble the same regarding the place of offerings for the gods. The plot duly selected is purified and a formula is chanted to scare away demons or ghosts. The trench, according to Āśvalāyana, should be twelve fingers deep, five spans wide and as long as the corpse with its hand uplifted. The kind of wood used, the size and the orientation of the pyres, and other things related to them are regulated by the sacred texts and nothing is left to the whims of the mourners. In the opinion of some writers the corpse should be disembowelled and the cavity filled with ghee.[49] The idea underlying this operation was to purify the corpse and to facilitate the cremation. Later on, however, this custom was regarded repulsive. At present, the pairing of hair and nails of the dead body and washing it with water are thought to be sufficient for purification. The corpse is now laid on the pyre, the threads that bind the thumbs are loosened, the cords that hold the bier together are cut off and the very bier is either flung into the water or placed upon the pyre.[50] The corpse in its hands, should have a piece of gold if it is of a Brahman, a bow if of a Kshattriya, a jewel if of a Vaiśya.[51] In the Vedic and the Sūtra periods, when everything was done according to the rule, the Anustaraṇī cow, as already said, was either slaughtered or let loose. Now this prescription is dropped altogether.

(12) *Lying of the Widow on the funeral pyre*

At this stage, a reference should be made to the custom of the lying of the widow on the funeral pyre with her husband, which, though obsolete now-a-days, was prevalent up to the time of the

48. Ibid,

49. अथास्य दक्षिणां कुक्षिमपावृत्य निष्पुरीषं कृत्वाऽद्भिः प्रक्षाल्य सर्पिषा अन्त्राणि पूरयित्वा दर्भैः संसीव्यति। B.P.S. i. 2–6.

50. A.G.S. iv.

51. Ibid: B.P.S. i. 8. 3-5.

Sūtras in ancient times.[52] The wife should lie down on the left side of the corpse according to Baudhāyana. Āśvalāyana recommends that she should be placed near the head on the north side. The chief mourner, or he who was to set fire to the pyre, should then address the dead saying, "O mortal, this woman, (your wife), wishing to be joined to you in a future world is lying by the corpse; she has always observed the duties of a faithful wife; grant her your permission to abide in this world, and relinquish your wealth to your descendants."[53] A younger brother of the dead, or a disciple, or a servant, should then proceed to the pyre, hold the left hand of the woman and ask her to come away, "Rise up, woman, thou liest by the side of the lifeless, come to the world of the living, away from the husband, and become the wife of him who holds thy hands and is willing to marry thee."[54]

The verses recited in connection with the above custom are first to be found in the funeral hymns of the Ṛgveda[54a] and the Atharvaveda.[55] Here we find the ritualistic survival of the Sati custom. During the earlier period gifts to the dead were buried or burnt with the corpse.[56] These gifts consisted of food, weapons, clothes and domestic animals. Sometimes slaves and even wife were also burnt or buried with the dead.[57] The Atharvaveda calls it "the ancient custom."[58] This inhuman custom, however, was discontinued in the Ṛgvedic time, though the formality of lying on the funeral pyre by the widow was retained. The Gṛhyasūtras prescribe the same ritualistic substitution for the real burning of the widow. The ritual literature since the time of the Ṛgveda is not in favour of burning the widow alive. The Paddhatis and the Prayogas on the funeral ceremonies have cancelled this custom, altogether, even not requiring the widow to attend the ceremonies performed at the ground of cremation. But the Satī custom never ceased entire and later on it was revived in certain tribes and families.[59]

---

52. Ibid.

53. Ibid.

54. A.G.S. iv. 2-4.

54a. X. 18. 8-9.

55. xviii. 3. 1-2.

56. Schrader, Aryan Religion, E.R.E., II, pp. 11—57; Indogermanea, 146.

57. Ibid.

58. धर्मं पुराणं परिपालयन्ती। xviii. 3.1.

59. It was mostly prevalent among the Rajputs. This custom was finally stopped by Lord William Bentinc in 1835.

When the ceremony of lying on the funeral pyre by the widow was finished, she was asked to bring away the gold referred to above from the hands of the dead with the following mantra, "For the promotion of thy wealth, and glory as a Brahman woman, and beauty and power, take the gold from the hand of the dead (and abide) in this (region); we (shall dwell) here well served and prospering, and overcoming all assailants."[60] The commentator on the Āśvalāyana Gṛhyasūtra says that the remover of the widow, and not the widow herself should take the gold, and that in the case of his being a slave, this and the two preceding verses should be repeated by the chief mourner. Wilson and Max-müller take it in the same sense,[61] though Sāyaṇa's comment is opposed to it. But whatsoever may be the difference in the interpretation, the removal of the widow and the articles was completed. No alternative is contemplated in the Āraṇyaka and the Sūtras. It clearly shows that when the Āraṇyaka was compiled, the inhuman practice of burning the living wife with her dead husband, had not obtained currency in the country. With the stoppage of the Sati custom, this ceremony automatically ceased to exist.[62]

During the times when the sacrificial rituals were followed regularly, the sacrificial vessels which the dead used to employ in his ceremonial rites were, now, to be placed on the different parts of his body. And so were the different members of the cow if she was killed; if not, they were substituted by cakes or by imitations of her organs made of rice and barley. These articles were burnt with the corpse, so that the dead might get them in the next world.

(13) *Cremation a Sacrifice*

When the preliminaries are finished, the cremation[63] begins, which is regarded as an offering into the Sacred Fire, conducting the corpse to heaven as a sacrificial gift.[64] When the pile is ready to be lighted, a fire is applied to it with the prayer, "Agni,

60. A.G.S. iv. 1-2.

61. The Journal of Royal Asiatic Society, vol. xvi (1854), pp. 201-14; for the opposite view see the remarks by Rājā Rādhākānta Deva on the above J. R. A. S., vol. xvii (1859), pp. 209–220; The Śuddhitattva by Raghunandana.

62. Ibid.

63. A.G.S. iv. 1-2; Bh. G.S. i. 2.

64. Ibid.

consume not this body to cinders; nor give it pain, nor scatter about its skin or limbs! O Jātavedas, when the body is fairly burnt, convey the spirit to its ancestors."[65] The prayer is followed by an address to the organs of the dead which runs as follows: "May the organ of vision proceed to the sun; may the vital air merge in the atmosphere; mayest thou proceed, according to the virtuous deeds to heaven or earth or the regions of water, whichever place is beneficial to thee; mayest thou there, provide with food, exist in corporeal existence."[66] This is a touching scene when the survivors send off their dead relative to the next world for ever but with every solicitude for his or her future happiness.

During the Sūtra period the cremation was performed by the flames of three or five fires kept by the householder and a divination took place as to where the dead had gone after the cremation. Note was taken of which fire reached the dead first, and it was argued therefrom whether the dead started for the world of the gods or the manes, or to somewhere else.[67] At present neither the different kinds of fires are preserved by a householder nor the relatives of the deceased bother about his future abode.

Among the followers of some Vedic schools, a knee-deep trench is dug, in which a certain water plant is placed.[68] In the opinion of A. Hillebrandt[69] it is 'Clearly an ancient superstition, the purpose of which was to cool the heat of the fire." The tradition explains this custom in this way. "The dead man rises from the trench and ascends along with the smoke to heaven."

According to the practices of other Vedic schools, the mourners leave the funeral pyre to burn itself away, and the chief mourner excavates three trenches to the north of the pyre, lines them with pebbles and sand and fills them with water brought in an odd number of jars. The people who joined the procession are now requested to purify themselves by bathing in the trenches. This being done, a yoke is put up with the Pāśa branches stuck in the ground and tied at the top with a piece of weak string. The mourners are made to

65. R.V. x. 16: 1.

66. A.V. xviii. 2. 7.

67. A.G.S. iv. 2–4.

68. H.G.S. 10. 1.

69. E.R.E. vol. 11. pp. 475. ff

pass under it. The chief mourner passes last and plucking out the yoke offers a prayer to the sun.[70]

(14) *The Return*

Then the funeral party moves off without looking around. The mourners are asked to restrain themselves from any expression of grief, and go forward with heads bent down, entertaining one another with consoling speeches and virtuous tales.[71] "Many tears" it is said, "burn the dead."[72] We learn from the Mahābhārata that Yudhiṣṭhira was rebuked by Vyāsa for bewailing the death of his nephew For the purpose of driving away the sorrows of the survivors the story-tellers are engaged.[73]

(15) *The Offering of Water*

The next ceremony is called the Udakakarma[74] or the offering of water to the dead. It is performed in a variety of ways. According to one authority, all the relatives of the dead down to the seventh or tenth generation bathe in the nearest stream and purify themselves by it and offer a prayer to Prajāpati. While bathing, they put on only a single garment and the sacred thread hangs over the right shoulder. Many authorities prescribe that the hair should be dishevelled and dust thrown upon the body. The mourners turn their face towards the south, plunge under the water and calling upon the dead person by name offer a handful of water to him. Then they get out of the water, put on dry clothes and wringing those that they had on before, they spread them out towards the north. The present day custom enjoins a very interesting item after the Udaka-Karma. Just after the bath some grains of boiled rice and peas are scattered on the ground for the crows. It recalls the primitive belief according to which the dead were supposed to appear as birds. This supposi-

70. A.G.S. iv. 2–4.

71. The Antyeṣṭipaddhati by Jayarāma on P.G.S. iii. 10.

72. V. viii. 86.

शोचमानास्तु सस्नेहा बान्धवाः सुहृदस्तथा ।
पातयन्ति जनं स्वर्गादश्रुपातेन राघव ॥ The Rāmāyaṇa quoted by Jayarāma on P.G.S. iii. 10.

73. cf. Liders, ZDMG. l. viii. 706 off.

74. P.G.S. iii. 10. 16–23.

tion is confirmed by the comparison of the Maruts (an offshoot of the Pitaras) with the birds.[75]

(16) *Regaling the Mourners*

After the bath the relatives of the dead retire to a clean and pure grassy spot. Persons conversant with the Itihāsas and the Purāṇas regale the mourners with the praises of the deceased and consoling stories from ancient lore.[76] They do not return to the village till the sunset or the appearance of the first star.[77] In the opinion of some, they do not go home before sunrise.[78] Then the young ones walk first and the old ones last—a procedure reverse of that followed when the procession goes to the cremation ground. When they arrive at their home, they touch, by way of purifying themselves, the stone, the fire, cow-dung, grain, til-seed, oil and water before they step in.[79] According to other authorities, at the door of the house, they chew leaves of the Pichumanda or the Neeṁ tree, rinse their mouth, touch water, fire, cow-dung etc. or inhale the smoke of a certain species of wood, tread upon a stone and then enter.[80] These magical performances symbolize the severance of relation with the dead, and the articles used in them are supposed to serve as barriers against the inauspicious spirit of the dead.

(17) *Impurity*

Now the period of Āśaucha,[81] pollution or defilement, begins. The death of a person entails a condition which can be adequately expressed by the Polynesian word, "taboo" which means "setting apart a thing or a person as shunned for a religious or a semi-religious reason." A corpse is everywhere regarded as a taboo and the greatest care is taken in approaching or dealing with it. It is not quite clear what is this taboo due to. Is the corpse feared in and for itself, or as a vehicle of death, or is it dreaded owing to its con-

---

75. वयो न सीदन्नधि बर्हिषि प्रिये । R.V. i. 85. 7.

76. P.G.S. iii. 10. 22.

77. Ibid. iii. 16. 35.

78. Ibid. iii. 10. 36.

79. B.P.S. i. 12. 6. says, "अथ गृहानायान्ति यच्चात्र स्त्रियः आहुस्तत्कुर्वन्ति ।"

80. P.G.S. iii. 10. 24.

81. Ibid. iii. 10. 27. ff; M.S. V. 58–105; Yāj. S. iii. 1; P.S. iii.

nection with the disembodied spirit? Whatsoever may be the religious or sentimental motive underlying the taboo, one thing is evident that, to a great extent, it was based on the contagious nature of the corpse. So the survivors, owing to their contact with the dead person during his sickness and with his corpse after his death, are severed from the society on the sanitary grounds. The prohibitions consequent on a death, however, reach far beyond the person who have been compelled to perform the last offices about a corpse. They extend to the whole house, the whole family, the whole clan, the whole village, nay, to the very fields and even sometimes to the heavens.[82] But generally speaking; though the whole village attends the cremation, it is more particularly the near relatives who are defiled by death pollution than distant ones. Moreover, the period of mourning and therefore of taboo varies among different peoples according to the relationship of the mourners to the dead or their various circumstances, from a few days to many months.[83]

The period and the scope of Āśaucha differs according to the caste, age and sex of the deceased. The Gṛhyasūtras do not make any distinction between the periods of Āśaucha for the Brahmans and the Kṣatriyas, the common period being ten days.[84] But they fix fifteen days for the Vaiśyas and one month for the Śudras as the periods of defilements.[85] This distinction was mainly based on the observance of the rules of purity and cleanliness in different castes. Option was, however, allowed for people of different circumstances. "Impurity caused by death lasts for three or ten days."[86] This Sūtra text is explained by Jayarāma with reference to a verse from the Parāśara-Smṛti :[87] "A Vipra (Brahman), who regularly performs Agnihotra and remains engaged in the study of the Vedas, is absolved from defilement in one day; one who studies the Vedas only, in three days; and one who neglects both, in ten days."[88] The later Smṛtis

82. Cf. E.S. Hartland, E.R.E. vol. iv. p. 418.

83. The period was determined by the standard of purity and the closeness of relation.

84. P.G.S. iii. 10. 30.

85. Ibid. iii. 10. 38.

86. Ibid. iii. 10. 29-30.

87. एकाहाच्छुध्यते विप्रो योऽग्निवेदसमन्वितः ।
त्र्यहात्केवलवेदस्तु निर्गुणो दशभिर्दिनैः ।। III. 5.

88. Ibid.

permits even exception from Āśaucha altogether. "Persons engaged in conducting a sacrifice, one initiated in a sacrifice, those performing similar ceremonies, men performing long sacrifices or undergoing some observances, students, one who has realized Godhood, artisans, artists, medical practitioners, maid-servants, slaves, kings and their servants become instantly purified."[89] The exception is entirely based on the social convenience. At present the period of defilement lasts ten days for a Brahman, twelve days for a Kṣatriya, fifteen days for a Vaiśya and one month for Śūdra.[90]

The periods as prescribed above are in the case of death of grown-up persons. The death of a child causes less impurity. According to the Gṛhyayasūtras, the death of a child under two inflicts defilement on parents only, for one night or three; the rest of the family or the clan are untouched.[91] The Smrtis, however, enjoin three days' defilement for all the Sapiṇḍas. "By the death of a child, whose teeth have come out and whose tonsure ceremony has been performed, all the Bāndhavas became impure."[92]. If a child dies before its naming ceremony no impurity is involved.[93]

The sex of the deceased is also a determining factor for fixing the period of defilement. This distinction is not known to the Gṛhyasūtras, and most probably it arose during the Smṛti period. The death of a boy after his Upanayana entails full-fledged defilement,[94] but a girl before her marriage is still regarded a child and her death causes defilement for a period of three days only;[95] if she dies before her tonsure, her death causes only one day's defilement. Impurity caused by the death of one's mother ends with the defilement caused by the death of one's father which takes place earlier, but

89. ऋत्विजां दीक्षितानां च यज्ञियं कर्म कुर्वताम्।
सत्रव्रति ब्रह्मचारिदातृ ब्रह्मविदां तथा।। Yāj. S. iii. 28.
कारवः शिल्पिनो वैद्याः दासीदासाश्च नापिताः।
राजानः श्रोत्रियाश्चैव सद्यःशौचा प्रकीतिताः। P.S. iii. 21-22.

90. Ibid. iii. 1-2.

91. P.G.S. iii. 10 2–5.

92. दन्तजातेऽनुजाते च कृतचूडे च संस्थिते।
अशुद्धा बान्धवाः सर्वे सूतके च तथोच्यते।। Quoted by Jayarāma on the above.

93. M.S. V. 70.

94. Yāj. S. III. 23.

95. M.S.V. 72.

such is not the case when the death of the mother takes place earlier than the death of the father, because in this case impurity begins from the latter occurrence.[96]

The observance of the rules of defilement for relatives and friends is optional in the Gṛhyasūtras. "It depends on one's wish to observe the rules of Āśaucha on the death of a family priest, the father-in-law, a friend, other relatives (matrimonial) and sons of the sister."[97] But the Dharmasūtras and the Smṛtis make it encumbent and the length of the periods differs according to the closeness of the relations with the dead.[98]

The rules to be observed during the Āśaucha are of two kinds–negative and positive. The negative rules[99] require the mourners to forego the many pleasures and comforts and even ordinary business of life and thus exhibit the feelings of grief and sorrow. They forbid certain things, such as the cutting of the hair and beard, study of Vedas, Gṛhya offerings etc. The positive rules[100] have also their origin in the aggrieved feelings of the survivors. They enjoin, for a period of three days, to observe continence, to sleep on the ground, to live on begged or purchased food, to eat only in the day time etc.

(18) *Asthi-Sañchayana*

The ceremony that follows the cremation is the Asthi-[101] Sañchayana[101] or the "Collection of Bones." It is the remnant of the ancient custom of burial. During the Sūtra period, a compromise between the burial and the cremation was introduced. According to the then current custom, the dead body was burnt, but, in order to preserve the old tradition, the remains began to be collected and buried after a few days. The Gṛhya-Sūtras contain a very detailed account of the ceremony. According to Āśvalāyana[102] the Asthi-Sañchayana ceremony should be performed on the thirteenth

96. A Smṛti quoted by Vijñāneśvara on Yāj. S. iii. 20.

97. P.G.S. iii. 10. 46-47.

98. Āp. D.S. i. vi.

99. P.G.S. iii. 10. 31. 32; Yāj. S. iii. 15; M.S. v. 73.

100. Yāj. S. iii. 16.

101. A.G.S. iv. 5; B.P.S. i. 14.

102. A.G.S. iv. 5.

or fifteenth day of the wane, while Baudhāyana[103] enjoins the third, fifth or seventh from the day of cremation. First of all, the cinders should be besprinkled with milk and water and the heap should be striken with an Udumbara staff to separate the bones. This should be done while repeating the mantras. The cinders should be then collected and thrown towards the south side leaving the bones behind. Three oblations should next be offered to Agni. According to the custom of the Taittiriyas, the duty of collecting the bones was performed by women, preferably by the senior wife of the deceased. Baudhāyana[104] enjoins that the women must attach a fruit of the Bṛhati plant to the left hand and with a dark blue and red thread, mount upon a stone, wipe their hands once with an Apāmārga plant and with closed eyes collect the bones with the left hand. The following verse was recited : "Arise hence, and assume a new shape. Leave none of the members of your body behind. Repair to whichever place you wish; may Savitā establish you there. This is one of your bones; be joined with the third in glory; having joined all bones be handsome in person; be beloved of the gods in a noble place."[105] The above formula is an appropriate commentary on the purpose of the ceremony. It shows that the dead were supposed to take a new shape in the other world for which it was thought necessary to send every part of the material body to the next world either by burning or burial.

The bones, then, were washed and deposited in an urn, or tied up in piece of black antelope skin. The pot containing the bones or the bundle was to be hung from the branch of a Śami tree. The bones of person who had performed sacrifices were, however, burnt again. The bones of others were accorded a burial. For this purpose, an urn was absolutely necessary. Āśvalāyana[106] recommends an urn with spout for females and one without it for males. The urn which was closed with a lid, was placed in a trench prepared in the same way as the ground of cremation, or it might be laid under the root of a tree. According to other authorities grass and yellow cloth were placed in the trench and the bones were thrown in.

After the Sūtra period the Asthi-chayana ceremony underwent a great change. During the Pauranic times, people had no regard

103. B.P.S. i. 14. 1.

104. Ibid. i. 14. 6.

105. Ibid.

106. A.G.S. iv. 5.

for the custom of burying the bones of every individual. The sanctity of rivers increased. The cremation began to take place generally on the bank of some river. The burial ceremony of the remains was simplified. From the later period we have an account of how the chief mourner, just after the cremation, puts the remains into a small earthen pot and throws them into the water, if there be any at hand, or if not, into some lonely place or desert.[107] Now it is regarded very meritorious for the dead to collect the bones on the day of cremation and subsequently throw them into the Ganges or other sacred rivers : "The virtuous one, whose bone floats on the water of the Ganges never returns from the Brahmaloka, to the world of the mortals. Those, whose bones are thrown into the Ganges by men, live in heaven for thousands of Yugas."[108]

(19) *Śānti-Karma*

The next ceremony to be noticed is called Śānti-Karma[109] or the pacificatory rites for the well-being of the living. The formulas uttered during it have regard to life and adverting of death. Effective measures are taken to ward off evil and to return to ordinary way of life. The mediaeval and the modern Smṛtikāras enjoin the shaving and pairing of nails and bathing.[110] But the Gṛhya-Sūtras prescribe a very long procedure. The ceremony should be performed on the morning following the ninth night after death, i.e., on the tenth day. Āśvalāyana,[111] however, recommends that it should be performed on the fifteenth of the wane. In the opinion of some authorities, the ceremony should take place at the burning ground, while the others leave it with the mourners to select any place out of a town, whether it be the burning ground or not, that may be convenient. The relatives by blood, both male and female, having assembled at the selected place, a fire should be kindled and they

107. The Antyeṣṭipaddhati by Harihara.

108. गंगातोये च यस्यास्थि प्लवते शुभकर्मणः।
न तस्य पुनरावृत्तिर्ब्रह्मलोकात्कदाचन॥
गंगातोये च यस्यास्थि नीत्वा संक्षिप्यते नरैः।
युगानां तु सहस्राणि तस्य स्वर्गे भवेद्गतिः॥ Yama quoted by Jayarāma on P.G.S. iii. 10.

109. A.G.S. iv. 5.

110. The Antyeṣṭipaddhati by Harihara.

111. A.G.S. iv. 5.

should be requested to sit down on a bullock hide of a red colour, spread on the ground, with its neck side facing the East, and its hair directed towards the North. The relatives should be requested in the following words:

"Ascend on this life-giving skin, as you wish to live to a decrepit old age. According to your seniority, attempt carefully to abide on it. May the well-born and well-adorned fire of this ceremony bestow long life on you. Even as days follow and seasons are attached to seasons; even as the young forsake not their elders, may Dhātā so prolong the life of these people according to their age."[112]

In the modern ritual, the females are not required to attend this ceremony, as they perform it separately from the males and the bullock-skin as a symbol of life is not utilised, because in modern Hinduism it has become repulsive. The party having properly seated, the chief mourner should offer four oblations to the fire. The relatives should rise up and recite the Mantras, while touching a red bull. In ancient times, the women were asked to put on collyrium with the following words:

"Let these women, who are not widowed, who have good husbands, apply the collyrious butter to their eyes; without tears, without disease, worthy of every attention, let these wives enter the house."[113]

At present, this item has been dropped, as the women do not participate owing to the Purdah system, and the popular currency of widowhood among the twice-born castes, which forbids any rejoicings on the part of the widow. Then the assembly should proceed towards East, leading the bull with the words:

"These men, forsaking the dead, are returning. This day we invoke the gods for our good, for success over enemies, and for our merriment. We proceed eastwards having well sustained long lives."[114]

---

112. Ibid.

113. इमा नारीरविधवा सुपत्नीरांजनेन सर्पिषा संविशन्तु।
अनश्रवोऽनमीवा सुरत्ना आरोहन्तु जनयो योनिमग्रे।। R.V. x. 18. 7.
The explanation of this verse is very controversial. According to some, it was recited when the women entered the home, while others hold that it was recited when the widows mounted the funeral pyre of their husband. See J.R.A.S. xvi. pp. 201–14; xvii. 209. 20.

114. A.G.S. iv. 5.

The Chief mourner then recites another Mantra, and with a Śami branch, effaces the foot-marks of the bull that precedes the party. On the departure of the last man, the Adhvaryu should place a circle of stones behind him as a wall to prevent death from overtaking those that have gone forward, praying, "I place this circle of stones for the living; May we and others not go beyond it in mid-life; may we all live a hundred autumns, driving death away from this heap."[115] The party then should repair to the house of the chief mourner. The fire that served the deceased is removed and extinguished outside. The new fire is kindled after the removal of the old. Now a feast takes place and the survivors follow the course of ordinary life.

(20) *The Śmaśāna*

Another funeral ceremony of the Hindus is the Pitṛmedha or Śmaśāna,[116] i.e., the building of a mound over the remains of a dead person. Burial of the dead is a custom whose origin can be traced back to the very early period of Aryan history.[117] It must have proved a great incentive for erecting a mound or tomb over the grave. Even at present, among the Christians and the Mohammadans, where burial is the universal custom, some kind of elevation is made over the body of the dead, and in the case of rich and notable persons tomb or mausoleum is built. Though the Indo-Aryans gradually abandoned the custom of burial, they were still fond of perpetuating the memory of their departed relatives by building a mound over their remains. In the Vedas we have no reference to this custom. But the omission is not a sure proof of its non-existence. The Brāhmaṇas that are mainly concerned with rituals refer to it. In the Śatapatha Brāhmaṇa[118] there is a detailed description of the Śmaśāna ceremony. Not all the Gṛhyasūtras describe it, which shows that it was not a universal practice. But the Gṛhyasūtras[119] that deal with it, adopt the procedure of the Śatapatha Brāmaṇa with some modifications. Among the Buddhists, however, the custom of raising a mound was very popular and the Hindu Śastrakāras reserved this honour for great saints, monks and Sanyāsins only. The Pad-

115. Ibid.

116. B.P.S. i. 18.

117. Schrader, Aryan Religion, E.R.E. vol. II. p. 11–57.

118. xiii. 8.

119. A.G.S. iv. 5.

dhatis make this custom optional and allot it a very insignificant position amidst the funeral ceremonies. In modern Hinduism, the raising of a mound is almost stopped and the building of the Samādhis or Stupas is limited to a few religious celebrities.

The questions for whom and at what time the Śmaśāna should be performed have given rise to ritual discussions and have been variously answered by different schools of ritual. The lapse of time after the death, the season of the year and the presiding constellations are all considered, and preference is given to the new-moon day.

After the spot is properly selected, on the day preceding the ceremony some plants are rooted up at that place. To the north of these plants earth is dug up and from this bricks, from six to twenty-four hundred, are made for building the mound besides the number employed for packing. Now the urn containing the ashes of the dead is brought and placed between three Palāśa twigs driven into ground and a hut is erected over it. If the bones are not found in the trench where they were deposited, a very quaint procedure is followed. Some dust is taken from the spot or the dead man is called upon from the bank of a river, and creature that happens to fall upon an outspread cloth is regarded as the representative of the bones. Over the Palāśa twigs a vessel with many holes is placed, through which sour milk and whey trickle upon the urn.

The ceremony proceeds with the trumpet blast and the sound of the lute. The company circumambulates the spot, striking the left thigh with hands. The relatives asssembled there fan the urn with the skirts of their garments. Some authorities prescribe songs and dance of females also. Variations and modifications of the above description are found in different schools.

The Śamśāna ceremony proper should take place during the first, the middle or the last part of the night. The party goes early in the morning to the place selected for the purpose. The spot must be cleared and surrounded by a rope supported by wood stakes. Its surface should be covered with small stones. On the ground furrows are opened with a plough drawn by six or more oxen and various seeds are cast into them. In the middle of the ground a hole is made, into which gravel or saliferous earth is cast. Some quantity of milk from a cow whose youngone is dead should be placed in the hole to serve as food for the dead person. A piece of reed is immersed in a trench dug to the south of the hole evidently to serve the purpose of boat to the dead. Next the darbha grass is arranged in the figure of a man and the remains are laid upon it and covered with an old cloth. Then, the vessel containing the ashes is broken and over the bones a monument is built according to a fixed plan. Where the monument is erected up to a certain height, food for the dead is enclosed within the walls. After the structure is completed, earth is piled over the Śamśāna and water is poured over it from the jars which are destroyed after their use. The mound or Stūpa thus built is the symbol of death and many devices are used to separate the world of living from that of the dead. The line of demarcation between them is drawn by means of lumps of earth, stones and branches of tree. Some formulas are also uttered to meet the same end.

(21) *Offerings to the dead*

The last item of the funeral ceremonies of the Hindus comprises those offerings to the dead which are made during the Āśaucha period.[120] The dead is regarded as still living in a sense. The efforts of the survivors are to provide him with food and guide his footsteps to the paramount abode of the dead.

During the Vedic periods, the Fathers were invited to partake the offerings in general,[121] but an individual invitation was hardly met with. This literary omission, however, does not negative the supposition that the offerings were made to the dead as the custom is prevalent in all religions of the world. The Sūtras[122] have got positive rules on the topic. They prescribe that a Piṇḍa or a "ball of rice" should be offered to the dead on the first day. The ball was called "Piṇḍa", because it was supposed to constitute the body of the Preta.[123] With the ball of rice water for ablution was poured out for him and he was called on by name. Milk and water were set out for him in the open air with the words, "Bathe here." Perfumes and drink were also offered as well as a lamp to facilitate his progress through the utter darkness that enshrouds the road to the city of Yama.[124] A feast, which contained dishes of meat also, was given to the Brahmans on the eleventh day.[125]

120. P.G.S. iii. 10. 27-28; The Kriyāpaddhati by Gadādhara.

121. R.V. x. 15.

122. P.G.S. iii. 10. 27-28.

123. पिण्डमवयवपूरकं दत्त्वा। जयराम on the above.

124. A.G.S. iv. 5.

125. P.G.S. iii. 10. 48.

The Paddhatis on the funeral ceremonies have fully developed this part of the ceremonies. They prescribed for every day after the cremation up to the twelfth, a particular kind of offering for a particular purpose. According to them, on the first day, should be offered a rice ball, a jar of water and food articles for satisfying the thirst and hunger of the dead and building the veins of the would-be body of the dead. Darbha grass for sitting, ointment, flowers, perfumes, and lamps should also be set out for the dead. On the second day, offerings are made for constituting the ears, eyes and nose of the dead; on the third day for neck, shoulders, arms and breasts, and so on up to the ninth day when the whole body of the dead is supposed to be completed. On the tenth day the hair, beard and the nails of the survivors are pared and the Piṇḍas offered to the dead and Yama for ending the Preta-state of the deceased. On the eleventh day follow a large number of ceremonies. In the beginning, ablutions are offered to the dead and Lord Viṣṇu is prayed to for the salvation of the Preta.[127] It is quite a new feature in the funeral ceremonies where heavenly blessings are substituted by salvation. The most prominent item of this day's procedure is the Vṛṣotsarga[128] or letting loose a bull and a heifer. Both the animals are bathed, adorned and branded with a discus and a trident. The following verse is uttered in the ears of the bull; "The four-footed Lord Dharma is Himself well-known as Vṛṣa or bull; I adore Him with devotion; may He protect me."[129] Then they are married by fastening a piece of cloth to them, with "This husband, the best among all, has been given by me; the most charming of all the wives, this heifer, has been given by me." After this the pair is let loose and driven to the Southern direction "for ending the Preta-condition of the dead and enabling him or her to cross the ocean of mortality."[130] The ceremony terminates with a feast to the Brahmans, who are called the Mahāpātras and are eleven in number. They receive ample Dakṣiṇā and all sorts of gifts that are supposed to be transported to the next world through

127. अनादिनिधनो देव शंखचक्रगदाधरः।
अक्षय्य पुण्डरीकाक्ष प्रेतमोक्षप्रदो भव॥
Quoted by Gadādhara on P.G.S. iii. 10.

128. The Vṛṣotsargapaddhati by Nārāyaṇa.

129. वृषो हि भगवान् धर्मश्चतुष्पादः प्रकीर्तितः।
वृणे हि तमहं भक्त्या स मां रक्षतु सर्वतः॥
Quoted in the Kriyāpaddhati by Gadādhara.

130. अमुक प्रेतस्य प्रेतत्वमुक्तये.... सन्तारयितुम्। Ibid.

them for the future felicity of the deceased. The provision of food is made for full one year, as the dead is believed to reach the abode of Yama in one year.

(22) *Sapiṇḍi-Karaṇa*

The ceremony of Sapiṇḍīkaraṇa[131] or 'uniting the Preta with the Pitaras' takes place either on the twelfth day after the cremation, at the end of three fortnights or on the expiry of the year. The first day is prescribed for those who maintain the sacrificial fire, the second and the third for the rest.

The soul of the dead person does not reach the world of the Pitaras at once. It remains separate from them for a time as a Preta or Spirit. During this period special offerings are presented to it. But after certain time, the dead man passes into the abode of the Fathers through the instrumentality of Sapiṇḍīkaraṇa.

On the dates prescribed for Sapiṇḍīkaraṇa the Ṣodaśa Śrāddhas are performed in the beginning. Then four pots are filled with sesame seeds, perfumes and water. Three of them are offered to the Pitaras and one to the Preta. The contents of the Preta-pot are poured into the Pitṛ-pot with the words, "These equal etc." and the ceremonies are over.

(23) *Special Cases*

Besides the normal ceremonies attendant on the natural death of an individual, many special cases are recorded in the Gṛhyasūtras and the Smṛtis. In the Vedic hymns the regular funeral ceremonies are described without any distinct reference to abnormal cases. Verses 2, 3, 4 and 35 of the Atharvaveda (xviii), however, may be assumed to point out such cases. The first of the above verses runs; "O Agni, bring here all the Fathers, buried, cast away, burnt or exposed, to enjoy the offerings." The most popular method of disposing of the dead in the Atharvavedic times was cremation, so the other cases mentioned above might have been abnormal. The burial, here, may refer to the burial of children and ascetics, custom known to later literatures on funeral; casting away may be the casting away of mandicants dying in a forest which is mentioned in

131. The Kātyāyana-śrāddha-Kalpasūtra V. 1-2. Antyeṣṭi paddhati by Nārāyaṇabhaṭṭa.

the Chāndogya-Upanishad,[132] or it may refer to merely depositing dead bodies in a Samādhi as recognized in Buddhism;[133] and the exposure may have been the exposure of the dead on trees as it is recorded in the Śatapatha Brāhmaṇa.[134] These cases cannot refer to very primitive method of casting away or exposure of the dead or disabled persons proving a burden on the family, as it is supposed by some scholars.[135] Rather they represent a special ceremonial in abnormal cases. This assumption can be supported by the fact that in the above Atharvavedic verses the Fathers are invited very affectionately and not remembered as cast away refuses. Coming down to the Brāhmaṇas, we find that the Śatapatha Brāhmaṇa,[136] as already pointed out, mentions the exposure of dead bodies on trees, a custom certainly followed in the cases of homeless ascetics and beggars, who did not leave heirs behind them to perform their funerals. The Taittirīya-Āraṇyaka[137] speaks of the rite of Brahmamedha, performed at the death of a Brahman who had realized Brahmanhood. From the Chāndogya-Upaniṣad[138] we know that sometimes dead bodies were left uncared for and no funeral ceremonies were performed specially in case of those who had entered into forest and pursued Brahmavidyā and went to Brahmaloka from where there was no return.

The most systematic treatment of the abnormal cases has been given in the Gṛhyasūtras, where, after a thorough classification, the ceremonies were codified. Baudhāyana[139] in his Pitṛmedhasūtras has described almost all the irregular cases of funeral ceremonies. The Smṛtis do not develop the ritual but prescribe different types of Āśaucha to be observed and the Prāyaśchittas to be performed in such cases. The later Paddhatis and the Prayogas follow the ritual described in the Gṛhyasūtras, though these have evolved a few new ceremonies e.g., the Jīvachhrāddha not found in the earlier literature.

---

132. vi. 16. 2. 3.

133. Buddhist India, pp. 78 ff.

134. iv. 5. 2. 13.

135. Zimmer, Alt. Leben, p. 402.

136. iv. 5. 2. 13.

137. iii.

138. vi. 6. 2. 3.

139. The B.P.S.

The first special funeral rite was that of the Āhitāgni or the householder, who maintained all the three Fires. He distinguished himself from the rest of the society by his religious regularity. So it was thought necessary to accord him special funeral. According to Baudhāyana,[140] Homas should be performed before and after his death and his sacrificial utensils should be burnt on a separate pyre with his effigy made of Kuśa grass. It should be noted that Āśvalāyana[141] prescribes the burning of sacrificial vessels with the dead body itself in a normal funeral. He, undoubtedly, records the earlier practice, when the sacrifices were offered more regularly. The Smṛtis differentiate between the cremation and Āśaucha of an Āhitāgni and of an Anāhitagni. Vṛddha-Yājnavalkya[142] says, "The Āhitāgni should be burnt with the Three Fires, Anāhitāgni with one and the rest with the Laukikāgni." In the opinion of Aṅgirā,[143] the period of impurity in the case of an Āhitagni should begin from his cremation (which may be postponed for certain reasons), but that of the Anāhitāgni from the day of his death. In modern practices, however, the distinction is not well preserved as the sacrificial religion has declined and only a few Agnihotrins maintain the Three Sacred Fires at present.

Another special rite is that of children. They are not full men, so their funeral must differ from that of the adult. Their tender body should be spared the fierce flames of fire; their innocent life neither inflicts so much impurity upon the family nor it requires so much purification as the worldly life of the householders. Children do not also require in the next world all the necessities of the terrestrial life, because they are not accustomed to them in this world. These ideas underly the special rite accorded to children. Baudhāyana[144] says that Pitṛmedha should not be performed in the case of the uninitiated boys and unmarried girls. According to him,[145] in the case of abortion, the abortive child should be buried and the performer becomes instantly purified after a bath with clothes on.

---

140. Ibid. iii. 1.

141. A.G.S.

142. Quoted by Vijñāneśvara on Yāj. S. iii. 1. 9.

143. Ibid. iii. 1. 21.

144. यथा एतन्न प्राक् चौलात्प्रमीतानां दहनं विद्यते चानुपनीतानां कन्यानां पितृमेध इत्युक्तम्। B.P.S. iii. 6. 1.

145. Ibid. iii. 6. 2.

In the opinion of Paingya,[146] however, the abortion entails empurity for a period of ten days upon the mother. A child, whose teeth have not come out, should be buried with the recitation of Parṇava[147] denied to the abortive child. A child before two, Pāraskara[148] says, should be buried without cremation. Manu[149] differs from the above authorities and prescribes that "The relations of the dead child below two should take it out of the village, should decorate its person with garland and clothes and leave it in open air (or bury it beneath the earth); collection of bones should not be done in this case. Neither the child should be cremated nor it should be offered water oblations." But he[150] allows an option in the case of a child whose teeth have come out, and Baudhāyana even recommends cremation if desired by the relatives.[151] At present the burial of children is performed in some localities, but in the majority of cases they are thrown away into rivers and no impurity is observed.

The next special rite is that of a Garbhiṇī or a pregnant woman who dies in her pregnancy. Baudhāyana[1152] says that she should be carried to the cremation ground. After saving the child she should be burnt properly with the additional gift of an Aṣṭakādhenu, a Tiladhenu and a Bhūmidhenu. The ceremonies following cremation should be the same as usual. At present in such cases no attemp is made to save the child and it is burnt with the mother, and the funeral ceremonies are the same as in normal cases. The modren Paddhatis[153] prescribe special ceremonies for a woman dying in her confinement or monthly course. According to them, her body should be bathed with water from a jar, in which Pañchagavya is mixed. It is, certainly, done to purify her body which is contaminated with the impurity of the childbirth or the menstural flow. Then the Prājāpatyāhutis are offered and the body is covered with

---

146. Quoted by Vijñāneśvara Yāj. S. iii. 1. 20.

147. B.P.S. iii. 6. 3.

148. P.G.S. iii. 10. 4. 5.

149. M.S. V. 67–70.

150. नात्रिवर्षस्य कर्तव्या बान्धवैरुदकक्रिया।
जातदन्तस्य वा कुर्युर्नाम्नि वापि कृते सति॥ M.S. v. 70.

151. B.P.S. iii. 6. 4.

152. Ibid. iii. 9. 1.

153. The Kriyāpaddhati by Gadādhara.

new clothes and burnt. But the cremation is distinguished by not burning the corpse entirely.[154]

The funeral of the Parivrājakas, retired ascetic and mendicants, form another class by itself. They are the persons, who have given up all worldly attachments and have realized the Brahman or the Universal Soul. Their goal in life is not the attainment of the Pitṛloka nor of the Svarga, but the acquirement of Brahmaloka or salvation. Therefore, both socially and religiously, they are above the ordinary householders. Hence their last sacrament must be different from that of those, who are after worldly pursuits and heavenly pleasures. The first mention of funeral of a realized Brahman is made in the Taittirīya Āraṇyaka[155] where it is called Brahmamedha. The Baudhāyana Gṛhyasūtra[156] describes the funeral ceremony of a Parivrājaka as follows. The dead body should be laid in a ditch and the begging bowl placed on his belly with the appropriate verses. Then his Kamaṇḍalu should be filled with water and put on his right hand. Next the ditch should be covered with earth and a mound should be raised on it to save the corpse from the carnivorous animals.[157] The performance of this duty to the Parivrājakas is regarded very meritorious.[158] The post-cremation ceremonies are prohibited in the case of a Sanyāsin.[159]

This custom is still followed in certain sects of the ascetics. But after the transition of Hinduism from Vedism or Brahmaṇism to Puranism and Tantraism, Sanyāsa came to be regarded as Kalivarjya. Though Śankarāchārya broke this prohibition by his example, Sanyāsa never became popular in Hinduism again. The modern Sadhus belong to different sects, following Jnānamārga or Bhaktimārga, and they cannot be properly called Sanyāsins. Some

154. "निःशेषस्तु न दग्धव्यः" इति वचनात् । Ibid.

155. The Taittirīya-Áraṇyaka, iii.

156. B.P.S. iii. 11.

157. शृगालश्ववायसाः खादन्ति चेद्दोषमाहारयेत्कर्तुः। तस्मादविशंकां वेदिं प्रच्छादयेदिति बौधायनः। iii. 11. 12. Later on in case of distinguished परिव्राजकऽ, this mound developed into a memorial.

158. इत्यशेषसंस्कारोऽश्वमेधफलं तत्रोदाहरन्ति । Ibid. iii. 11. 1.

159. त्रयाणामाश्रमाणां च कुर्याद्दाहादिकाः क्रियाः।
यतेः किञ्चिन्न कर्तव्यं न चान्येषां करोति सः।। Quoted by Gadādhara in his Kriyāpaddhati.

of the sects practise burial but the majority of them prefer water-burial and their last offices are completed with a grand feast to the Sadhus and the Brahmans. The present custom of breaking the skull of an ascetic is based on the Upanisadic belief that the soul of a Brahmajnānī escapes through the Brahmarandhra or a hole on the top of head.[160] So the skull is broken to facilitate the departure. The Sanyāsins are not cremated, because being purified by the fire of spiritual knowledge and merged in Brahman, they do not require material fire to sanctify their body and convey the soul to the next world.[160a]

Men, dying in distant lands away from their homes, form another category. Here too Baudhāyana[161] is the first Sūtrakāra who describes the ceremonies in detail. The relations, when informed of the death, should bring the dead body, if preserved, or the bones for the proper funeral. In the latter case, thirty three bones should be selected from different limbs, as the man was supposed to consist of thirty-three.[162] But when the bones were not available and only the directon was known,[162] the Preta was called by name from that direction, an effigy of the man was made on the black deerskin, sacrificial vessels were placed on it, Kuśa grass was scattered on these articles and the cremation was performed. When no clue of the person gone abroad was found and he was believed to be dead, his funeral ceremonies were performed as described above. In such cases, sometimes, a few of the supposed dead persons came back home. They had got to be revived again with the proper Saṁskāras,[163] from the Conception to the Vivāha, as they were socially dead and no body would keep contact with them. At present the same ritual is followed but people do not evince any hurry about the funeral of missing persons, and their Antyeṣṭi performed when the possibility of their return is over.

A peculiarly novel practice of Jīvachchhrāddha[164] has come into existence in modern time. By an orthodox Hindu it is believed

160. शतं चैका हृदयस्य नाडयस्तासां मूर्द्धानमभिनिःसृतैका।
तयोर्ध्वमायन्नमृतत्वमेति विष्वङ्कन्या उत्क्रमेण भवन्ति॥ Ch. U. viii. 66.

160a. Vide the Yatisaṁskāra a part of the Pratāpanarasiṁha, B.B.R.A.S. cat. p. 222 nos. 700—703.

161. B.P.S. iii. 6.

162. "त्रयस्त्रिंशत्पुरुषः"। Ibid. iii. 6. 2.

163. Ibid. iii. 7.

164. The Jivacchrāddhaprayoga by Nārāyaṇabhaṭṭa.

that his proper funeral is essential for his Sadgati, (heaven or salvation). In case he has got no sons, or when he is doubtful whether his Antyeṣṭi will be properly performed by his children or not, he becomes anxious to see that it is duly done in his life-time. His person is represented by an effigy and the entire ceremonies are performed as usual. There is, however, a popular superstition that persons, whose Anteyṣṭi is performed in their life-time, die very soon. So only a few dare to do so.

Those who die of accidents are also treated as special cases. According to Baudhāyana,[165] those, who die of wounds caused by weapons, administration of poison, choking by a string, drowning in water, fall from a mountain or a tree etc., do not deserve a funeral. Most probably they were thrown away into water or cast away into forests. At present, however, they are accorded funeral ceremonies after performing certain Prāyaśchittas. The idea underlying the denial of funeral in this case was that these persons could not be admitted into the Pitṛloka; therefore it was futile to undergo the botherations of tedious ceremonies.[166] But the Gautama-Dharmasūtra says that the survivors could perform the Udakakarma etc. if they liked.[167] The majority of the Smṛtis, however, prohibit the observance of Āśaucha and performance of ceremonies, as no impurity is caused by their death.

The patitas or fallen are also recorded as special cases. According to Manu,[168] an apostate, a man born of Pratiloma marriage, a suicide, a Pāṣaṇḍa, an adultress, a woman causing abortion or hating her husband etc. should not be given a funeral. Yājñavalkya includes thieves also in the same class. The reason behind this prohibition is that these people are lost to society on account of their unsocial habits and, therefore, they are not entitled to the

---

165. B.P.S. iii. 7. 1. He recognizes an exception देशान्तरमृते संग्रामहते व्याघ्रहते शरीरमादाय विधिना दाहयेत्। Ibid iii. 7. 2.

166. उदकं पिण्डादानं च प्रेतेभ्यो यत्प्रदीयते।
नोपतिष्ठत्ति तत्सर्वमन्तरिक्षे विनश्यति ॥
Quoted by Vijñāneśvara on the Yāj. S. iii. 1. 6.

167. प्रायोऽनाशकशस्त्राग्निविषोदकोद्बन्धप्रपतनैश्चेच्छताम्। Ibid.

168. V.M.S. 87–90.

169. पाषण्डयनाश्रिताः स्तेना भर्तृघ्न्यः कामगादिकाः।
सुराप्य आत्मघातिन्यो नाशौचोदकभाजनाः ॥ Yāj. S. iii. 1. 6.

social privilege of deriving benefit from a Saṁskāra. At present such cases are not detected or publicly accepted, and many of the fallen pass as ordinary householders.

(24) *The Primitive Nature of the Ceremonies*

The funeral ceremonies, though often repeated and tedious, are of the simplest type. In no other field of Hinduism the primitive beliefs regarding life and death survive so insistently as in the naive funeral operations. The next world is nothing but the replica of this earth, and the needs of the dead are the same as those of the living. Throughout the ceremonies the prayers are offered for the sensuous enjoyments and ease of the dead. We do not find any indication of the desire for his or her spiritual benefit, salvation or beatitude. The prayer for freedom from the cycles of birth and death is very casual and could be discovered only in the latest phase of the ritual. The whole performance is of the most primitive kind, and speaks of a period of remote antiquity.

CHAPTER X

CONCLUSION

(1) *Life a Mystery and an art*

Life has been a great mystery to man. Its origin, growth, decadence and disappearance have always exercised his thoughts and emotions. The Hindu Saṁskāras were just an attempt to fathom and to facilitate the flow of this mystery. Through observations and experiences and through faltering and confidence of ages the ancient Hindus realised that life was an art like any other art in the world. It required cultivation and refinement. Man born and left to himself was a mass of elements, crude and brutal and slightly removed from his fellow-citizens of the forest. His life stood in need of as much care, protection and cultivation as a plant in a garden, crops in a field and an animal in a cattle-farm. The Saṁskāras involved conscious efforts to meet this need. The seers and the sages of yore, to their light and resources, tried to transform crude animality into refined humanity.

(2) *Life a Cycle*

As in philosophy so in rituals life was regarded as a cycle. It starts where it ends. From birth to death it is a continuous series of incidents moving round a nucleus of desire to live, to enjoy, to think and ultimately to retire. All the Sāṁskāras and their ceremonies emanate from the centre of life and are concurrent with its circumference. The Gṛhyasūtras, the oldest manuals of the Saṁskāras start with the Vivāha (Marriage Ceremonies), because marriage was supposed to be the centre of life which supports and sustains all social activities. The Smṛtis, however, begin with the conception of a child in the womb of its mother, as, obviously, the life of an individual germinates here and they end with the Antyeṣṭi (Funeral Ceremonies), which apparently mark the end of an individual life. Between births and deaths like life, the Saṁskāras revolve.

(3) *Dogma a Conscious Development*

In the beginning, the Saṁskāras, though not automatic, were spontaneous. There was no dogma and there was no code. Precedent was the only authority; the question of rationale did not arise. When in course of time the various ceremonies connected with the

Saṁskāras developed and they were amplified according to the social sentiments and needs, a conscious attempt was made at the codification of the Saṁskāras and dogmas were fixed. This provided for the stability of the institutional aspect of the Saṁskāras, but it hindered its spontaneous growth which resulted in its stultification and decay.

(4) *The Procedure of the Saṁskāras*

The forms and procedure of the Saṁskāras were suggested by observation and reasoning. Even in early times there were elaborate and distinct procedures of the Saṁskāras. Their precise origin is lost in the depth of antiquity but it is certain that they originated in social needs and in course of time they assumed a relgious garb. Symbols and taboos played an important part in the procedural development of the Saṁskāras.

(5) *The Place of the Saṁskāras in Hinduism*

(*i*) *Saṁskāras took Life as a whole*

In the beginning of civilizations life was much simpler than it is at present and it was not divided into compartments. Social institutions, beliefs, sentiments, arts, sciences etc. were all closely interwoven. The Saṁskāras covered all these fields of life. Religion was an all-embracing factor in ancient times and rituals were giving sanctity and stability to all possible incidents in life, and to this end, they are utilising all the moral and materal resources of the world to which man had an access. The aim of the Saṁskāras was to create conditions for the development of an integrated personality of an individual, who can adjust himself with the world around him believed to be full of human and superhuman forces.

(*ii*) *Saṁskāras and the Three Paths of Life*

When in course of time the complexities of life increased and distinctions in action came to be made, the Hindus recognized three definite paths of life—(1) Karma-mārga (the Path of Action), (2) Upāsanā-mārga (the Path of Meditation and Worship) and (3) Jñāna-mārga (the Path of Knowledge). Though the Saṁskāras were sufficiently comprehensive in their scope originally, they came to be included, later on, in the Path of Action (Karma-mārga alone. The first Path of life was a preparatory step to the second and the third ones, meant for the purification of mind (Chitta-śuddhi). Therefore though the saṁskāras were not of the highest importance in life, they were of the primary importance and thus essential for every individual. As a matter of fact they provided a necessary training for a higher type of culture intellectual and spiritual.

(ii) *Philosophical Indifference and Hostility towards the Saṁskāras and their reconciliation with Philosophy*

Indian philosophical attitude towards life centred round the idea that temporal life, in its last analysis, is futile and that a permanent state of consciousness transcending the earthly existence is to be reached. The Saṁskāras which blessed the Mundane affairs of life were looked down upon by retiring aspirants after the transcendental values of life. Some of the Upaniṣadic thinkers derided all sacrifices, including the Saṁskāras, and compared them with frail boats unfit for crossing the ocean of mortality. But the classical Hindu mind, being synthetic and taking a balanced view of life, was able to reconcile ritualism with philosophy and under the same sacrificial canopy, side by side with most elaborate sacrifices, the highest metaphysical questions were raised and discussed. The Chārvakas (Materialists), the Buddhists and the Jains (Heterodox Religions) attacked rituals in vain. The Chārvākas, having no rituals and dogmas to rest upon, died out. The Buddhist and the Jain churches developed their own rituals, leaving their laity to follow the popular rituals current in the society. The Brahmanical thinkers never tried to discard them, perhaps, thinking that people could not live without some kind of ceremonies; the Saṁskāras, being the best of them, received their approval.

(iv) *Saṁskāras and Puranic Hinduism*

The development of Puranic Hinduism synchronized with the decline of the Vedic religion and the gravity of religious life shifted from home—the venue of the Saṁskāras—to the places of pilgrimage and the temples. The emphasis was laid on idol-worship. But though the big sacrifice fell into disuse, the Saṁskāras survived with the change that some of them, e.g., the Tonsure and the Upanayana, in some cases, came to be performed at a temple instead of at home. The Saṁskāras were so closely associated with the personal life of an individual that they clung to him or her through all changes and vicissitudes. Their hold on life was so strong that even some of the deities had to undergo some of these Saṁskāras.

(6) *The Achievements of the Saṁskāras*

The Saṁskāras helped in the refinement and purification of human life, facilitated the development of personality, imparted sanctity and importance to human body, blessed all material and spiritual aspirations of man and ultimately prepared him for an easy and happy exit from this world of complexities and problems. They also helped in the solution of the many social problems of importance. For example, the Garbhādhāna (Conception) and other pre-natal Saṁskāras were connected with sex-hygiene and eugenics. When the latter had not developed as independent branches of science, the Saṁskāras were the only educative agencies in these matters. Similarly, the Vidyārambha (Learning of Alphabets) and the Saṁskāras beginning from the Upanayana (Initiation) to the Samāvartana (Returning Home from the Teacher's) are all of highly educational importance. In early societies there was no secular agency to enforce compulsory education upon the masses. The Saṁskāras, being compulsory, served this purpose. Every child, if he was not mentally and physically invalid, was to undergo a compulsory course of education involving learning and strict discipline. This maintained the intellectual and cultural level of the ancient Hindus. The Vivāha Saṁskāra (Marriage) regulated a number of sexual and social problems by laying down definite rules on the types and forms of marriage, the limitations of marriage, the selection of parties and the nuptials. No doubt, these rules tended to make society static but they also added to the stability and happiness of social groups and family life. The last Saṁskāra, the Antyeṣṭi (Funerals) combined the duties of a house-holder towards the dead and the living. It was a wonderful combination of family and social hygiene and consolation for the survivors. Thus, the Saṁskāras operated in the practical life as a graduated scheme of human life and its development.

(7) *The Decline of the Saṁskāras*

Like other socio-religious institutions the Saṁskāras also, after serving their purpose for a long time, declined in course of time due to their internal weaknesses and external circumstances, which developed in the history of the Hindus. The creative stage of the Saṁskāras was followed by the critical, conservative and imitative ones, when the Saṁskāras were codified, commented upon, compiled and confusedly and poorly imitated. The result was that they became static and stultified and lost their power of elasticity and adaptation. The time and ideology under which they evolved were left far behind and new social and religious forces were operating in the society, which did not fully conform to old social and religious institutions. Buddhism, Jainism and the many new cults of devotion diverted the attention of the people from ritualistic exactitude to devotional practices of worship. The linguistic difficulty was also responsible for the decline of the Saṁskāras. The Mantras recited in the Saṁskāras were from the Vedas and the procedure of the Saṁskāras was couched in archaic Sanskrit and the both have continued to be so till to-day. Though Sanskrit has ceased to be the popular language of India and is intelligible to only a few learned persons, the priests have never cared to change the language of the Saṁskāras, as they are always anxious to preserve the mystic and obscure nature of the religious ceremonies. The natural consequence is the apathy and indifference of the masses towards the Saṁskāra, which have become a sealed book to them.

A far-reaching cause of the decline of the Saṁskāras was the development of the society from its primitive conditions and the bifurcation and specialisation of the different branches of human activities. Originally the Saṁskāras combine religious beliefs and practices, social customs and laws, educational schemes, rules regarding health and hygiene etc. In course of time all these aspects of human life developed more or less independently. So the Saṁskāras lost most of their contents and importance; only its religious sanctity survived in its truncated form. The Saṁskāras, which once constituted a serious attempt at the reformation of man, were reduced to mere ceremonies. The Saṁskāras to-day are in the majority of cases a matter of routine benefit of effective influence.

Hinduism assimilated foreign elements in its fold throughout its long history. These elements conformed to the broad outline of Hinduism, but they did not find minute ritualistic details congenial to them. They performed the most important Saṁskāras like the Vivāha (Marriage) and the Antyeṣṭi (Funeral), which they could not escape, but they had little use of the minor ones. The advent of Islam in India eclipsed Hindu culture and in the major part of the country there was no free opportunity to perform religious rites. For their safety the masses abstained from ostentacious ritualistic procedure and only a few orthodox families performed them at their great risk. The later and modern impact of materialism from the west has attacked Hinduism on a different plane. Through western educational system and foreign medium of instruction it has uprooted the majority of young people receiving this new education from their moorings both intellectually and emotionally. It has made its converts hostile towards the traditional life of the country, sceptic towards spiritual values of the life and impatient of any religious discipline. They are getting lost to the very sacramental conception of life. This constitutes the gravest menace to the Saṁskāras. The only saving feature for the Saṁskāras is the reaction which is visible to-day against materialism in a serious section of humanity, which may restore the religious and spiritual values to man in future again.

(8) *Revivalism and the Saṁskāras*

In the nineteenth century in India the impact of western influences was on the one hand, capturing the mind of a large number of young people, on the other hand, it created a reaction against it led by nationalistic cultural movements. The more orthodox of them, like the Arya Samāja and the Sanatana Dharma movements, sought to defend the Hindu community firstly by retorting to the charges hurled by the foreigners against the Hindu religion and culture and secondly by reviving the old social and religious institutions with some reforms and simplification, so that they might attract the educated people intellectually. The Saṁskāras were revived with a zeal and they appealed to the people for some time, but they are loosing their influence again. The real question is not the West versus the East; it is the Old versus the New. The Saṁskāras originated in the hoary past when the problems and the needs of the society were different from what they are to-day; the mind of the people was working under an ideology which was peculiar to its age. To-day the society has changed; the man has changed accordingly; his beliefs, sentiments and aspirations have all undergone change. Unless the Saṁskāras are also transformed in the light of new developments, they cannot appeal to the new mind.

(9) *Prospects*

The Saṁskāras were the expression of human beliefs, sentiments, aspirations, hopes and fears, and they catered for human needs. With changes in life they are bound to change. To-day the very conception of life has undegone change. By scientific discoveries many mysteries of life have been solved and man's control over his environment has immensely increased. Many natural forces which were feared or respected have become docile servants of man. Material resources of life are getting multiplied. Many fields of life which were regarded sacred have now become secular. So, the awe and reverence with which the religious rites were performed are diminishing gradually. But in spite of all these changes in the material aspects of the world, certain central mysteries of life and some fundamental needs of human existence will remain. Though the evolutionary process of life has been analysed and studied, the origin of life, its constituents and their combinations are still puzzling the human mind, and there does not seem to be any possibility of solving the central problem of life satisfactorily. At the source of life man is even to-day experiencing the mystic touch of the invisible. This fact will keep alive the religious sentiments in man.[1] Though the magic hold of religion in some fields of life will be loosened, the human heart will not part with that sanctity which is imparted by religious sanction. The consecration of life will never cease. Similarly the fact that life is an art and it requires conscious and planned efforts for its cultivation and refinement will never die out. The art of race-culture and nation-building will always form an important part of human progress. The Saṁskāras will change their old garbs and will assume new shapes.

1. Cf. "The most beautiful thing we can experience is the mysterious. It is the source of all true art and science. He to whom this emotion is stronger, who can no longer pause to wonder and stand wrapt in awe, is as good as dead: his eyes are closed. The insight into the mystery of life, coupled though it be with fear, has also given rise to religion. To know that what is impenetrable to us really exists, manifesting itelf as the highest wisdom and the most radiant beauty which our dull faculties can comprehend only in their most primitive forms—this knowledge, this feeling, is at the centre of true religiousness. In this sense, and in this sense only I belong to the ranks of devoutly religious men."

—Albert Einstein, I Believe, Unwin Books, 1962

BIBLIOGRAPHY

I. SANSKRIT TEXTS

(I) THE VEDAS

1. The Ṛgveda Saṁhitā
2. The Sāmaveda Saṁhitā
3. „ Yajurveda „
4. „ Atharvaveda „
5. „ Vājasaneyī „
6. „ Taittirīya „
7. „ Maitrāyaṇī „
8. „ Kāṭhaka „

(II) THE BRĀHMAṆAS

1. The Aitareya Brāhmaṇa
2. The Śatapatha Brāhmaṇa
3. „ Gopatha „
4. „ Taittirīya „
5. „ Pañchaviṁśa „
6. „ Sāmaveda-Mantra Brāhmaṇa

1. The Taittirīya Āraṇyaka

(IV) THE UPANIṢADS

1. The Bṛhadāraṇyaka
2. The Chāndogya.
3. „ Maitrāyaṇī.
4. „ Śvetāśvatara.
5. The Taittirīya.

(V) THE GṚHYASŪTRAS

1. The Ātharvaṇa G. S.
2. The Āpastamba G. S.
3. The Āśvalāyana G. S.
4. Kāṭhaka G. S.
5. The Kauśika G. S.
6. The Kauśītaki G. S.
7. The Khadira G. S.
8. The Gobhila G. S.
9. The Jaimini G. S.
10. The Pāraskara G. S.
11. The Baudhāyana G. S.
12. The Bhāradvāja G. S.

13. The Mānava G. S.
15. The Śāṅkhyāyana G. S.
15. The Śāṅkhyāyana G. S.
16. The Hiraṇyakeśi G. S.
17. The Vaikhānasa Smārta S. (7 Praśnas of Gṛhya).

(VI) THE GṚHYAKALPAS

1. The Mānava Śrāddha K.
2. The Paippalāda Ś. K.
3. The Kātyāyana Ś. K.
4. The Baudhāyana Ś. K.
5. The Hiraṇyakeśi Ś. K.
6. The Gautama Ś. K.

(VII) THE GṚHYAPARIŚIṢṬA

1. The Gṛhyasaṅgraha Pariśiṣṭa (of Gobhilaputra).

(VIII) THE DHARMASŪTRAS

1. The Āpastamba D. S.
2. The Baudhāyana D. S.
3. The Gautama D. S.
4. The Hārīta D. S.
5. The Hiraṇyakeśi D. S.
6. The Mānava D. S.
7. The Śaṅkha Likhita D. S.
8. The Vaikhānasa Smārta D. S.
9. The Vasiṣṭha D. S.
10. The Viṣṇu D. S.

(IX) THE EPICS

1. The Rāmāyaṇa.
2. The Mahābhārata.

(X) THE ARTHAŚĀSTRA

1. The Kauṭilya Arthaśāstra.

(XI) THE SMṚTIS

1. The Atri Smṛti
2. The Aṅgiras Smṛti
3. „ Āpastamba „
4. „ Āśvalāyana Dharmaśāstra
5. „ Āśvalāyana „
6. „ Ṛṣyaśṛṅga Smṛti
7. „ Kapila „
8. „ Kātyāyana „
9. „ Gobhila „
10. „ Gautama „
11. „ Chaturviṁśatimata
12. „ Dakṣa „
13. „ Devala „
14. „ Nārada „

15. „ Parāśara „ 16. „ Pitāmaha „

17. „ Pulastya „ 18. „ Paiṭhīnasi „

19. „ Prachetas „ 22. „ Prajāpati „

21. „ Bṛhatpārāśara „ 32. „ Bṛhadyama „

23. „ Bṛhaspati „ 24. „ Baudhāyana „

25. „ Bhāradvāja „ 26. „ Manu „

27. „ Marīci „ 28. „ Yama „

29. „ Yājñavalkya „ 30. „ Laghu-Parāśara „

31. „ Laghu-Yama „ 32. „ Laghu-Bṛhaspati „

33. „ Laghu Vasiṣṭha „ 34. „ Laghu-Viṣṇu „

35. „ Laghu-Vyāsa „ 36. „ Laghu-Śaṅkha „

37. „ Laghu-Śātātapa „ 38. „ Laghu-Śaunaka „

39. „ Lagh-Hārīta „ 40. „ Laghvatri „

41. „ Laghu-Āśvalāyana 42. „ Likhita „

43. „ Lohita „ 44. „ Laugākṣi „

45. „ Vasiṣṭha „ 46. „ Viśvāmitra „

47. „ Viśveśvara „ 48. „ Viṣṇu „

49. „ Vṛddha-Parāśara Saṁhitā 50. „ Vṛddha-Śātātapa „

51. „ Vṛddha-Hārīta „ 52. „ Vṛddhātri „

53, „ Vṛddha-Gautama 54. „ Vaiṣṇava Dharmaśāstra

55. „ Vyāsa „ 56. „ Śaṅkha-Likhita „

57. „ Śankha „ 58. „ Śāṇḍilya „

59. „ Śātātapa „ 60. „ Śaunaka „

61. „ Śamvarta „ 62. „ Hārīta „

(XII) THE PURĀNAS

1. The Bhaviṣya Purāṇa 2. The Garuḍa Purāṇa

3. The Liṅga „ 4. The Padma „

5. The Skanda „ 6. The Viṣṇu „

(XIII) THE COMMENTARIES

1. On the Āpastamba G. S.
   (a) Anākulā by Haradatta.

2. On the Āśvalāyana G. S.
   (a) Anāvilā by Haradatta.
   (b) Vimalodayā by Jayasvāmin.
   (c) C. by Devasvāmin.
   (d) C. by Nārāyaṇa.

3. On the Kauśika G. S.
   (a) C. by Bhattāri Bhaṭṭa.
   (b) C. by Darila.
   (c) C. by Vāsudeva.

4. On the Khadira G. S.
   (a) C. by Rudraskanda.

5. On the Gobhila G. S.
   (a) C. by Nārāyaṇa Bhaṭṭa.
   (b) C by Yaśodhara.
   (c) C. by Sāyaṇa.

6. On the Gautama Dh. S.
   (a) Mitākṣarā by Haradatta.

7. On the Jaimini G. S.
   (a) Subodhinī by Śrinivāsa.

8. On the Dakṣa Smṛti.
   (a) C. by Kṛṣṇanātha.

9. On the Parāśara Smṛti.
   (a) C. by Mādhava.

10. On the Pāraskara G. S.

(a) C. by Haradatta.

(b) C. by Gadādhara.

11. On the Baudhāyana Dh. S.

(a) C. by Govinda Svāmin.

(b) C. by Parameśvara Parivrājaka.

12. On the Manu Smṛti.

(a) Manu-muktāvali by Kullūka.

(b) Mānavāśayānusāriṇi by Govindarāja.

(c) Nandini by Nandanāchārya.

(d) C. by Medhātithi.

13. On the Yājñavalkya Smṛti.

(a) C. by Aparārka.

(b) C. by Kulamaṇi Śukla.

(c) C. by Devabodha.

(d) Mitākṣarā by Vijñāneśvara.

(XIV) THE TREATISES

1. The Anūpavilāsa (Saṁskāra-Ratna) by Dharmāmbodhi.

2. The Aṣṭādaśa-Saṁskāra by Chaturbhuja.

3. The Aṣṭādaśa-Smṛti-Sāra.

4. The Karma Tattva-Dīpikā by Kṛṣṇa Bhaṭṭa.

5. The Kṛtya-Chintāmaṇi by Chaṇḍeśvara.

6. The Govindārṇava (Saṁskāra-Vīchi) by Śeṣanṛsiṁha.

7. The Chaturvarga-Chintāmaṇi by Hemādri.

8. The Chamatkāra-Chintāmaṇī by Vaidyanātha.

9. The Jaṭṭamalla-Vilāsa by Śrīdhara.

10. The Nirṇayasindhu by Kamalākara Bhaṭṭa.

11. The Vīramitrodaya by Mitramiśra.

12. The Ṣoḍaśa-Saṁskārāḥ (according to Āśvalāyana).
13. The Ṣoḍaśa-Saṁskārāḥ by Kamalākara.
14. The Ṣoḍaśa-Saṁskārāḥ by Chandrachūḍa.
15. The Ṣoḍaśa-Saṁskāra-Setu by Rāmeśvara.
16. The Saṁskāra-Kalpadruma by Jagannātha Yājñika.
17. The Saṁskāra-Kaumudī by Giribhaṭṭa.
18. The „ Kaustubha by Anantadeva.
19. The „ Tattva by Raghunandana.
20. The „ Nirṇaya by Nanda Paṇḍita.
21. The „ Nṛsiṁha by Narahari.
22. The „ Pradīpa.
23. The „ Pradīpikā by Viṣṇuśarma Dīkṣita.
24. The „ Bhāskara by Khaṇḍe Bhaṭṭ.
25. The „ Mayūkha by Nīlakaṇṭha.
26. The „ Ratna by Khaṇḍe-rāya.
27. The „ Ratna-Mālā by Gopinātha Bhaṭṭa.
28. The „ Ratnākara (Pāraskarīya).
29. The „ Saṅkhyā.
30. The Smṛti-Kaumudī by Madanapāla.
31. The Smṛti-Kaustubha by Anantadeva.
32. The Smṛti-Chandrikā by Āpadeva Mīmāṁsaka.
33. The Smṛti-Chandrikā by Devaṇṇa Bhaṭṭa.
34. The Smṛti-Tattva by Raghunandana.
35. The Smṛti-Nibandha by Nṛsimhabhaṭṭa.
36. The Smṛti-Ratnākara by Viṣṇubhaṭṭa.
37. The Smṛti-Sāra by Yājñikadeva.

(XV) THE PADDHATIS

1. The Āpastamba-Paddhati by Viśveśvara Bhaṭṭa.
2. The Kauśika-Gṛhyasūtra-Paddhati of Keśava.

3. The Garga-Paddhati.

4. The Garbhādhānādi-Daśakarma-Paddhati by Śaunaka.

5. The Daśa-Karma-Paddhati by Paśupati.

6. „ by M. M. Kālesi.

7. „ by Gaṇapati.

8. „ by Pṛthvidhara.

9. „ by Bhavadeva Bhaṭṭa.

10. „ by Rāmadatta Maithila.

11. The Daśa-Karma-Vyākhyā by Halāyudha.

12. The Pāraskara-Gṛhya-Paddhati by Kāmadeva.

13. The Pāraskara-Gṛhya-Paddhati by Vasudeva.

14. The Baudhāyana-G. S. Paddhati by Keśava Svāmin.

15. The Maitrāyaṇa- G. S. Paddhati.

16. The Śāṅkhyāyana-G. S. Paddhati by Viśvanātha.

17. The Śāṅkhyāyana G. S. Paddahati by Vasudeva.

18. The Ṣodaśa-Karma-Paddhati by Ṛṣibhaṭṭa.

19. The Ṣodaśa-Saṁskāra-Paddhati by Ānandarāma Dīkṣit.

20. The Saṁskāra-Paddhati by Kamalākara.

21. „ by Amṛta Pāṭhaka.

22. „ by Ānandarāma—Yājñika.

23. „ by Nārāyaṇa Bhaṭṭa.

24. The Sāmavedīya-Saṁskāra-Paddhati by Vireśvara.

25. The Saṃskāra-Vidhi by Svāmi Dayānanda Sarasvatī.

26. The Ṣodaśa-Saṁskāra-Vidhi by Paṇḍita—Bhīmasena Śarma.

(XVI) THE PRAYOGAS

1. The Āpastamba-G.S. Prayoga.

2. The Āśvalāyana-G.S. Prayoga.

3. The Pāraskara-G.S. Prayoga.

4. The Prayoga-Kaustubha by Ganeśa Pāṭhaka.

5. The Prayoga-Chandrikā by Vīrarāghava.
6. The Prayoga-Tattva by Raghunātha.
7. The Prayoga-Darpaṇa by Nārāyaṇa.
8. The Prayoga-Dīpa by Dayāśaṁkara.
9. The Prayoga-Dīpikā by Ramakṛṣṇa Bhaṭṭa.
10. The Prayoga-Paddhati by Gaṅgādhara.
11. The Prayoga-Paddhati by Dāmodara Gārgya.
12. The Prayoga-Paddhati by Raghunātha.
13. The Prayoga-Pārijāta by Nṛsiṁha.
14. The Prayoga-Pārijāta by Puruṣottama Bhaṭṭa.
15. The Prayoga-Maṇi by Keśava Bhaṭṭa.
16. The Prayoga-Ratna by Ananta.
17. " by Kāśinātha Dīkṣita.
18. " by Keśava Dīkṣita.
19. " by Nārāyaṇa Bhaṭṭa.
20. " by Nṛsiṁha Bhaṭṭa.
21. " by Maheśa.
22. " by Mahādeva.
23. " by Harihara.
24. The Prayogasāra by Bālakṛṣṇa.

(XVII) THE KĀRIKĀS

1. The Āśvalāyana G. S.–Kārika by Sudarśana.
2. The Āśvalāyana G. S.–Paribhāṣā.
3. The Kātyāyana G. S.–Kārikā.
4. The Khadira G.S.–Kārika by Vāmana.
5. The Baudhāyana G. S.–Kārikā by Kanaka-Sabhāpati.
6. The Sāmavedīya G. S.–Kārikā by Bhūvaka.
7. The Gṛhyasūtra–Kārikā by Karka.
8. The Gṛhyasūtra–Kārikā by Reṇuka.

9. The Drāhyāyaṇa G. S.–Kārikā.

10. The Pāraskara G. S.–Kārikā by Reṇukāchārya.

11. The Śāṅkhyāyana G. S.–Kārikā.

12. The Śaunaka Kārikā.

(XVIII) SPECIAL WORKS ON DIFFERENT SAMSKĀRAS

THE JĀTAKARMA

1. The Āpastamba–Jātakarma by Bāpaṇṇa Bhaṭṭ.

2. The Janmadina-Kṛtya-Paddhati.

3. The Janma-divasa-Pūjāpaddhati.

4. The Sūtaka–Nirṇaya of Bhattoji.

THE ANNAPRĀŚANA

1. The Annaprāśana.

2. The Annaprāśana Prayoga.

THE CHŪḌĀKARAṆA

1. The Chūḍākaraṇa–Keśānta.

2. The Chūḍākarma by Dattapaṇḍita.

3. The Chūḍākarma-Prayoga.

4. The Chaulopanayana.

5. The Chaulopanayana Prayoga.

THE KARṆAVEDHA

1. The Karṇavedha-Vidhāna (from the Prayoga-Pārijāta).

THE UPANAYANA

1. The Upanayana-Karma-Paddhati.

2. The Upanayana-Kārikā.

3. The Upanayana-Chintāmaṇi by Viśvanātha.

4. The Upanayana-Tantra by Gobhila.

5. The Upanayana-Tantra by Rāmadatta.

6. The Upanayana-Tantra by Laugākṣi.
7. The Upanayana-Paddhati by Rāmadatta.
8. The Upanayana-Paddhati by Viśvanātha.
9. The Punarupanayana.
10. The Punarupanayana-Prayoga by Divākara.
11. The Yajñopavīta-Paddhati by Rāmadatta.
12. The Vrātya-Prāyaśchitta-Nirṇaya (an extract from the Prāyaśchittenduśekhara of Nāgoji Bhaṭṭa).
13. The Vrātya-Śuddhi-Saṁgraha.
14. The Vrātyastoma-Paddhati by Mādhavāchārya.
15. The Aśvatthopanayana-Vidhi.

THE KEŚĀNTA

1. The Godānavidhi-Saṁgraha by Madhusūdana Gosvāmī.

THE SAMĀVARTANA

1. The Samāvartana-Prayoga by Śyāmasundara.

THE VIVĀHA

1. The Aṅkurārpaṇa (from the Prayoga-Ratna of Nārāyaṇa Bhaṭṭa).
2. The Udvāha-Kanyā Svarūpa-Nirṇaya.
3. The Udvāha-Chandrikā by Govardhana Upādhyāya.
4. The Udvāha-Tattva (C. by Kāśirāma-Vachaspati-Upādhyāya).
5. The Udvāha-Nirṇaya by Gopāla Nyāya-Pañcharatna.
6. The Udvāha-Lakṣaṇa.
7. The „ Viveka by Ganes'abhaṭṭa.
8. The „ Vyavasthā.
9. The „ Vyavasthā-Saṁkṣepa.
10. The Udvāhādi-Kālanirṇaya by Gopīnātha.
11. The Kanyādāna-Paddhati.
12. The „ Prayoga.

13. The Kanyā-Vivāha.

14. The Kanyā Saṁskāra.

15. The Gotra-Nirṇaya by Bālambhaṭṭa.

16. The Gotra-Nirṇaya by Mahādeva Daivajña.

17. The Gotra-Pravara-Khaṇḍa (from Āpastamba S.).

18. The Gotra-Pravara-Dīpa by Viṣṇupaṇḍita.

19. The Gotra-Pravara-Nirṇaya by Anantadeva (from the Saṁskāra-Kaustubha).

20. The Gotra-Pravara-Nirṇaya by Kamalākara.

21. „ by Jīvadeva.

22. „ by Nāgeśabhaṭṭa.

23. „ by Nārāyaṇa Bhaṭṭa.

24. „ by Bhaṭṭoji.

25. „ by (Abhinava) Mādhavāchārya.

26. „ by Viśvanātha.

27. The Gotra-Pravara-Māñjarī by Keśava.

28. „ by Puruṣottama Paṇḍita.

29. „ by Śaṁkara Tāntrika.

30. „ by Śaṁkara Daivajña.

31. The Gotra-Pravara-Ratna by Lakṣmaṇa Bhaṭṭa.

32. The Gotra-Pravaroccāra (from Audīcya-Prakāśa).

33. The Pravara Kāṇḍa (Āśvalāyana).

34. The Pravara-khaṇḍa (Āpastambīya).

35. The Pravara-khaṇḍa (Vaikhānasa in one Praśna).

36. The Pravara-Darpaṇa by Kamalākara.

37. The Pravara-Nirṇaya by Bhattoji.

38 The Pravarādhyāya from the Viṣṇudharmottara.

39. The Maṇḍapodvāsana-Prayoga by a son of Dharaṇīdhara.

40. The Vivāha-Karma by Agnihotrī Viṣṇu.

41. The „ Chaturthi-Karma.

42. The „ Tattva by Raghunandana.

43. The „ Dvirāgamana-Paddhati.

44. The „ Nairūpaṇa by Nandabhaṭṭa.

45. „ Nairūpaṇa by Vaidyanātha.

46. The „ Paṭala by Śārṅgapāṇi.

47. The „ Paddhati (Gobhilīya).

48. „ „ by Gaurīśaṅkara.

49. „ „ by Chaturbhuja.

50. „ „ by Jagannātha.

51. „ „ by Narahari.

52. „ „ by Nārāyaṇa Bhaṭṭa.

53. „ „ by Rāma Chandra.

54. „ „ by Rāmadatta–Rājapaṇḍita.

55. The Vivāha-Ratna by Haribhaṭṭa.

56. The „ Ratna-Saṁkṣepa by Kṣemaṅkara.

57. The „ Vṛndāvana by Keśavāchārya.

58. The „ Saukhya by Nīlakaṇṭha.

59. The „ Kanyā-Svarūpa-Nirṇaya by—
Anantarāma Śastrin.

60. The Sāpiṇḍya-Kalpa-Latā by Sadāśivadeva.

61. The „ Dīpikā by Nāgeśa.

62. The „ Nirṇaya by Bhaṭṭoji.

63. „ by Rāmakṛṣṇa.

64. „ by Rāmabhaṭṭa.

65. „ by Srīdhara Bhaṭṭa.

THE ANTYEṢṬI

1. The Antya-karma-dīpikā by Hariharabhaṭṭa Dīkṣita.

2. The Antya-kriyā-Vidhi by Manurāma.

3. The Antyeṣṭi-Paddhati by Anantadeva.

4. „ by Keśava.

5. „ by Maheśvara Bhaṭṭa.

6. „ by Rāmāchārya.

7. „ by Harihara, son of–Bhāskara.

8. „ by Bhaṭṭanārāyaṇa, son of Rāmeśvara or Aurdhvadehika Paddhati.

9. The Antyeṣṭi Paddhati by Viśvanātha, son of Gopāla.

10. The Antyeṣṭi-Prakāśa by Divākara.

11. The Antyeṣṭi-Prayoga (Āpastambīya).

12. „ (Hiraṇyakeśīya) by Keśavabhaṭṭa.

13. „ by Nārāyaṇa Bhaṭṭa.

14. „ by Viśvanātha.

15. The Āśaucha-Prakāśa.

16. The Āśaucha-Sāra by Satpaṇḍita Śri Balabhadra.

17. The Āśaucha by Veṅkateśa.

18. The Āśaucha-Kāṇḍa by Vaidyanātha Dīkṣita.

19. The Āśaucha-Gaṅgādharī by Gaṅgādhara.

20. The Āśaucha- Dīdhiti by Anantadeva (from the Smṛti Kaustubha).

21. The Āśaucha-Nirṇaya by Ādityāchārya.

22. „ by Kauśikāchārya.

23. „ by Govinda.

24. „ by Nāgoji Bhaṭṭa.

25. „ by Bhaṭṭoji.

26. „ by Raghunandana.

27. „ from Smṛti-Kaustubha.

28. „ from Smṛti-Saṁgraha.

29. The Āśaucha-Śataka by Nīlakaṇṭha.

30. The Āhitāgnimarṇe-Dāhādi (Āśvalāyanīya).

31. The Āhitāgner-Dāhādi-Nirṇaya by Rāmabhaṭṭa.

32. The Āhitāgnyantyeṣṭi-Prayoga.
33. The Ekādaśāha-Kṛtya.
34. The Ekoddiṣṭa-Śrāddha-Prayoga.
35. The Ekoddiṣṭa-Sāriṇī by Ratnapāṇi Miśra.
36. The Aurdhvadehika-Kalpavalli by Viśvanātha.
37. The Aurdhvadehika Kriyā-Paddhati by Viśvanātha.
38. The Aurdhvadehika-Paddhati by Kamalākara Bhaṭṭa.
39. The Antyeṣṭi-Paddhati by Nārāyaṇa Bhaṭṭa.
40. The Sapiṇḍīkaraṇa for Mādhyandinīyas.
41. The Pitṛmedha-Prayoga.
42. The Pitṛmedha-Bhāṣya (Āpastambīya) by Gārgya Gopāla.
43. The Pitṛmedha-Vivaraṇa by Raṅganātha.
44. The Pitṛmedhasūtra by Gautama.
45. The Paitṛmedhikasūtras by Bhāradvāja.
46. The Preta-Dīpikā by Gopīnātha Agnihotrin.
47. The Preta Pradīpa by Kṛṣṇamitrāchārya.
48. The Preta-Mañjarī or Preta-Paddhati by Yadu-Miśra.
49. The Maraṇa-Karma-Paddhati ascribed to the Yajurvedīya G.S.
50. The Maraṇa-Sāmayika-Nirṇaya.
51. The Vṛṣotsarga-Kaumudi by Rāmakṛṣṇa.
52. The Vṛṣotsarga-Tattva by Raghunandana.
53. The Vṛṣotsarga-Paddhati ascribed to Śaunaka.
54. „ by Nārāyaṇa.
55. The Vṛṣotsarga-Prayoga by Anantabhaṭṭa.
56. The Vṛṣotsarga-Vidhi by Madhusūdana Gosvamin.
57. The Vaitaraṇī-Dāna (Stein's Cat. p. 104).
58. The Śuddhi-Kaumudī by Maheśvara.
59. The Śuddhi-Tattva of Raghunātha.
60. The Śapiṇḍīkaraṇa-Vidhi.

II. GENERAL WORKS

1. Abbot, J. .. The Keys of Power, Mathuen, London, 1932.

2. Aldrich, C. R. .. Primitive Mind and Modern Civilization, Kegan Paul, London.

3. Alberuni's India, Tr. by Sachau, London, 1914.

4. Altekar, A. S. .. Education in Ancient India. The Indian Book-Shop, Benares 1934.

5. .. The Position of Women in Hindu Civilization, Culture Publication House, Benares Hindu University.

6. Ancient India, as described by Megasthenes and Arrian Tr. by M'crindle, London 1877.

7. Bader, C. .. Women in Ancient India. Kegan Paul, London 1925.

8. Banister, H. .. Psychology and Health, Cambridge University Press, London, 1935.

9. Barth, A. .. Religions of India. Trübner Oriental Series, London, 1914.

10. Bloomfield, M. .. The Religion of the Veda. Nickerbocker Press, 1908.

11. Bose, P. N. .. Survival of Hindu Civilization. Newman, Calcutta, 1913.

12. Buch M.A. .. The Spirit of Ancient Hindu Culture, Baroda, 1921.

13. Caland .. Ancient Indian customs about the Funeral Witchcraft of Ancient India.

14. Carr-Saunders, A. M. .. Eugenics. Home University 1926.

15. Chakaldar, H. C. .. Social Life in Ancient India: Studies in Vātsyāyana Kāmasūtras, Greater India Society, Calcutta, 1929.

16. Crawby, E. ... The Mystic Roses. 2nd ed. Theodore Besterman, vols. I & II, Mathuen Co. London, 1927.

17. Das, A. C. .. Ṛgvedic Culture. R. Cambray & Co. Calcutta, 1925.

18. Das S. K. .. The Educational System of the Ancient Hindus. Mitra Press, Calcutta, 1930.

19. Dawson .. The Ethical Religion of Zoroaster. New York, 1931.

20. Dubois, A. J. A. & Beauchamp, H. K. .. Hindu Manners, Customs and Ceremonies. Clarandon Press, Oxford, 1906.

21. Dutt, R. C. .. History of Civilization in Ancient India, vols. I & II. Kegan Paul, London, 1893.

22. Encyclopaedia of Religion and Ethics, Ed. by J. Hastings. vols. I-XIII T. T. Clark, Edinburg, 1925–34.

23. Farquhar, J. N. .. Religious Life in India. Oxford University Press, London, 1916.

24. Fick, R. .. The Social Organization in N. E. India in Buddhist Time. Tr. by S. K. Maitra, University of Calcutta, 1920.

25. Frazer, Sir, J. G. .. The Golden Bough–Macmillan, London, 1925.

26. ,, .. Totemism and Exogamy. Macmillan, London 1935.

27. Frend, S. .. Totem and Taboo. New Republic Inc. New York, 1927.

28. Gates, R. R. .. Heredity and Eugenics. Constable, London, 1923.

29. Glotz .. Ancient Greek at work. London, 1926.

30. Ghurye, G. S. .. Caste and Race in India. Kegan Paul London, 1932.

31. Geiger .. Civilization of the Eastern Iranians, London, 1895.

32. Goldenweiser, A. A. .. Anthropology. Harrop. London, 1937.

33. Hillebrandt .. Ritual Literature Vedische.

34. Hopkins .. Religions of India.

35. .. Epic India.

36. Howard .. A History of Matrimonial Institutions, vols I—III, Chicago, 1904.

37. Jayaswal, K. P. .. Manu and Yājñavalkya Butterworth, Calcutta, 1930

38. Jolly, J. .. Hindu Law and Custom. Tr. by B. K. Ghosh. Greater India Society, Calcutta, 1928.

39. Kane, P. V. .. History of Dharmaśāstra, vols. I & II Bhandarkar Oriental Research Institute, Poona.

40. Keay, F. E. .. Ancient Indian Education, Oxford University Press, London, 1918.

41. Keith, A. B. .. The Religion and Philosophy of the Veda and the Upaniṣads, vols. I. II.
Harvard University Press, Cambridge, Massachusettes, U.S.A.

42. Keyserling, Count H. .. The Book of Marriage, Jonathan Cape, London, 1927.

43. Macdonell, A. A. .. Vedic Mythology. V. Von K. J. Tübner, Strassburg, 1897.

44. Macdonell, A. A. and Keith, A. B. .. Vedic Index, vols. I & II. John Murray, London, 1912.

45. Majumdar, R. C. .. Corporate Life in Ancient India. Second ed. University of Calcutta, 1922.

46. Marret, R. R. .. Sacraments of Simple Folk, Clarandon, Oxford, 1933.

47. Maiyne, J. D. .. A Treatise on Hindu Law and Usage. Madras, 1914.

48. Mess, G. H. .. Dharma and Society, Luzac & Co. London, 1935.

49. Meyer, J. J. .. Sexual Life in Ancient India, Vols. I & II. Routledge, London, 1930.

50. Monier Williams, M. .. Indian Wisdom, Fourth Ed. Luzac & Co. London, 1836.

51. Mookerjee, Radha Kumud .. Hindu Civilization, Longmans, Green & Co., London, 1936.

52. Müller-Lyre, F. .. The Evolution of Modern Marriage. Allen and Unwin, London, 1930.

53. Max Müller .. The Family Allen and Unwin, London, 1931.

54. Max Müller .. History of Ancient Sanskrit Literature.

55. On Yuan Chwang .. Tr. by Watters London, 1904.

56. O' Malley, L. S. S. .. India's Social Heritage, 1934.

57. .. Indian Caste Customs. Cambridge University Press, London, 1932.

58. Puntambekar, S. V. .. An Introduction to Indian Citizenship and Civilization Nand Kishor & Bros., Banaras.

59. Radhakrishnan, S. .. The Hindu View of Life, Allen and Unwin, London, 1927.

60. .. Indian Philosophy, vols. I & II, Allen and Unwin, 1927.

61. Ragozin, Z. A. .. Vedic India T. Fisher Union, London, 1899.

62. Rapson, E. J. .. Cambridge History of India, vol. I. Cambridge University Press, London.

63. Risley, H. H. .. The People of India, Second Ed. Tacker and Co., Calcutta, 1915.

64. Roy, S. .. Customs & Customary Law in British India, Published by the author Calcutta, 1911.

65. Russel, Bertrand .. Marriage and Morals. Allen & Unwin, London, 1930.

66. Sarkar, B. K. .. The Positive Background of Hindu Sociology. Panini Office, Allahabad, 1921.

67. Sarkar, S. C. .. Some Aspects of the Earliest Social History of India. Oxford University Press, London, 1928.

68. Seal, B. N. .. The Positive Sciences of the Ancient Hindus. Longmans, London, Bombay and Calcutta, 1915.

69. Sen Gupta, N. C. .. Sources of Law and Society in Ancient India. Art Press, Calcutta, 1614.

70. Spencer .. Principles of Sociology, Edinborough, 1893.

71. Stevenson, Mrs. Sinclair .. Rites of the Twiceborn.

72. Tripathi, R. S. .. History of Ancient India, Nand Kishor & Bros. Banaras.

73. Tripathi, G. M. .. Marriage Forms under Ancient Hindu Law, Bombay, 1906.

74. Vaidya, C. V. .. Epic India. Bombay Book Depot. Bombay 1933.

" " .. A History of Sanskrit Literature, Bombay.

75. Venkateshwar, V. .. Indian Culture Through The Ages, Vols. I & II. Longmans, London, Bombay, 1928.

76. Westermark, E. .. History of Human Marriage, Vols. I–III. Fifth Ed. Macmillan, London, 1921.

77. Winternitz .. A History of Indian Literature, Vol. I. Calcutta University.

III. JOURNALS

1. Allahabad University Studies, Allahabad.
2. Annals of the Bhandarkar Oriental Research Institute, Poona.
3. Indian Antiquary.
4. Indian Culture, Calcutta.
5. Indian Historical Quarterly, Calcutta.
6. Journal of the American Oriental Society, Yale Uni. U.S.A.
7. Journal Asiatique.
8. Journal of the Asiatic Society of Bengal, Calcutta.
9. Journal of the Bihar and Orissa Research Society, Patna
10. Journal of the Bombay Branch of the Royal Asiatic Society.
11. Journal of the Bombay Historical Society.
12. Journal of Oriental Research, Madras.
13. Journal of the Royal Asiatic Society of Great Britain and Ireland.
14. Man in India, Ranchi.
15. New Indian Antiquary.
16. Quarterly Journal of the Mythic Society.
17. Proceedings of the All India Oriental Conferences.
18. Proceedings of the Indian History Congress.

GENERAL INDEX

A

H

T

W

Y